THE FAR SIDE OF PARADISE

A BIOGRAPHY OF F. SCOTT FITZGERALD

BY ARTHUR MIZENER

The Far Side of Paradise

The Sense of Life in the Modern Novel

EDITED BY ARTHUR MIZENER

Afternoon of an Author,
by F. Scott Fitzgerald

The Fitzgerald Reader

Modern Short Stories

THE FAR SIDE OF
PARADISE

A BIOGRAPHY OF
F. SCOTT FITZGERALD

by

Arthur Mizener

ILLUSTRATED

SENTRY EDITION

HOUGHTON MIFFLIN COMPANY BOSTON

C 10 9 8 7 6 5 4

ISBN: 0-395-08395-8

This book is for my mother

FOREWORD
TO THE REVISED EDITION

SINCE THE ORIGINAL publication of *The Far Side of Paradise* in 1951, a good deal of published and of unpublished information about Fitzgerald has accumulated. Of the published material the most striking is the story of Fitzgerald and Sheilah Graham in *Beloved Infidel* by Miss Graham and Mr. Gerold Frank. I was familiar with this story in its main outlines when I wrote *The Far Side of Paradise*, but I was persuaded by friends of Miss Graham (one of them a psychiatrist) that it would be a serious mistake to discuss the matter with Miss Graham or to tell what I already knew. I therefore omitted the story. I do not even now see how I could have done otherwise, since Miss Graham's friends may have been right about her feelings in 1951, and the very possibility that they were made it impossible for me to consult Miss Graham. Further silence on the subject has, however, been made unnecessary by the publication of *Beloved Infidel*, and I have therefore rewritten the last two chapters of *The Far Side of Paradise* for this edition in order to include the story of Miss Graham and Fitzgerald.

The most revealing account of Fitzgerald that has been published since the original publication of *The Far Side of Paradise* is Morley Callaghan's story of his friendships with Fitzgerald and Hemingway during the spring and summer of 1929 in *That Summer in Paris* (1963). Only less valuable is

Hemingway's *Moveable Feast* (1964) with its beautifully written and curiously one-eyed view of Fitzgerald, a view which can, I think, be fully understood only in the light of Mr. Callaghan's portrait of Hemingway. There have also been useful glimpses of Fitzgerald in such books as James Drawbell's *The Sun Within Us* (1963) and such articles as James Thurber's for *The Reporter* in 1951; and there has been Andrew Turnbull's subsequent biography, *Scott Fitzgerald* (1963), and his selection of Fitzgerald's letters (1963).

In addition a good many people to whom I am particularly grateful have written me to correct my descriptions of episodes in Fitzgerald's life for which I unwarily accepted Fitzgerald's own somewhat romanticized recollections; a good example is Major Palmer's account of Fitzgerald's first meeting with Zelda, a less dramatic but more convincing one than Fitzgerald's own, which I accepted in the original edition of this book and which has been repeated by other writers.

I have, then, revised this edition of *The Far Side of Paradise* to include all the new information of this kind, published and unpublished, that is now available to me, and I have made such changes in the book's conception of Fitzgerald as this new knowledge suggests. For the reader's convenience I have also introduced into the notes page references to the selection of Fitzgerald's letters edited by Mr. Turnbull for Scribner's, when letters I have quoted appear in that selection.

Arthur Mizener

Cornell University
September, 1964

FOREWORD
TO THE FIRST EDITION

THIS BOOK could obviously not have been written without a great deal of assistance from a great many people, many more than I can hope to name here. It could, quite literally, not have been written at all had not Mrs. Frances Fitzgerald Lanahan made available to me with the greatest generosity everything she had which bore on her father's life and work. In his case this included nearly all the most significant material — Mrs. Lanahan's own recollections of her father, Fitzgerald's Ledger, his Scrapbooks and Albums, his manuscripts, his files of letters, above all, perhaps, his magnificent letters to Mrs. Lanahan herself. Nor would I have attempted to write this book without the approval and the help of Mr. Edmund Wilson, who has given more time to my problems than I like to remember. I also owe a special debt to Mr. H. D. Piper, who turned over to me his large collections of notes about Fitzgerald.

I am only less indebted to those people who gave me their impressions of Fitzgerald and their permission to quote from letters, among whom were Mrs. Maxwell Perkins, Mrs. Bayard Turnbull, Mr. Ludlow Fowler, Mr. Charles W. Donahoe, Mr. and Mrs. C. O. Kalman, Mrs. Francis Butler, Mr. and Mrs. Norris Jackson, Mr. Robert Clark, Mr. Richard Washington, Mr. and Mrs. Arthur Hartwell, Mr. Stephen Dunning, Mr. and Mrs. Gerald Murphy, Mrs. John Peale Bishop, Mrs. John

Pirie, Mrs. Maurice Flynn, Mr. Thomas Daniels, Mrs. Lois Moran Young, Doctor Benjamin Baker, Doctor Thomas Rennie, Mrs. Frances Kroll Ring, Miss Marie Shank, and Mrs. Newman Smith.

I owe a special debt to Mr. Ernest Hemingway, Mr. Budd Schulberg, and Mrs. Marjorie Kinnan Rawlings for letting me use material which might well have had a professional value for them. I owe a personal debt to Professor Willard Thorp and Mr. Allen Tate who in different ways persuaded me to write this book. How much I am indebted to Mr. Charles Scribner for allowing me access to Fitzgerald's correspondence with Maxwell Perkins and to Harold Ober, Fitzgerald's agent, for allowing me to read Fitzgerald's letters to him can be estimated by a glance at the notes to this book. I owe a similar debt to Judge John Biggs, who, as the Trustee of the Fitzgerald estate, made Fitzgerald's papers available to me, and to Mr. Julian Boyd and the staff of the Princeton University Library, who gave me unasked more privileges in the library than I would ever have dared to ask for.

Mr. Malcolm Cowley and Mr. Reed Whittemore read this book from beginning to end in manuscript and saved me from a host of blunders.

I am deeply grateful to Houghton Mifflin for granting me one of their Literary Fellowships and to the Trustees of Carleton College for the generous leave which allowed me to take advantage of that Fellowship.

I am indebted to *The Atlantic Monthly*, *Partisan Review*, *Furioso*, and *The Kenyon Review* for permission to use material which has already appeared in their pages. I am also indebted to *New Directions* for permission to quote from *The Crack-Up*, to Harcourt, Brace and Company and Faber & Faber for permission to quote from T. S. Eliot's *Four Quartets*, and to Charles Scribner's Sons for permission to quote from Fitzgerald's books.

Probably no twentieth-century writer will ever be so well

documented as Fitzgerald; his own records of his life, made to help him in his work, are minute and painstaking; he was a great preserver of the symbols of the past, from Plaza hat checks to the thousands of pages of manuscript that remain from the writing of *Tender Is the Night*. None of these records would have been available to me without the generosity of the people I have just been naming. It is no fault of theirs if I have often felt, as William Faulkner has said, that "they are like a chemical formula exhumed along with letters from that forgotten chest . . . almost indecipherable, yet meaningful, familiar in shape and sense, the name and presence of volatile and sentient forces; you bring them together in the proportions called for, but nothing happens; you re-read, tedious and intent, poring, making sure that you have forgotten nothing, made no miscalculation; you bring them together again and again nothing happens; just the words, the symbols, the shapes themselves, shadowy inscrutable and serene, against that turgid background of a . . . mischancing of human affairs." "There never was," as Fitzgerald said in his Notebooks, "a good biography of a good novelist. There couldn't be. He's too many people if he's any good."

Arthur Mizener

Carleton College
Northfield, Minnesota

CONTENTS

ILLUSTRATIONS

(following page 194)

INTRODUCTION

THERE ARE three concentric areas of interest in a study of Scott Fitzgerald. At the heart of it is his work. His work was the major interest in his life, for he was a natural writer if only in the sense that from his grade-school days until the end of his life nothing was ever quite real to him until he had written about it. That work ought to be the essential interest of any book about him, not simply because it bulks larger but because it is more valuable than anything else in his life.

He always, however, wrote about himself or about people and things with which he was intimate. As a consequence his life is inextricably bound up with his work. He made a habit of jotting down notes of his experiences and feelings in the month-by-month record he kept in his Ledger. The nine stories he wrote about Basil Duke Lee, with their brilliant and minute recreation of his boyhood, are a good illustration of how he could transform these bare bones into fiction. Moreover, his life is of considerable interest in itself. He was a personality, a being of great charm and influence, despite the unforgivable things he occasionally did. "I didn't have the two top things — great animal magnetism or money," he once noted with perfect objectivity. "I had the two second things, tho', good looks and intelligence. So I always got the top girl." He lived a colorful life and, in the end, a disastrous one, which is no less moving because much of the disaster was of his own making. "There were four or five Zeldas and at least eight Scotts," as James Thurber once put it, "so that their living room was forever tense with the presence of a dozen desperate personalities, even when they were alone in it. Some of these Fitzgeralds were characters out of a play or a novel, which made the lives of the multiple pair always theatrical, sometimes unreal, and often badly overacted." [1] This is the second area of interest for a study of him, only less absorbing than the first, and, because his imagination worked so immediately from his experience, very closely related to it.

The third area of interest is the time and place in which he lived. This area is not merely the early years of the twenties and the upper middle class in America. Fitzgerald became a figure for them almost by accident. As such he has his interest, for that time and place appear more and more as we get away from them a turning point in the history of American culture. But the person who was, in the popular, superficial sense, the "laureate of the Jazz Age" was a relatively insignificant part of Fitzgerald. He was the exceptional yet representative figure for a far deeper quality of the time and a far larger group of people than these. His time and place haunted him every minute of his life and the effect of this preoccupation is what most obviously distinguishes his work from that of the good sociological novelists like Dos Passos on the one hand and, on the other, from that of the emotional and self-regarding novelists.

It is not easy to get a clear view of Fitzgerald's career and of his talent; it is not even easy — despite its pervasive influence — to define his achievement. There are a good many reasons for this blurring, but perhaps the most important of them is Fitzgerald's curious ability to get close to the reader. He was, as a person, probably no less odd and alone than most people, but he had a talent for intimacy. In his personal relations he created a sense of unguarded impulsiveness — perfectly genuine even when it was used consciously — which was hard to resist, as many people who hated his reputation and disapproved of his conduct and yet were won over by him have testified. He created an air of interest in those he was with, when he chose to, which is rarely provided for anyone except by himself. He did so because, with his quick imagination, he always saw what others were feeling and sympathized with them, especially if he himself had imposed on them one of his obsessions or muddled their lives with his drunken disorder or hurt them by some sharpness when they failed to respond to him as he had decided it was proper for them to.

There is a story in Morley Callaghan's *That Summer in Paris* that illustrates this quality very clearly. Callaghan and his wife had sought out the Fitzgeralds in Paris and their first evening together had been far from a success. After it Callaghan wrote Fitzgerald a letter apologizing for having upset them, though it was Fitzgerald who had been rude; when Callaghan had failed to respond enthusiastically as Fitzgerald read him a passage from *A Farewell to Arms*, Fitzgerald had said gently, "Would this impress you, Morley?" dropped to the floor and attempted to stand on his head (he was not quite sober enough to bring it off).

When Callaghan told Hemingway this story, Hemingway said, "Well, that's Scott." That was true enough as far as it went, but there was more to Fitzgerald than Hemingway's judgment allowed. He spent most of the day he got Callaghan's letter trying to find him; when the Callaghans got back from dinner that night they found three *pneumatiques* from Fitzgerald, and almost immediately he and Zelda arrived at their flat. "Morley," said Fitzgerald, "I got your note. This is terrible. All afternoon we've looked for you."

Then Scott, taking me by the arm again amid all our protestations of goodwill and self-depreciation, made one of those generous remarks which few other men could have made, and which seemed to come so easily out of his heart. "You see, Morley," he said simply, "there are too few of us."

This pattern of tipsy inconsiderateness and deeply sympathetic, sober repentance occurs again and again in every one of Fitzgerald's personal relations, though much of the time it is only the thoughtless behavior that gets reported in the anecdotes. Most of the anecdotes in Hemingway's *A Moveable Feast*, for example, show Fitzgerald only at his worst — obsessed with hypochondriacal anxiety over "congestion of the lungs" or extravagant anxiety over "the way I was built" — but Hemingway had clearly known the rest of the pattern too. "When [Scott] was drunk," he tells us, "he would usually come to find me and, drunk, he took almost as much pleasure interfering with my work as Zelda did interfering with his. This continued for years but, for years too, I had no more loyal friend than Scott when he was sober." [2]

This power of understanding and of sympathy, with the feeling of intimacy it bred, that Fitzgerald at his best brought to his personal relations carries over into his best stories and gives these stories an effect unique in twentieth-century fiction. "Almost everything I write in novels," as he once put it quite truly himself, "goes, for better or worse, into the subconscious of the reader." [3] This is a confusing effect because, by itself and independently of other qualities, it is likely to affect very powerfully our response to the story. Fitzgerald's work is full of precisely observed external detail, for which he had a formidable memory, and it is this gift of observation which has led to the superficial opinion that he was nothing but a chronicler of the social surface, particularly of the twenties. Yet, for all its concrete external detail, his work is very personal.

The events of his stories are nearly always events in which Fitzgerald has himself participated with all his emotional energy: "My own happiness . . . often approached such an ecstasy," he wrote in *The Crack-Up*, "that I could not share it even with the person dearest to me but had to walk it away in quiet streets and lanes with only fragments of it to distil into little lines in books. . . ." [4] At the same time, though his stories are full of these intense feelings, both their events and the feelings which surround them are observed with an almost historical precision; nothing is concealed, nothing ignored. "He [had]," as John Peale Bishop put it, "the rare faculty of being able to experience romantic and ingenuous emotions and half an hour later regard them with satiric detachment." [5] "Even the breaking of his own heart," as Bishop added on another occasion, "was a sound to be listened to and enjoyed like the rest." [6] At its best, his mind apprehended things simultaneously with a participant's vividness of feeling and an intelligent stranger's acuteness of observation.

Because he thus wrote about the things he had participated in without any prudence whatever ("To record one must be unwary," he said) we too participate in them.[7] To some readers this experience is a revelation, the opening of a door for the first time into the world of imagination. Oftener than not these are unsophisticated readers, and, as Glenway Wescott remarked of *This Side of Paradise*, "a book which college boys really read is a rare thing, not to be dismissed idly or in a moment of severe sophistication." [8] Still, as Mr. Wescott would be the first to add, the judgments of college boys are not quite final, either. It is a considerable tribute to Fitzgerald that not only college boys but all sorts of other unusual readers have provided for him that "illiterate audience" for which Eliot and Yeats have yearned, but the effect of a special and quite undiscriminating Fitzgerald cult which is also a result of their admiration has only harmed his reputation.

This sense readers have that they are participating intimately in the experiences of his stories is also what makes certain of them seriously underrate Fitzgerald. His knowledge is that naïve and disturbing kind possessed by the child in Andersen's fairy story who was not "wise" enough not to say that the king was naked. His stories give the reader a feeling of exposure, of a revelation of the commonness and weakness and even smallness of what we all are. To certain minds this feeling is both unpleasant and insignificant. As one of the finest living American poets, Allen Tate, once said, "It was his very romanticism which kept him from ever learning more about the American rich [who were his subject] than a little boy knows about cowboys and Indians." [9] But this opinion ignores the judgment in Fitzgerald's work and exaggerates the romance in a way that is very unlike Mr. Tate. "There are always those," as Fitzgerald himself remarked, "to whom all self-revelation is contemptible. . . ." [10]

This sense of participation in Fitzgerald's stories confuses the judgment, because it offends some readers extravagantly, and because there are some who enjoy it too much. Fitzgerald's creation of it cannot be ignored; it is a characteristic and important part of his work and it must be taken account of and evaluated. But it is a feeling that has to be controlled if we are to evaluate fairly the other aspects of his talent and achievement.

It is no help to this end that he began his career with a great popular success. *This Side of Paradise* connected him in many people's minds with "the Jazz Age," so that he was for them both the historian — "the laureate" — of the post-war generation and its exemplar. Perhaps the strongest mark of the early twenties is the widespread conviction — so much stronger than their superficial cynicism — that anyone could do anything; it was a wonderful and inspiriting conviction and encouraged all sorts of people to achievements they might never otherwise have attempted. Fitzgerald himself once remarked half jokingly, "Hugh Walpole was the man who started me writing novels. One day I picked up one of his books while riding on a train from New York to Washington. After I had read about 100 pages I thought that 'if this fellow can get away with it as an author I can too.' . . . After that I dug in and wrote my first book." [11] This is entirely in the spirit of the times, if not literally true. Only in such an atmosphere could Fitzgerald have been mistaken for the spokesman of a conscious and cultivated attitude. Fitzgerald "really created for the public the new generation," as Gertrude Stein said, by quite innocently being it; he was as surprised as anyone else to discover that in *This Side of Paradise* "he had written a 'bible of flaming youth.' " [12]

Partly because of certain qualities very deep in his nature, partly from sheer bewilderment, Fitzgerald himself became for a short time a victim of the popular delusion that he was a spokesman — and perhaps he never altogether escaped from this rôle's special appeal to him for the rest of his life.

> For just a moment, before it was demonstrated that I was unable to play the role, I, who knew less of New York than any reporter of six months standing and less of its society than any hall-room boy in a Ritz stag line, was pushed into the position not only of spokesman for the time but of the typical product of that same moment. I, or rather it was "we" now, did not know what New York expected of us and found it rather confusing.[13]

For three or four years they did their best to be what appeared to be expected of them, and at least until 1930 they were responding to calls for statements on "Making Monogamy Work" (1924), "What Became of Our Flappers and Sheiks" (1925), and "Who Can Fall in Love After Thirty" (1928).

On this note Fitzgerald faded from the consciousness of the general public to a really remarkable extent, with the result that when he died in 1940 the obituaries made it evident that for the newspapers and their public Fitzgerald and his work represented "the Jazz Age." As *The New Yorker* pointed out: "Not only were they somewhat uninformed (note to the New York *Times*: 'The Beautiful and Damned' is not a book of short stories, and it isn't called 'The Beautiful and the Damned,' either) but they were also inclined to be supercilious." [14] In this Fitzgerald was perhaps only a victim of circumstances and the American need to think of all writers

as either Great, with a very large G, or something to be condescended to with all the force of one's own uncertainty.
Since, in 1940, the twenties seemed as remote to many people
as the world of Trollope, and since Fitzgerald was remembered, not even as having understood them, but as representing them he was condescended to on every hand, from *The
Nation* to *College English*, with a kind of smartness and disregard for the question of genuineness which is shocking.[15]
The greatest arrogance was shown by Westbrook Pegler's
notice, with its talk of Fitzgerald's "group or cult of juvenile
crying-drunks" and of the far-off time "when Scott Fitzgerald's few were gnawing gin in silver slabs and sniffing
about the sham and tinsel of it all." [16] But nearly everyone
appeared inclined to write about him as if his life had consisted of the years from 1920 to 1928 and the people of that
period had not been real people whose lives had consequences
but merely the raw materials of a period musical comedy to
which, by a grotesque accident, an unhappy but extremely
improving ending out of some work like *The London Mer-
chant* had got affixed.

As a consequence of this widespread opinion about the
twenties in general and Fitzgerald in particular, there is a
tendency on the part of even informed readers to be more
aware than they ought to be of how well Fitzgerald caught
what Paul Rosenfeld called "the pitch and beat" of a time
and place and to remember disproportionately how, in two
novels and two volumes of short stories, all produced in three
short years, he did this for the period immediately after the
first war.

The circumstances of Fitzgerald's own production, of
course, made this distorted view of him much easier. There
had always been the possibility that he might turn out, at
worst, merely a popular writer or, at best, a promising writer
with a few solid achievements early in his career who petered
out as ignominiously as did many of the easily acclaimed gen-

iuses of the twenties. He did not in fact do either of these things; indeed there is a serious argument to be made for the notion that the work of the last five or six years of his life is the finest he ever did. But after *The Great Gatsby* there was a long spell when he appeared to be petering out; and then, when *Tender Is the Night* came along, we were in the midst of the proletarian decade. Not many people read *Tender Is the Night* at the time; it sold less than 13,000 copies in its first two years. And since everyone was looking for the noble-savage kind of proletarian hero and a dialectical view of American society, the feeling about *Tender Is the Night*, even among those who did read it, seemed to be, as Fitzgerald said, "that my material was such as to preclude all dealing with mature persons in a mature world." When he was driven, he would say, "But, my God! it was my material, and it was all I had to deal with." [17] When he was less angry he saw how everything that had conspired to make him far more popular than he deserved to be in the twenties conspired equally to make him far less popular than he deserved to be in the thirties.

In addition to this impression that Fitzgerald was petering out, which both his own weaknesses and the weaknesses of the times conspired to create, he suffered the kind of denigration which in serious critical circles is reserved for writers who produce regularly for the slick magazines. More often than not, perhaps, this denigration is deserved, and probably no writer altogether escapes the debilitating effect of commercial writing; certainly Fitzgerald did not. Most serious critics, however, do not read the slick magazines, with the result that they are likely to think the gap between them and avant-garde fiction is greater than it is and to suppose that a writer who produces for them regularly is hopelessly damned. Fitzgerald wrote enough mediocre stories — even a few downright bad ones — for the commercial magazines to give the impression of a full-sized career of commercial mediocrity.

The result is a general impression that while Faulkner was a formidable romantic genius lurking in a decadent social jungle in Oxford, Mississippi, and Hemingway a serious man who got the maximum out of a fine but circumscribed talent, Fitzgerald was a gifted writer who was corrupted by *The Saturday Evening Post*.

This simplified view of what was in fact a very complicated situation is clearly represented by Hemingway's story of how Fitzgerald told him that "he wrote what he thought were good stories, and which really were good stories for the *Post*, and then changed them for submission, knowing exactly how he must make the twists that made them salable magazine stories. I had been shocked at this and I said it was whoring." [18] It is possible Fitzgerald did say something like this: he was always inclined to play the role he thought his listener expected of him, and he worried himself about his magazine writing, not because he had any romantic notions about his artistic chastity, but because he resented the time that writing for magazines took from his novel writing.

But only Hemingway's Manichean view of the writer's world could make him believe Fitzgerald wrote his magazine stories this way; there is no evidence at all to support this conception of how he wrote them and a great deal to suggest that he wrote them exactly as he did his novels. Some of them, especially some of those written in the middle thirties, are hastily written and he was thoroughly ashamed of such stories; he often grew angry, too, over how much easier it was to sell for high prices what he knew to be bad stories than to sell what he knew to be good ones. But Hemingway's Jekyll-and-Hyde conception of Fitzgerald's relation to his work is a grossly oversimplified view of it.[19]

Even careful and unprejudiced readers seem to have missed the fact that all through the late twenties and the thirties, besides the half-written and aborted stories, Fitzgerald was also writing a number of very fine ones for commercial magazines.

"Rich Boy" was in *Red Book* in 1926, "Babylon Revisited" and "Family In the Wind" were in *The Saturday Evening Post* in 1931 and 1932, "The Long Way Out" and "Financing Finnegan" and "The Lost Decade" were in *Esquire* in 1937, 1938, and 1939 — the list could be extended.

Fitzgerald himself contributed to the impression that he was frittering away his talent in hack work. His standards were very high; "I want to be one of the greatest writers that ever lived, don't you?" he said to Edmund Wilson when he was an undergraduate; and though he lost the naïveté of this, he never lost its substance.[20] In 1933 he was quoting to a correspondent Ford Madox Ford's remark that "Henry James was the greatest writer of his day; therefore, for me, the greatest man," and adding: "That is all I meant [in a previous conversation] by supereority. T. S. Elliot seems to me a very great person — Mrs. Lanier seems to me a very fine character."[21] Against this standard he was always measuring himself and finding himself wanting. "I now get 2000 a story and they grow worse and worse and my ambition is to get where I need write no more but only novels," he wrote John Peale Bishop in the spring of 1925, and a few years later he called himself "a first-rate writer who has never produced anything but second-rate books."[22] He went on repeating this conviction to the end of his life, when he wrote Max Perkins, with that terrifyingly casual past tense of his later life, "in a *small* way I was an original."[23] Whether it is true that he might have done better work even than his best or much more as good as his best had he not done so much commercial work is another question — and probably an unanswerable one; the point here is the extent to which such remarks contributed to the impression that Fitzgerald was not a serious writer at all.

In the thirties, when, as one publisher remarked, it was smart to be Marxist, to be neither Marxist nor avant-garde was bad; but to be, in addition, a commercial success in the slick magazines was worse. Fitzgerald failed the critics in these ways and they became uncertain whether to take him as a serious writer who was sometimes popular or as a popular writer who was occasionally serious. Even today, when the tribute of imitation has been paid him by so many able writers, and when *The Crack-Up* and the careful comments it elicited have had their effect, it is still difficult to see Fitzgerald quite clearly as a serious writer. While Hemingway was producing "the first forty-nine stories" and Faulkner around fifty, Fitzgerald was producing one hundred and sixty — not to mention thirty-odd articles, a scattering of poems, plays, and radio work, and a three years' supply of movie scripts. Of Fitzgerald's one hundred and sixty stories, at least fifty are serious and successful stories, and perhaps half of these are superb. Even if we assume that Hemingway's forty-nine and Faulkner's fifty are all first-rate — and this is evidently a false assumption — Fitzgerald as a serious writer of short stories compares very favorably with them both. The same thing is true of his novels. All this appears to have been by no means clear.

THE FAR SIDE OF PARADISE

A BIOGRAPHY OF F. SCOTT FITZGERALD

CHAPTER I

FITZGERALD'S LIFE has, apart from its close connection with his work, a considerable interest of its own; it was a life at once representative and dramatic, at moments a charmed and beautiful success to which he and his wife, Zelda, were brilliantly equal, and at moments disastrous beyond the invention of the most macabre imagination. The moral of its history is the teasing puzzle any human history is; but the forces of flawed character and of chance are revealed in Fitzgerald's life with remarkable fullness, both because it was a dramatic life lived with all the lack of caution which characterized Fitzgerald and because he spent his life representing what he understood of it. Just as his life illuminates his work, so his work does his life.

He was born at three-thirty in the afternoon of September 24, 1896, in a house on Laurel Avenue in St. Paul, Minnesota. He weighed ten pounds and six ounces: it was the only period in his life when he was the physical superior of his contemporaries. His father, Edward Fitzgerald, had been born in 1853 on a farm named Glenmary near Rockville in Montgomery County, Maryland, and was descended, on his mother's side, from Scotts and Keys who had been in this country since the early seventeenth century and had regularly served in the colonial legislatures. Edward Fitzgerald's great-grandfather, Philip Barton Key, had been a member of the

Congress under Jefferson; his aunt, Mrs. Suratt, was hanged for complicity in the murder of Lincoln. Francis Scott Key was a remote cousin of his mother. At the close of the Civil War, when he was no more than twelve or fifteen, he went west. Eventually he arrived in St. Paul, where, by the eighties, he was running a small wicker furniture business. In one of the panics of the nineties this business failed and he went to work as a salesman for Procter and Gamble. He was a small, quiet, ineffectual man with beautiful Southern manners, "very much the gentleman," as his contemporaries said, "but not much get up and go." [1] He was, in any event, no match for his wife who, according to the gossip of the times, had persuaded him to propose to her by threatening to throw herself into the Mississippi, along which they were taking a walk. "Molly," he used to say of Mrs. Fitzgerald, who was not very attractive, "just missed being beautiful." [2]

Mary McQuillan was the oldest of the four children of Philip McQuillan, an Irish immigrant who, after a start in Galena, Illinois, where he married his employer's daughter, came on to St. Paul. Here, as a wholesale grocer, he eventually "reared a personal fortune estimated at from three to four hundred thousand dollars," as the St. Paul papers put it, before he died at the age of forty-four of Bright's disease. Fitzgerald's Grandmother McQuillan's imposing Victorian mansion then stood on Summit Avenue near Dale Street. It represented the solidity and permanence of wealth to a boy whose childhood was spent moving from apartment to apartment and hotel to hotel at the rate of better than one move a year, largely because of his father's economic insufficiency. But the McQuillans did not represent breeding, for in addition to being "straight 1850 potato famine Irish" (as Fitzgerald once put it) they were eccentric, and their eldest daughter added to this eccentricity a directness which was also marked in her only son. "Whatever came into her head," as one of her in-laws remarked, "came right out of her mouth." She dressed carelessly and had her hair flying about her head in disorder. She was capable of appearing on a formal occasion wearing one old black shoe and one new brown one, on the principle that it is a good idea to break in new shoes one at a time (she had foot trouble and had to have her shoes made to order).[3] She was an omnivorous reader of bad books and when Fitzgerald did a little piece about her at the time of her death, he made Alice and Phoebe Cary her favorite poets.[4] Fitzgerald's contemporaries remember her from their child-hood as a witchlike old lady who carried an umbrella, rain or shine, and seemed always to be walking back and forth to the lending library with an armful of books. She was devoted to her only son and spoiled him in a way which could only be partly counteracted by his maiden Aunt Annabel Mc-Quillan. Near the end of his life he said: "I was fond of Aunt Annabel and Aunt Elise [Delihant, his father's sister], who gave me almost my first tastes of discipline, in a peculiar way in which I wasn't fond of my mother who spoiled me."[5]

His mother's treatment was bad for a precocious and imag-inative boy, and as Fitzgerald confessed to his daughter after she had grown up, "I didn't know till 15 that there was any-one in the world except me. . . ."[6] He was thirty before experience succeeded in convincing him that "life was [not] something you dominated if you were any good."[7] "Even if you mean your *own* life," as a friend wrote him when she read this remark in Fitzgerald's autobiographical essay, "The Crack-Up," "it is arrogant enough, — but life!"[8] But it was something more complicated than arrogance. About Fitzger-ald's writing there was always an element of play, of imitative representation, as when he wrote a relative with whom he quarreled, "I will try to resist the temptation to pass you down to posterity for what you are" (and did not succeed; he put her in a story shortly afterwards), or when he re-marked to his daughter of a passage in *The Way of All Flesh*, "My God — what precision of hatred is in those lines.

I'd like to be able to destroy my few detestations . . . with such marksmanship as that." [9] Perhaps some conviction of "The Omnipotence of Thought" exists in all writing. In Fitzgerald's case it carried over, like so much else, into his life, so that about everything he did for a long time there was an element of play, of an extravagance and simplicity of expectation which can only be described as childlike. It was this side of his nature which made him a lifelong practical joker and capable of enjoying success and pleasure as few people can.

As a small boy Fitzgerald lived, as he said later, "with a great dream" and his object was always to try to realize that dream. When he was four or five, for instance, he described his pony to his Grandmother McQuillan in minute detail; she was horrified that so small a child should have a pony, and it was not easy, after Scott's persuasive description, to convince her that the pony was quite imaginary. With his gift for imagining games and his energy in executing them, he sought to be the leader wherever he went. As a child he had a hard time understanding that other children did not exist simply as material for his uses, and when they asserted their own egos with the brutal directness of children, he was always unprepared for it and deeply wounded. One of the bitterest memories of his childhood was his sixth birthday party, in Buffalo. To the vision of himself in his long-trousered sailor suit playing the suave and gracious host his imagination had given itself for days; he was now to enter at last into the world of society. He was out early to meet his guests. Nobody came. All afternoon he waited with his freshly pressed suit, his clean hands, his carefully brushed hair; but nobody ever came, and at last he went "sorrowfully in and thoughtfully consumed one complete birthday cake, including several candles (for I was a great tallow eater until I was well over fourteen)." [10]

It is a consequence of this habit of projecting his wishes that he retained all his life the important emotional commitments of his growing up. It is partly because, as Americans, we all have similar commitments and because it never occurred to Fitzgerald, as it does to us, that he ought to pretend to have outgrown these commitments, that his work has such remarkable immediacy for us. He never buried his past because he was too naïve to realize that you are supposed to believe it is dead. It is not easy to convey the extraordinary energy with which his imagination responded and reached out to experience; he got something of what he felt into an incident — only the names are not actual — he used in *The Romantic Egotist*.

> . . . one night . . . with Nancy Collum . . . I sat in a swaying motor-boat by the club-house pier [at White Bear], and while the moon beat out golden scales on the water, heard young Byron Kirby propose to Mary Cooper in the motor-boat ahead. It was entirely accidental, but after it had commenced, wild horses could not have dragged Nancy and me from the scene. We sat there fascinated. Kirby was an ex-Princeton athlete and Mary Cooper was the popular debutante of the year. Kirby had a fine sense of form and when at the end of his manly pleading she threw her arms about his neck and hid her face in his coat, Nancy and I unconsciously clung together in delight. . . . when finally, unable to keep the secret, I told Kirby about it, he bought me three packages of cigarettes, and slapped me on the back telling me to be a sport and keep it very dark. *My enthusiasm knew no bounds, and I was all for becoming engaged to almost anyone immediately.*[11]

Given Fitzgerald's capacity for hero-worship, for identifying himself with some person he admired and then imagining himself as that person, he was bound to make an heroic image for himself of the athlete, and the process by which he did so can be traced step by step. It began when he was very young, at a small Y.M.C.A. basketball game. "The Captain of the losing side was a dark, slender youth of perhaps fourteen, who played with a fierce but facile abandon that . . . sent him everywhere around the floor pushing, dribbling, and shooting impossible baskets from all angles. . . . Oh, he was fine, really one of the finest things I ever saw. . . . after I saw him all athletes were dark and devilish and despairing and enthusiastic. . . ." [12] Here was a concrete instance of the romantic heroism vaguely outlined by Fitzgerald's imagination, and the image and the idea were fused by this experience. With his habit of struggling stubbornly to achieve in his own life the ideals he imagined, he went out himself for basketball and, trying to play with the "fierce but facile abandon" of his ideal, got a reputation for being a ball hog.

This vision of the heroic athlete was rapidly given an elaborate context by the boys' books he read and acquired a heavy burden of conventional detail. The hero was a prep-school or college boy, a male cinderella, small and discriminated against, who by some dramatic and unlikely display of pluck won the big game for St. Regis or Princeton. This dream was only gradually modified and never wholly uprooted by the hard realities of prep-school and college life. It put him on the Newman football team despite his dislike of the game and sent him out for Freshman football at Princeton — at one hundred and thirty-eight pounds. Every so often the ideal would achieve a new personification: Sam White in the Princeton-Harvard game of 1911; Hobey Baker, the Princeton captain of 1913, "slim and defiant"; "the romantic Buzz Law whom I had last seen one cold fall twilight in 1915, kicking from behind his goal line with a bloody bandage round his head," the mere sight of whom, "a slender, dark-haired young man with an indolent characteristic walk," could make "something stop inside" Fitzgerald when they passed on the Champs Elysées ten years after they had left college.[13] In these figures he found, as he put it once about Hobey Baker, "an ideal worthy of everything in my enthusiastic admiration, yet consummated and expressed in a human being who stood within ten feet of me." [14]

This is a characteristic instance of the process by which Fitzgerald's imagination took hold of — or was taken hold of by — the concrete particulars of American experience and gradually made out of them symbols for the whole of human experience. There may not be potential in Buzz Law much of the full moral value of the tragic hero, but he does have the advantage of being, as hero, genuine and indigenous; such as it was, his kind of heroism is something every American knows at first hand, and something that Fitzgerald responded to with his whole nature.

All his life he retained this kind of imaginative innocence. The most vivid image of aristocratic pride and self-possession he had ever seen was his boyhood rival, Reuben Warner, sitting with "aloof exhaustion" at the wheel of his Stutz Bearcat "with that sort of half-sneer on [his] face which I had noted was peculiar to drivers of racing cars."[15] Fitzgerald could joke about how he had slouched "passionately" at the wheel of the family car in an effort to realize this image himself. But the image nonetheless remained to haunt him all his life, as did all the deeply felt experiences of his youth. "It was on the cards," he would say to his daughter, "that Ginevra King should get fired from Westover — also that your mother should wear out young."[16] In any objective sense, the coupling of Zelda's tragedy and Ginevra King's departure from Westover is ludicrous. But their essential meaning was the same, and Fitzgerald, having felt both deeply, tended to ignore the discrepancy in objective importance.

If it was natural enough for Fitzgerald to apply to the normal boy's dream of social achievement and athletic success his habit of energetic idealization, it was also natural that others should resent his efforts to use them as bit players in his drama. But this resentment was something that his home environment had not in the least prepared him for. On the contrary, his mother's undiscriminating admiration had quite the opposite effect.

This situation was the source of two important characteristics of the adult Fitzgerald. Here, in the first place, was the beginning of that deep-seated social self-consciousness which is marked in his adult years. The ambition to lead, to succeed, to fulfill his dream of being a first-rate man had necessarily to be realized in the world he lived in. Whatever his scorn of that world — and it was considerable — he could not ignore it. At the same time the very intensity of his idealization of it and of his efforts to succeed puzzled and alienated his contemporaries who, the moment he ceased to charm them, turned on him. Not understanding, even as an adult, these sudden changes, he became uncertain of his social standing early in life. This uncertainty shows up clearly in his school days.

This situation must also have been the source of his unusual feelings about his mother. Even as a young boy he alternated between being ashamed of her eccentricity and being devoted to her. When he got away to school and realized how bitterly he had to suffer because of the way she had spoiled him, he was very angry at her. Yet when she died in 1936, at a time when his morale was at its lowest point and he was in serious financial straits, he remarked that "she was a defiant old woman, defiant in her love for me in spite of my neglect of her and it would have been quite within her character to have died that I might live." [17] After he finished *The Great Gatsby* he started to write a novel about matricide called *The Boy Who Killed His Mother*, on which he worked for four years without making much headway. While he was at work on it his mother came to Paris to visit him, and he anticipated her arrival by going around Paris telling all his friends what a dreadful old woman she was (though his friends, to their surprise, found her perfectly all right when she finally appeared). This attack on her may have been partly a product of his social uncertainty; but it was partly a product of his personal feelings about her. At about this time he also wrote a comic ballad about a dope fiend of sixteen who murdered his mother.

In a dear little vine covered cottage
On Forty-second Street
A butcher once did live who dealt
In steak and other meat.

His son was very nervous
And his mother him did vex
And she failed to make allowance
For his matricide complex
And now in old Sing Sing
You can hear that poor lad sing.

Just a boy that killed his mother
I was always up to tricks
When she taunted me I shot her
Through her chronic appendix
I was always very nervous
And it really isn't fair
I bumped off my mother but never no other
Will you let me die in the chair? . . .

It was dope that made me do it
Otherwise I wouldn't dare
'Twas ten grains of morphine that made me an orphine
Will you let me die in the chair?

With his considerable amateur talent for acting, Fitzgerald used to deliver this ballad at parties, his face powdered white, a cigarette dangling from his mouth, and his hands trembling.

In the spring of 1898, when he was two years old, the Fitzgeralds were moved to Buffalo by Procter and Gamble. Except for two and a half years from 1901 to 1903 when they lived in Syracuse, they remained in Buffalo until 1908. In March of that year Mr. Fitzgerald was fired. The experience was a terrifying one for his young son who, when the news came, prayed silently that they might not have to go to the poorhouse. In July they moved back to St. Paul. Mrs. Fitzgerald took her son on frequent trips during this period, to Orchard Park, Atlantic City, the Catskills and Adirondacks, and Chautauqua. They feared, not without reason, that he was consumptive. He was also taken to visit Randolph, his Aunt Eliza Delihant's place in Montgomery County, Maryland, and there, in April, 1903, he was a ribbon holder at the wedding of his cousin Cecilia, with whom he later fell in love when she was a young widow living in Norfolk and he was an undergraduate; she turns up in *This Side of Paradise* as Clara.

When he was four his parents tried to send him to school but he cried so hard they took him out after one day, and when he was sent to the Holy Angel's Convent in Buffalo at the age of seven it was with the understanding that he need go only half a day — either half he chose. He had a childhood horror of dead cats and remembered all his life a vacant lot in Syracuse that was full of them. He also developed a curious shame of his own feet and refused to go barefoot or even to swim because it involved exposing them. His father encouraged in him an interest in American history so that he remembered from his sixth year books about the Revolution and the Civil War, and, after seeing a play on the subject, spent hours in the attic dressed in a red sash which, he was convinced, made him look like Paul Revere. As he grew older, however, he turned the attic into a gymnasium and persuaded his family to give him a football outfit, complete with shinguards.

In school he was always in trouble with his teachers. An episode in one of the unpublished Basil stories which is a recollection of his own experience at Miss Nardon's Academy shows why.

"So the capitol of America is Washington," said Miss Cole, "and the capitol of Canada is Ottawa — and the capitol of Central America — "

" — is Mexico City," someone guessed.

"Hasn't any," said Basil absently.

"Oh, it must have a capitol," said Miss Cole looking at her map.

"Well, it doesn't happen to have one."

"That'll do, Basil. Put down Mexico City for the capitol of Central America. Now that leaves South America."

Basil sighed.

"There's no use teaching us wrong," he suggested.

Ten minutes later, somewhat frightened, he reported to the principal's office where all the forces of injustice were confusingly arrayed against him.

The forces of injustice continued to array themselves against him in this way for the rest of his academic career at St. Paul Academy and Newman and Princeton.

Though the influence of his mother and his energetically pious Aunt Annabel was probably as great as the influence of his father, Fitzgerald's early memories are all of what he learned from his father. The code of the Southern gentleman which his father taught him at this time — the belief in good manners and right instincts — stayed with him as an ideal all his life. Nick Carraway, the narrator in *The Great Gatsby* who is from St. Paul, Minnesota, has been told by his father to remember, when he is tempted to criticize others, that "a sense of the fundamental decencies is parcelled out unequally at birth";[18] in *Tender Is the Night* Dick Diver's father, a clergyman from Buffalo, New York, has taught him the need for " 'good instincts,' honor, courtesy, and courage," those "eternal necessary human values" which, as Fitzgerald said in "Echoes of the Jazz Age," were inadequately provided by the hedonistic twenties.[19] All these were the direct product of his own father's example.

I loved my father — he wrote later — always deep in my subconscious I have referred judgments back to him, what he would have thought, or done. He loved me — and felt a

deep responsibility for me — I was born several months after
the sudden death of my two elder sisters & he felt what the
effect of this would be on my mother, that he would have to
be my only moral guide. . . . What he told me were simple
things.

"Once when I went in a room as a young man I was confused so I went up to the oldest woman there and introduced
myself and afterwards the people of that town always thought
I had good manners." He did that from a good heart that
came from another America — he was much too sure of what
he was . . . to doubt for a moment that his own instincts
were good. . . .

We walked down town in Buffalo on Sunday mornings
and my white ducks were stiff with starch & he was very
proud walking with his handsome little boy. We had our
shoes shined and he lit his cigar and we bought the Sunday
paper. When I was a little older I did not understand at all
why men that I knew were vulgar and not gentlemen made
him stand up or give the better chair on our verandah. But
I know now. There was new young peasant stock coming up
every ten years & he was one of the generation of the col-
onies and the revolution.[20]

He tried to tell his son stories which would embody the feelings he inherited from his past, but his son did not think them
very good stories at the time; "[my father] came from tired
old stock, with very little left of vitality and mental energy,"
he wrote in *The Romantic Egotist*. Later he understood
better; "his own life," he wrote Harold Ober in 1926, "after
a rather brilliant start back in the seventies has been a 'failure'
— he's lived always in mother's shadow and he takes an im-
mense vicarious pleasure in any success of mine."[21]

By the time the Fitzgeralds moved back to St. Paul in July,
1908, when Scott was twelve, he had got well started on most
boyhood interests. He had fallen in love with a girl at Mr.
Van Arnem's dancing school, had organized a play in a neigh-

bor's attic, had collected stamps and cigar bands, played football on a neighborhood team ("guard or tackle and usually scared silly"), written a detective story and the beginning of a history of the United States (it never got past the battle of Bunker Hill), sung for visitors (at his mother's insistence) "Way Down in Colon Town" and "Don't Get Married Any More," told his first lie at confession "by saying in a shocked voice to the priest 'Oh, *no*, I *never* tell a lie'" — exactly as does the little boy in "Absolution." He was like Basil Duke Lee at the same age, "by occupation actor, athlete, scholar, philatelist and collector of cigar bands." [22]

2

The Fitzgeralds' return to St. Paul opened a new world to their son. Up to that time his family had moved regularly every September, so that he had hardly lived in a single neighborhood long enough to become a part of it. But for the next ten years of his life he was to be one of the group of children who lived in the neighborhood of Summit Avenue. As usual the Fitzgeralds moved each year — from 294 Laurel Avenue to 514 Holly Avenue; then to 509 and 499 Holly. Here they stayed for three years before they moved again into 593 Summit Avenue, one of a row of brownstone-front houses near Dale Street. Summit Avenue is St. Paul's show street, "a museum," as Fitzgerald later called it, "of American architectural failures." [23] Dale Street, however, is just about where Summit Avenue lapses into a quite ordinary street, a decline which is signaled by the row of narrow-fronted, attached houses in one or the other of which — they moved from 593 to 599 in 1918 — the Fitzgeralds lived the rest of their lives in St. Paul. None of these moves within St. Paul, however, took them out of the Summit Avenue community. Thus, as Fitzgerald grew up, his family moved gradually around the periphery of St. Paul's finest residential district, settling finally at the end of its best street. The symbolism is almost too neat, and Fitzgerald was acutely aware of it. When *This Side of Paradise* was accepted in 1919, for instance, he sat down at once to write his childhood friend, Alida Bigelow, about his success. The letter is headed:

> (599 Summit Avenue)
> In a house below the average
> Of a street above the average
> In a room below the roof.
> I shall write Alida Bigelow. . . .[24]

For if St. Paul had then a great deal of the simple and quite unself-conscious democracy of the old middle-western cities, it also had its wealth and its inherited New England sense of order. The best people in St. Paul are admirable and attractive people; but they are, in their quiet way, clearly the best people. They do not forget the Maine or Connecticut "connection"; they send their children to Hotchkiss or Hill or Westover, to Yale or Princeton, to be educated; they are, without ostentation or affectation, cosmopolitan.

At the top — Fitzgerald once wrote of St. Paul — came those whose grandparents had brought something with them from the East, a vestige of money and culture; then came the families of the big self-made merchants, the "old settlers" of the sixties and the seventies, American-English-Scotch, or German or Irish, looking down somewhat in the order named — upon the Irish less from religious difference — French Catholics were considered rather distinguished — than from their taint of political corruption in the East. After this came certain well-to-do "new people" — mysterious, out of a cloudy past, possibly unsound.[25]

This was the world Fitzgerald grew up in, desiring with all the intensity of his nature to succeed according to its standards and always conscious of hovering socially on the edge of it, alternating between assertion and uncertainty because of his acute awareness that his foothold was unsure. None of the things that bothered him would have made a serious impression on him had it not been for his already established insecurity. Fitzgerald's younger sister, Annabel, for instance, appears to have settled happily and without self-consciousness into the social life of the community. She was a pretty girl, very quiet and self-possessed. Fitzgerald's imagination seems to have fixed itself for a time on her and to have sought through her, as it was so often in later life to seek its satisfactions through the lives of others, the "interior security" and exterior success which he felt he never quite achieved in his own person. He believed that only her quietness prevented her achieving the romantic social success in which he took such innocent delight. To remedy this deficiency he provided her with a fashionable "line" with which she would amaze her dance partners. Annabel eventually married a young naval officer, Clifton Sprague, who was later to distinguish himself as the commander of the tin-can fleet which fought gallantly at the battle of Leyte Gulf in 1944.

It would be an exaggeration to suggest that Fitzgerald was not often happily at ease socially too. Still, when he came to use his childhood memory of White Bear in the summer of 1911 for "Winter Dreams," he made the hero a caddy. Gradually, as he grew older, he became more and more self-conscious about the small social gestures which ought to become more and more habitual. The end of this development was his lifelong habit of attacking the task of conducting himself like a gentleman with nervous anxiety. The habit was all the more remarkable because he had great personal charm when he chose to exert it, and because a part of his mind understood the situation perfectly, knew that one does not become a gentleman by acting the part consciously, understood that alienation is self-induced.

A great many things in his boyhood situation had pitfalls for him. He was embarrassed by his mother; and he was troubled by his father's trade. His father was now a wholesale grocery salesman, a job he probably obtained through the old McQuillan connection. It was said in St. Paul that he made just about enough to pay for the desk in his brother-in-law's real estate office from which he conducted his business. Mr. Fitzgerald was even required to charge his postage stamps at the corner drugstore. Such things were a constant humiliation to his son, who loved him and never forgot his mother's "Well, if it wasn't for [Grandfather McQuillan] where would we be now?" [26]

> I am — Fitzgerald wrote long afterward — half black Irish and half old American stock with the usual exaggerated ancestral pretensions. The black Irish half of the family had the money and looked down upon the Maryland side of the family who had, and really had, that . . . series of reticences and obligations that go under the poor old shattered word "breeding". . . . So being born in that atmosphere of crack, wise crack and countercrack I developed a two cylinder inferiority complex. So if I were elected King of Scotland tomorrow after graduating from Eton, Magdelene the Guards, with an embryonic history which tied me to the Plantagonets, I would still be a *parvenue*. I spent my youth in alternately crawling in front of the kitchen maids and insulting the great. [27]

Thus, very conscious of a dubious gentility and an inadequate family income, he set out to make his way in St. Paul and at St. Paul Academy. He was a small, handsome, blue-eyed boy, full of energy and invention and already so determined to make a success that the school magazine, *Now and Then*, quickly tagged him as the man who knew exactly "How to Run the School," and asked rather quarrelsomely if there were not someone who would "poison Scotty or find some means to shut his mouth." [28] "He wasn't popular with his schoolmates," said his headmaster. "He saw through them too much and wrote about it." [29]

On the long, wonderful summer visits at White Bear Lake with his friends Cecil Read and Robert Clark—whose families could afford places at White Bear—he was constantly being beaten at games, even by girls. Nonetheless, as he was to do all his life, he stuck grimly to it. He played football, first with a corner-lot team which he and his friends organized (and got a broken rib), and then on intramural teams. Once in the fall of 1909 he got into an Academy game; "The Academy outweighed the 'Summits' about sixty pounds," says *Now and Then*. "On account of this the Academy put some of their lightest men on the line." He was on the third-string "Blue" basketball team and was the second-string pitcher for the Academy's third team, which had a disastrous season that year.

But if his athletic career was an unbroken series of unadmitted defeats, he had some success in an extracurricular way and as a literary man. He was the leader and idea man for a club, known first as the Scandal Detectives and later as the Gooserah, which had its headquarters in the loft of his friend Cecil Read's barn on Holly Avenue and later in the attic of the Reads' new house on Summit. Here, when Fitzgerald was reading *The Three Musketeers*, they were taught by him to fence and, when he read *Arsène Lupin*, to be detectives: everything he read had to be lived. Under the stimulus of romances about the Ku Klux Klan, the Gooserah also organized "adventures." One of these was an attack on another boy of their own age, Reuben Warner, who had captured the affections of the girl Fitzgerald admired. Their skillfully conceived piece of terrorization, which ended with Mr. Warner's calling out the police, was used by Fitzgerald in his story "The Scandal Detectives" in *Taps at Reveille*.[30]

It was widely known in these circles, too, that Scott kept,

locked in a box under his bed, a manuscript known as his "Thoughtbook," which was believed to contain candid and destructive accounts of all his contemporaries. This document still exists, fourteen pages torn from a notebook and covered with Fitzgerald's boyish scrawl. It was the source for the "Book of Scandal" Basil kept, though its main preoccupation is neither scandal nor his friends but girls. As the work of a fourteen-year-old boy it is remarkable for the minuteness of its analyses of people and of Fitzgerald's feelings about them; its interest in the small shifts of power within his social group is unflagging. "[Paul Ballion]," he will write, "was awfully funny, strong as an ox, cool in the face of danger polite and at times very interesting. Now I dont dislike him. I have simply out grown him." Or: "Since dancing school opened this last time I have deserted Alida [Bigelow]. I have two new Crushes. To wit — Margaret Armstrong and Marie Hersey. . . . The 2nd is the prettiest the 1st the best talker. The 2nd the most popular with T. Ames, L. Porterfield, B. Griggs, C. Read, R. Warner ect. and I am crazy about her. I think it is charming to hear her say, 'Give it to me as a comp-pliment' when I tell her I have a trade last for her. I think Una Baches is the most unpopular girl in dancing schools. Last year in dancing school I got 11 valentines and this year 15." The battle, as this passage shows, was for general popularity. It was the age of character books and the lock of hair and Fitzgerald showed great curiosity as to how many girls listed him as their "favorite boy" or the one they would "like to kiss most." He was also a tireless collector of locks of hair, which he would mount on pins and wear on his coat lapel. His success was considerable, for he was an attractive boy.

As they grew older, the crowd began to gather regularly in the yard of the Ames house on Grand Avenue which Fitzgerald later described with such fidelity in "The Scandal Detectives." It was here that he had, as he put it in his Ledger, his first "faint sex attraction."

Basil — he wrote of the character to whom he ascribed this experience — rode over to Imogene Bissel and balanced idly on his wheel before her. Something in his face then must have attracted her, for she looked up at him, looked at him really, and slowly smiled. . . . For the first time in his life he realized a girl completely as something opposite and complementary to him, and he was subject to a warm chill of mingled pleasure and pain. It was a definite experience and he was immediately conscious of it. . . .

"Can you come out tonight?" he asked eagerly. "There'll probably be a bunch in the Whartons' yard."

"I'll ask mother." . . .

"Listen," he said quickly, "what boys do you like better than me?"

"Nobody. I like you and Hubert Blair best."

Basil felt no jealousy at the coupling of this name with his. There was nothing to do about Hubert Blair but accept him philosophically. . . .

"I like you better than anybody," he said deliriously.

The weight of the pink dappled sky above him was not endurable. He was plunging along through air of ineffable loveliness. . . .[31]

Meanwhile he had begun to write and had become St. Paul Academy's star debater (no one had found a means to shut him up). Having had to read Sir Walter Scott in school, he turned out a complicated story of knights and ladies called "Elavo"; and having become an expert on the detective story on his own initiative, he wrote "The Mystery of the Raymond Mortgage." This story was printed in *Now and Then* in September, 1909; it was his first published work. It is, for a schoolboy, a skillfully plotted little murder story and, in its sedulous imitation of the style of such works, often unconsciously very funny. "The morning after I first saw John Syrel, I proceeded to the scene of the crime to which he had alluded"; " 'What have you heard?' I asked. 'I have an agent in Indianous,' he replied, 'in the shape of an Arab boy whom

I employ for ten cents a day' "; this is the quintessence of the Doyle style. ". . . through some oversight," as Fitzgerald himself remarked later, "I neglected to bring the [mortgage] into the story in any form"; but no one seemed to notice.[32] This success was followed by two romantic Civil War stories, "A Debt of Honor" and "The Room with the Green Blinds," and a football story called "Reade, Substitute Right Half."

He also became a playwright. He had always loved plays, from the time he had enacted Paul Revere in his red sash in the attic in Buffalo, and he never tired of reading the parts for his friend Tubby Washington's toy theater while Tubby was reduced to moving the cardboard figures around the stage. When he was reading *Arsène Lupin*, he wrote and managed to produce a half-hour detective play in the Ames' living room; its cast — Slim Jim, Anne the girl, Mike a police-man — foreshadows the more ambitious "Captured Shadow" written two years later. The great moment came, however, when Miss Elizabeth Magoffin, a St. Paul lady of romantic tendencies with an interest in the theater, organized a modest children's performance of a comedy called "A Regular Fix." It was produced at the Academy in August, 1911. She had hardly reckoned on the effect of this experience on Fitzgerald, who sat down at once and wrote a melodramatic western called "The Girl from Lazy J," of which he was both star and director. The ever-faithful Tubby drove direc-tor Fitzgerald to despair with his repeated failure, as the vengeful Mexican bandit, to pause at the break in his key line, "Now I will have revenge — but wait."

These multifarious extracurricular activities had seriously affected Fitzgerald's school work. He was incapable of learn-ing anything which did not appeal to his imagination and always depended on his wealth of scattered information about American history and certain areas of literature to distract attention from his failure to have prepared the day's assign-ment. But since he had become a writer he had taken to

scribbling on the blank pages of his textbooks throughout all
his classes, and it became apparent that drastic measures would
have to be taken. A family conference was held and it emerged
that Aunt Annabel was prepared to foot the bill for a boarding school, provided it was a good Catholic school. Plans
were therefore laid to send Fitzgerald to Newman in the fall
of 1911.[33]

He faced this prospect with his usual burst of imaginative
fervor. All his knowledge of boarding school life, as he had
learned about it from Ralph Henry Barbour and others, was
summoned to the task of providing an adequate dream of social and athletic success in this glittering eastern world. At
the same time some need of his imagination for thinking of
himself now as a man asserted itself. He had acquired his first
adult long trousers and he began to make those characteristic
American middle-class boys' experiments with sex which are
always conducted with working-class or lower middle-class
girls — "chickens" they were then called. This was the summer
he picked up a "chicken" at the State Fair with the result
described in "Basil at the Fair." [34] During this summer he and
Tubby took to picking up such girls regularly; they would
get, as they supposed, very drunk on a bottle of drugstore
sherry and make tentative sexual ventures.

3

Fitzgerald's two years at Newman were a repetition on a
larger scale of his experience at St. Paul Academy. He set off
for Newman full of dreams of success and popularity and yet
acutely aware of his divided nature. He once recalled in detail his judgment of himself at this time.

. . . Physically — I marked myself handsome; of great athletic *possibilities*, and an extremely good dancer. . . . Socially . . . I was convinced that I had personality, charm,

magnetism, poise, and the ability to dominate others. Also I was sure that I exercised a subtle fascination over women. Mentally . . . I was vain of having so much of being talented, ingenious and quick to learn. To balance this, I had several things on the other side: Morally — I thought I was rather worse than most boys, due to a latent unscrupulousness and the desire to influence people in some way, even for evil . . . lacked a sense of honor, and was mordantly selfish. Psychologically . . . I was by no means the "Captain of my fate." . . . I was liable to be swept off my poise into a timid stupidity. I knew I was "fresh" and not popular with older boys. . . . Generally — I knew that at bottom I lacked the essentials. At the last crisis, I knew I had no real courage, perseverance or self respect.[35]

This is a remarkably honest account of himself; it shows, as he observed later in *The Romantic Egotist*, that "all my inordinate vanity . . . was on the surface . . . and underneath it, came my own sense of lack of courage and stability."

He was, in short, the Basil of "The Freshest Boy." "Basil . . . had lived with such intensity on so many stories of boarding-school life that, far from being homesick, he had a glad feeling of recognition and familiarity." "With what he consider[s] kindly intent" he makes to the older boy he is traveling to school with "the sort of remark that creates lifelong enmities":

"You'd probably be a lot more popular in school if you played football," he suggested patronizingly.

Lewis did not consider himself unpopular. He did not think of it in that way at all. He was astounded.

"You wait!" he cried furiously. "They'll take all that freshness out of you."

"Clam yourself," said Basil, coolly plucking at the creases of his first long trousers. "Just clam yourself."

"I guess everybody knows you were the freshest boy at the Country Day!"

"Clam yourself," repeated Basil, but with less assurance. "Kindly clam yourself."

"I guess I know what they had in the school paper about you —"

Basil's own coolness was no longer perceptible. . . . [Lewis's] reference had been to one of the most shameful passages in his companion's life. In a periodical issued by the boys of Basil's late school there had appeared, under the heading Personals:

> If someone will please poison young Basil, or find some means to stop his mouth, the school at large and myself will be much obliged.[36]

So too, Fitzgerald arrived at Newman, and, repeating his mistakes at St. Paul Academy, made himself the most unpopular boy in the school. "He saw now that in certain ways he had erred at the outset — he had boasted, he had been considered yellow at football, he had pointed out people's mistakes to them, he had shown off his rather extraordinary fund of general information in class."[37] Football was a particularly sore point. "Newman was just a small school and football was practically a form of exercise in which everyone took part," said one of his classmates years later; "but it was a key to prestige and that was the inducement [for Fitzgerald]. Fitz himself was ordinarily quite an indifferent player without real zest for the game and never went out for football at college, but by then there were other avenues for obtaining prestige for which he was better equipped."[38] His extreme good looks — even four years later he collected a painful number of votes as the prettiest member of his class at Princeton — helped to win him a quick reputation as a sissy. Within a month of his arrival he had had several fights forced on him, with the crowd always against him, and had been lectured on his freshness by a fellow student named Herbert Agar. His roommate remembered him years later as having had "the most impenetrable egotism I've ever seen": he was constantly aware that "he was one of the poorest boys in a rich boys' school." [39] He had the faculty as well as the students against him: he was never on time for classes or meals, and he could not be prevented from reading after lights; he was constantly on bounds. Ten years later he wrote of this time:

I was unhappy because I was cast into a situation where everybody thought I ought to behave just as they behaved — and I didn't have the courage to shut up and go my own way, anyhow.

For example, there was a rather dull boy at school named Percy, whose approval, I felt, for some unfathomable reason, I must have. So, for the sake of this negligible cipher, I started out to let as much of my mind as I had under mild cultivation sink back into a state of heavy underbrush. I spent hours in a damp gymnasium fooling around with a muggy basket-ball. . . .

And all this to please Percy. He thought it was the thing to do. If you didn't go through the damp business every day you were "morbid." . . . I didn't want to be morbid. So I became muggy instead. . . .

The worst of it is that this same business went on until I was twenty-two. That is, I'd be perfectly happy doing just what I wanted to do, when somebody would begin shaking his head and saying:

"Now see here, Fitzgerald, you mustn't go on doing that. It's — it's morbid." [40]

But while a part of Fitzgerald did rebel from the start against the narrowness and tyranny of boarding-school life, a part of him was exactly like Percy. Some years later a shrewd observer who knew him at Officers' Training School remarked of Fitzgerald that "he was eager to be liked by his companions and almost vain in seeking praise. At the same time he was unwilling to conform to the various patterns of dullness and majority opinion which would insure popularity." [41] At Newman, too, though he never gave up the pursuits which were supposed to lead to success, he could never quite do them in the conventional and accepted way.

During his first fall there he stuck grimly to his job on the scrub football team, struggled with stubborn courage to live down his unpopularity, and suffered deeply, as the "Incident of the Well-Meaning Professor" in *This Side of Paradise* shows. His greatest consolation was to escape from school to the theater in New York. His notes for this period are full of references to plays seen — *The Little Millionaire*, with George M. Cohan, *Over the River*, *The Private Secretary*, and above all, *The Quaker Girl* with Ina Claire and *Little Boy Blue* with Gertrude Bryant. He now added to his ambitions the intention to produce a great musical comedy and began to scribble librettos in his spare time. He went home for a brief, wonderful Christmas vacation and came back to find that his poor marks had put him back on bounds. But he settled down to try to make a new start. "It was a long hard time. . . . An indulgent mother had given him no habits of work and this was almost beyond the power of anything but life itself to remedy, but he made numberless new starts and failed and tried again." [42] Gradually his unpopularity waned and in the spring he won the Junior Field Meet, which gave him a tiny triumph to cling to. He went home for the summer chastened and improved.

During the summer he went through the characteristic cycle once more. "All one can know," he once said of the age of fifteen, "is that somewhere between thirteen, boyhood's majority, and seventeen, when one is a sort of a counterfeit young man, there is a time when youth fluctuates hourly between one world and another — pushed ceaselessly forward into unprecedented experiences and vainly trying to struggle back to the days when nothing had to be paid for." [43] In St. Paul his newly discovered consideration for others was, he found, a great social asset; for just a moment he was the most popular boy in the crowd. Then, realizing he was making a success, he began to talk about himself and quickly destroyed his popularity. He never forgot a dance at White Bear this summer which began with his having to beg a ride out with some boys who did not much want him — they were at the age when the possession of a car was immeasurably important — and ended with his being left out of a party which was organized right under his nose.

Happily, however, there was a diversion from this trouble. During the previous Christmas vacation he had seen a production of *Alias Jimmy Valentine* which had inspired him to write (on the train coming home for the summer) a similar drama called "The Captured Shadow." This was to be the summer's production of The Elizabethan Dramatic Club, a group of about forty young people organized for the purpose by Fitzgerald and directed by Miss Elizabeth Magoffin. Miss Magoffin was so carried away by the young author that she gave him her picture inscribed "To Scott 'He had that spark — Magnetic mark —' with the best love of the one who thinks so," and added to her tribute an effusion entitled "The Spark," which begins:

He was handsome — and straightness and firmness of form;
His lucid eyes shown with a light nigh divine;
His body enwrapping a soul big and warm,
A head and a heart — he was master of mind.

It was enough to try the modesty of any fifteen-year-old.

The play, which was performed at Mrs. Backus' School on August twenty-third, was a great success. As Fitzgerald said in the story he wrote fifteen years later and called "The Captured Shadow," "he had followed his models closely, and for all its grotesqueries, the result was actually interesting — it was a play"; it is.[44] The action is carefully planned and there is plenty of plausible if conventional movement to the plot. It has its drunks, its comic gangsters, its elderly spinster, its Irish policeman and French detective. After originally casting himself for the second male lead, Fitzgerald was persuaded to play the suave gentleman burglar himself and "much favorable comment was elicited by the young author's cleverness," as the local press put it, from an audience of several hundred. The charity selected to provide a nominal cause for the production was the richer by sixty dollars. Thus Fitzgerald returned to Newman with a success behind him.

His second year at Newman was happier than his first. He made the football team, though not as a regular, and was even commended for his "fine running with the ball" in the *Newman News'* account of the Kingsley game. But he was still without enthusiasm for the game and, on one occasion during the Newark Academy game, he avoided an open-field tackle so obviously that the quarterback, Donahoe, came over to him and said: "You do that again and I'll beat you up myself." With his wonderful Irish sense of the absurd and his ability to see it in his own experience, Fitzgerald loved to repeat this story about himself, and usually concluded his narration by remarking that he was so much more scared of Donahoe than of any ball carrier that he played a brilliant defensive game the rest of the afternoon. He made a good friend of Donahoe, and all his life admired with his characteristic generosity Donahoe's possession of the persistence and self-control which he imagined — often quite wrongly — that he himself lacked. Respect for Donahoe's modesty made him omit his name when he said in "Handle with Care" that he "represented my sense of the 'good life,' though I saw him once in a decade . . . . in difficult situations I . . . tried to think what *he* would have thought, how *he* would have acted." [45]

Meanwhile, still under the influence of *The Quaker Girl* and *Little Boy Blue*, he had gone on writing musical comedies. He read all the Gilbert and Sullivan he could get hold of and filled his notebooks with ideas for songs and plots. Then sometime during the spring he picked up a musical score which he found on the top of a piano. It was for a show called "His Honor the Sultan" and, he discovered, had been produced by something called the Triangle Club of Princeton University. "That," he wrote later, "was enough for me. From then on the university question was settled. I was bound for Princeton." [46] * It was not quite that easy; Aunt Annabel was still financing his schooling and did not want him to go to a Protestant college. She was, however, eventually talked around. Meanwhile Fitzgerald won the school Elocution Prize, played the part of Johann Ludwig, King of Schwartzbaum-Altminster, in a one-acter called "The Power of Music" which the Comedy Club produced, became an editor of the *Newman News*, won the Senior Field Day, pitched for the second team, and, in general, established himself as a respected if not brilliant member of the school community. In May he took his examinations for Princeton and "did a little judicious cribbing and never forgot it afterwards." [47] Even so he did not do well enough to assure his admission.

He went home for the summer to study for his September make-up examinations, to fall in love once more, and to work on another play for The Elizabethan Dramatic Club. This time he produced a Civil War melodrama called "The Coward" about a young Southerner who is "unwilling to don a

---

* But on another occasion he said it was seeing Sam White beat Harvard (in 1911, 8-6, by scoring a touchdown on a blocked kick) which decided him for Princeton. White's touchdown was exactly the kind of sudden, brilliant, individual act which would have struck his imagination, especially as it occurred for him against a background of gallant defeats. "I think what started my Princeton sympathy," he said on another occasion, "was that they always just lost the foot-ball championship. Yale always seemed to nose them out in the last quarter by superior 'stamina' as the newspapers called it. . . . . I imagined the Princeton men as slender and keen and romantic, and the Yale men as brawny and brutal and powerful." A decade later he was to make Tom Buchanan "one of the most powerful ends that ever played football at New Haven"; he is the contrasting type to "the romantic Buzz Law."

uniform and fight for the independence of the South." "Playwright Fitzgerald . . . appear[ed] in the role of Lieut. Douglas," a minor figure, but, though Miss Magoffin's name still appears as the "Directress," Mr. Scott Fitzgerald has crept in as Stage Manager, and the yellow posters for the performance announce that "Gustave B. Schurmeier presents LAURANCE BOARDMAN in SCOTT FITZGERALD'S COMEDY 'THE COWARD' . . ."[48] The performance, on August 29, was a great success and this time the Baby Welfare League benefited by one hundred and fifty dollars from the first performance alone. There was a second at the White Bear Yacht Club a week later.

During this summer the youthful bottle of drugstore sherry began to give way to more adult drinks, and twice during the year Fitzgerald was drunk enough to remember the occasions as special ones. He began to be known around St. Paul as "a man who drank," a reputation which gave him a certain romantic interest which he undoubtedly enjoyed. There was one sensational occasion when he scandalized St. Paul by disturbing the Christmas service at St. John's, the most correct of Episcopal churches.

I entered quietly — Fitzgerald remembered afterwards — and walked up the aisle toward [the rector], searching the silent ranks of the faithful for some one whom I could call my friend. But no one hailed me. In all the church there was no sound but the metalic rasp of the buckles on my overshoes as I plodded toward the rector. At the very foot of the pulpit a kindly thought struck me — perhaps inspired by the faint odor of sanctity which exuded from the saintly man. I spoke.

"Don't mind me," I said, "go on with the sermon."

Then, perhaps unsteadied a bit by my emotion, I passed down the other aisle, followed by a sort of amazed awe, and so out into the street.

The papers had the extra out before midnight.[49]

CHAPTER II

FITZGERALD came on to Princeton in the middle of September of 1913 to take the examinations which would determine whether he was to be admitted. On the twenty-fourth he was able to wire his mother: ADMITTED SEND FOOTBALL PADS AND SHOES IMMEDIATELY PLEASE WAIT TRUNK.[1] He settled for his freshman year into the rambling stucco warren at 15 University Place.

The Princeton to which he was then admitted was a very different place from the present Princeton. It was essentially an undergraduate college, though the Graduate College was dedicated the fall Fitzgerald arrived. Its enrollment was around 1500; it had a good undergraduate library of about 300,000 volumes; it had just begun to feel the effect of the preceptorial system introduced under President Wilson, who had recently escaped from an unhappy situation at the University into the governorship of New Jersey and had been replaced by John Grier Hibben.

Physically Princeton still centered in the old campus above the transverse line set by McCosh Walk, though some of the new dormitories on the lower campus such as Little, Patton, and Cuyler had been built. The railroad station still stood at the foot of Blair steps, and the old Casino, where the Triangle Club rehearsed, stood not far off. The rickety but partly eighteenth-century façade of Nassau Street had not yet been replaced by faked Georgian; Nassau Street itself was unpaved. The modern undergraduate commons on the corner of University Place and Nassau Street would not be built for two more years; Palmer stadium was under construction and would first be used for the Dartmouth game in the fall of Fitzgerald's sophomore year (Fitzgerald first saw "the romantic Buzz Law kicking from behind his own goal line with a bloody bandage round his head" on University Field on Prospect Street).

> Pause some evening — wrote V. Lansing Collins in 1914 — beneath the windows of any dormitory on the campus. . . . From one room comes the rapid clicking of a typewriter where someone is getting out a report or an essay . . . in another room are three or four men hotly arguing some triviality of college politics; across the way a talking machine is reproducing the latest Broadway success; elsewhere an impromptu quartet of piano, violin, guitar, and mandolin is reminding nobody of the Kneisels or the Flonzaleys. . . .[2]

This sounds typical of undergraduate life at almost any time, save that the overtones of the age of guitar and mandolin are still evident. They were soon to fade, however. The Princeton modification of hazing, known locally as "horsing" — it consisted in forcing freshmen to sing or recite, or to march to commons in "lockstep express" — was officially abolished altogether in the spring of 1914. The rushes — battles between freshmen and sophomores — continued for only a few years longer, though Fitzgerald was proud to have his picture taken to show his battered condition after one of them. The fact revealed by "an official census" that there were only six undergraduate automobiles in Princeton in 1913 was soon to seem astonishing. It was, as Dean Gauss remarked years later, "the Indian Summer of the 'College Customs' era in our campus life," an era which was gradually dying and was to be abruptly closed by the country's entrance into the war.[3]

Meanwhile, however, it was a small world, as perhaps the

undergraduate world always is. Most of its standards and traditions had come down to it very little changed from the nineties and this was largely true of the curriculum as well as of undergraduate mores. ". . . Ernest Dowson and Oscar Wilde were the latest sensational writers who had got in past the stained glass windows [of the library]," as Edmund Wilson remembered.[4] John Peale Bishop, a sympathetic observer, described it as a place where

> . . . nothing matters much but that a man bear an agreeable person and maintain with slightly mature modifications the standards of prep school. Any extreme in habiliment, pleasures or opinions is apt to be characterized as "running it out," and to "run it out" is to lose all chance of social distinction. . . .
>
> These somewhat naive standards may be violated on occasion by the politician or the big man, but to the mere individualist they will be applied with contempt and intolerance.[5]

Football was a deadly serious affair; the Big Three were still really big, so that football, it could be felt, was a game conducted by gentlemen in a kind of Tennysonian Round-Table spirit. No editorial writer on the *Daily Princetonian* ever questioned the idea that the success or failure of a university year depended on the results of the Yale and Harvard games, and Fitzgerald, at a time when he was by no means a simple disciple of the conventional Princeton attitude, could write in *This Side of Paradise*: "There at the head of the white platoon marched Allenby, the football captain, slim and defiant, as if aware that this year the hopes of the college rested on him, that his hundred-and-sixty pounds were expected to dodge to victory through the heavy blue and crimson lines."[6] Questions of the intercollegiate regulation of major sports were conducted at the high diplomatic level by consultations among the captains of the Big Three teams and their decisions were solemnly canvassed at the universities and in the metropolitan press.

Football was the best means to social distinction on the campus, and social distinction, as the quotation from John Peale Bishop shows, was the main preoccupation of the first two years of an undergraduate's career. The competition was no less fierce because its most inviolable requirement was that the contestants should appear quite unconcerned with social prestige. Beneath this pretense of indifference the game of becoming a Big Man was carried on day in and day out by everyone who had, by local standards, good sense. "From the day when, wild-eyed and exhausted [from the rush], the . . . freshmen sat in the gymnasium and elected some one from Hill School class president . . . up until the end of sophomore year it never ceased, that breathless social system, that worship, seldom named, never really admitted, of the bogey 'Big Man.'" ". . . all the petty snobbishness within the prep-school, all the caste system of Minneapolis, all were here magnified, glorified and transformed into a glittering classification." [7]

There were besides football other, though less powerful, means of becoming a Big Man; other sports which drew crowds counted, though, as Bishop noted, "Closet athletics, such as wrestling and the parallel bars, are almost a disadvantage." [8] After football the most powerful organization socially was the Triangle Club which, by an incredible consumption of undergraduate time and energy, produces annually a commonplace musical comedy. After the Triangle Club, the *Daily Princetonian* was the most reputable pursuit for an undergraduate, and after that what Bishop called "the Y.M.C.A. in a Brooks suit" — the Philadelphian Society — and *The Tiger*.

All this energetic pursuit of extracurricular activities received its reward at the time of club elections in the middle of the sophomore year. The Princeton clubs come as near to being purely social institutions as such organizations ever can, and it is this very purity which sets the limits to their influence. A Yale senior society or an ordinary fraternity chapter, which does perform a serious function however limited or misdirected it may be, offers its members something to work for and even believe in. A Princeton club, apart from providing a place to eat, to play billiards, and to take a girl on week-ends (and nowadays, though not in Fitzgerald's day, a bar and a television set), does not even pretend to offer anything. The function of the Princeton clubs is to provide a system of grading people according to social distinction at the middle of the sophomore year. Once that is done, their serious purpose has been fulfilled. Perhaps the classic statement about the Princeton clubs was made by the group of sophomores who refused to join any club in the spring of 1917. "Making a club is usually considered the most important event in college life. Not to make a club constitutes failure; and a man's success is measured by the prestige of the club to which he is elected. In order to achieve this success, a man must repress his individuality enough to conform to the standards which the upper-classmen may determine" — "standards," as a sympathetic *Princetonian* editorial added, ". . . which . . . have been uniformly bad, almost as bad as they could be." [9] For the last two years of an undergraduate's life the clubs then provide him with a gathering place patterned on the best country-club models where he eats and enjoys the wonderful leisure of undergraduate years in luxurious surroundings with congenial companions — if in the scramble of other considerations he has been lucky enough to fall among friends.

But if this was the dominant world of the University, Princeton was also a place in which Scott Fitzgerald, going out for dinner during the September examination period before commons were open, could sit down at the Peacock Inn next to an aristocratic-looking boy, and while "in the leafy street outside the September twilight faded [and] the lights came on against the paper walls, where tiny peacocks strode and trailed their tails among the gayer foliations," he and Bishop could talk and talk about books, about Stephen Phillips and Shaw and Meredith and the Yellow Book.[10] It is true that as they talked Fitzgerald appears to have worried for fear the "St. Paul's crowd at the next table would . . . mistake *him* for a bird, too . . ." and he would injure his social standing.[11] Still, that intellectually admirable world was there. It had been built up through two college generations under the leadership of T. K. Whipple and Edmund Wilson and it was, before the war broke its tradition too, to include, besides Bishop, the versatile Stanley Dell, John Biggs, Jr., and Hamilton Fish Armstrong. Fitzgerald was going to turn to this group at the end of his college career and to say many years later, without qualification and undoubtedly with some exaggeration: "I got nothing out of my first two years [in college] — in the last I got my passionate love for poetry and historical perspective and ideas in general (however superficially), that carried me full swing into my career." [12]

But if this is an oversimplified view of his career it is a tribute to what this group did for him which is deserved; they gave him the only education he ever got, and, above all, they gave him a respect for literature which was more responsible than anything else for making him a serious man. The voice of conscience which had taken form under these pressures spoke when Fitzgerald wrote sadly to his old friend, John Biggs, about Biggs' appointment to the Third Circuit Court of Appeals as the youngest judge in the history of that court: "I hope you'll be a better judge than I've been a man of letters." This was a professional conscience. If Princeton was a place of provincial social competition for two years and of charming relaxation for two more, and if it was academically a place where, as Fitzgerald himself remarked, too often "in the preceptorial rooms . . . mildly poetic gentlemen resented any warmth of discussion and called the prominent men of the class by their first names," it was also a place where people with intellectual interests could educate themselves.[13]

These people were committed to high standards and maturity of judgment; they wrote for each other as best they could without embarrassment or inhibition. Some of the literary expectations of the time have been betrayed by changes in ambition or personal defeats; but very few of its judgments seem, thirty years after, to have been wrong. They belonged, these writers, as Edmund Wilson remarked long after,

> to a kind of professional group, now becoming extinct and a legend, in which the practice of letters was a common craft and the belief in its value a common motivation. . . . [They] saw in literature a sphere of activity in which they hoped themselves to play a part. You read Shakespeare, Shelley, George Meredith, Dostoevsky, Ibsen, and you wanted, however imperfectly and on however infinitesimal a scale, to learn their trade and have the freedom of their company. I remember Scott Fitzgerald's saying to me, not long after we got out of college: 'I want to be one of the greatest writers who have ever lived, don't you?' I had not myself really quite entertained this fantasy because I had been reading Plato and Dante. Scott had been reading Booth Tarkington, Compton Mackenzie, H. G. Wells and Swinburne; but when he later got to better writers, his standards and achievements went sharply up, and he would always have pitted himself against the best in his own line that he knew. I thought his remark rather foolish at the time, yet it was one of the things that made me respect him; and I am sure that his intoxicated ardor represented the healthy way for a young man of talent to feel.[14]

However far this world was, in its essential values, from the ordinary social world of Princeton, the two of course overlapped; Princeton was a small place. Both Wilson and Bishop were in the Triangle Club. Wilson even wrote the book for the Triangle's 1915-1916 show called "The Evil Eye." He started with the idea that he could do something brilliant and ended with the feeling that, under the usual pressures, he had produced just another musical comedy. "I am sick of it myself," he wrote Fitzgerald when he had finished the first draft. "Perhaps you can infuse into it some of the fresh effervescence of youth for which you are so justly celebrated." [15] For by this time Fitzgerald was a considerable figure in the Triangle Club and was as a matter of course to write the lyrics for what Dean Gauss was later to call the "most serious of all [Wilson's] literary *pêchés de jeunesse*."

It was Dean Gauss too, however, who remarked with amusement that, for all Wilson's boredom with the play, it was "a bit too exotic and literary . . . [for] the older wearers of Triangle charms." [16]

One could not, to be sure, be a really big man without pretty well accepting the mores of the social world and going out for the right things and avoiding the wrong, but the two worlds tolerated each other, so that the *Princeton Pictorial Review* could write an editorial supporting "running it out," and the *Nassau Lit* could take up questions of campus politics. If Wilson went his sure way toward his unobtrusive, thorough, and humane learning and toward the mastery of a craft whose demands he had always understood and never underrated, he could at the same time participate in the life of the social world, writing, not very seriously perhaps, his Triangle show, being elected to a good but not big club, being good-humoredly selected by his classmates at the end of four years as "the worst poet" they knew. It is typical of the social world's kind of tolerance that Fitzgerald should have remembered the undergraduate Wilson as "the shy little scholar of Holder Court." [17] It is also typical of the literary world that Wilson, thinking of how Fitzgerald first called on him with a story, should have remembered that

> *I climbed, a quarter-century and more*
> *Played out, the college steps, unlatched my door,*
> *And, creature strange to college, found you there:*
> *The pale skin, hard green eyes, and yellow hair —*
> *Intently pinching out before a glass*
> *Some pimples left by parties at the Nass;*
> *Nor did you stop abashed, thus pocked and blotched,*
> *But kept on peering while I stood and watched.*[18]

The two worlds thus lived together with only the occasional strain of a rebellion against the club system to mar their sympathy, and many undergraduates doubtless lived out their college careers according to the ostensible conventions of the society largely unaware of how a man really becomes Big. It was a perfectly healthy society set in an old and homogeneous small town. Years after, in a passage in his Notebooks, Fitzgerald compared it with modern Princeton:

Once upon a time Princeton was a leafy campus where the students went in for understatement, and if they had earned a P, wore it on the inside of the sweater, displaying only the orange seams, as if the letter were only faintly deserved. The professors were patient men who prudently kept their daughters out of contact with the students. Half a dozen great estates ringed the township, which was inhabited by townsmen and darkies — these latter the avowed descendents of body servants brought north by southerners before the Civil war.

Nowadays Princeton is an "advantageous residential vicinity" — in consequence of which young ladies dressed in riding habits, with fashionable manners, may be encountered lounging in the students' clubs on Prospect Avenue. The local society no longer has a professional, almost military homogeneity — it is leavened with many frivolous people, and has "sets" and antennae extending to New York and Philadelphia.[19]

As such a society, the old Princeton had, within the narrow area of activity established by its ideals, its conceptions of honor and duty, its heroes and men of integrity, its occasions of difficult moral choice. Its worst fault was its failure, inherent in the conditions necessary to education, to provide extracurricular activities with practical consequences in the real world, thus forcing the ordinary, unintellectual undergraduate to devote his energy to social achievement and games. It is certainly better for undergraduates to see football players and Triangle authors and Princeton gentlemen, all of whom have skills and gifts of a kind, as heroic figures of a serious world, in the way Fitzgerald did, than to take the cynical attitude toward these things of later, more sophisticated undergraduates. It committed them to a kind of order; "For at Princeton, as at Yale, football became, back in the nineties, a sort of symbol . . ." as Fitzgerald said. "It became something at first satisfactory, then essential and beautiful. It became . . . the most intense and dramatic spectacle since the Olympic games. The death of Johnny Poe with the Black Watch in Flanders starts the cymbals crashing for me, plucks the strings of nervous violins as no adventure of the mind that Princeton ever offered." [20]

Fitzgerald plunged eagerly into the life of Princeton. His first impulse was to accept its standards, to admire its heroes, to use his imagination to make his participation in it seem even more dazzling than it otherwise would have. As the university where the *honnêtes hommes* of the American bourgeoisie were supposed to concentrate — as contrasted with Yale, the university where the ambitious went, and Harvard, the university of intellectuals and individualists — Princeton had a special appeal for Fitzgerald, with his feelings of social uncertainty and his desire for social success and security. That it was also the university of Southern gentlemen only strengthened his admiration of it. "I think of Princeton," said Amory Blaine in *This Side of Paradise*, "as being lazy and good-looking and aristocratic." [21] Fitzgerald's acceptance of Princeton did not, of course — such commitments never did — prevent the shrewd, observing part of his mind from seeing what the forces which made for success were; but neither did his almost Machiavellian grasp of the political realities of the system and the worth of some of its big men affect his admiration of it or his determination "to become one of the gods of the class." [22] All his life he made this kind of approach to a new world.

[His winter dreams] — as he wrote later of the hero of "Winter Dreams" — persuaded [him] . . . to pass up a business course at the State university . . . for the precarious advantage of attending an older and more famous university in the East, where he was bothered by his scanty funds. But do not get the impression, because his winter dreams happened to be concerned at first with musings on the rich, that there was anything merely snobbish in the boy. He wanted not association with glittering things and glittering people — he wanted the glittering things themselves. Often he reached out for the best without knowing why he wanted it. . . . [23]

The Fitzgerald of 1913 — he was seventeen years old the day he was admitted to Princeton — was a small boy (five feet seven), slight and slope-shouldered in build, almost girlishly handsome, with yellow hair and long-lashed green eyes which seemed, because of the clearness of their whites, to stare at people with a disconcerting sharpness and curiosity. "He had rather a young face, the ingenuousness of which was marred by the penetrating green eyes fringed with long dark eyelashes," says *This Side of Paradise* of Amory Blaine at this age;[24] and

> *The glitter of the hard and emerald eyes*[,]
> *The cornea tough, the aqueous chamber cold,*

is the clearest detail in Wilson's memory of Fitzgerald's physical appearance as an undergraduate. His remarkable pallor
reinforced the effect of his eyes. He wore the correct clothes
and labored to acquire the proper manners and mannerisms,
the high stiff Livingston collar with the narrow opening and
rounded points or the equally high button-down collar with
the deliberate bulge, the dark tie, the narrow-cuffed white
flannels, or the tight knickers, the high-buttoned vest and
jacket, the casual almost slouching posture, the swooping
handshake. But the very earnestness with which he stalked
convention betrayed him. All the energy of his disturbing
talent for transforming imaginatively the actual world into
an adequate vehicle for his immature but deeply felt vision
of the good life had been applied to the Princeton ideal of
the gentleman, so that the very completeness of his conform-
ity and the dramatic intensity of his performance of the part
of an average undergraduate made him stand out as an odd
and unusual person. It was the essence of the Princeton manner to appear not to take the deadly game of social competition seriously; but Fitzgerald, with his lifelong habit of "taking things hard," his anxiety to succeed and to be liked and
admired, could not manage that most essential part of the
pose. He worried, much too visibly, over the details of his
performance; it was a failing he never conquered: twenty-five
years later he was still fussing at his hostess at a house party
in Tryon to know if his sports jacket were "all right." ("A
gentleman's clothes may be right or wrong," his hostess remarked, "but he is never self-conscious about them and he
certainly never talks about them.")[25] "I can't drift," says
Amory Blaine "—I want to be interested. I want to pull
strings, even for somebody else, or be Princetonian chairman
or Triangle President. I want to be admired, Kerry."[26] So did
Fitzgerald.

One of his classmates remembers an occasion early in their freshman year when Joe McKibben, an upperclassman from St. Paul, took him and Fitzgerald walking along the old canal with another upperclassman. Fitzgerald bounded around and was boyish and talkative in a harmless way. The next day when they met outside a classroom Fitzgerald rushed up to his friend and said: "Do you know who that was we were walking with yesterday? — That was George Phillips, the varsity tackle!" His classmate said he knew that. "But my gosh, why didn't you tell me! I made a fool of myself, didn't I?" [27] To discuss the matter in this open way was to disregard the decencies of the situation.

As the telegram announcing his admission indicates, Fitzgerald began by trying to be a football hero, but at one hundred and thirty-eight pounds his chances of success were not good even had he had any natural talent or liking for the game. He lasted just one day on the freshman squad.[28] The initial failure did not daunt him at the time, but it meant there was one kind of god he would never be and the realization left its scar, a lifelong habit of daydreaming a story which he had first written out as a student at St. Paul Academy.[29] He described this dream in his essay on insomnia called "Sleeping and Waking."

"Once upon a time" (I tell myself) "they needed a quarterback at Princeton, and they had nobody and were in despair. The head coach noticed me kicking and passing on the side of the field, and he cried: 'Who is *that* man — why haven't we noticed *him* before?' The under coach answered, 'He hasn't been out,' and the response was: 'Bring him to me.'

". . . we go to the day of the Yale game. I weigh only one hundred and thirty-five, so they save me until the third quarter, with the score — "

— But it's no use — I have used that dream of a defeated dream to induce sleep for almost twenty years, but it has worn thin at last.[30]

But there were other ways to prestige. He went out for *The Tiger* and—probably at Bishop's urging—for a part in the English Dramatic Association's annual play. Though he was tentatively cast, he quickly dropped out of the EDA; it was not an organization with much prestige. But he had a contribution in the first issue of *The Tiger*. Most important of all, he went to the organization meeting of the Triangle Club in October and was busy for the next two months helping with suggestions for lyrics and laboring over the lights during rehearsals in the old Casino. By February he was hard at work on a libretto which he hoped would be accepted for the next year's Triangle show. By that date he was also deep in academic difficulties. As early as October 7 the dean had called him into consultation on this question and now the midyear examinations showed the full extent of his troubles; he had failed three subjects, acquired fifth groups in three others, and made one fourth group—in English.* This dismal record resulted in spite of his having devised what was considered to be the perfect stall for the question which caught him napping in class: "It all depends on how you look at it. There is the subjective and objective point of view." [31]

Throughout the spring he continued to work hard on his Triangle show and grew intimate with Walker Ellis, a handsome and romantic junior from New Orleans who was now the president-elect of the Triangle. Through the spring he watched with fascination the club elections and, carried away by the wonderful New Jersey spring, began to think of himself as a dedicated romantic nature and to discuss all the aspects of this commitment with his friend Sap Donahoe. He also took to walking in the beautiful gardens of the Pyne estate and watching the swans in the pools. Father Fay, a converted Episcopalian who had taken Fitzgerald up when he had been a student at Newman, came to the campus from

* Grades at Princeton run downward from first to seventh group. Groups one to five are passing, six and seven failures. The groups span approximately ten points each on a scale of one hundred.

time to time during the year and took him out to dinner with a few other carefully selected undergraduates. That spring he invited Fitzgerald to his mother's home at Deal for a weekend and Fitzgerald was dazzled by the mixture of luxury and intellectual life he found. With his usual combination of innocence and calculation he played the eager, ingenuous boy; one guest who met him at Deal called him "a prose Shelley." There was of course much very real naïveté in him at this point in his career and all his life he appeared more naïve than he was because he was so direct and effervescent. Moreover, he had had very little experience of the sophisticated eastern rich and Fay's world doubtless seemed to him the perfect fulfillment of the simpler St. Paul society in which he had never felt secure. To be intimately at home in Fay's world was really to succeed.

Father Fay was a man of taste and cultivation who, having never known anything but the life of the well-to-do, had that unconscious ease and security in it which Fitzgerald always envied and never could achieve. In addition to these qualities he was something of an eighteen-nineties aesthete, a dandy, always heavily perfumed, and a lover of epigrams. To a schoolboy of both social and literary ambitions this combination of characteristics must have been nearly irresistible. As a convert to Catholicism Fay could sympathize with Fitzgerald's dislike of the dreary side of his Irish Catholic youth and also show him a Catholicism which was wealthy and cultivated and yet secure in its faith. ". . . he [Shane Leslie] and another [Fay], since dead," Fitzgerald wrote several years later, "made of that church a dazzling, golden thing, dispelling its oppressive mugginess and giving the succession of days upon gray days, passing under its plaintive ritual, the romantic glamour of an adolescent dream." [32]

As a man of taste and intellectual interests, Father Fay understood all Fitzgerald's ambitions and doubts. At the same time he had a gift for getting on an intimate footing with young men of Fitzgerald's age, and, delighting in him, exercised that talent so that Fitzgerald found him sympathetic and understanding and talked with him as an equal.[33] Fay was presently to be a Monsignor and, as a friend of Cardinal Gibbons and the occasional diplomatic representative of the Vatican, he had already considerable position and influence in the church. He was a romantically satisfying figure. There is no doubt that Fay did a great deal for what Shane Leslie, the Irish novelist and critic, called "the crude, ambitious schoolboy" who arrived at Newman from St. Paul, and, until he died very suddenly in the influenza epidemic in 1919, Fay was probably the greatest single influence on Fitzgerald. How much Fitzgerald admired him is clear from the portrait of him as Father Darcy in *This Side of Paradise* and from the dedication of the book to him (even though his name is misspelled in it).[34] Such need as there was in Fitzgerald's nature for a father was fully satisfied by him. ". . . the jovial, impressive prelate who could dazzle an embassy ball, and the green-eyed, intent youth . . . accepted in their own minds a relation of father and son within a half-hour's conversation," says Fitzgerald of Monsignor Darcy and Amory Blaine.[35]

The flavor of their relation can still be felt in Fay's letters. They are addressed to "Dear Old Boy" or "Dear Boy" and a characteristic one runs:

July 9, 1917

I was very glad to get your letter. It was an amusing letter, although one can see that you are frightfully bored.

I am jolly glad about the poetry. Do get it done as quickly as possible and let me know about the commission. . . . We had a good jaw at the club, did we not? I enjoyed it immensely. It is always so entertaining to talk about oneself. . . .

What you say about the Manlys is most amusing. . . . That is so like what I would have done at your age.

Do write me soon. I mean to say, whenever the spirit
moves you.

Best love,

CYRIL FAY

"So they talked," as *This Side of Paradise* says, "often about
themselves, sometimes of philosophy and religion, and life as
respectively a game or a mystery. The priest seemed to guess
Amory's thoughts before they were clear in his own head, so
closely related were their minds in form and groove." [36] The
account of Amory and Darcy in *This Side of Paradise*, with
its amazing honesty, shows more clearly than anything the
tangle of affection and sympathy, of social and intellectual
snobbery, of literary attitudinizing and wisdom, of innocence
and calculation which constituted the relation between Fitzgerald and Fay.

"I think when we write one another," said Fay, "we ought
always to think of the possibility of the other person some
day publishing that letter." He was right. Fitzgerald used
three of Fay's letters and one of his poems in *This Side of
Paradise* with only the slight changes necessary to make them
fit the fictional situation. [37] What is even more surprising is the
revelation of how Fay talked to Fitzgerald; the episode of
Eleanor Savage, for example, was an experience of Fay's youth
he had told Fitzgerald about. When Fitzgerald sent Fay his
version of the episode for *The Romantic Egotist*, Fay was
unperturbed, indeed fascinated: "The two chapters . . . gave
me a queer feeling. I seemed to go back twenty-five years.
Of course you know that Eleanor's real name was Emily. I
never realized that I told you so much about her. . . . How
you got it in I do not know. . . . Really the whole thing is
most startling. . . . I suppose this is most ill-advised talk on
my part, but really I cannot be bothered with the hypocracy
of an elder. . . ." [38] Thus Fitzgerald was probably right when
he told Shane Leslie that "I really don't think he'd have
minded" about the letters and the poems. [39]

With this important visit with Fay at Deal Fitzgerald completed his freshman year. The rest of his life he liked to remember that he had flunked practically everything that year
in order to write the Triangle show. "I spent my entire freshman year," he said later, "writing an operetta for the Triangle
Club. To do this I failed in algebra, trigonometry, coördinate
geometry and hygiene."[40] But in fact three of these four
failures were in the first term and his June record, with only
one failure, was a great improvement over February; he even
raised his English mark to a third group. He took forty-nine
cuts, the maximum allowed without penalty.

That September the Elizabethan Dramatic Club staged the
last of its annual plays. This time Fitzgerald wrote for them
a farce about a man who wishes to buy a house and tries to
get it cheap by persuading the owners it is haunted. The
elaborate make-believe of other years as to organization and
purpose was continued: "Assorted Spirits" was "produced
under the management of G. B. Schurmeier"; it was "Presented by the Elizabethan Dramatic Club for the Benefit of
the Baby Welfare Association"; it was directed by Miss
Elizabeth Magoffin. But all these names were really fronts for
Scott Fitzgerald. He wrote the play, organized the production, directed, and acted. The play was apparently a competent farce, and, together with the public interest in what the
society pages liked to call "juvenile St. Anthony Hill," made
for a success. The Baby Welfare Association netted three
hundred dollars and the play was given a second time at the
White Bear Yacht Club. On this second occasion there was a
near panic. In the midst of one of the ghost scenes the main
fuse burned out with a loud explosion; women shrieked and
prepared to faint. "Scott Fitzgerald the 17-year-old playwright proved equal to the situation however and leaping to
the edge of the stage quieted the audience with an improvised
monologue. . . . The youthful playwright actor held the attention of the 200 men and women and in a few minutes the
electrician had repaired the lights and the play proceeded."[41]

Fitzgerald used the experience of this little crisis in his story "The Captured Shadow."

Meanwhile, in spite of all the work he was doing on "Assorted Spirits," he managed to get in enough tutoring to go back to Princeton early and to pass off enough conditions to become a sophomore in precarious "good standing." The Committee on Non-Athletic Organizations, however, found his standing too insecure to allow him to participate officially in the Triangle Club. It puzzled and angered him to find that important things like the Triangle Club and his career as a Big Man could be interfered with by the academic authorities and he was presently to write a story about this experience of taking make-up examinations called "The Spire and the Gargoyle," in which the Spire is the imitation Gothic architecture of Princeton which stands for all the romantic success Fitzgerald dreamed of and the Gargoyle the instructor who graded his make-up examination. The irony of the story depends on the absurdity of a superior and more sensitive person like Fitzgerald's finding himself at the mercy of this pathetic worm. This is the perennial undergraduate attitude, of course, but Fitzgerald's version of it has a kind of classic perfection.

For the moment, however, the gargoyle was cowed and Fitzgerald promptly forgot the possibility that he might vent his spleen again later, for he was swept away in the excitement of having his Triangle show accepted in September. His friend Walker Ellis was partly responsible for his triumph, but having done some revision on the dialogue — mostly, as a faculty reviewer noted in the *Princetonian*, the addition of faintly disguised borrowings from Wilde and Shaw — Ellis put himself down as the author of the book, leaving Fitzgerald credit only for the lyrics.[42] Unable to accept the part he had been cast for or to go on the Christmas trip because of his ineligibility, Fitzgerald nonetheless threw himself into the work of producing the show, pulling wires for others instead of himself when it came to parts, working to get his friends into the chorus, and devoting the better part of a solid month to rehearsals. In the intervals he worried about the club elections which would come in the spring.

The show itself — entitled *Fie! Fie! Fi-Fi!* — is a Graustarkian melodrama about a prime minister of Monaco who is ousted by an ex-gangster and saloonkeeper from Chicago and reinstated through the machinations of the gangster's estranged but undivorced wife, temporarily a manicurist at the hotel. It had a successful tour and Fitzgerald's lyrics were much praised. He had been studying his Gilbert as the "Chatter Trio" of Act I shows:

> *I'd like to hear a reason for this terrible commotion, —*
> *But if you try to talk so much I can't get any notion;*
> *So restrain yourselves and take your time and let's discuss the*
>   *question.*
> *You act as though you had a touch of chronic indigestion —*
> *And as I need a lot of time for ev'ry mental action;*
> *Kindly ease your flow of English, or you'll drive me to*
>   *distraction.*[43]

His remarkable verbal facility stood him in good stead in this business; once, when Hooper, the coach, found fault with a song, Fitzgerald went to the back of the old Casino and, while the chorus ran through a number, produced a new and better lyric.

While the Triangle was touring as far west as Chicago and St. Louis in the customary haze of alcohol and débutantes, Fitzgerald went home to St. Paul for Christmas. By now he had become a figure there, a somewhat uncertain quantity, perhaps, but a handsome young man who was making a success at Princeton and likely to become a Big Man. When it became known that "Midge" Hersey was bringing home for a vacation visit her Westover roommate, Ginevra King, it was expected that an interesting passage at arms between her and Fitzgerald was bound to occur. Ginevra King was a celebrity, a beautiful and wealthy girl from Chicago who had already acquired a reputation for daring and adventurousness. Fitzgerald let it be known that, though he had originally not planned to spend the vacation in St. Paul, he might undertake to stay if Miss King interested him. Thus warily the two champions approached one another. It was not, however, till January fourth, at a dinner at the Town and Country Club, that they met. The scene is described with great precision in a story Fitzgerald wrote for the *Nassau Lit* two years later: "Isabelle and Kenneth were distinctly not innocent, nor were they particularly hardened. . . . When Isabelle's eyes, wide and innocent, proclaimed the ingenue most, Kenneth was proportionally the less deceived. He waited for the mask to drop off, but at the same time he did not question her right to wear it. She, on her part, was not impressed by his studied air of blase sophistication. She came from a larger city and had slightly an advantage in range. But she accepted his pose. It was one of the dozen little conventions of this kind of affair. . . . So they proceeded, with an infinite guile that would have horrified the parents of both." [44] Nevertheless, up to the limit of his still immature capacity, Fitzgerald fell in love. For Ginevra, he became for a time the most important of her many conquests. As she said herself many years later, ". . . at this time I was definitely out for quantity not quality in beaux, and, although Scott was top man, I still wasn't serious enough not to want plenty of other attention!" [45] For all that he was in love, Fitzgerald understood her attitude. "The future vista of her life," he wrote of Isabelle, "seemed an unending succession of scenes like this: under moonlight and pale starlight, and in the backs of warm limousines and in low, cosey roadsters stopped under sheltering trees — only the boy might change. . . ." [46] But for Fitzgerald the girl would not. There were, of course, plenty of other girls, for he was at the age when social life consists largely of mild flirtations, and he had a dozen such encounters at house parties and during vacations in the next couple of years. But in his schoolboy way he never faltered in his devotion to his Westover Cynara. To the end of his life he kept every letter she ever wrote him (he had them typed up and bound; they run to 227 pages). Born and brought up in the best circumstances in Chicago and Lake Forest, Ginevra moved for him in a golden haze of habit, assumption, gesture, made up of a lifetime of wealth and ease, of social position always taken for granted, of country clubs and proms which she dominated as if such authority were her natural prerogative. When Fitzgerald wanted to realize this feeling in his story, "Winter Dreams," he portrayed himself as Dexter Green, whose father was a grocer and whose "mother's name had been Krimslich . . . a Bohemian of the peasant class . . . [who] had talked broken English to the end of her days"; Dexter Green had been a caddy, worked his way through college, and was as a young businessman "making more money than any man my age in the Northwest." Fitzgerald portrayed Ginevra in the story as Judy Jones, whom Dexter saw always in a "soft deep summer room" peopled with the men who had already loved her, "the men who when he first went to college had entered from the great prep schools with graceful clothes and the deep tan of healthy summers," or swimming in the moonlight alone and moody at expensive summer resorts, or at dances, "a slender enamelled doll in cloth of gold" who had just "passed through enchanted streets, doing things that were like provocative music." "Whatever Judy wanted, she went after with the full pressure of her charm." [47] Like Gatsby with Daisy, Dexter knew she "was extraordinary, but he didn't realize [until he knew her well] just how extraordinary a 'nice' girl could be." [48]

Ginevra, the extraordinary "nice" girl, the beautiful, magnetic girl who was always effortlessly at ease and sure seemed like this to Fitzgerald, with his imagination, his genteel poverty, and his uncertainty. The other men were part of her charm, for though she conquered everywhere quite deliberately, she remained essentially untouched, free. This was the girl he was, without much conscious intention, to make the ideal girl of his generation, the wise, even hard-boiled, virgin who for all her daring and unconventionality was essentially far more elusive than her mother — and, in her own way, far more romantic. He could see the naïveté and innocence of this girl temporarily in search of pleasure but seriously desiring some not very clearly defined romantic future, and it only made her seem to him more poignant: Judy Jones is wholly defeated in the end. Thus Fitzgerald was something more than one of Ginevra's conquests; what he loved was the substance she gave to an ideal to which his imagination clung for a lifetime. To the end of his days the thought of Ginevra could bring tears to his eyes, and when, twenty years after they had parted, he saw her again in Hollywood, he very nearly fell in love all over again with that imagined figure.

Thus, he fell in love; tentatively, as if he understood the consequences of complete commitment, he focused his imagination on her as he was to do finally with Zelda a few years later. He went back to college to write Ginevra at Westover enormous daily letters full of the touching incoherence of young lovers. ". . . Oh, it's so hard to write you what I really *feel* when I think about you so much; you've gotten to mean to me a *dream* that I can't put on paper any more. . . ."[49]

At Princeton his main concern was the clubs. At midyears he managed to pass everything except chemistry, and in March he went triumphantly into Cottage Club as one of the important men in its section, having turned down bids from Cap and Gown, Quadrangle, and Cannon. Cottage represented the type of social success Fitzgerald had dreamed of; Walker Ellis, with his personal charm, his apparently effortless embodiment of all the qualities of elegance and superiority which were the Princeton ideal, was the president of Cottage:

it was the logical climax to Fitzgerald's social career. Years later he wrote a friend he was trying to advise for her son's sake that "though I might have been more *comfortable* in Quadrangle, for instance, where there were lots of literary minded boys, I was never sorry about my choice." [50] At the section party he passed out cold for the first time in his life.

In many ways this was one of the happiest times in his whole life. On February twenty-sixth he had been elected secretary of the Triangle and he began to look forward to being the club's president in his senior year with a confidence which — except for his disregard of the Gargoyle — was justified. In May he was elected to the editorial board of *The Tiger*. He anticipated election to the Senior Council, that most select gathering of the leaders of the senior class. He was in love and on the whole happy about it; there was one wonderful moment in early June when he met Ginevra in New York. They went to *Nobody Home* and to the Midnight Frolic. The glittering urban splendor of a metropolitan evening was the perfect setting for Ginevra and he always remembered how "for one night . . . she made luminous the Ritz Roof on a brief passage through [New York]." [51] He was also beginning to make his way among the serious writers; that occasion described in Wilson's poem on which he had brought "the shy little scholar of Holder Court" his first contribution for the *Nassau Lit*, "Shadow Laurels," had taken place and before the spring was out he had appeared twice in the *Lit*. He was happy among his friends at Cottage, and they topped off a spring of easy, lazy gaiety with an epic visit to Asbury Park which Fitzgerald duly recorded in *This Side of Paradise*.[52] Because he was successful and confident of the future, he was at ease about everything. Consequently he was unmoved by the first faint signals of disaster which could be seen in his term-end report. Again he failed three subjects; he had taken in the first term alone more than the forty-nine cuts allowed in any two successive terms. Moreover, the ebullient delight he always took in his own success had brought on his old habit of talking too much about himself — it was only when he verbalized his experience that it seemed completely real to him — to such an extent that even his old friends grew impatient with him. One of them sent him an "Ode to Himself, by F. S. F.":

> *I can pull off a line of sob-stuff*
> *I'm a typical Parlor Snake*
> *At cards I'm a regular devil*
> *When there's anything much at stake.*
> *My motto is "I should worry"*
> *And before I stop I'll say —*
> *I'm a peach of an 'all 'round' fellow*
> *I'm Perfect in Every Way!* [53]

CHAPTER III

DURING THE SUMMER VACATION he went west to visit his old friend Sap Donahoe at the Donahoe's ranch near White Sulphur Springs, Montana. This visit provided the background for "The Diamond as Big as the Ritz." While he was there he played cowboy in a Stetson, gauntlets and puttees, won fifty dollars at poker and on one occasion got drunk and climbed on a table to sing to the amused cowmen of White Sulphur Springs a song called "Won't You Come Up." He was not hearing from Ginevra, but his anxiety was somewhat relieved when he was told that his chief rival was "poor as a church mouse."

In the fall he returned to Princeton ready to go on to the climactic triumphs of his undergraduate career. As always, however, when he was most full of confidence, the enemy struck; he flunked make-up examinations in Latin and chemistry, and he had one of those familiar conferences with the Committee on Non-Athletic Organizations and found himself ineligible. The situation was more serious now; his academic deficit had been accumulating for two years and this was the year for the crucial elections, the final rewards of three years of labor in the Triangle Club and on *The Tiger*.[1] Still, though he had moments of despair, the situation was not yet irretrievable. There was Ginevra at Westover and they dined happily at the Elton in Waterbury after the Yale-Princeton game at

New Haven in October; he worked hard as the Triangle's secretary, coaching his friends in their parts as a substitute for playing a part himself and doing much of the organizing and directing of the show while President Heyniger played football; he was secretary of the Bicker Committee in Cottage. What was in the sequel the most ironic event of the fall occurred when, in October, the Triangle had a series of photographs made of him as a Show Girl; these photographs were widely used for publicity over such captions as "Considered the Most Beautiful 'Show Girl' in the Princeton Triangle Club's New Musical Play 'The Evil Eye.' . . ." But Fitzgerald was of course never in the show.

In November he went to the infirmary with a high fever, got out after a week or so, and then had to return. His trouble was diagnosed at the time as malaria, which was more or less endemic at that time in Princeton, with its swamps and mosquitoes and its Negro slums down Witherspoon Street. When, in 1929, he had what subsequently proved to have been a tubercular hemorrhage, and later investigations showed the scars of even earlier attacks, he decided that this malaria had been tuberculosis. But since there is evidence of a mild attack of tuberculosis in 1919 also, there is little reason to suppose that there was anything more the matter with him than the malaria which he certainly had. His illness was perfectly real, but it also gave him an opportunity to leave college for a respectable reason at a time when the odds on his flunking out at midyears were prohibitive.[2] His plan was to drop out for the rest of the year and to return the next September to start his junior year over again. On November 28 he attended his last class of the year therefore and departed for St. Paul. Still trying to save something from the wreckage of his social career, he persuaded Dean McClenahan to write him an official statement that "Mr. F. Scott Fitzgerald withdrew from Princeton voluntarily . . . because of ill-health and that he was fully at liberty, at that time, to go on with his class, if his health had permitted." "Dear Mr. Fitzgerald," said the Dean's covering letter, "This is for your sensitive feelings. I hope you will find it soothing."[3] "Almost my final memory before I left," Fitzgerald wrote later, "was of writing a last lyric on that year's Triangle production while in bed in the infirmary with a high fever."[4]

But the career was beyond redemption. ". . . it took them," he said twenty-five years later, still hating vigorously the malicious and impersonal "them," "four months to take it all away from me — stripped of every office and on probation — the phrase was [it was written on his heart like Philip and Calais] 'ineligible for extra-curricular activities.' "[5] In February he came on to Princeton for a visit; both the club elections and the Triangle elections were impending. But there was nothing to be done. "To me," he wrote twenty years later, "college would never be the same. There were to be no badges of pride, no medals, after all. It seemed on one March afternoon that I had lost every single thing I wanted — and that night was the first time that I hunted down the spectre of womanhood that, for a little while, makes everything else seem unimportant."[6]

For all the trivial objective content of the experience, this was one of the great blows of his life. He had committed himself imaginatively to this world — or had had his imagination committed to it by circumstances — and the occasion's value was determined for him by what his imagination had made of it. He brought with him to Princeton for exorcism the ghosts of all his past failures. To have succeeded at Princeton would have been to triumph in a world so superior to the Middle West that he could have taken the Middle West for granted. And he had succeeded at Princeton; he had made Cottage, had every reason to believe he would be president of the Triangle, an editor of *The Tiger*, perhaps even a member of the Senior Council. Then, just as he was about to receive these tangible evidences of his success and at last feel at ease in a world which satisfied the needs of his nature, the Gargoyle, with his gift for perfectly timed malice, struck, and for the third time he was defeated. Had he had his rewards, his badges and medals, he would no doubt quickly have seen them for what they were. But he did not get them, so that all his life he remembered the deprivation and could not get out of his mind an extravagant sense of the value of these medals or a feeling that somehow he had never quite known what it was to be a Princeton man, had not penetrated to the innermost sanctum which his imagination dimly conceived, was still only a very good imitation of a man accepted and at ease in the aristocratic world. ". . . a typical gesture on my part," he wrote John O'Hara twenty years later, "would have been, for being at Princeon and belonging to one of its snootiest clubs, I would be capable of going to Podunk on a visit and being absolutely booed and overawed by its social system, not from timidity but because of some inner necessity of starting my life and my self justification over again at scratch in whatever new environment I may be thrown." [7] Like Dick Diver, the hero of *Tender Is the Night*, at Yale, he went "through [Princeton] almost succeeding but not quite"; instead of removing his sense of social insecurity, this experience fixed it permanently. "I was always trying to be one of them!" as he told James Drawbell years later. "That's worse than being nothing at all!" [8]

For the young man who set it down that "if I couldn't be perfect I wouldn't be anything" this "not quite" was worse than no success at all. That all this disaster should have resulted from the Gargoyle's suddenly turning on him again seemed to him the grossest kind of injustice. Eventually he was going to describe this period in his Ledger as "A year of terrible disappointments & the end of all college dreams. Everything bad in it was my own fault." [9] Even when he wrote *This Side of Paradise* he had Monsignor Darcy chide Amory over his inability to "do the next thing" and described Amory's failure by saying: "The fundamental Amory, idle, imaginative, rebellious, had been nearly snowed under. He had conformed, he had succeeded, but as his imagination was neither satisfied nor grasped by his own success, he had listlessly, half-accidentally chucked the whole thing and become again . . . the fundamental Amory." [10] But when, five years later, President Hibben wrote him a letter of mild remonstrance at the impression given by *This Side of Paradise* "that our young men are merely living for four years in a country club and spending their lives wholly in a spirit of calculation and snobbery," Fitzgerald was still so angry at the Gargoyle's outrageous injustice that he replied:

> [*This Side of Paradise*] was a book written with the bitterness of my discovery that I had spent several years trying to fit in with a curriculum that is after all made for the average student. After the curriculum had tied me up, taken away the honors I'd wanted, bent my nose over a chemistry book and said, "No fun, no activities, no offices, no Triangle trips — no, not even a diploma "if you can't do chemistry" — — after that I retired.[11]

At moments all the rest of his life this feeling of helpless rage — not really at others so much as at life, for having refused him what he had earned — would come back. In 1940, when he finally ran across Bishop's article, "The Missing All," and read its quite truthful assertions that he was "dropped from the class [of 1917]" and that "he had an ailment, which served as an excuse for his departure," he was in a rage.[12] "I left on a stretcher in November — you don't flunk out in November," he wrote Hemingway.[13] At the same time he was writing his daughter: "I wore myself out on a musical comedy there [at Princeton] for which I wrote book and lyrics, organized and mostly directed while the president played football. Result: I slipped way back in my work, got T. B., lost a year in college — and, irony of ironies, because of [a] scholastic slip

I wasn't allowed to take the presidency of the Triangle."
". . . no Achilles heel ever toughened by itself," as he remarked to her on another occasion. "It just gets more and
more vulnerable." [14]

His friends on the *Lit* summed up his career with less
sympathy:

> *I was always clever enough*
> *To make the clever upperclassmen notice me;*
> *I could make one poem by Browning,*
> *One play by Shaw,*
> *And part of a novel by Meredith*
> *Go further than most people*
> *Could do with the reading of years;*
> *And I could always be cynically amusing at the expense*
> *Of those who were cleverer than I*
> *And from whom I borrowed freely,*
> *But whose cleverness*
> *Was not of the kind that is effective*
> *In the February of sophomore year. . . .*
> *No doubt by senior year*
> *I would have been on every committee in college,*
> *But I made one slip:*
> *I flunked out in the middle of junior year.* [15]

The next eight months were unhappy and aimless ones for
him. He sat in the audience when "The Evil Eye" played in
St. Paul; he had mumps; he occasionally got drunk. In February he put on his Show Girl make-up and went to a Psi U
dance at the University of Minnesota with his old friend Gus
Schurmeier as escort. He spent the evening casually asking for
cigarettes in the middle of the dance floor and absent-mindedly
drawing a small vanity case from the top of a blue stocking.
This practical joke made all the papers, but it was an inadequate substitute for the flowers he had looked forward to as

"the Most Beautiful 'Show Girl' in the Triangle Club." * In
March he was preoccupied with Ginevra's leaving Westover
after Miss Hillard, the headmistress, had accused her of scandalous conduct and had later retracted the charge.[16] The play
he wrote for the Triangle that spring was rejected. In August
he paid Ginevra an unhappy visit at Lake Forest. "Poor boys,"
someone told him, "shouldn't think of marrying rich girls." [17]

In September he was back at Princeton to begin over again
in his stubborn and courageous way. He was still ineligible,
but Paul Nelson, who had been elected to the presidency of
the Triangle Club which he had expected to get, suggested
there was still hope for him despite the rejection of his book,
and he set to work once more to write the songs for the show;
once more the Show Girl pictures were got out and printed
in the newspapers, though he was not to be in this new show
either. He wrote endlessly for *The Tiger* despite his lack of
any official connection with it and conceived and wrote most
of an issue of the *Nassau Lit* which burlesqued *Cosmopolitan*.
Ginevra came down for the Yale game, but they were quarreling now and when they met again in January, she was no
longer interested; they quarreled, so far as she was concerned,
finally. ("I have destroyed your letters," she wrote him that
summer in reply to a request from him, ". . . I'm sorry you
think that I would hold them up to you as I never did think
they meant anything.")[18]

His interests were gradually shifting from the social to the
intellectual world. He began to see more of Bishop and John
Biggs, who in March succeeded Bishop as editor of the *Lit*.
He became friendly with David Bruce and with Henry
Strater, who read Tolstoi and Edward Carpenter and Walt

---

* "At the Chicago performance of 'The Evil Eye,'" said The *Daily
Princetonian* on January 7, 1916, "300 young ladies occupied the front rows
of the house and following the show, they stood up, gave the Princeton
locomotive and tossed their bouquets at the cast and chorus." "They sent
flowers too," Fitzgerald wrote his daughter twenty-five years later of his
attack of malaria, " — but not to the footlights, where I expected them —
only to the infirmary."

Whitman and seemed to take them quite seriously. These two, together with Richard Cleveland, the president's son, led a famous sophomore rebellion against the clubs in the spring, a rebellion in which ninety sophomores bound themselves "not to join any elective eating club while members of Princeton University," and, with the sympathy of the *Princetonian*, whose editorial editor, Alec McKaig, supported them boldly, they managed to reduce by twenty-five per cent the number of sophomores joining clubs and might have worked a permanent change in the system had not the interruption of the war destroyed their work.

Fitzgerald was fascinated by Strater; Strater seemed to be utterly unaffected by social disapproval, going about the business of doing what he thought right without regard for prestige; he seemed to see better than anyone the absurdity of the defenders of the clubs who solemnly accused him of trying to bring about a situation in which "the entire College dined in an atmosphere of Utopian socialistic love." [19] He suggested to Fitzgerald a new conception of superiority, a conception of moral and intellectual integrity which Strater's dramatic assertion made colorful and appealing to him, especially when Strater, sticking firmly to his Tolstoian position, came out as a pacifist in the face of our declaration of war. Fitzgerald never wholly gave in to Strater, but he listened to him, often all night, and took out his puzzlement by contributing liberally to an issue of *The Tiger* which satirized impartially both the clubs and the reformers.[20] He was especially amenable to the appeal of Strater's kind of distinction because, with the failure of his social career, he had begun to write for the first time in his life with the mature intention of realizing and evaluating his experience.

During the previous term, while he had been out of college, he had written "The Spire and the Gargoyle," which is, for all its naïveté, an attempt to deal with his own failure. Writing made him realize a little how much he had been deprived of by the desire to conform, and until after he had written *The*

Beautiful and Damned he thought of Strater as the "greatest influence in his writing." [21] "My idealism," he said, "flickered out with Henry Strater's anticlub movement at Princeton." [22]

In February he went to New York to see Wilson in his Eighth Street apartment and thought Wilson had found the ideal man's world, at once "released . . . from all undergraduate taboos" and yet "mellow and safe, a finer distillation of all that I had come to love at Princeton." [23] He had begun to read voraciously in Tarkington, Shaw, Wells, Butler, and, above all, Compton Mackenzie. He was enchanted by *Youth's Encounter* and *Sinister Street* and began a period of seeing himself as Michael Fane and all his friends as appropriate subsidiary figures. Wilson and his other New York friends fitted in admirably, as did Fay, who took him to dine in suave splendor at the Lafayette and got confused in Fitzgerald's exuberant imagination with Mr. Viner. Thus with his imagination full of the romance of *Sinister Street*—so that, seeing a man disappear silently into a doorway in Greenwich Village one night he had an almost physical sense of the pressure of evil —and with his head "ringing with the meters of Swinburne [and, he ought to have added, Tennyson] and the matters of Rupert Brooke," he plunged into being a writer.[24] He deluged the *Nassau Lit* with his work and before he was through they had published nine poems, five reviews, and eight short stories.

With this shift, he completed for the first time what was to be the characteristic pattern of his relation to his experience. In one of the best articles written at the time of *The Crack-Up's* publication, Malcolm Cowley noticed what he called Fitzgerald's "double vision." "It was as if," he said, "all his novels described a big dance to which he had taken . . . the prettiest girl . . . and as if at the same time he stood outside the ballroom, a little Midwestern boy with his nose to the glass, wondering how much the tickets cost and who paid for the music." [25]

This is an important insight for an understanding of Fitzgerald the talented novelist. His nature was divided. Partly he was an enthusiastic, romantic young man. Partly he was what he called himself in the "General Plan" for *Tender Is the Night*, "a spoiled priest." This division shows itself in nearly every aspect of his life. The romantic young man was full of confidence about his own ability and the world's friendliness; the spoiled priest distrusted both himself and the world. The romantic young man wanted to participate in life and took delight in spending himself and his money without counting the cost ("All big men have spent money freely," he wrote his mother when she tried to caution him in 1930, "I hate avarice or even caution"); but the spoiled priest, shocked by debt and fearing the spiritual exhaustion Fitzgerald was later to call "Emotional Bankruptcy," wanted to stand aside and study life. The spoiled priest compared the romantic young man — as his author compared Gatsby — to Trimalchio, the rich and vulgar upstart in Petronius' *Satyricon.*

But the talented novelist, whose books Fitzgerald sometimes read "for advice" ("How much," he said, "I know sometimes — how little at others")[26] would not have existed without them both. All his best work is a product of the tension between these two sides of his nature, of his ability to hold in balance the impulses "to achieve and to enjoy, to be prodigal and open-hearted, and yet ambitious and wise, to be strong and self-controlled, yet to miss nothing — to do and yet to symbolize."[27] Not until 1936 did he lose faith in his ability to realize in his personal life what he called "the old dream of being an entire man in the Goethe-Byron-Shaw tradition, with an opulent American touch, a sort of combination of J. P. Morgan, Topham Beauclerk and St. Francis of Assisi. . . ."[28] He never lost his conviction that "the test of a first-rate intelligence is the ability to hold two opposed ideas in the mind at the same time, and still retain the ability to function."[29]

If Fitzgerald's imagination owes its force and penetration

to the spoiled priest, however, it was the kind which works successfully only when it has personal experience to deal with; Fitzgerald was a romantic in the sense that for him "the divine," as Hulme put it, "is life at its intensest." "Taking things hard—from Genevra to Joe Mank—" he said, remembering his whole life, from his first love (Ginevra King) to his last battle (with Joseph Mankiewicz, the Hollywood producer) to preserve the integrity of his work: "That's the stamp that goes into my books so that people can read it blind like brail." [30] Understanding was for him the awareness of a constellation of feelings and of the objects to which they attached themselves in a moment of actual experience. "After all," as he said, "any given moment has its value; it can be questioned in the light of after-events, but the moment remains. The young princes in velvet gathered in lovely domesticity around the queen amid the hush of rich draperies may presently grow up to be Pedro the Cruel or Charles the Mad, but the moment of beauty was there." [31] Thus the direct experience of the romantic young man who plunged eagerly and unwarily into the life about him provided the novelist with his material.

This material the spoiled priest struggled throughout Fitzgerald's life to understand. When he was young this struggle sometimes gave Fitzgerald an almost priggish air. Once, for instance, when he was an undergraduate he watched a friend leave a group of classmates on Nassau Street to pursue a young lady. After a long silence, he said: "That's one thing Fitzgerald has never done!" [32] This attitude gave his early critics their most obvious target. ". . . a chorus girl named Axia," said Heywood Broun in his review of *This Side of Paradise*, "laid her blond head on Amory's shoulder and the youth immediately rushed away in a frenzy of terror and suffered from hallucinations for forty-eight hours. The explanation was hidden from us. It did not sound altogether characteristic of Princeton." [33] This moral earnestness was also partly responsible for Fitzgerald's changing his title from *The Romantic Egotist* to *This Side of Paradise*: "Well, this side of Paradise! . . . There's little comfort in the wise." Rupert Brooke's lines in "Tiare Tahiti" imply more than "we glamorous young people live practically in heaven"; they also mean "the world is very imperfect and the prudent wisdom of the old is perhaps no better than the imprudent sincerity of the young."

Ernest Boyd was, for all his fancy writing, observing shrewdly when he said of Fitzgerald in 1924: "There are still venial and mortal sins in his calendar, and . . . his Catholic heaven is not so far away that he can be misled into mistaking the shoddy dreams of a radical millennium as a substitute for Paradise. . . . His confessions, if he ever writes any, will make the reader envy his transgressions, for they will be permeated by the conviction of sin, which is much happier than the conviction that the way to Utopia is paved with adultery." [34] At the end of his life Fitzgerald himself wrote his daughter: "Sometimes I wish I had gone along with [Cole Porter and Rodgers and Hart and that gang], but I guess I am too much a moralist at heart, and really want to preach at people in some acceptable form, rather than to entertain." [35]

These are the forces which constitute what he called "luxuriance of emotion under strict discipline." They are logically contradictory impulses, but much of the time, and always when he was at his best, they functioned together in Fitzgerald. When his child was born in 1921, his emotional involvement with Zelda in her suffering was intense; he was, as the friend who waited with him at the hospital said, all prospective fathers rolled into one. At the same time he had his notebook out — "I might be able to use this" — and was taking down everything Zelda said. What he took down was: "Oh God, goofo I'm drunk. Mark Twain. Isn't she smart — she has the hiccups. I hope it's beautiful and a fool — a beautiful little fool." [36] When Daisy, the heroine of *The Great Gatsby*, is first showing the soft spot in her nature, what Nick calls her "basic insincerity," the talented novelist was indeed able to use this.

"Oh yes." She looked at me absently. "Listen, Nick; let me tell you what I said when [the baby] was born. Would you like to hear?"

"Very much."

"It'll show you how I've gotten to feel about — things. Well, she was less than an hour old and Tom was God knows where. I woke up out of the ether with an utterly abandoned feeling, and asked the nurse right away if it was a boy or a girl. She told me it was a girl, and so I turned my head away and wept. 'All right,' I said, 'I'm glad it's a girl. And I hope she'll be a fool — that's the best thing a girl can be in this world, a beautiful little fool. . . .' "

The instant her voice broke off, ceasing to compel my attention, my belief, I felt the basic insincerity of what she had said. . . .[37]

This act of uninvolved understanding at a moment of maximum involvement is of a piece with hundreds of others, from the compassionate but devastating portrait of Ring Lardner which he used as a foundation for the character of Abe North in *Tender Is the Night* to the many frank and disapproving portraits he made of himself in various guises in his fiction. You always wonder, as Glenway Wescott wondered of "The Crack-Up," "if he himself knew how much he was confessing."[38] But of course he did. "You've got to sell your heart," he wrote a young writer, trying to explain what he did. ". . . In 'This Side of Paradise' I wrote about a love affair that was still bleeding as fresh as the skin wound on a haemophile."[39] It was only one example from a lifetime's accumulation.

The stories he wrote during this period of seeking to understand his life at Princeton are, apart from "The Spire and the

Gargoyle" and one war story, about Ginevra.[40] Like all his deeply felt experiences, this one would not let him rest, and he was struggling to understand what he and Ginevra had been and why they had acted as they had. Each of the stories has a conventional, even banal framework, which is often very naïvely handled — the young lover who climbs the rain pipe to talk to his girl, the alcoholic but indefinably charming bohemian uncle with a secret sorrow — but at the heart of each is a version of himself and Ginevra, genuine, alive, and, at each reimagining, more fully understood.

All through this spring of 1917 a preoccupation with the war had been growing at Princeton. A large delegation of undergraduates had gone off to join the mosquito fleet; another was, with the assistance of experienced military men like Professor Robert Root of the English Department, drilling energetically on the campus. With the immediate support of Strater's pacifism and John Biggs' common sense, Fitzgerald took little part in this excitement. He never did participate in the rotarian kind of war hysteria — "wine-bibbers of patriotism," he called such people, "which, of course, I think is the biggest rot in the world."[41] He had his own pose, built partly out of Rupert Brooke and partly out of what he called "the short, swift chain of the Princeton intellectuals, Brooke's clothes, clean ears, and, withall, a lack of mental prigishness . . . Whipple, Wilson, Bishop, Fitzgerald. . . ."[42] Its form was: "This insolent war has carried off Stuart Wolcott in France, as you may know and really is beginning to irritate me — but the maudlin sentiment of most people is still the spear in my side. In everything except my romantic Chestertonian orthodoxy I still agree with the early Wells on human nature and the 'no hope for Tono Bungay' theory."[43] The two sources of the attitude are interesting, since Fitzgerald's attitude, deepened by their experience of the war and of the activities of the Palmers and the Volsteads and the Doughertys, was to emerge in the twenties as the younger generation's.

Fitzgerald went on, with enforced calm noting the names of classmates he had admired who were already being killed in France during the winter and spring of 1916-1917 and trying to decide whether to enlist in the air force or the infantry. In June he visited Fay at Deal and heard the first of a scheme which was to occupy him for some time. The scheme was surrounded by a great deal of mystification, but on some authority — there are hints in Fay's letters that it was the very highest — Fay was going to Russia, ostensibly as the head of a Red Cross mission but actually to see what he could do for the Roman Church in Russia during the disturbance of the Kerensky revolution. His plan was to take Fitzgerald along, in the guise of a Red Cross lieutenant, as his confidential assistant. The boyish, E. Phillips Oppenheim air with which he and Fitzgerald managed to invest the affair can be seen from Fay's letters:

> Now, in the eyes of the world, we are a Red Cross Commission sent out to report on the work of the Red Cross, and especially on the State of the civil population, and that is all I can say. But I will tell you this, the State Department is writing to our ambassador in Russia and Japan, the British Foreign Office is writing. . . . Moreover I am taking letters from Eminence to the Catholic Bishops. . . .
>
> As soon as you have read this letter and shown it at home, burn it.[44]

He and Fay had another conspiratorial conference in Washington late in the month to discuss costs — they were to pay their own way — and the important matter of the uniform (they agreed that only Wetzel could do the case justice). Fitzgerald then went on to spend a literary month with Bishop at his home in Charles Town, West Virgina, where he "wrote a terrific lot of poetry mostly under the Masefield-Brooke influence." [45] One of these outpourings, entitled "The Way to Purgation," was sold to *Poet Lore* in the fall; it was the first piece of writing he ever sold, though *Poet Lore* never printed it.[46]

Late in July he was back in St. Paul, where he went out to Fort Snelling and took the necessary examinations for a provisional appointment as a second lieutenant in the regular army. At the same time he was getting his passport for Japan and Russia to go with Fay. Early in September there came a hasty letter from Fay in Washington: "We can not go to Russia because of the new Revolution. . . . But there is another reason which is that you and I are to be sent to Rome. Do not breathe a word of this and burn this letter. . . . I cannot put details on paper." [47] This turned out to be a mission from Cardinal Gibbons to the Pope to lay before him the American Catholic attitude toward the war, "which is most loyal—barring the Sien-Fien—40% of Pershing's army are Irish Catholics," as Fitzgerald summed it up.[48] But this scheme, too, hung fire (Fay finally got to Rome the following February); he had further consultations with Fay at Deal Beach, but there was nothing to do but return to Princeton for his senior year and wait restlessly for his commission. He roomed with John Biggs who, like him, was on *The Tiger* and the *Lit*. Together they sometimes produced whole issues of *The Tiger* between darkness and dawn and wrote a great deal of the *Lit*.[49]

His commission was finally issued on October 26. His first move on receiving it was to sign the Oath ("My pay started the day I signed the Oath of Allegiance and sent it back which was yesterday"); his second to go up to New York, to Brooks Brothers, and order his uniforms.[50] Presently his orders came and he prepared to depart for Fort Leavenworth on November 20. He maintained the proper attitude, writing his mother:

> About the army please lets not have either tragedy or Heroics because they are equeally distastful to me. I went into this perfectly cold bloodedly and dont sympathize with the

"Give my son to country" ect
      or   ect
"Hero stuff"   ect

because *I just went* and purely for *social reasons*. If you want to pray, pray for my soul and not that I wont get killed — the last doesn't seem to matter particularly and if you are a good Catholic the first ought to.

To a profound pessimist about life, being in danger is not depressing. I have never been more cheerful.[51]

This letter is colored by his special feelings about his mother: he was afraid that she might make some ill-timed assertion of conventional patriotism in St. Paul and that would hurt him because he suffered from his mother's being foolish almost as much as from his own being so. He had to discipline her. "I could now be sympathetic to Mother," he had written the year before, "but she reacts too quickly." [52] Yet the attitude this letter expresses represents, in spite of its affectations, motives that were very real in Fitzgerald. "Updike from Oxford or Harvard," he wrote his cousin Ceci, "says 'I die for England' or 'I die for America' — not me I'm too Irish for that — I may get killed for America — but I'm going to die for myself." [53] Moreover, for all his dislike of conventional patriotism he was appealed to by the romantic idea of the gallant individual confronting and dominating danger and death. His not getting overseas and into action came gradually to seem to him a great deprivation. "It was as if, when he came later to read books about it," as Edmund Wilson has said, "he decided that he had been greatly to blame for not having had any real idea of what had been going on at that time, and he suddenly produced his old trench helmet which had never seen the shores of France and hung it up in his bedroom at Wilmington and would surprise his visitors there by showing them, as if it were a revelation, a book of pictures of horribly mutilated soldiers." [54] (As part of her education he required his eleven-year-old daughter to look these pictures over at La Paix in 1932, and the book was still in his library when he died.)

Nor was the loss of a romantic occasion the only loss Fitzgerald imagined; the war had a curiously social quality for him too. Missing out on it was for him a little like his never having, as an undergraduate, got into the inner sanctum of the Big Men at Princeton.

> "God damn it to hell," he once said, "I never got over there. I can't tell you how I wanted to get over. I wanted to belong to what every other bastard belonged to: the greatest club in history. And I was barred from that too. They kept me out of it. . . . Oh, God, I've never made it in anything!"

This feeling of deprivation, with its curious mixture of romantic and social frustrations, is dramatized in the story he wrote about it twenty years later called " 'I Didn't Get Over.' "[55] " 'I Didn't Get Over' " is the story of Captain Hibbing, who is snubbed during a training exercise by an officer named Abe Danzer who had been a prominent figure when they had been at college together. Hibbing is thrown off by this snub, loses his head, and asserts his authority by forcing the troops to cross a river in a leaky ferry which sinks with the loss of several men. All the heroism of the story belongs to Abe Danzer, but Fitzgerald identifies himself with Hibbing, who was thrown off by Danzer's snubbing him and acted badly as a consequence, just as Fitzgerald sometimes did in similar circumstances. The experience Hibbing has to tell about is far more dramatic than anything that happened to those who did get over and "spent most of [the time] guarding prisoners at Brest." But it was not, as Hibbing put it, "the big time." Training camp was a hopelessly inadequate setting for the heroism Fitzgerald had imagined.[56]

His departure from Princeton was, he thought, the end of

youth, the end of experiments with life and fresh starts under-
taken with easy confidence that there was plenty of time, the
end of the period when one is irretrievably committed to
nothing. These were the things he meant when he talked
about youth, when he said at the age of twenty-one, "God!
how I miss my youth — that's only relative of course but
already lines are beginning to coarsen *in other people* and
that's the sure sign." [57] There were many social influences to
encourage this attitude in the twenties — the revolt of the
"Younger Generation," the heritage from the hedonism of
the Nineties. But Fitzgerald's feelings about youth went much
deeper than that; because his commitment to any experience
was always unguarded, he could appreciate, as few people
ever have, his youth, which had no commitments of invested
vitality, no past, no unredeemable times "lost, spent, gone."
Though he loved experience, he hated the indelible "marks of
weakness, marks of woe" it left. Even through the pose of
the young man off to the wars and writing to a pretty cousin,
you can feel this conviction: "On the whole I'm having a
fairly good time — but it looks as if the youth of me and my
generation ends sometime during the present year, rather
summarily — If we ever get back, and I don't particularly
care, we'll be rather aged — in the worst way. After all life
hasn't much to offer except youth and . . . every man I've
met who's been to war, that is this war, seems to have lost
youth and faith in man. . . ." [58]

Fitzgerald's directness in asserting these feelings made it
easy to misunderstand him. "You put so damned much value
on youth," Hemingway wrote him nearly twenty years later,
"it seems to me that you confused growing up with growing
old. . . ." [59] But it was not, of course, a desire to avoid maturity that determined Fitzgerald's feeling. What he wanted
to do was to keep his emotional capital intact, and this desire
was in turn the result of his fear of bad investment rather
than of any timorousness in the face of experience. He had

begun to understand very early in life how dependent he was on emotional energy and to be disturbed by its extravagant expenditure. "I was always," he said later of his young manhood, "saving or being saved — in a single morning I would go through the emotions ascribable to Wellington at Waterloo." [60] This ability to care intensely was his great personal charm; everyone you talk to who knew him as a young man will try to make you understand that charm. They will laugh at their memory of his unguarded eagerness and excitement over parties and his dashing but inaccurate dancing — he could not carry a tune and he had a very uncertain sense of rhythm. But like Jay Gatsby's, his life was modeled on "his Platonic conception of himself." No one ever remembers except with a certain envy the way he could say to the girl he was dancing with, "My God, you're beautiful! You're the most beautiful girl I know!" — and mean every word of it.

But he also knew how extravagant this expenditure of vitality was. Later in his life he would work out a theory of what he called "Emotional Bankruptcy"; it is the most pervasive idea he ever had and it derives directly from his own knowledge of himself. Neither *Tender Is the Night* nor *The Last Tycoon* makes very good sense unless you realize how deeply embedded in them this idea is. Even at the age of twenty-one he had the essentials of it worked out. He summed them up in a poem called "Princeton — The Last Day" which, if it is still borrowing heavily for its style, states accurately his feeling that at this point in his life he was leaving for good the endless pause of youth.

> *No more to wait the twilight of the moon*
> *In this sequestrated vale of star and spire;*
> *For one, eternal morning of desire*
> *Passes to time and earthy afternoon.*
> *Here, Heracletus, did you build of fire*
> *And changing stuffs your prophecy far hurled*
> *Down the dead years. . . .*[61]

Just before he left Princeton, he brought Dean Gauss the manuscript of a novel. He wanted Dean Gauss to recommend the book to his publisher, Scribner's. Gauss, after reading it, told Fitzgerald frankly that he could not do so. Fitzgerald argued that he would probably be killed in the war and wanted it published. This conviction had taken a strong hold on his imagination; as late as 1923 he was telling a reporter that he had been "certain all the young people were going to be killed in the war and he wanted to put on paper a record of the strange life they had led in their time." [62] Dean Gauss finally talked him out of trying to publish. He remembers that the first part of this novel was much like the first part of *This Side of Paradise*, the remainder a series of unconnected anecdotes, satires, and verse about Princeton life, such as "The Spire and the Gargoyle" and the satire on Alfred Noyes' class in *This Side of Paradise*.[63]

But Fitzgerald was not through with the novel. He carried over into Officers' Training Camp precisely the attitude he had been maintaining at Princeton. He did not fail to note, half in earnest and half ironically, that "in my right hand bunk sleeps the editor of *Contemporary Verse* (ex) Devereux Joseph, Harvard '15 and a peach — on my left side is G. C. King a Harvard crazy man who is dramatizing *War and Peace*; but you see I'm lucky in being well protected from the Philistines" [64] — and, he might have added, that great mass of people who had not gone to Harvard, Yale, or Princeton. But his main preoccupation was his novel. At about the time he was showing the first version of his book to Dean Gauss, Fay, about to depart for Europe, confided Fitzgerald to Shane Leslie's care and Fitzgerald showed Leslie his poems and later wrote him his plans for a "novel in verse." The minute he was settled at Leavenworth, he started to rewrite his novel, at first by concealing a pad within his copy of *Small Problems for Infantry* and later, after he had been caught at this, by working weekends amidst the smoke and conversation and rattling of newspapers at the Officers' Club.

"I would begin work at it every Saturday afternoon at one and work like mad until midnight. Then I would work at it from six Sunday morning until six Sunday night, when I had to report back to barracks. I was thoroughly enjoying myself." [65] Working in this way he wrote a novel of one hundred and twenty thousand words, twenty-three chapters, of which four were in verse, "on the consecutive week-ends of three months"—that is, while he was at Fort Leavenworth; he was transferred to Camp Taylor, Kentucky, in February, 1918. It is hardly any wonder that he was remembered at Leavenworth as "a sandy-haired youngster . . . the world's worst second lieutenant." [66]

Fitzgerald's statement that *The Romantic Egotist* was completed by January is a slight exaggeration; he still had five of his twenty-three chapters to go. [67] But in spite of being on leave that month, he got the rest finished by March, doing part of the job in Cottage Club during his leave and sending the final installment to Bishop in March. [68] He sent the book to Leslie who, after spending ten days correcting the punctuation and grammar, sent it along to Scribner's with a recommendation and a request that, if they did not like it, they keep it anyway so that Fitzgerald "could go to France believing his book had been accepted." [69] By June the book was being read by Scribner's.

The Romantic Egotist was a very crude book, yet it was an original and striking book, too. "I don't think you ever realized at Princeton," he wrote Wilson while he was at work on it, "the childlike simplicity that lay behind all my petty sophistication and my lack of a real sense of honor." [70] A good deal of this combination of simplicity and petty sophistication was in *The Romantic Egotist*. But it also had Fitzgerald's penetration and honesty. The book's worst faults were its lack of structure and, in the early parts, of concrete particulars. "Each scene—chapter or what you will should be significant in the development either of the story or the hero's character and I don't feel that yours are," Bishop wrote him. "You see Stephen does the things every boy does. Well and good. . . . But the way to get it is to have the usual thing done in an individual way. You don't get enough into the boy's reactions to what he does. . . . You see what I mean? Each incident must be carefully chosen—to bring out the typical: then ride it for all it's worth." But if the book had faults, it should also be remembered that a great deal of what is now *This Side of Paradise*, including some of the best of it, such as the chapters about Princeton and the Isabelle and Eleanor episodes, was carried over into that book with only minor revisions from *The Romantic Egotist*.[71]

In August Scribner's returned the book to Fitzgerald with a long and encouraging letter. ". . . we are," they said, "considerably influenced by the prevailing conditions, including a governmental limitation on the number of publications . . . but we are also influenced by certain characteristics of the novel itself." [72] They then went on to make a number of detailed suggestions and concluded by urging him to submit the book again. Fitzgerald attempted to meet these suggestions and returned the manuscript to Scribner's, but at the end of October they finally rejected it. Of the editors only Perkins was really for it; both Brownell and Burlingame favored its rejection.[73]

At the same time he had been getting on with his career as the worst second lieutenant in the army. In February he got a leave and made a flying trip east to visit Princeton. He returned to Camp Taylor, Kentucky, where he found Bishop, who showed him around Louisville and talked poetry with him into the small hours. In April he was transferred again, to Camp Gordon, Georgia, and, in June, yet again to Camp Sheridan near Montgomery, Alabama. Here, in June, he received the news that Ginevra was to be married in September.

Then one Saturday night at the country club he noticed a girl dancing with his friend Major Dana Palmer. She was young, so young that she had not put up her hair and wore the frilly sort of dress that used to be reserved for young girls. As he looked at her, he always recalled afterward, everything inside him seemed to melt. The minute the dance was over, he got hold of Major Palmer and had himself introduced to Zelda Sayre. In his precise way where emotions were concerned he noted in his Ledger that he "fell in love on the 7th" of September. Like Amory Blaine, who stopped at the door of the Knickerbocker bar to check his watch before he got drunk because Rosalind had finished with him, Fitzgerald always "wanted particularly to know the time, for something in his mind that catalogued and classified liked to chip things off cleanly." [74]

CHAPTER IV

WHEN FITZGERALD met her Zelda Sayre was just eighteen, a beautiful girl with marvelous golden hair and that air of innocent assurance attractive Southern girls have. The Sayres were an undistinguished but solid and respectable Southern family; Zelda's father had become a Judge of the City Court of Montgomery in his early thirties and was later appointed to the Supreme Court of Alabama, on which he served for thirty years. His children were brought up quietly and conservatively in what was the small-town Southern society of Montgomery (Montgomery was then a town of about 40,-000). As a girl Zelda often resented her father; he was aloof, Olympian, abstractly just. She baited him to try to destroy his reserve and sometimes succeeded: the first time Fitzgerald dined at the Sayres Zelda drove Judge Sayre into a rage Fitzgerald never forgot. But these successes against the "older generation" were rare. Usually Judge Sayre was calm and certain; if he often seemed to Zelda inhumanly perfect, he provided for her a solid assurance of how things ought to be done which was always there to return to, however often she took small moral flights of her own. Later the heroine of Zelda's novel, *Save Me the Waltz*, was to say that she "didn't know how to go about asking the Judge to pay the taxi [when he visited them in New York] — she hadn't been absolutely sure of how to go about anything since her marriage had precluded the Judge's resented direction." [1]

With the Judge's solid convictions always in the background to support her, and with her own beauty to give her confidence, she found it possible to do, quite simply, without hesitation or self-consciousness, whatever came into her head. From the time she was a young girl she seems to have thought of herself as "two simple people at once, one who wants to have a law to itself and the other who wants to keep all the nice old things and be loved and safe and protected." [2] Until her marriage she could be both these people at once without serious strain, and the result was that she quickly became a famous figure in the community, a girl with innumerable daring and unconventional exploits to her credit who had already left "the more or less sophisticated beaux and belles of Atlanta . . . gasping for air when she struck the town." [3]

All this was a preparation for wartime Montgomery. With the coming of war, Camp Sheridan and Camp Taylor filled up with officers from all over the country and from what was for those times — and perhaps especially for Montgomery — a startling range of social classes. Overnight the social life of Montgomery took on an excitement, a feeling that anything was possible, which made every date a poignant moment of limitless romantic possibilities. It only added to the excitement that you never knew whether the handsome officer who cut in at the Country Club dance was a streetcar conductor, like the Earl Schoen of Fitzgerald's story, "The Last of the Belles," or a Harvard man of distinguished Boston ancestry, like Bill Knowles. The new ideas about manners which were developing all over the country at the time found their perfect occasion in wartime Montgomery. And Zelda — or at least the Zelda who wanted to be a law to herself — was the ideal heroine for this world; she was beautiful and witty, she was just seventeen, and there was nothing she did not dare do.

She took this larger and much more unstable world in her stride and quickly became its central figure. So regularly did flyers from Camp Taylor stunt over her house that it became necessary for the commanding officer to issue an order specifically forbidding this kind of courtship of Miss Sayre.[4] Something of the attitude with which she met experience at this time can be seen in her later "Eulogy of the Flapper":

How can a girl say again, "I do not want to be respectable because respectable girls are not attractive," and how can she again so wisely arrive at the knowledge that "boys *do* dance most with the girls they kiss most," and that "men *will* marry the girls they could kiss before they had asked papa?" Perceiving these things, the Flapper awoke from her lethargy of sub-deb-ism, bobbed her hair, put on her choicest pair of earrings and a great deal of audacity and rouge and went into the battle. She flirted because it was fun to flirt and wore a one-piece bathing suit because she had a good figure, she covered her face with paint and powder because she didn't need it and she refused to be bored chiefly because she wasn't boring. She was conscious that the things she did were the things she had always wanted to do.[5]

Zelda's extreme popularity and the competitive situation it created were an initial attraction to Fitzgerald. Like the Princess in the fairy story, though she did not have to be awakened with a kiss when he reached her side, she was barricaded and remote behind her host of admirers, a challenge to the unregarded younger son who was determined to marry the Princess and be a success. Moreover, Zelda's habit of doing without hesitation "the things she had always wanted to do" appealed to something deep in Fitzgerald, to his conviction that "if you don't know much — well, nobody else knows much more. And nobody knows half as much about your own interests as *you* know";[6] this side of paradise there's little comfort in the wise.

So, because she attracted him enormously, because she was desired by many, because she seemed to feel exactly as he did — and to have far more courage to do what she felt —

Fitzgerald fell in love with her. And as with every important act of his life, he made out of falling in love with her an act of identification and dedication. Like Gatsby, "he took [her] one still . . . night . . . [and] found that he had committed himself. . . . He felt married to her, that was all." [7] He was head over heels in love, by turns jealous, charmed, ecstatic.

> Lolling down on the edge of time
> > Where the flower months fade as the days move over,
> Days that are long like lazy rhyme
> > Nights that are pale with the moon and the clover,
>
> Summer there is a dream of summer
> > Rich with dusks for a lover's food —
> Who is the harlequin, who is the mummer,
> > You or time or the multitude?
>
> Still does your hair's gold light the ground
> > And dazzle the blind till their old ghosts rise? . . .
> Part of a song, a remembered glory. . . .
> > Kisses, a lazy street — and night. [8]

Zelda too was in love. "There seemed to be some heavenly support beneath his shoulder blades that lifted his feet from the ground," she remembered when she wrote her novel, "as if he secretly enjoyed the ability to fly but was walking as a compromise to convention. . . . The pressure of masculine beauty equilibrated for twenty-two years had made his movements conscious and economized as the steps of a savage transporting a heavy load of rocks on his head." [9] She was fascinated by his extravagant gestures, such as his carving on the doorpost of the country club (instead of on a tree) a legend in which his name bulked much larger than hers ("David, David, David, Knight, Knight, Knight, and Miss Alabama Nobody" is the version she gives in her novel, *Save Me the Waltz*).[10] But she was also determined to dominate the relation. The Saturday night after their first meeting, again at the country club, she suddenly dragged her escort into a lighted telephone booth and started kissing him passionately. When she stopped abruptly he said, "What's the idea of this outburst?" and Zelda said, "Oh, Scott was coming and I wanted to make him jealous." Most of all, perhaps, she was fascinated by the assurance with which he predicted his future fame, for like Sally Carrol of "The Ice Palace," who is a portrait of her, she "want[ed] to live where things happen on a big scale." [11]

In her way she was as ambitious as he was; it made for certain difficulties. Though she was in love with him, she did not, for all her yielding, commit herself as he did. She was not perfectly sure. ". . . except for the sexual recklessness," Fitzgerald remembered with his remarkable clarity long afterwards, "Zelda was cagey about throwing in her lot with me before I was a money-maker, and I think by temperament she was the most reckless of all [the women he had known]. She was young and in a period when any exploiter or middle-man seemed a better risk than a worker in the arts." [12] Zelda wanted, just as Fitzgerald did, a luxury and largeness beyond anything her world provided and she had a certain, almost childlike shrewdness in pursuing it.

At the end of October the advance detachment of the Ninth Division got its overseas orders and early in November they arrived at Camp Mills, Long Island. At one point during their stay they even entrained for Quebec but were pulled off the train again and told their departure would be postponed. (Fitzgerald liked to remember marching onto a transport, steel helmet slung at his side, but that was dramatic license.) While they waited on Long Island there were a great many parties in New York; Fitzgerald as usual provided a good deal of the fun and some of the serious trouble. He rode a cab horse through Times Square to the delight of his friends in the cab and, on another occasion, started turning cartwheels in Bustanoby's, eventually landing in the ladies' room.

On another occasion he borrowed a friend's room at the

Astor on the plea that he was broke and had no place to go, and then managed to get himself and a girl from Princeton caught there, completely naked, by the house detective. After considerable negotiation Fitzgerald offered the detective a hundred dollars to let them go and when the detective accepted, thrust a tightly folded bill into the detective's hand and fled with the girl. Too late the detective found himself with a one-dollar bill in his hand, which did not make things any easier for the friend from whom Fitzgerald had borrowed the room when the detective finally caught up with him. Fitzgerald was saved from arrest by the New York police only by his commanding officer's putting him under military arrest at Camp Mills. But when the unit entrained for Montgomery a few days later, Fitzgerald had disappeared. One of his friends told the commanding officer he thought Fitzgerald had gone to Princeton and Washington, and, in fact, when the train stopped at Washington, there was Fitzgerald sitting on the next track in the classic pose, a girl on either side of him and a bottle in his hand.[13]

"I think," said one of Fitzgerald's friends of this time, "Scott abused the kindness and friendship of nearly everyone, but at that time, one could not help liking him very much." Here is the first clear display of the pattern of behavior that was to continue throughout Fitzgerald's life, the wild conduct and the total lack of consideration for its consequences either for himself or others alternating with the sober sensitivity and considerateness that made it impossible for people not to be very fond of him. It makes it clear that from the beginning Fitzgerald had almost no resistance to alcohol. "Like many others who got the name of being drunkards," as Louis Bromfield, who knew him later, put it, "[Scott] simply couldn't drink. One cocktail and he was off. It seemed to affect him as much as five or six drinks affected Hemingway or myself. Immediately he was out of control and there was only one end . . . that he became thoroughly drunk, and like many Irishmen, when he became drunk he usually became very disagreeable and rude and quarrelsome, as if all his resentments were released at once." By the time Bromfield knew him, there were serious resentments to be released, but from the beginning Fitzgerald acted out his fantasies in a most astonishingly literal way when he was drunk.[14]

Back at Camp Sheridan he was made aide-de-camp to the commander, General A. J. Ryan. All through December and January he and Zelda walked in the woods together, went to the vaudeville at the Grand Theatre and sat in the back so they could hold hands, "gazed at each other soberly through the chorus of 'How Can You Tell!'" when they saw *Hitchy-Koo*, danced, and swam in the moonlight. Fitzgerald called her so often that he remembered the Sayres' telephone number all his life. Still, Zelda was not easy to win. She let him read her diary (eventually he used parts of it in *This Side of Paradise* and *The Beautiful and Damned*; like all she wrote it was brilliant, amateur work); she let him spend Christmas day with her in a charmed anticipation of domesticity. But at the same time she continued to go to all the local dances with others, and to attend proms at Auburn and Georgia Tech.[15] On these occasions Fitzgerald would get drunk, and later they would quarrel and Zelda would question whether he was ever going to make enough money for them to marry and live as she wished to. She "held him firmly at bay" (the phrase is Fitzgerald's own).[16]

On February 14, 1919, his discharge came through. For a long time he had been thinking of that fine man's world he had seen Edmund Wilson enjoying in Eighth Street in the spring of 1917, and he and Bishop had been planning to set themselves up in a similar apartment in New York. Before the armistice, he had written Bishop suggesting the idea (Bishop was overseas) and Bishop had replied:

Will you honestly take a garret (it may be a basement but garret sounds better) with me somewhere near Washington Square? Shall we go wandering down to Princeton on fragrant nights in May? . . . We'll have a drunk — what if the bars are closed. I am bringing back a trunk locker. We'll wander about New York . . . then go down to Princeton, climb the stairs of Witherspoon and bellow down the Nass. We'll chant Keats along the leafy dusk of Boudinot Street and come back to talk the night away.[17]

But now there was the serious business of making a fortune to be attended to promptly, for Zelda was not going to wait forever. When he reached New York on February 19 he wired her with anxious enthusiasm: DARLING HEART AMBITION ENTHUSIASM AND CONFIDENCE I DECLARE EVERYTHING GLORIOUS THIS WORLD IS A GAME AND WHILE I FEEL SURE OF YOU[R] LOVE EVERYTHING IS POSSIBLE I AM IN THE LAND OF AMBITION AND SUCCESS. . . . In the land of ambition and success he began tramping the streets in search of a job. His notion was to "trail murderers by day and write short stories by night," so he canvassed every newspaper in town, carrying the scores of his Triangle shows under his arm as evidence of his talent. "The office boys," he said later, "were not impressed."[18] He finally settled for a job with the Barron Collier agency writing advertising slogans, mainly for streetcar cards. His biggest success, however, was a slogan for a steam laundry in Muscatine, Iowa: "We Keep You Clean in Muscatine." "It's perhaps a bit imaginative," he remembered the boss's saying, "but still it's plain that there's a future for you in this business."[19]

He settled into a room at 200 Claremont Avenue — "one room in a high, horrible apartment-house in the middle of nowhere" — to live temporarily on his ninety dollars a month and to make his fame and fortune writing stories at night. He produced nineteen of them between April and June, but "no one bought them, no one sent personal letters. I had one hundred and twenty-two rejection slips pinned in a frieze about my room."[20] In June he sold a story to the *Smart Set*, which

George Jean Nathan and H. L. Mencken were making the liveliest magazine in America. But the story was "Babes in the Woods," which he had written more than two years earlier for the *Lit*. He used the thirty dollars it brought him to buy a pair of white flannels; he still had them, stored away like a bartender's first dollar, in 1934.[21] Meanwhile Zelda was becoming more and more what she called, in an ominous circumlocution, "nervous." "He knew what 'nervous' meant — that she was emotionally depressed, that the prospect of marrying into a life of poverty and struggle was putting too much strain upon her love."[22] Fame and fortune did not seem to be materializing on schedule for Fitzgerald, and Zelda was fretting her time away in Montgomery wondering if she ought not to marry one of her more eligible and financially better equipped admirers.

It was all much too clear to Fitzgerald. In March he had sent her an engagement ring which must have been pathetically modest under the circumstances, and twice during the spring Zelda's nervousness reached a point where frequent telegrams no longer calmed her and Fitzgerald had to go to Montgomery to see her. "I used to wonder," he noted bitterly, "why they locked Princesses in towers." Now that solution of the difficulty struck him as so admirable that Zelda had to write him: "Scott, you've been so sweet about writing — but I'm so damned tired of being told you 'used to wonder why they kept princesses in towers' — you've written that verbatim in your last six letters!"[23]

. . . in a haze of anxiety and unhappiness [he recalled afterwards] I passed the four most impressionable months of my life. . . . As I hovered ghost-like in the Plaza Red Room of a Saturday afternoon, or went to lush and liquid garden parties in the East Sixties or tippled with Princetonians in the Biltmore Bar I was haunted always by my other life — my drab room in the Bronx, my square foot of the sub-

way, my fixation upon the day's letter from Alabama —
would it come and what would it say? — my shabby suits,
my poverty, and love. . . . I was a failure — mediocre at
advertising and unable to get started as a writer.

The fact that "the returning troops marched up Fifth Avenue
and girls were instinctively drawn East and North toward
them" so that you felt "this was the greatest nation and there
was gala in the air" only made matters worse.[24] When it was
all over, he sat down and summed it up in "May Day," the
first of those beautifully balanced impressionistic stories he
was to write from time to time all his life. "May Day" covers
the whole range of his experience, from his most personal and
private feelings, through his awareness of the mixed lives of
farm boys, waiters, party girls, prom trotters, and college
boys, to his acute sense of the times, of the pride and pros-
perity and repression of post-war America. The Jazz Age, he
remarked much later, "began about the time of the May Day
riots in 1919."[25] Gordon Sterrett, with his frayed shirt cuffs
and his poverty, his inability to get started as a cartoonist and
his alcoholic deterioration, is Fitzgerald's exaggeratedly con-
demnatory portrait of himself. Gordon's suicide after Philip
Dean refuses to lend him money reflects Fitzgerald's moments
of acute despair over his financial situation. Gordon is the
story's projection of Fitzgerald's private consciousness, but
the story as a whole covers the full complex of experience at
a significant moment in the history of Fitzgerald's time.

Instead of committing suicide like Gordon Sterrett, Fitzgerald escaped into innumerable parties with his college
friends, some of them full of the delight and extravagance
of undergraduate revelry, all of them, no doubt, haunted for
him by his other life, as Gordon Sterrett's parties with his
old college friends are haunted. The most colorful of these
parties grew out of the interfraternity dance at Delmonico's
in May, 1919, which provided the material for Mr. In and

Mr. Out in "May Day." It began with Fitzgerald sitting quietly in the Fifty-Ninth-Street Childs carefully mixing hash, dropped eggs, and catsup in his companion's derby. When he was interrupted he insisted on climbing on a table and making a speech, and after he had been dragged from the table and out of Childs he wanted to explain to everybody that the façade of the buildings around Columbus Circle does not really curve; it only seemed to because he was drunk. Later he and a college friend, Porter Gillespie, returned to the party at Delmonico's and played their game of Mr. In and Mr. Out. Well into the next morning they breakfasted on shredded wheat and champagne, carrying the empty bottles carefully out of the hotel and smashing them on the curb for the benefit of the churchgoers along Fifth Avenue.[26]

In June Zelda sent him a print of a picture he had paid to have taken which she had inscribed affectionately to Bobby Jones. This must have been another of her calculated maneuvers, like the telephone-booth business at the country club, since Mr. Jones has said that he never even had a date with Zelda. Nevertheless, when Fitzgerald responded to this inscribed photograph with an outburst of jealousy, she again became so "nervous" that he felt he had to go to Montgomery to see her.[27] But this time it did not work; Zelda had had enough of the strain of an engagement which every day looked less as if it were going to lead to a marriage. She told him flatly she was not prepared to go on. Fitzgerald took the situation very badly. "He seized her in his arms and tried literally to kiss her into marrying him at once," he wrote when he described his conduct in " 'The Sensible Thing.' " "When this failed, he broke into a long monologue of self-pity, and ceased only when he saw that he was making himself despicable in her sight. He threatened to leave when he had no intention of leaving, and refused to go when she told him that, after all, it was best that he should."[28] When Zelda finally saw him off at the station, he climbed into a Pullman and then sneaked through into the daycoach, which was all he could afford for the trip back to New York.[29] It was a desperate irony for the man who had just been trying to persuade his girl he was rich enough for her. "He had met [her] when she was seventeen," he wrote when he came to sum up this experience, "possessed her young heart all through her first season . . . and then lost her, slowly, tragically, uselessly, because he had no money and could make no money; because, with all the energy and good will in the world, he could not find himself; because, loving him still, [she] had lost faith and begun to see him as something pathetic, futile and shabby, outside the great, shining stream of life toward which she was inevitably drawn." [30] This was Zelda's attitude as Fitzgerald understood it, an attitude with which he sympathized, which he felt to be unavoidable in the kind of girl he admired. She was "inevitably drawn" toward "*the* . . . stream of life*," a stream with such a high concentration of money in it that it shone.

He came back to New York and went on an epic three-weeks' drunk which provided him with one of the best scenes in *This Side of Paradise*.[31] Physical exhaustion and the advent of prohibition put an end to this cure, but it had, as he said of Amory's drunk, "done its business; he was over the first flush of pain." When he sat down to take stock of his situation, he decided he might as well try his hand once more at a novel. "The idea of writing [*This Side of Paradise*]," he said shortly afterwards, "occurred to me on the first day of last July. It was a sort of substitute form of dissipation." [32] But the remarkably optimistic young man had not, in spite of his recent blow, altogether given up his dream of success; he took up the idea of writing his novel over again in part because he still hoped to produce a best seller, win Zelda back, and become famous and admired.

He quit his advertising job with relief and, on July 4, left for St. Paul, having made an arrangement with his mother that he could have his old room on the third floor. There he settled down to rewrite *The Romantic Egotist* according to a schedule which he had pinned to the curtain before his desk. Not even an appeal from Edmund Wilson could interrupt his work. Wilson and Stanley Dell were trying to put together a volume of realistic war stories, and Wilson wrote Fitzgerald an amusing and penetrating request for a contribution:

> No Saturday Evening Post stuff, understand! Let us have the Army, as it is, — Come now! clear your mind of cant! brace up your artistic conscience, which was always the weakest part of your talent! forget for a moment the phosphorescences of the decaying Church of Rome! Banish whatever sentimentalities may still cling about you from college! Concentrate in one short story a world of tragedy, comedy, irony and beauty!!! — I await your manuscript with impatience.[33]

Fitzgerald replied: "I have just finished the story for your book. It's not written yet."[34]

It never was; he stuck to his schedule for the novel until it was finished. He revised carefully every scene he retained from *The Romantic Egotist* and added a good many new ones, including practically all of Book Two of *This Side of Paradise*.[35] He worked hard through two hot summer months in his third-floor front room at 599 Summit, with the result that by the end of July he was able to write Maxwell Perkins at Scribner's that he had completed the first draft of the revision; "This is a definite attempt at a big novel," he wrote, "and I really believe I have hit it. . . ."[36] By the end of August he had been through the whole manuscript again. On September 3 he wrapped it up, hugged it to him, and with his invariable feeling for the drama of an occasion, cried to his friend Tubby Washington, "Tubby! Maybe this is it!"[37] The manuscript seemed to him too precious to trust to the mails, and he persuaded an acquaintance, Mr. Thomas Daniels, to carry it to Scribner's.

Meanwhile he had, of necessity, been living very quietly. He spent occasional evenings down the block at 513 with John Briggs (later the headmaster of St. Paul Academy) and Donald Ogden Stewart, two young men who were as full of modern literature as he; they would discuss the latest books and argue over what Fitzgerald was doing in *This Side of Paradise*; or they would wander out to see Father Joe Barron, an intelligent and sympathetic priest, and argue with him into the small hours about such things as the ascetic ideals of the thirteenth century. Stewart's elaborate jokes — his obviously faked ventriloquist act and his parody illustrated lectures — never failed to delight Fitzgerald. But most nights he walked quietly down to the corner drugstore and let Tubby buy him a coke and cigarettes. The cokes distressed his Aunt Annabel: she was sure he was ruining his health. He lived thus off Tubby because his family, angry because he refused to enter on a proper business career, would not give him pocket money.

It was a misery to them, too, that he hardly pretended to be a good Catholic any more. He was never very devout, though like most people he had moments as he was growing up when his imagination was appealed to by religion ("Became desperately Holy," he noted of himself at fourteen), and occasionally he was attracted by a colorful piece of Catholic history and the sense of a great and socially impressive tradition which it gave him. Still he had been brought up a Catholic, with all that means in the way of habitual convictions. If it is too simple to say, as one of his contemporaries did, that "when Scott ceased to go to mass he began to drink," it is true that his unfaltering sense of life — and especially his own life — as a dramatic conflict between good and evil was cultivated, if not determined, by his early training. As he wrote Wilson at this time: "I am ashamed to say that my

Catholicism is scarcely more than a memory—no that's wrong it's more than that; at any rate I go not to church nor mumble stray nothings over chrystaline beads." [38] It takes a sense of sin which lies far deeper than any nominal commitment to a doctrine to be as powerfully affected by immoral conduct, especially his own immoral conduct, as Fitzgerald was. "Poor Scott," as one shrewd friend remarked, "he never really enjoyed his dissipation because he disapproved intensely of himself all the time it was going on." [39] At the same time, of course, the very significance thus lent to dissipation made it seem fascinating and important to him, so that he sometimes appeared to have almost a compulsion to shock himself.

However damned this attitude may be, it could exist only in a man whose basic feeling for experience was a religious one. This was hardly clear to his family. What they did see was what he was at no pains to conceal. "There is no use concealing the fact," he wrote Shane Leslie a year later, "that my reaction a year ago last June [i.e., June, 1919] to apparent failure in every direction did carry me rather away from the church. My ideas now are in such wild riot that I would flatter myself did I claim even the clarity of agnostisism." [40] That last sentence is polite evasion, for at about the same time he assured President Hibben in the letter he wrote him about *This Side of Paradise* that "my view of life, President Hibben, is the view of [the] Theodore Dreisers and Joseph Conrads—that life is too strong and remorseless for the sons of men." [41] Such talk shocked and angered his family.

Their disapproval of his opinions was not decreased when a St. Paul firm, Griggs Cooper, offered him the position of advertising manager at a very good salary and he refused it. [42] This refusal shows how much he was prepared to stake on *This Side of Paradise* and how intolerable, to his imagination as well as Zelda's, merely moderate success was. Not even the possibility that the Griggs Cooper position might tempt

Zelda moved him — or perhaps he knew, from his own feelings, that in the long run it would not provide a life that
would satisfy her.

While he waited to hear from Scribner's he did, however,
take a job. His old friend Larry Boardman, who had worked
up to a supervisory position in the Northern Pacific carbarn,
got it for him. He told Fitzgerald to report in old clothes.
Fitzgerald arrived in dirty white flannels, polo shirt, sweat-
shirt, and a blue cap, and complained to Boardman that he
did not seem to be able to make conversation with the men.
Eventually he caught on and bought a pair of overalls and
learned not to offend the foreman by sitting down when he
hammered nails. After a few days, however, he decided he
was not cut out for this kind of work and quit. The day he
did so, his new, four-dollar overalls were stolen, a misfortune
which wiped out practically everything he had earned.[43]
Luckily he did not have to wait very long to hear from
Scribner's; this time Perkins was enthusiastic about the book
and, with the help of Charles Scribner, Jr., persuaded the
elder Mr. Scribner to accept it. He wrote Fitzgerald special
delivery on September 16:

> I am very glad, personally to be able to write you that we
> are all for publishing your book, "This Side of Paradise."
> Viewing it as the same book that was here before, which in
> a sense it is, though . . . extended further, I think that you
> have improved it enormously. As the first manuscript did,
> it abounds in energy and life and it seems to me to be in
> much better proportion. . . . The book is so different that
> it is hard to prophesy how it will sell, but we are all for
> taking a chance and supporting it with vigor.

Fitzgerald was overwhelmed. "Of course I was delighted to
get your letter," he wrote Perkins two days later, "and I've
been in a sort of trance all day. . . ." He was so excited that

day that he ran up and down Summit Avenue stopping cars and telling all his friends and a good many mere acquaintances that his book had been accepted.[44] His battered morale revived and he was once more full of confidence. The possibility that the novel might not shake the world but, like most first novels, slip quietly into the great silence simply never occurred to him. A month or so later, when he called on Scribner's in New York, he assured them he would be quite satisfied with a sale of 20,000 copies in the first year.*

From the very beginning he kept at Perkins for immediate publication; his reasons for this impossible request are revealing:

> . . . one thing I cannot relinquish without a slight struggle. Would it be utterly impossible for you to publish the book Xmas — or say by February? I have so many things dependent on its success — including of course a girl — not that I expect it to make me a fortune but it will have a psychological effect on me and all my surroundings. . . . I'm in that stage where every month counts frantically and seems a cudgel in a fight for happiness against time.[45]

Not that Zelda was abnormally hardhearted and determined about the fortune; Fitzgerald was ready to marry even with poor financial prospects, but he understood and sympathized with Zelda's attitude. It is worth observing that the position ascribed to her in his letter to Perkins is Fitzgerald's conception of her attitude: the letter was written only two days

* The book actually did far better than that. Published March 26, 1920, it had sold 32,786 copies by November 8, 1920, 39,786 by February 1, 1921. Before the original sale died down, about the middle of 1923, it had sold better than 50,000 copies. A cheap reprint sold another 20,000 copies during the next year. "The book didn't make me as rich as I thought it would nor as you would suspect from the vogue and the way it was talked about," Rascoe reported Fitzgerald as saying. ". . . its actual sale wasn't more than 30,000 copies the first year." (*We Were Interrupted*, p. 20.) Despite the inaccurate figure, this probably represents Fitzgerald's feeling. For a famous book, *This Side of Paradise* did not sell very well.

after the novel had been accepted, before Zelda could even have heard the news, to say nothing of responding to it. "I can't," says Rosalind to Amory, "be shut away from the trees and flowers, cooped up in a little flat, waiting for you. You'd hate me in a narrow atmosphere. I'd make you hate me. . . . I wouldn't be the Rosalind you love. . . . I like sunshine and pretty things and cheerfulness — and I dread responsibility. I don't want to think about pots and kitchens and brooms. I want to worry whether my legs will get slick and brown when I swim in the summer." [46] Part of what Fitzgerald loved very much in Zelda was the integrity of her belief in her rights as a beauty to have pretty things and to let others take the responsibility. Long after he remarked that this being "one of the eternal children of this world" was "a thing people will stand until they realize the awful toll exacted from others." [47] How soon he realized what this toll was is shown by the portrait of Luella Hemple in "The Adjuster" (written in December, 1924). "We make an agreement with children," says Doctor Moon, "that they can sit in the audience without helping to make the play, but if they still sit in the audience after they're grown, somebody's got to work double time for them, so that they can enjoy the light and glitter of the world." [48] This is Fitzgerald's view of Zelda, no doubt true as far as it goes, but, for all its sympathy, a partial view. We have no similar record of Zelda's view of his shortcomings, and as his favorite author, Samuel Butler, remarked in his "Apology for the Devil," "It must be remembered that we have heard only one side of the case. God has written all the books." [49] In any event, the appeal of Zelda's imperiousness was at this time much stronger than its power to disturb him, because its demands on life were so very like his own.

The bubbling excitement in which he lived during the period immediately after the acceptance of *This Side of Paradise* can be seen in the letter he wrote his childhood friend, Alida Bigelow, then a student at Smith, a few days after the news reached him. The letter is headed: "Ist Epistle of St. Scott to the Smithsonian, Chapter the I, Verses the I to the last," and under the date there is a piece of doggerel which begins:

> *What's a date!*
> *Mr. Fate*
> *Can't berate*
> *Mr. Scott.*
> *He is not*
> *Marking time. . . .*

Time was not, after all, getting the better of him; he was sure now that he was showing life he was a good enough man to dominate it. The body of the letter then goes on to assert a series of melancholy attitudes with such ebullience as to deny them in the very act of stating them.

Most beautiful, rather-too-virtuous-but-entirely-enchanting Alida:

Scribner's has accepted my book. Ain't I smart! . . . In a few days I'll have lived one score and three days in this vale of tears. On I plod — always bored often drunk, doing no penance for my faults — rather do I become more tolerant of myself from day to day, hardening my chrystal heart with blasphemous humor and shunning only toothpicks, pathos, and poverty as being the three unforgivable things in life. . . .

I am frightfully unhappy, look like the devil, will be famous within 1 12 month and, I hope, dead within 2.

Hoping you are the same
I am
With Excruciating respect
F. Scott Fitzgerald

P.S. If you wish you may auction off this letter to the gurls

of your collidge — on condition that the proceeds go to the
Society for the drownding of Armenian Airdales
Bla!

F. S. F.[50]

On the crest of this wave of enthusiasm he began to write
like mad; he got some work done on a new novel which he
tentatively entitled *The Demon Lover* ("A very ambitious
novel . . . which will probably take a year"), but mostly he
wrote short stories.[51] Between September and December he
produced nine stories — one of them was written in a single
evening — and polished up another one that had been written
in the spring and rejected everywhere.[52] He was still anxious
to demonstrate that he was a money-maker, and the quickest
way to swing a cudgel in his "fight for happiness against
time" was to produce salable short stories in impressive quantity. During October he managed to make $215 — mostly
from *The Smart Set* — and to pay off his "terrible small
debts." [53] Even small debts like these were terrible to him.
One of the most persistent manifestations of his divided nature
is the way he was always in debt, often seriously so, and yet
never ceased to be deeply shocked by the fact.

The Smart Set's $215, together with $300 that Bridges, the
editor of *Scribner's Magazine*, paid him on November 1 for
two stories, made him a man of means and he felt ready to
see Zelda again. In the middle of November, therefore, he
returned to Montgomery in subdued triumph. He and Zelda
walked in the Confederate cemetery and sat again on the
remembered couch in the Sayres' living room. Everything
was the same; it was the renewal he had dreamed of so long.
Only everything was not the same. For one thing, "I was a
professional and my enchantment with certain things that she
felt and said was already paced by an anxiety to set them
down in a story — it was called *The Ice Palace*. . . ." [54] For
another thing, the magic was gone. As he wrote afterward in
" 'The Sensible Thing' ":

There was nothing changed — only everything was changed. . . . He saw [the sitting room] was only a room, and not the enchanted chamber where he had passed those poignant hours. He sat in a chair, amazed to find it a chair, realizing that his imagination had distorted and colored all these simple familiar things. . . . He knew that that boy of fifteen months before had had something, a trust, a warmth that was gone forever. The sensible thing — they had done the sensible thing. He had traded his first youth for strength and carved success out of despair. But with his youth, life had carried away the freshness of his love. . . . He could never recapture those lost April hours. . . . Well, let it pass, he thought; April is over, April is over. There are all kinds of love in the world, but never the same love twice.[55]

These feelings were genuine but, as the title of his story suggests, less sensible than Zelda's. ". . . *don't* try so hard," she wrote him, "to convince yourself that we're very old people who've lost their most precious possessions. . . . That first abandon couldn't last, but the things that went to make it are tremendously alive . . . so don't mourn for a poor little forlorn memory. . . ." But it was not in Fitzgerald's nature to be sensible about his emotional investments, and Zelda knew that; she understood Fitzgerald's divided nature quite clearly. Earlier she had written him about another problem: "I know you've worried — and enjoyed doing it thoroughly — and I didn't want you to. . . . I know it's depriving you of an idea that horrifies and fascinates — you're so morbidly exaggerative. . . . Sort of deliberately experimental and wiggly."

Thus they became engaged again, informally; they would be married when Fitzgerald's book came out. With that unconscious irony absolute accuracy often produces, Fitzgerald described the situation to Perkins by saying: "I'm almost sure I'll get married as soon as my book is out."[56] With this much assurance about Zelda, he went on to New York, where Paul Reynolds, the literary agent, agreed to handle his work. He was assigned to the immediate care of a young man named Harold Ober, and so conscientiously did Ober handle the sales of Fitzgerald's stories and their author's confused and often desperate financial affairs that when he set up an agency of his own in September, 1929, there was no question about Fitzgerald's going with him. He began auspiciously by selling "Head and Shoulders" to the *Post* for $400, nearly three times as much as Fitzgerald had ever been paid before. At the same time Metro made a flattering movie offer. On the strength of these successes Fitzgerald got roaring drunk and flooded his hotel by leaving the tap on in his bathroom.

He returned to St. Paul "in a thoroughly nervous alcoholic state" which did not, however, prevent his celebrating at the Christmas parties.[57] He had now given up the ambitious writing schemes he had worked out in his enthusiasm the previous fall.[58] Instead he revised two of the old rejected stories and Reynolds promptly sold them to the *Post* for $1000. Then, with one of those incredible bursts of energy on which he was to come more and more to depend, he managed to turn out a mildly amusing story about a drunk who had gone to the wrong party as one end of a camel. "12,000 words," as he wrote Perkins, ". . . begun eight o'clock one morning and finished at seven at night and then copied between seven and half past four and mailed at 5 in the morning."[59] This burst of energy gave him enough money to go to New Orleans "because I'm afraid I'm about to develop tuberculosis."[60] Probably he was right, for a later medical examination showed the scars of a mild attack. At the same time he was writing Perkins: "I want to start [a new book] but I don't want to go broke in the middle and start in and have to write short stories again . . . for money."[61] He had not been able to pay for a Coca-Cola five months before, and had since made a couple of thousand dollars and could look forward to the profits of his novel, but he was a man who half consciously assumed that the necessities of life did not have to be calculated as expenses and was thus able to look on the main portion of his income as available for "free" expenditure, with the result that, to his continual astonishment, he always lived well beyond his income.

He arrived in New Orleans in the middle of January, settled into a boarding house on Prytania Street, and started another novel; in less than a month he had given it up.[62] He did not like New Orleans. "O. Henry said this was a story town," he said, "—but its too consciously that—just as a Hugh Walpole character is too consciously a character."[63] He did, however, turn out two stories which were again promptly sold to the *Post*. His wooing of Zelda, conducted to a considerable extent by telegram, consisted largely of reports of these sales: THE SATURDAY EVENING POST HAS JUST TAKEN TWO MORE STORIES PERIOD ALL MY LOVE, he would wire; or: I HAVE SOLD THE MOVIE RIGHTS OF HEAD AND SHOULDERS TO THE METRO COMPANY FOR TWENTY FIVE HUNDRED DOLLARS I LOVE YOU DEAREST GIRL.[64] It would be hard to say whether his own delight in success or his desire to sooth any incipient "nervousness" in Zelda weighed more heavily in this curious form of wooing.

This delight in success was, in any event, only a part of his attitude toward his work, a part that was to conflict all his life with a desire to write not just profitably but well. As early as December, 1919, he had asked Harold Ober, "Is there any market at all for the cynical or pessimistic story except *Smart Set* or does realism bar a story from any well-paying magazine no matter how cleverly it is done?" Two years later he had reached the point of asserting that, despite his talent, he was determined to grit his teeth and make money:

I am rather discouraged—he wrote Ober—that a cheap story like *The Popular Girl* written in one week while the baby was being born brings $1500.00 & a genuinely imaginative thing into which I put three weeks real enthusiasm like

The Diamond in the Sky ["The Diamond as Big as the Ritz"] brings not a thing. But, by God and Lorimer, I'm going to make a fortune yet.[65]

This conflict was to haunt his career from beginning to end. From the time he wrote "The Curious Case of Benjamin Button" ("altogether too unusual for us to publish," said the *Post*) to the time he wrote "Crazy Sunday" (which, according to the *Post*, "didn't get anywhere or prove anything"), his best work was hard to sell.[66] But it was frighteningly easy to sell his competent, mediocre, and even his bad work. He never stopped trying to write good stories, but when he became desperate for money, he found it hard to resist selling stories he was ashamed of, such as "Your Way and Mine," of which he wrote Ober in 1926: "This is one of the lousiest stories I've ever written. Just *terrible! . . . Please* — and I mean this — don't offer it to the *Post*. . . . I'd rather have $1000. for it from some obscure place than twice that and have it seen. *I feel very strongly about this!*" [67] This was the most he could afford his conscience.

Twice during January, 1920, he came up from New Orleans to Montgomery to see Zelda. The second time their engagement was put on a formal basis, and he brought a batch of Sazaracs all the way from New Orleans to celebrate the occasion.[68] The *Post* had just taken four more of his stories. Again he went on to New York to complete the sale of *Head and Shoulders* to the movies, an event which he celebrated in two very characteristic ways. With the help of an old friend, Ruth Sturtevant, he bought Zelda an expensive feather fan; and he treated himself, like a child in a candy shop, to all the luxuries of New York.[69] When two old friends looked him up they found him having himself bathed by two bellboys. When he finally got himself dressed, he insisted on taking them to "his" bootlegger on Lexington Avenue and buying them each a pint of Scotch. This gesture was impressive in

1920; bootleggers did not become standard equipment until several years later. At dinner-time Fitzgerald announced that he had a date. His preparations for it included fixing hundred-dollar bills in his vest pockets in such a way as to expose them prominently. Since he had been hinting that this date was a daring one, his friends felt this piece of conspicuous display was ill-timed. They finally got the bills away from him and put them in the hotel vault; they amounted to $500 or $600. He was drunk with the excitement of money.

At the same time he saw his own rise from poverty to afflu-ence as an illustration of the terrible, meaningless power of money. It was not his nature to deduce from this understand-ing a conviction that society needed to be totally recon-structed; but, as he recalled in 1936 when he went back over his life trying to explain his crack-up, "the man with the jingle of money in his pocket who married the girl a year later would always cherish an abiding distrust, an animosity, toward the leisure class — not the conviction of a revolutionist but the smouldering hatred of a peasant. In the years since then I have never been able to stop wondering where my friends' money came from, nor to stop thinking that at one time a sort of *droit de seigneur* might have been exercised to give one of them my girl." [70]

In March he went down to Princeton to stay at Cottage until Zelda came up for the wedding. There he finally realized that dream of renewing his undergraduate life which he and Bishop had shared throughout the war. He went to the Prom and did a good many other things which had been luxuries or impossibilities for him when he was an undergraduate. [71] The illusion of undergraduate days was easy to create because so many of his contemporaries were back in college from the war completing the work for their degrees. In his spare time he worked, and worked with that complete seriousness and concentration of his talent which he always seemed to be able to summon in the odd intervals of exhausting and irrelevant activities. "Can't work here," he wrote Perkins from Cottage, "so have just about decided to quit work and become an ashman. Still working on that *Smart Set* novelette." The *Smart Set* novelette was "May Day" and it was completed before he left Princeton.

On March 20 the Sayres announced the engagement and Fitzgerald sent Zelda her first orchid.[72] They were now planning to be married as soon as possible. On March 26 *This Side of Paradise* was published.

CHAPTER V

THIS SIDE OF PARADISE depends indirectly on Fitzgerald's personal experience, but "we must not forget," as one critic has put it, "that the artist may 'experience' life differently in terms of his art." [1] If Amory Blaine, the hero of *This Side of Paradise*, like Fitzgerald, settled in New York after the war, worked for an advertising firm, and had a love affair which ended in disaster and an epic three-week drunk, we would nonetheless be wrong to conclude that what he felt about his experience was what Fitzgerald felt about his. Fitzgerald was in love with the daughter of an Alabama judge, and he felt nagging doubts — no less strong because he defied them — about Zelda's ability as well as his own to stand up socially in the world he longed to conquer. The story of Anthony Patch and Dorothy Raycroft in *The Beautiful and Damned* and the story of Ailie Calhoun ("The Last of the Belles") and Lieutenant Earl Schoen, with their wonderful feeling for class and custom, derive in their devious ways from Fitzgerald's feelings about himself and Zelda too. These feelings are a far cry from Amory's feelings for Rosalind, the smart and socially triumphant sister of Amory's Princeton classmate, the assured citizen of Fitzgerald's Lost City, the gallantly philosophical flapper. Not that Amory and Rosalind have not their roots in Fitzgerald's feelings about himself and Zelda too, as do many other quite different characters in his fiction.

The very variety of these characters shows how dangerous it would be to confuse any of them with him and Zelda. What it is important to see in *This Side of Paradise* is the way Fitzgerald got the possibilities of his life, his "heightened sensitivity to the promises of life," into it without betraying its actuality.

The idea of a book about a young man's college experience and his coming of age was suggested to him by books like Owen Johnson's *Stover at Yale* as he eagerly confessed in his unselfish way to Johnson the first time they met.[2] But Fitzgerald's conception of his subject was very different from Johnson's. Stover's great problems were those of "the team" and the need to create class unity and the difficulties of making a senior society without sacrificing self-respect. Through all these crises he was earnestly supported by the heroine, Jean Story. When as a sophomore he "forgot" himself and told Jean he loved her and she met "the shock of his blunder" with "dignity and gentleness," Stover "put out his hand and gently took the end of the scarf which she wore about her shoulders, and raised it to his lips."[3] This is not quite the way Amory and Isabelle make love. Nor is Johnson's feeling that, when Skull and Bones taps Stover in spite of his independence, the world has been proved sound like the feeling with which Fitzgerald leaves Amory on the highway near Princeton, thinking, "here was a new generation . . . grown up to find all Gods dead, all wars fought, all faiths in man shaken."[4]

Fitzgerald's feelings about his subject were very much influenced by Compton Mackenzie's *Sinister Street*. Unfriendly reviewers like Frances Newman thought that "[if] 'Sinister Street' was until very lately the apple of one's eye and if even the discovery of a new apple [this was *Jurgen*] has not caused one to love it less, the perusal of 'This Side of Paradise' becomes nothing less than agony";[5] and after reading the manuscript of *This Side of Paradise* in November, 1919, Wilson wrote Fitzgerald half jokingly that it was "like an exquisite burlesque of Compton Mackenzie with a pastiche of Wells thrown in at the end." [6] These influences, too, Fitzgerald was anxious to admit. "I sent the novel to Mencken," he wrote Frances Newman, "with the confession that it derives itself from Mackenzie, Wells and Tarkington," and six years later he was still being careful to list, among the books which had influenced him greatly, "At 20, 'Sinister Street' — Compton Mckenzie. At 22, 'Tono Bungay' — H. G. Wells." [7]

For most readers these influences were hardly visible, and *This Side of Paradise* struck them like a bombshell. "My how that boy Fitzgerald can write!" said Harry Hansen, then the literary editor of the Chicago *Daily News*, "I have just had a wonderful evening with 'This Side of Paradise.' It is probably one of the few really American novels extant." [8] Whether readers thought, as some did, that "the boy was a cad" and the girl an insult to her sex, or, as others did, that "the fine open eyed outlook that the boy has on his generation" and "the keen sense for details of contemporary psychology" gave readers "the very essence of youth" made little difference; they were fascinated. It is possible to argue, as Burton Rascoe recently has, that there was nothing very novel about the life described in *This Side of Paradise*, that casual drinking and petting had been going on for several years.[9] They had; Frederick Lewis Allen thinks " 'the petting party' had been current as early as 1916"; and Fitzgerald himself later said it dated from 1915.[10] But the historical fact is not the point. Fitzgerald was the first to describe this life in detail and to represent these activities as new, daring, and admirable. They cease to be in his book merely casual, occasional gestures and become the acts of a generation which was making a sincere effort to live more fully and happily than their parents and to be honest and unhypocritical about what they were doing.

To this generation's extravagance and courage and to the romance of the idea that one could do anything if one only tried, Fitzgerald responded with enthusiasm; these were his convictions, too. At the same time he was surprised by a great many things that the assertion of independence led others to do. What stands out most strongly in his own memory of his attitude in the early twenties is his sense of separation from them. This curious yet characteristic combination of feelings makes *This Side of Paradise* much more interesting than other books on the same subject like Dorothy Speare's *Dancers in the Dark* or Percy Marks' *The Plastic Age*, or even Benét's *The Beginning of Wisdom*. In Fitzgerald's book there is the constant play of an ingrained moral sense which, for all the charm and poignancy he finds in the life he portrays, places and evaluates it. He writes like some kind of impassioned and naïve anthropologist, recording with minuteness and affection and at the same time with an alien's remoteness and astonishment.

This was always his attitude toward his material. The myths for his fiction were made out of the concrete experiences and the social ideals of his world, into which he poured his ambition for goodness and his idealizing imagination. At every stage of his career he made a hero out of the most representative and brilliant man he knew, out of Reuben Warner, the leader of his little set in St. Paul when he was a child; out of Walker Ellis during the years in college when his dream was to make Cottage Club and the Triangle; out of Henry Strater in the last two years of college; out of Gerald Murphy on the Riviera; out of Irving Thalberg in Hollywood. "At certain moments," he wrote in one of his notes for *The Last Tycoon*, "one man appropriates to himself the total significance of a time and place." With this man, in each place he knew, Fitzgerald sought to identify himself; this was the way his imagination came to grips with the world. "When I like men," he wrote in his Notebooks, "I want to be like them — I want to lose the outer qualities that give me my individuality and be like them. I don't want the man [;] I want to absorb into myself all the qualities that make him attractive and leave him out. I cling to my own inards." [11]

Just as he found his heroes in the everyday world, so he found his moral and social ideals; and in exactly the same way he adapted them to the hard inner core of his own ego, which was never affected by his superficial adaptability: he clung to his own innards. Thus he organized a world which had the integrity of his own finely coordinated feelings and was, at the same time, vividly actual.

But if he knew this society, he was also subject to it; his imaginative commitment was the source of his power to realize it. As a subject for fiction it was — except for a brief period in the twenties — unfashionable. By the time *The Great Gatsby* was published critics were complaining that Fitzgerald was not writing about the American peasant ("a stubborn seeking for the static in a world that for almost a hundred years has simply not been static," he called this fad).[12] This complaint grew louder during the thirties. But Fitzgerald could not have pretended to a world he had never lived in even if he had wanted to. He knew the American middle-class life of his time as few writers have ever known their material; "the people were right, the talk was right, the clothes, the cars were real," as John O'Hara put it. About such things Fitzgerald was never wrong. And in his imagination they took on shape and color and meaning almost automatically. He could make something like an American folktale out of them:

> *There'd be an orchestra*
> *Bingo! Bango!*
> *Playing for us*
> *To dance the tango,*
> *And people would clap*
> *When we arose,*
> *At her sweet face*
> *And my new clothes.*[13]

With this kind of material Fitzgerald was likely to fail as a writer, when he did so, rather with the Victorians than with the followers of Flaubert and James. His instinct was to write what James called in "The New Novel" the novel of "saturation" (James' illustrations included Wells and Mackenzie) rather than the novel with a clear "centre of interest" and "a sense of the whole." The very purity of his imagination and the tenacity with which it fixed itself on the life about him only made more obvious his failure to organize all his imagined experience. Not till he wrote his third book did he produce a novel in which the form is adequate to the realized life.

This was the way he knew the life he described in *This Side of Paradise*; he understood it — within the limits of the standards it set for him — completely. He knew the absurdity of confusing its trivial manners and its serious morals, of supposing that a particular way of dancing was "an offense against womanly purity" and rolled stockings identical with sexual promiscuity. He knew from experience that within the emerging system of manners the old distinctions still held, that among his contemporaries there were still the wise and the foolish, the brave and the cowardly, the good and the bad.

This sympathetic respect for his subject and his conviction that, like all human experience, it mattered immensely give the book its permanent interest. However immature his feelings, they are fully represented and convincing, and such full realization has some value, however inadequately the experience so realized is judged. The book's account of Amory's first days at Princeton and of the gay trip to Deal Beach, for example, are overwhelmingly true to undergraduate life. The Princeton scenes taken altogether, in spite of occasional over-dramatization and sentimentalization, trace very penetratingly the invisible pressures and stresses of a society.[14] If Fitzgerald failed to understand just how limited a society this one was, he still realized it vividly.

Moreover, he had been struggling since the failure of *The Romantic Egotist* to discover how to communicate more completely what he saw and felt, to find the kind of events which would give his sense of experience full play, to feel his way to the proper rhythm of scene and summary, to discover, above all, the right detail and the right tone. He had a fine ear, and the speech of the characters in *This Side of Paradise* is completely convincing. The immaturity of the conversations on supposedly intellectual subjects between Burne Holiday and Amory or the touchingly egocentric lovemaking of Amory and Rosalind is as evident as it is because Fitzgerald's dialogue is very good. The love letter Amory writes Isabelle is so convincing that you suspect Fitzgerald of using one of his own letters to Ginevra King for just this purpose as he used Father Fay's letters for another:

> Oh, Isabelle, dear — it's a wonderful night. Somebody is playing "Love Moon" on a mandolin far across the campus, and the music seems to bring you into the window. Now he's playing "Good-by, Boys, I'm Through," and how well it suits me. For I *am* through with everything. I have decided never to have a cocktail again, and I know I'll never again fall in love. . . . Oh, *dearest* Isabelle (somehow I can't call you just Isabelle, and I'm afraid I'll come out with the "dearest" before your family this June)[15]. . . .

And so on and on.

These virtues in the book are the products of great honesty, of a determination to record what he saw and felt at any cost. The cost, at this stage in his development, was considerable. The distance between Amory and his creator, so far as values are concerned, is always very narrow, and sometimes non-existent. It is not only Amory who is full of unrecognized intellectual affectations and emotional immaturities; it is, much of the time, the author; in these respects the book itself is hardly wiser than its hero. The case against *This Side of Para-*

dise was never more firmly made than by Fitzgerald's friend Edmund Wilson, writing at the very height of the book's fame.

> [Amory Blaine] — he wrote — was . . . an uncertain quantity in a phantasmagoria of incident which had no dominating intention to endow it with unity and force. . . . [The book] is very immaturely imagined: it is always just verging on the ludicrous. And, finally, it is one of the most illiterate books of any merit ever published. . . . It is not only full of bogus ideas and faked literary references but it is full of English words misused with the most reckless abandon.[16]

That Fitzgerald took such hard hitting from Wilson without complaint shows his fundamental humility.

Because of the book's success and because people who disliked its account of the Younger Generation wanted to belittle it, its mechanical defects were made much of. FPA ran lists of Fitzgerald's errors in his column, heading the first one with the observation that " 'This Side of Paradise' is sloppy and cocky; impudent instead of confident; and verbose." [17] There were a great many errors in the book, for Fitzgerald was incapable of submitting to the ordinary routines of education. "Aside from his literary talent," as Glenway Wescott put it " — literary genius, self-taught — I think Fitzgerald must have been the worst educated man in the world." [18] His mind moved with great subtlety among the concrete experiences he had known well and felt deeply, but he had almost no capacity for abstract ideas or arguments and could enter into other people's attitudes only when he had known them in his own experience. He was not proud of being so constituted and tried to think of himself as an intellectual. It was only late in his life that, writing ironically about his own career, he had the narrator in "Financing Finnegan" say, "It was only when I met some poor devil of a screen writer who had been trying to make a logical story out of one of his books that I realized

[Finnegan] had his enemies. 'It's all beautiful when you read it,' this man said disgustedly, 'but when you write it down plain it's like a week in the nuthouse.' " [19] By then Fitzgerald was himself a "poor devil of a screen writer" in Hollywood. But when he wrote *This Side of Paradise* he was anxious to conceal this deficiency and filled the book with what Wilson called "bogus ideas and faked literary references."

He was also a startlingly bad speller. To the end of his life he wrote *ect.* for *etc.* and spelled his friend's name Hemming-way or Hemingway indifferently. He made all the standard mistakes, such as "dissapoint," and seemed not to know when he was spelling correctly. "Excuse the pencil," he wrote Perkins August 25, 1921, "but I'm feeling rather discouraged tonight and I haven't the energy to use ink — ink the ineffable destroyer of thought, that fades an emotion into that slatternly thing, a written down mental excretion. What ill-spelled rot!" His grammar was equally erratic.

It was not, of course, simply that he was impervious to the mechanics of the English language, though he was that; it was also that he wrote under the guidance of his delicate sense of the pitch and tone of English sentences. This sense is the secret of his marvelously evocative prose, and compared to it a deficiency in the textbook mechanics of the language is insignificant. His power comes out even in his fooling:

> Please don't say you can't come the 25th but would like to come the 29th. We never receive people the 29th. It is the anniversary of the 2nd Council of Nicea when our Blessed Lord, our Blessed Lord, our Blessed Lord, our Blessed Lord —
>
> It always gets stuck in that place. . . .
>
> Pray gravity to move your bowels. Its little we get done for us in this world. Answer.[20]

In Fitzgerald's best work this power is in every sentence. Toward its realization all the work of revision in his manuscripts was directed. It is an interesting process to watch.*

He had counted on Scribner's to correct the errors in his manuscript and was badly upset when he realized they had not. By July he had gathered from various sources "approximately *100* mispellings and misprints" and was saying to Perkins, "It was rather humiliating this morning to get a letter wondering 'whether they left the mistakes in just as they did in the Young Visitors to keep the spirit of the original.'" [21] Critics of the book's substance also endorsed Wilson's judgment. The *Times Literary Supplement* said: "As a novel, it is rather tiresome; its values are less human than literary, and its characters . . . with hardly an exception, a set of exasperating *poseurs*, whose conversation, devoted largely to minute self-analysis, is artificial beyond belief." Heywood Broun made the same point when he wrote in the New York *Tribune:* "The self-consciousness of Fitzgerald is a barrier which we are never able to pierce. He sees himself constantly not as a human being, but as a man in a novel or in a play. Every move is a picture and there is a camera man behind each tree." [22]

The very honesty with which Fitzgerald presents his experience and his feelings about it only makes evident the immaturity to which these comments point. Some allowance must, to be sure, be made for the conventions of the period, especially in matters of sex, in judging Fitzgerald. Benét's *The Beginning of Wisdom*, a far more mature book than *This Side of Paradise*, written at almost exactly the same time on the same subject (it even mentions *This Side of Paradise* in the last few pages), makes its females epicene ("as beautiful and sexless a thing as the flight of a gull over waves") and its love affairs boyish ("a passion that was curiously comradely"). ". . . the quest of slenderness," as Frederick Lewis Allen has said, "the flattening of the breasts, the vogue of short skirts (even when short skirts still suggested the appearance of a

* See Appendix A.

little girl), the juvenile effect of the long waist, — all were signs that, consciously or unconsciously, the women of this decade worshiped not merely youth, but unripened youth. . . ." [23]

Still, making every allowance, the immaturity of Amory's love affairs is remarkable — and ironic, considering how daring the book was supposed to be. Fitzgerald's lovers are concerned with something called "kissing," an act which is dissociated from any other physical action and in itself involves almost no physical sensation; the concomitants of kissing are for these lovers metaphysical, a generalized sense of wickedness and romance. Apart from kissing they spend their time making long speeches about themselves, full of sentiments from Swinburne and Rupert Brooke and of sweeping generalizations about "Life"; as lovers they show the hypnotized egocentricity and intellectual immaturity of college freshmen. Something of this attitude stayed with Fitzgerald as late as *Tender Is the Night:* Rosemary's "body hovered on the edge of childhood."

But however immature they are these lovers are not dull characters; on the contrary, they are hauntingly and embarrassingly real. They make us aware of how we would remember ourselves, had we Fitzgerald's gift for remembering the precise feelings which belonged to our experience as we lived it. He remembered these feelings as precisely as he remembered the clothes, the cars, the furniture, the songs, the slang. This is the value of *This Side of Paradise.* But it is largely a historical rather than a literary value. Not that *This Side of Paradise* is only social history; it is the history of a good deal more than that. But it is still a kind of history, a remarkably accurate account of what happened, in feeling as well as fact, rather than an evaluating formal organization of things that might have happened. What justifies the *Times* and the critics who agreed with it is not the characters themselves but Fitzgerald's acceptance as author of their point of view, the fact that he not only takes them perfectly seriously but, when speaking in his own person, thinks exactly as they do.

The general ideas in terms of which Fitzgerald reasoned about his experience were suggested to him by his reading, so that his book appeared, superficially, "an exquisite burlesque" with overt values that were "less human than literary." Yet the experience itself was all Fitzgerald's own, and the failure of critics like Frances Newman — who said quite rightly of her review that it was "assault with intent to murder" — to distinguish where what is second-hand leaves off and what is first-hand begins is the characteristic failure of people who are literary in the bad sense.[24] For all the book's inadequacies and affectations, it is not essentially a bad book. "Looking it over," Fitzgerald wrote Perkins twenty years later, "I think it is now one of the funniest books since 'Dorian Gray' in its utter spuriousness — and then, here and there, I find a page that is real and living."[25] Such pages come when he is drawing directly on his minutely detailed memory, of every feeling during that awful conference with the headmaster when he was so very unpopular at Newman, of every crisis in the fierce drama of his life at Princeton, of every word he and Ginevra King had ever said to one another. If he took it all, much of the time, with childish solemnity, that was because it had mattered so much to him; if he "philosophized" over it absurdly, that was because he was trying to find in it a meaning equivalent to his feeling of its importance. And some of the time he did neither. On almost the first page of the book the fundamental quality of his imagination appears in the description of Beatrice O'Hara, a description which is alive with the fascination and horror of wealth which Fitzgerald first fully realized for our period and which is a permanent part of our American feelings:

All in all Beatrice O'Hara absorbed the kind of education that will be quite impossible ever again; a tutelage measured

by the number of things and people one could be con-
temptuous of and charming about; a culture rich in all arts
and traditions, barren of all ideas, in the last of those days
when the great gardener clipped the inferior roses to produce
one perfect bud.[26]

Here there is a genuine, experienced attitude; the sense of the
romance and shoddiness, the charm and waste, that is Beatrice
O'Hara is present even in the half-nostalgic, half-ironic ca-
dence of a small phrase like "quite impossible ever again."
Beatrice O'Hara was Fitzgerald's sharp memory of an actual
person, "the mother of a friend of mine, whose name I cannot
mention." [27]

The genuine subject of *This Side of Paradise*, then, is the
sort of transmuted biography which was always Fitzgerald's
subject. Throughout the book, amidst all the cocksure badness
of judgment, the immaturity of sentiment, the affectations of
knowledge and style, this subject keeps reasserting itself, the
incorruptible heart of Fitzgerald's imagination which he was
so busy trying to beautify with borrowed feathers. Sixteen
years later, still remembering what Edmund Wilson, who
"had been my literary conscience" all his life, had said about
the book's bogus ideas and faked references, Fitzgerald remarked: "A lot of people thought it was a fake, and perhaps
it was, and a lot of others thought it was a lie, which it was
not." [28]

Though Perkins wrote him temptingly that "the pyramid
we have made of [*This Side of Paradise*] in our window [on
Fifth Avenue] is striking," Fitzgerald wanted to be in Princeton the day his book was published.[29] Scribner's advertising
department ran a small ad in the *Daily Princetonian:* "The
First Novel of F. SCOTT FITZGERALD '17 . . . A Story
About a Princeton Man," it asserted boldly. As an advertising
man with a long experience in selling the services of the
Muscatine, Iowa, Steam Laundry, Fitzgerald was disgusted by

this conservative policy. But there was something like a stampede in the Princeton University Store the day of publication.

Plans for his wedding were now pretty well completed. At Mrs. Sayre's suggestion they were to be married in New York. "She wants me to come to New York," Zelda wrote, "because she says you'd like to do it in St. Patrick's. . . . I told Mamma I might just come and surprise you, but she said you mightn't like to be surprised about 'your own wedding' — I rather think it's *my* wedding." Fitzgerald accepted Mrs. Sayre's generous suggestion happily and wired Zelda: I HAVE TAKEN ROOMS [for Zelda and her sister] AT THE BILTMORE AND WILL EXPECT YOU FRIDAY OR SATURDAY WIRE ME EXACTLY WHEN. Then he added his usual conclusion: BOOK SELLING ALL MY LOVE. Two days later they were still arguing about the date, but by announcing that he would BE AWFULLY NERVOUS UNTIL IT IS OVER and that the FIRST EDITION OF THE BOOK IS SOLD OUT . . . LOVE, Fitzgerald prevailed on Zelda to arrive in New York in time to be married on Saturday, April 3.[30]

When Zelda arrived in New York she seemed to Fitzgerald's friends, as she was, charmingly and romantically Southern, but Fitzgerald, sensitive as always to such things, was upset by her clothes and immediately called in his old St. Paul friend Marie Hersey, who was in school in New York. "My God, Marie," he said to her in an anguish of social distress, "You've got to help me! Zelda wants to buy nothing but frills and furbelows and you can't go around New York in that kind of thing; you go shopping with her." [31] So Marie went shopping with Zelda and tactfully guided her to a Patou suit. "There was a rippling sun along Fifth Avenue the day it was bought," Zelda remembered fifteen years later, "and it seemed very odd to be charging things to Scott Fitzgerald. The thing was to look like Justine Johnson at the time and it still seems a fine way to have looked. The shopper was two days out of Alabama. From the shop we went to tea in the Plaza Grill." [32]

On April 3 they were married in the rectory of St. Patrick's cathedral; Ludlow Fowler, one of Fitzgerald's college friends, and Zelda's sisters Rosalind, Marjorie, and Clotilde were the only others present. After the ceremony the priest said to them: "You be a good episcopalian, Zelda, and, Scott, you be a good catholic, and you'll get along fine." It was, Fitzgerald always remembered wryly, the last advice he ever got from a priest.[33] During their honeymoon they went to *Enter Madame* "and the actors were cross because our tickets were in the front row and we laughed appreciatively at the wrong places and uproariously at the jokes we made up as the show went along." They went to the midnight roof and "thought the man was real who straggled into the show dressed like a student and very convincingly got himself thrown out." [34]

They also went to a great many parties, and then, for the week-end of April 25, they went down to Cottage to chaperone houseparties. Fitzgerald started the week-end off with one of his practical jokes, by solemnly introducing Zelda to everyone as his mistress. Since they appeared at the club dances in a condition such that, as one observer remarked, a draft would have blown them down, the joke convinced more people than it should have; then there was "a rather gay party staged conspicuously in Harvey Firestone's car of robin's-egg blue" at which Fitzgerald acquired a very black eye; there was also a dinner at Cottage.[35] It was all quite innocent and harmless, but it offended what Dean Gauss later called "blue-nosed respectability."

On May 1, the *Nassau Lit* scheduled a banquet of old editors. It was a beautiful spring day, and Stanley Dell, Bishop, Wilson, and Fitzgerald drove down from New York for the occasion. All of them except Dell, who was driving, got a little drunk on the way down. They had set out with the idea of celebrating the spring, and had purchased in New York a supply of gilt laurel wreaths, lyres, and pipes of Pan. When they stopped for a moment outside Princeton on the old Lincoln Highway Fitzgerald, having entered into the occasion with characteristic enthusiasm, made an ecstatic speech in praise of the spring, Princeton, and his friends. In this state of mind they arrived in Princeton, where they sought out Dean Gauss. They found him on his front lawn, and there crowned him with a laurel wreath, to the accompaniment of extempore verses on the occasion from Fitzgerald. They then separated to go to their various clubs until the banquet that night; the last anyone saw of Fitzgerald was when he went dancing up the walk of Cottage, a laurel wreath askew on his head and the pipes of Pan at his lips. It was, for all its innocence, precisely the image of him that was already in the mind's eye of respectable members of his club. He was quickly approached by the president and told that he was suspended from membership. He went straight to the station and back to New York, as hurt as he had been when, a child of six in Buffalo, he had approached a crowd of children and been told to go away, they did not want him around.[36]

It is difficult not to sympathize with Fitzgerald's feeling that "the unctuousness and hypocrisy of the proceedings was exasperating." Years later, when he himself was under attack for suppressing a vicious undergraduate riot, Dean Gauss remembered this occasion and wrote Fitzgerald: "I remember with a good deal of feeling how a number of years ago a number of respectable evangelists in the cause of letters came down to Princeton crowned with laurel to reestablish the cult of Apollo and what a scandal this was to bluenosed respectability. Yet the aim then in view was a worthy one. . . ."[37]

Presently the Fitzgeralds moved from their honeymoon cottage at the Biltmore to the Commodore and settled down to another round of parties. They celebrated the move by whirling about in the revolving doors for half an hour.[38] With such gestures of innocent ebullience the period Fitzgerald was to name "the Jazz Age" began. "The uncertainties of 1919 were over" he said in "Early Success" " — there seemed little doubt about what was going to happen — America was going on the greatest, gaudiest spree in history. . . . The whole golden boom was in the air — its splendid generosities, its outrageous corruptions and the tortuous death struggle of the old America in prohibition." [39] Of this gaudy spree the people who were of an age with the century counted on having their share. They did not lack social generosity or political idealism, as the Sacco-Vanzetti case was to show a little later. Even Iris March, the heroine of *The Green Hat*, was capable of giving her feelings about the older generation a political turn, as when she says to Sir Maurice: "To you, it seems a worthy thing for a good man to make a success in the nasty arena of national strifes and international jealousies. To me, a world which thinks of itself in terms of puny, squalid, bickering little nations . . . is the highest indignity that can befall a good man, it is a world in which good men are shut up like gods in a lavatory." [40] But we do not remember Iris March's attitude as a political one any more than those who remember Ford Madox Ford's more brilliant portrait of Sylvia Tietjens remember how politically conscious her hatred of Christopher is. [41] For the twenties the situation did not define itself in these terms. ". . . in spite of the fact," wrote Fitzgerald in 1931, "that now we are all rummaging around in our trunks wondering where in hell we left the liberty cap — 'I know I *had* it' — and the moujik blouse . . . it was characteristic of the Jazz Age that it had no interest in politics at all." [42]

For what it was worth, Amory Blaine was a socialist. "We fancied ourselves," said Joseph Freeman of the most earnest people of the twenties, "disinterested devotees of art, revolution and psychoanalysis. All these seemed indiscriminately to point the way to universal human freedom from external oppression and internal chaos." [43] Max Eastman could pin his faith simultaneously on *The Masses* and *The Enjoyment of Poetry*, and Floyd Dell could write a Compton Mackenzie quest novel about the education of a middle-western socialist; the realities of the Russian revolution and the poetry of T. S. Eliot — both of which Max Eastman came to hate — were not yet evident. It took ten years for this split between Marxism and literature to make its appearance in the general thought of the period, so that Fitzgerald would write, jokingly but revealingly, to Wilson: "[Alec] told me to my amazement that you had explained the fundamentals of Leninism, even Marxism the night before, & Dos tells me that it was only recently made plain thru the same agency to the *New Republic*. I little thought when I left politics to you & your gang in 1920 you would devote your time to cutting up Wilson's shroud into blinders! Back to Mallarmé!" [44]

For the most part the attitude was far less earnest than Freeman's and Eastman's. For a moment after the war it looked as if the political strain this generation had inherited from Wells and Shaw would predominate over the aesthetic, as if the interest which would, in the thirties, produce Edmund Wilson's *To the Finland Station* would anticipate the interest which, in the twenties, produced his *Axel's Castle*. The response to John Dos Passos' *Three Soldiers*, in 1921, showed the feelings which could have led to this result. Fitzgerald's own review of the book is typical. "[The reader]," he says, "will hear [in *Three Soldiers*] the Y.M.C.A. men with their high-pitched voices . . . he will see these same obnoxious prigs charging twenty cents for a cup of chocolate. . . . He will see filth and pain, cruelty and hysteria and panic, in one long three-year nightmare and he will know that the war brought the use of these things . . . to himself and to his OWN son. . . ." At the same time, he speaks of the war in that tone which Mencken made stylish, as "the whole gorgeous farce of 1917-1918." [45] "When the police rode down the demobilized country boys gaping at the orators in Madison Square [on May Day in 1919]," Fitzgerald recalled later, "it was the sort of measure bound to alienate the more intelligent young men from the prevailing order. . . . If goose-livered business men had this effect on the government, then maybe we had gone to war for J. P. Morgan's loans after all. But, because we were tired of Great Causes, there was no more than a short outbreak of moral indignation. . . ." [46]

Instead of indignation there was a carefully cultivated air of amused indifference to the whole business of public affairs. In a general way you thought the socialists were right about our society, and you were sickened by the earnest hypocrisy of politicians and professional moralists, but public affairs seemed remote and insignificant, and, for the most part, quite hopelessly absurd; Mencken compared the superior intellectual in America to a man in a zoo. Fitzgerald documented this view in a characteristic passage in *The Beautiful and Damned:*

> [Anthony] tried to imagine himself in Congress rooting around in the litter of that incredible pigsty with the narrow and porcine brows he saw pictured sometimes in the roto-gravure sections of the Sunday newspapers, those glorified proletarians babbling blandly to the nation the ideas of high-school seniors! Little men with copy-book ambitions who by mediocrity had thought to emerge from mediocrity into the lustreless and unromantic heaven of a government by the people. . . . [47]

"Life," as he recalled long afterwards, "was largely a personal matter," [48] and this personal matter consisted mostly of an assertion, often deliberately extravagant and calculated to shock the old lady from Dubuque, of the virtues of hedonism. Very few stopped to wonder, with Walter Lippmann, "Who knows, having read Mr. Mencken and Mr. Sinclair Lewis, what kind of world will be left when all the boobs and yokels have crawled back into their holes and have died of shame?" [49] As long as the boom lasted, as Malcolm Cowley has pointed out, it was possible to ignore American society as an obscure mess, to concentrate on the cultivation of the pleasant life.

Americans who made a heroine of Iris March liked to think it was all *pour le sport* and that they were much too committed to doing what was fun or "interesting" ever to sink to earnestness about a career or society. "Suppose," said Cole Porter with devastating finality to the suggestion that he make a career of music, "I had to settle down on Broadway for three months just when I was planning to go to Antibes." [50]

Carl Van Vechten's Campaspe represents the attitude which the period wanted to affect:

> The tragedies of life, she reflected, were either ridiculous or sordid. The only way to get the sense of this absurd, contradictory, and perverse existence into a book was to withdraw entirely from the reality. . . . *On n'apprend qu'en s'amusant*, according to Sylvestre Bonnard. . . . She mentally decided that Hilaire Belloc's The Mercy of Allah gave a better picture of a modern millionaire, because the book was good humored . . . than the more solemn performances of W. L. George . . . and Theodore Dreiser. . . . It was this same lack of humor, this sentimental adherence to a rigid point of view which in her eyes spoiled Three Soldiers. . . . An attempt to trump up tears for the victims would always fail with a sophisticated audience, but when ridicule was aimed at the real offender, modern democracy or the church, a sense of tragic irony ensued. Something might even happen, although she was extremely dubious about this. [51]

On n'apprend qu'en s'amusant; practically this meant for the twenties parties, and for a few years — until people began to say like Dick Diver, "So much fun — so long ago" — life was for them a nearly continuous party. "Topics of the Times" carried a little essay on how the word "party" had taken on a new significance and had "come to mean a gathering of persons who have a 'good time' only when highly stimulated by strong waters" and suggested to its readers that they study "that remarkable book" *The Beautiful and Damned* if they wished to understand the nature of these affairs.[52] And Zelda wrote later of this period:

"We're having some people," everybody said to everybody else, "and we want you to join us," and they said, "We'll telephone."

All over New York people telephoned. They telephoned from one hotel to another to people on other parties that they couldn't get there — that they were engaged. It was always tea-time or late at night.

. . . Up they went, humming the New Testament and Our Country's Constitution, riding the tide like triumphant islanders on a surf board. Nobody knew the words to "The Star-Spangled Banner." [53]

CHAPTER VI

AT THE MIDDLE of this whirl of parties stood the Fitzgeralds. The boy from Minnesota who, as he said himself,
"knew less of New York than any reporter of six months
standing and less of its society than any hall-room boy in a
Ritz stag line," and his girl from Montgomery, Alabama, were
an immediate and brilliant success in New York.[1] With the
publication of *This Side of Paradise* Fitzgerald had become a
hero to his generation. To the young people who found in the
book a glorious expression and a justification of the life they
believed in and longed for, he became, as Glenway Wescott
put it, "a kind of king of our American youth."[2] For this
role he appeared to be almost ideally equipped. He was strik-
ingly handsome, gracefully casual and informal; he loved
popularity and responded to it with great charm; his strong
sense of responsibility for the success of a social occasion made
him exercise his Irish gift of gay nonsense until it seemed as
if the fun he could invent was inexhaustible. He was in his
own person a triumphant justification of the way of life he
described in his book. So, too, was Zelda. In no way a professional beauty, or, like some Southern girls, consciously feminine, she had with her striking red-gold hair an "astonishing
prettiness."[3] Like Amory Blaine's Rosalind, she loved to be
sunburned and healthy and fresh. As a young woman she used
little make-up; her nails were, like a sensible child's, clipped

and unpolished. The combination of her unself-conscious and fresh young prettiness with the wit and unconventionality of her attitude was invariably fascinating. With her quick intelligence she immediately adjusted herself to the manners and customs of the New York world without losing the special attraction of her southernness and her independence; she was, as one of their friends put it, "a barbarian princess from the South."

"The other evening at a dancing club," one of their contemporaries wrote, "a young man in a gray suit, soft shirt, loosely tied scarf, shook his tousled yellow hair engagingly, introduced me to the beautiful lady with whom he was dancing and sat down. They were Mr. and Mrs. Scott Fitzgerald, and Scott seemed to have changed not one whit from the first time I met him at Princeton, when he was an eager undergraduate bent upon becoming a great author. He is still eager. He is still bent upon becoming a great author." [4] Ring Lardner was, therefore, expressing precisely the period's feelings about the Fitzgeralds when, in his modernized versions of familiar fairy stories, he called the prince Scott and Cinderella Zelda, —

> *None had such promise then, and none*
> *Your scapegrace wit or your disarming grace;*
> *For you were bold as was Danaë's son,*
> *Conceived like Perseus in a dream of gold,*

as John Peale Bishop wrote of Scott.[5]

Like a fairy-story hero and heroine they lived in a world in which the important things were romance and thrills — both of which could be bought on a roof garden in New York if you just had enough money. The attitude comes through very clearly in "Rags Martin-Jones and the Pr—nce of W—les." "So I go in with my purse full of beauty and money and youth," says Rags, "all prepared to buy. 'What have you got for sale?' I ask [the merchant], and he rubs his hands together and says: 'Well, Mademoiselle, to-day we have some perfectly be-*oo*-tiful love.' Sometimes he hasn't even got that in stock, but he sends out for it when he finds I have so much money to spend." [6] So the hero of the story, a bright young executive, gives Rags an evening at a roof garden where he fools her into thinking she has met the Prince of Wales and she thanks him for "the second greatest thrill" of her life and marries him. Thus wrote the romantic young man in Fitzgerald, who guided him during these wonderful months of triumph and success. What the spoiled priest was thinking of it all was another matter. A decade later he was to say in "Babylon Revisited" of the man who locked his wife out in the snow after a drunken quarrel: ". . . the snow of twenty-nine wasn't real snow. If you didn't want it to be snow you just paid some money." [7]

The Fitzgeralds went about New York spending money and "doing what they had always wanted to do" with a youthful innocence and gusto which made whatever they did seem a part of their charm. They were as likely to be two or three hours late to a dinner party as on time and even more likely not to come at all. They went to people's houses, carefully greeted their hosts, and then sat down quietly in a corner and, like two children, went fast asleep. [8] They rode down Fifth Avenue on the tops of taxis because it was hot or dove into the fountain at Union Square or tried to undress at the *Scandals*, or, in sheer delight at the splendor of New York, jumped, dead sober, into the Pulitzer fountain in front of the Plaza. [9] Fitzgerald got in fights with waiters and Zelda danced on people's dinner tables. [10] "When Zelda Sayre and I were young," said Fitzgerald, "the war was in the sky," [11] and with his incurable honesty he always remembered how optimistic and assured they all felt about life as they actually lived it in the early twenties "when we drank wood alcohol and every day in every way grew better and better, and there was a first abortive shortening of the skirts, and girls all looked alike in sweater dresses, and people you didn't want to know said 'Yes, we have no bananas,' and it seemed only a question of a few years before the older people would step aside and let the world be run by those who saw things as they were." [12] It was for them a time "when the fulfilled future and the wistful past were mingled in a single gorgeous moment." [13] Fitzgerald had achieved his dream of writing a famous book, marrying Zelda, and making a success in New York. For a moment the delights of anticipation remained a part of the achievement. At the same time Fitzgerald knew that fulfillment destroys the dream. In the middle of this achieved "orgiastic future," as he calls it in *The Great Gatsby*, he sat alone one day, riding through New York "between very tall buildings under a mauve and rosy sky," and "bawl[ed] because I had everything I wanted and knew I would never be so happy again." [14] It was not simply that the orgiastic future which "year by year recedes before us" drove him to "run faster, stretch out his arms farther" in a pursuit that he half understood was self-defeating even as he gave more and more of his time and energy to it; it was also that the man who wanted to "achieve . . . to be . . . wise, to be strong and self-controlled" always stood at the elbow of the man who wanted "to enjoy, to be prodigal and open-hearted . . . to miss nothing," reminding the former that he was marking time, that he was not doing anything except waste his gift and strain his resources writing commercial stories under terrible pressure in order to pay for the party.[15]

Moreover, in spite of their success, they were often lonely and confused; "Within a few months after our embarkation on the Metropolitan venture we scarcely knew any more who we were and we hadn't a notion what we were," Fitzgerald said.[16] This confusion was the result not simply of the social situation but also of themselves, or at least of Fitzgerald. He was not exactly a shy man so much as one who was never wholly at his ease socially. For ease he substituted a kind of dramatic power on which he depended to charm and entertain people. He did not expect people to believe most of what he said; part of the fun was that it was not true. He delighted in such occasions as the one on which he hurried in half an hour late for an engagement at the Manhattan Bar and said, with anxious apology: "I'm very sorry I'm late. You see, I got run over by a bus." When his friend said: "My God, Scott, are you all right," he was heroically superior to the whole affair; "yes, yes" — brushing himself off casually — "I just picked myself up." [17] But it required energy and inventiveness to carry off this role constantly, especially as it was part of Fitzgerald's very real generosity as well as of his pleasure in shining that he was always anxious to be entertaining. "Once," as he wrote Max Perkins years later, "I believed in friendship, believed I *could* (if I didn't always) make people happy and it was more fun than anything." "It is in the thirties that we want friends," he added in the Notebooks. "In the forties we know they won't save us any more than love did." [18]

In the delight and confusion of this life, Fitzgerald's old habit of falling into a mood of lofty assurance in which he innocently advised all comers for their own good and talked endlessly about himself reasserted itself. He was like Richard Carmel in *The Beautiful and Damned*, who, in this respect, is half a portrait and half a gloomy prediction — for Fitzgerald exaggerated his faults in this mood — of his creator's future. (Richard Carmel actually wrote the novel called *The Demon Lover* which Fitzgerald had projected a year before.)

The author, indeed, spent his days in a state of pleasant madness. The book was in his conversation three-fourths of the time — he wanted to know if one had heard "the latest"; he would go into a store and in a loud voice order books to be charged to him, in order to catch a chance morsel of recognition from clerk or customer. He knew to a town in what sections of the country it was selling best; he knew exactly what he cleared on each edition, and when he met any one who had not read, or, as it happened only too often, had not heard of it, he succumbed to moody depression.[19]

He read all the publicity about his being "the youngest writer for whom Scribner's have ever published a novel" and was even persuaded to say that *This Side of Paradise* was "a novel about Flappers written for Philosophers." [20] Heywood Broun, better than any critic in New York, put his finger on this brash quality in both the book and Fitzgerald's conduct, though he seems not to have felt its authentic charm:

We have just read F. Scott Fitzgerald's "This Side of Paradise" (Scribner's) — he wrote — and it makes us feel very old. According to the announcement of his publishers Mr. Fitzgerald is only twenty-three, but there were times during our progress through the book when we suspected that this was an overstatement. Daisy Ashford is hardly more naive. . . . None of Fitzgerald's characters ever puts his hands down for a second. There is too much footwork and too much feinting for anything solid and substantial being accomplished. You can't expect to have blood drawn in any such exhibition as that.[21]

". . . for some days [after this attack]," Fitzgerald remembered, "I was notably poor company." [22] Nonetheless, he tried to meet Broun's onslaught by inviting him to lunch and, as he himself put it later, "in a kindly way [telling] him that it was too bad he had let his life slide away without accomplishing anything. He had just turned thirty. . . ." [23] Broun's response to this well-meant advice was to print one of Fitzgerald's interviews in which he told how he had become a great writer, and to remark at the end of it: "Having heard Mr. Fitzgerald, we are not entirely minded to abandon our notion that he is a rather complacent, somewhat pretentious and altogether self-conscious young man." [24] Fitzgerald was not consoled by Perkins' tactful suggestion that "we consider all this sort of thing as advantageous." [25] The boy who, full of dreams of the glories of prep-school life and of his own heroic role in it, had quickly made a bad name for himself at St. Paul Academy and Newman had reappeared; no one had yet found a means to shut Scotty's mouth. So amused were Bishop and Wilson by this sudden excess of greatness that they sent Fitzgerald a list of items for a "Proposed exhibit of Fitzgeraldiania for Chas. Scribner's Sons." It included "Three double malted milks from Joe's [a popular undergraduate eating place in Princeton] . . . Overseas cap never worn overseas . . . 1 bottle of Oleaqua [a much publicized hair tonic sold by Jack Honoré's barber shop in Princeton] . . . Entire Fitzgerald library consisting of seven books, one of them a notebook and two made up of press clippings . . . First yellow silk shirt worn by Fitzgerald at the beginning of his great success . . . Mirror." [26]

In May he and Zelda decided to achieve peace and to collect their souls in the country; they began investigating Westchester County and near-by Connecticut. They needed a car, and "a man sold [them]" — the phrase is eloquent of what happened — a second-hand Marmon.[27] Zelda did not improve the car when she "drove it over a fire-plug and completely de-intestined it." "About once every five years," as Fitzgerald said, "some of the manufacturers put out a Rolling Junk, and their salesmen come immediately to us because they know that we are the sort of people to whom Rolling Junks should be sold." [28] Eventually they settled in Westport in a comfortable gray-shingled house known locally as the Burritt Wakeman place.

But peace did not descend; instead weekend guests descended. One night, out of some kind of boredom, Zelda put in a fire alarm and when the department arrived and asked where the fire was, she struck her breast dramatically and said, "Here."²⁹ "There were people in automobiles all along the Boston Post Road," Zelda said afterwards, "thinking everything was going to be all right while they got drunk and ran into fire-plugs and trucks and old stone walls. Policemen were too busy thinking everything was going to be all right to arrest them."³⁰ Through May and June they saw a host of old and new friends, college friends of Scott's like John Biggs and Townsend Martin, new acquaintances like Charles Towne. George Jean Nathan came for a weekend and immediately announced that their Japanese servant, Tana, had whispered to him that his real name was Lieutenant Emile Tannenbaum and that he was a German Intelligence Officer;³¹ he kept urging on them parties which were hard to resist; "Can't we all have a party during the week? Mencken will be here and I should like to have you meet him. I have laid in three more cases of gin," he would write.³² He flirted gaily with Zelda. But for all his high spirits, he aroused Fitzgerald's jealousy and Fitzgerald picked a quarrel with him. Though they were very much in love, both Fitzgeralds were, in their different ways, easily made jealous. Scott's was a lover's jealousy, and when it was aroused, all the old-fashioned morality of his upbringing, which was not very far below the surface of his nature at any time, came out. Zelda, on the other hand, was often unhappy when Scott was lionized, for she liked to be the center of things as much as he did. "They love[d] each other . . . desperately, passionately. They [clung] to each other like barnacles cling to rocks, but they want[ed] to hurt each other all the time . . ." says Simone of David and Rilda (who are contemporary portraits of the Fitzgeralds) in Van Vechten's *Parties*.³³ This was the impression they gave people.

Gradually the division in Fitzgerald's nature was being reinforced by the life they were living, by Zelda's delight in it and her appeal to the old feeling, left over from his wooing, that her love required it.

When I was your age — he wrote his daughter in 1938 — I lived with a great dream. The dream grew and I learned how to speak of it and to make people listen. Then the dream divided one day when I decided to marry your mother after all, even though I knew she was spoiled and meant no good to me. I was sorry immediately I had married her, but being patient in those days, made the best of it and got to love her in another way. You came along and for a long time we made quite a lot of happiness out of our lives. But I was a man divided — she wanted me to work too much for her and not enough for my dream.[34]

This account of his feelings is distorted by the opinions of the much older Fitzgerald who wrote it. What he said about the Anthony and Gloria of *The Beautiful and Damned* in 1921 is probably closer to what he felt at the time. "The idyl passed," he said of them. ". . . But, knowing they had had the best of love, they clung to what remained. Love lingered — by way of long conversations at night . . . by way of deep and intimate kindnesses they developed toward each other, by way of their laughing at the same absurdities and thinking the same things noble and the same things sad."[35] But those who worried about Fitzgerald's career worried about his working for Zelda, and the spoiled priest in Fitzgerald did too. "Scott was extravagant," said Max Perkins, "but not like her; money went through her fingers like water; she wanted everything; she kept him writing for the magazines."[36]

All this Fitzgerald understood better than he has sometimes been given credit for, but he was, as he said in his Notebooks, "too many people" to act wholly on the judgment of any one of them. One night about this time, in a speakeasy, he struck up a casual acquaintance with James Drawbell and the two of them went off to Drawbell's "small back airless room on the top floor [of a] grubby brownstone house" to talk. "Don't be stuffy," Fitzgerald said when Drawbell apologized for the room. "You're not the only one. I put up at a dreadful hole once." "Parties," he then said, thinking of the one he had just walked out on, "are a form of suicide. I love them, but the old Catholic in me secretly disapproves. I was going to the world's lushest party tonight." A moment later he was saying, "Nice to get away from the gang and meet another bewildered and despairing human soul," and when Drawbell said, "Bewildered, yes. . . ." Fitzgerald added, "The rest will come. Wait till you're successful." [37]

Gradually, however, in the midst of all this bewilderment, Fitzgerald's writer's conscience, his serious ambition, began to assert itself; what that conscience thought of Scott and Zelda Fitzgerald was to come out in his portrait of Anthony and Gloria Patch in his next novel. "My new novel," he wrote Mr. Scribner a little later, "called 'The Flight of the Rocket' concerns the life of Anthony Patch between his 25th and 33rd years (1913-1921). He is one of those many with the tastes and weaknesses of an artist but with no actual creative inspiration. How he and his beautiful young wife are wrecked on the shoals of dissipation is told in the story." [38] This description points up the share which Fitzgerald's feelings about himself and Zelda played in *The Beautiful and Damned*. If you were carried away by the glamour of Gloria you could even say, as Grace Moore did, that "[Zelda] and Scott always seemed to me straight out of *The Beautiful and Damned*." [39]

There was some encouragement for this view in Zelda's wonderfully entertaining and very personal review of the book.

To begin with, — she wrote — every one must buy this book for the following aesthetic reasons: First, because I know where there is the cutest cloth of gold dress for only $300 in a store on Forty-second Street, and also if enough people buy it where there is a platinum ring with a complete circlet, and also if loads of people buy it my husband needs a new winter overcoat, although the one he has has done well enough for the last three years.

A little later in the review she remarks: "It seems to me that on one page I recognize a portion of an old diary of mine which mysteriously disappeared shortly after my marriage, and also scraps of letters which, though considerably edited, sound to me vaguely familiar. In fact, Mr. Fitzgerald — I believe that is how he spells his name — seems to believe that plagiarism begins at home." [40] This suggestion that the book is biographical was also encouraged by Hill's generalized but easily recognizable portraits of the Fitzgeralds on the dust-wrapper. Fitzgerald was half amused and half angry over this wrapper, not, characteristically, because it exploited their private lives, but because he was annoyed by the portrait of himself; he wrote Perkins one of his comically enraged letters about it: "The more I think of the picture on the jacket the more I fail to understand [Hill's] drawing that man. The girl is excellent of course — it looks somewhat like Zelda but the man, I suspect, is a sort of debauched edition of me. . . ." He went on to observe that though Anthony is "just under six feet . . . here he looks about Gloria's height with ugly short legs" and that though Anthony is dark-haired, "this bartender on the cover is light-haired." [41] Fitzgerald had always wanted to be dark-haired and had always been sensitive about his inadequate five feet eight inches of height, which was mainly a matter of short legs. ("Perfection," he had noted in his sophomore year in college, "black hair, olive skin and tenor voice.") [42]

This suggestion that the book had its scandalous side was encouraged by the newspaper paragraphers; "Readers may satisfy their curiosity . . ." and ". . . if there is so much smoke . . ." they said. But one had to be as simple-minded as Grace Moore to know the Fitzgeralds and still be victimized by this idea. Gloria and Anthony were not the Fitzgeralds;

they were what the spoiled priest in Fitzgerald thought the Fitzgeralds might become. "Gloria," he wrote his daughter years later, "was a much more trivial and vulgar person than your mother. I can't really say there was any resemblance except in the beauty and certain terms of expression she used, and also I naturally used many circumstantial events of our early married life. However the emphases were entirely different. We had a much better time than Anthony and Gloria did." [43]

They did. They were both at ease as New Yorkers now, and they were having a wonderful time. Moreover, they wanted to see others having a good time. Between them they could create — like young and unhaunted Divers — a charmed and happy world, and they loved doing it. So they played their parts as prince and princess of the confident and eager kingdom of youth with what one of their friends called "an almost theatrical innocence." These were, of course, expensive roles to play. "It costs more," as Zelda remembered, "to ride on the tops of taxis . . . [and] Joseph Urban skies are expensive when they're real." [44]

They were expensive, so expensive that Fitzgerald began about this time a lifelong habit of borrowing from his agent. At first his requests that Ober "deposit a thousand" would be made when he could say "am mailing story today." But gradually he came to anticipate the production of a story, so that for twenty years he was almost constantly behind with Ober. About these calls for help Ober was unfailingly generous, and again and again Fitzgerald would write him: "I must owe you thousands — three at least — maybe more. . . . I honestly think I cause you more trouble and bring you less business than any of your clients. How you tolerate it I don't know — but thank God you do." [45] Ober's generosity went beyond mere money, as Fitgerald was to realize at the end of his life when he asked for more help than Ober could give. Ober not only lent Fitzgerald money; he took the responsibility for

Fitzgerald's financial difficulties as if they were his own. His "we" in the following letter was habitual: "I realize this solves our difficulties only temporarily but if you can finish rewriting the fourth section of the story [*Tender Is the Night*] in eight or ten days and then take a little rest, I think it would probably be much easier for you to do a short story and I am sure we can survive some way until that is done." [46]

Though Fitzgerald was aware even in 1920 that their financial problem was more than a joke, he could not help seeing the comedy of it.

. . . after we had been married for three months I found one day to my horror that I didn't have a dollar in the world. . . .

I remember the mixed feelings with which I issued from the bank on hearing the news.

"What's the matter?" demanded my wife anxiously, as I joined her on the sidewalk. "You look depressed."

"I'm not depressed," I answered cheerfully; "I'm just surprised. We haven't got any money."

"Haven't got any money," she repeated calmly, and we began to walk up the Avenue in a sort of trance. "Well, let's go to the movies," she suggested jovially.

It all seemed so tranquil that I was not a bit cast down. The cashier had not even scowled at me. I had walked in and said to him, "How much money have I got?" And he had looked in a big book and answered, "None."

That was all. There were no harsh words, no blows. And I knew there was nothing to worry about. I was now a successful author, and when successful authors ran out of money all they had to do was to sign checks. I wasn't poor — they couldn't fool me. [47]

But he was disturbed by this early discovery that the minute he started a novel, or any piece of work that took any time, he sank over his ears in debt. Thus on December 31, 1920, he wrote Perkins:

The bank this afternoon refused to lend me anything on the security of stock I hold — and I have been pacing the floor for an hour trying to decide what to do. Here, with the novel within two weeks of completion, am I with six hundred dollars worth of bills and owing Reynolds $650 for an advance on a story that I'm utterly unable to write. I've made half a dozen starts yesterday and today and I'll go mad if I have to do another debutante which is what they want.

I hoped that at last being square with Scribner's I could remain so. But I'm at my wit's end. Isn't there some way you could regard this as an advance on the new novel rather than on the Xmas sale [of *This Side of Paradise*] which won't be due me till July? And at the same interest that it costs Scribner's to borrow? Or could you make it a month's loan from Scribner and Co. with my next ten books as security? I need $1600.00.

Anxiously

When everything proper has been said about Fitzgerald's being in this financial mess after making over eighteen thousand dollars in 1920 and about the transparent exaggeration that *The Beautiful and Damned* was two weeks from completion (it was not finished until the following April), this remains a touching letter: it is so oviously shocked itself by the amount required that once the awful sum is mentioned it turns tail and runs.

This particular crisis was soon over. *This Side of Paradise* was at the peak of its sales and Scribner's were glad to make a little advance against his accumulated royalties; the movies came forward to buy two more stories and to pay three thousand for an option on Fitzgerald's future output.[48] But this kind of rescue by fresh funds solved nothing permanently. It was not until the end of his life that Fitzgerald faced the fact that he had never been "any of the things a proper business man should be" and recognized how "crippled . . . I am by my inability to handle money." [49]

Paradoxical as it may sound, Fitzgerald did not care enough about money ever to manage it in a businesslike way. What he did care for was that vision of the good life which he had come to feel was, at least in America, open only to those who command the appurtenances of wealth. Like the Dalyrimple of his own story, who went wrong so successfully, "he had a strong conviction that the materials, if not the inspiration of happiness, could be bought with money." [50] He strove, therefore, to become a member of the community of the rich, to live from day to day as they did, to share their interests and tastes. "For sixteen years," he wrote in 1936, "I have lived pretty much as this . . . person, distrusting the rich, yet working for money with which to share their mobility and the grace that some of them brought into their lives." He was speaking the simple if complicated truth when he wrote Hemingway, after Hemingway had made a joke about him and the rich in "The Snows of Kilimanjaro," "Riches have *never* fascinated me, unless combined with the greatest charm or distinction." [51]

But, loving the life of mobility and grace which he saw was open to the rich and which he tried to achieve for himself, he could find nothing to interest him in the means to that life; in fact, the spoiled priest in him had a deep-seated moral distrust of the whole process of money-making, and it is an image of this distrust that Gatsby, with his incorruptible dream of the good life, achieves the means for it by all sorts of underworld activities. Fitzgerald never seriously condemns Gatsby's illegal business life; he even makes us sympathize with Gatsby when he defends that life against Tom's condemnation. Fitzgerald could see no real distinction between bootlegging and dealing in stolen liberty bonds on the one hand and, on the other, the kinds of transactions he suspected, after the Harding scandals, that most businessmen were a party to. He was not at all sure, much of the time, that he could distinguish between these people and a writer with a great gift who wrote superficial stories for the commercial magazines.

The virtues he respected were "honor, courtesy, and courage," and, in a phrase he marked heavily in his copy of Mencken's *Prejudices*, "interior security." It was the full opportunity for the realization of these virtues in the life of the rich which appealed to him. He admired deeply the rich people who practiced them, and in his generous and unselfish way he gave all rich people the benefit of the doubt, wanting to believe in their heroism. "How I envied you when you knew those people!" he said to Max Perkins once when, walking around a great estate near Baltimore, they met the owner and found he and Perkins had been classmates at Harvard.[52] But such people often disappointed him, and the spoiled priest in him could be very hard on them when they did. They roused in him, as he said, "not the conviction of a revolutionist but the smouldering hatred of a peasant." [53]

They are — he wrote his daughter late in his life — homeless people, ashamed of being American, unable to master the culture of another country; ashamed, usually, of their husbands, wives, grandparents, and unable to bring up descendants of whom they could be proud, even if they had the nerve to bear them, ashamed of each other yet leaning on each other's weakness, a menace to the social order in which they live. . . . If I come up and find you gone Park Avenue, you will have to explain me away as a Georgia cracker or a Chicago killer. God help Park Avenue.[54]

"The idea of the grand dame slightly tight," he observed on another occasion, ". . . is one of the least impressive in the world. You know: 'The foreign office will hear about this, hic!' " [55]

The tension of this "double vision" is apparent in all his heroes. It is in his portrait of Gatsby, the newly rich bootlegger who had grown up on a Minnesota farm and had none of the superficial charm or confidence of the really rich but did have his "heightened sensitivity to the promises of life"; it is in his portrait of Dick Diver, whose father was an impoverished clergyman from Buffalo who nonetheless taught Dick his trick of the heart; it is in his portrait of Stahr, the dispossessed Jew who had fought his way up from the slums of Erie, Pennsylvania, but who had the aristocrat's gift for understanding and command. The rich, as he remarked at the beginning of one of his finest stories, "are different from you and me" (the second pronoun is important) and this difference fascinated him all his life because for his understanding the circumstances of the very rich provided the perfect occasion for the conflict of good and evil.

There is a fine — though I think largely unconscious — revelation of Fitzgerald's attitude toward this central subject matter in the ending he sketched but never got written for *The Last Tycoon:* everything he found in the life of the rich is in it — the opportunity their life offers for the realization of the dream of happiness, the fascination and glitter of its appurtenances, the immorality of its brutal acquisition, and, above all, the crucial moral choice with which it confronts those who live it. A plane in which Stahr is flying from Hollywood to New York crashes in Oklahoma in November. Everyone in it is killed and it remains undiscovered except by two boys, Jim and Dan, who are about fifteen, and a somewhat younger girl, Frances. "Frances comes upon a purse and an open travelling case which belonged to the actress. It contains things that to her represent undreamt of luxuries . . . a jewel box . . . flasks of perfume that would never appear in the town where she lives, perhaps a negligee or anything I can think of that an actress might be carrying which was absolutely the last word in film elegance. She is utterly fascinated. Simultaneously Jim has found Stahr's brief-case — a briefcase is what he has always wanted, and Stahr's briefcase is an excellent piece of leather — and some other travelling appurtenances of Stahr's. . . . Dan makes the sug-gestion of 'Why do we have to tell about this? We can all come up here later, and there is probably a lot more of this stuff here. . . .' Show Frances as malleable and amoral in the situation, but show a definite doubt on Jim's part, even from the first, as to whether this is fair dealing even toward the dead." Eventually Jim's conscience drives him to tell the authorities of their discovery. "There will be no punishment of any kind for any of the three children. Give the impression that Jim is all right — that Frances is faintly corrupted and may possibly go off in a year or so in search of adventure and may turn into anything from a gold digger to a prostitute, and that Dan has been completely corrupted and will spend the rest of his life looking for a chance to get something for nothing." [56]

This is to see, in a way not unlike Henry James', that one of the central moral problems is raised in American life in an acute form among the rich, in the conflict between the op-portunities for being "all right" and for being "completely corrupted" which exist for them. Thus the spoiled priest in Fitzgerald found the conflict he was seeking at the very heart of the world the romantic young man's imagination responded to with such eagerness.

CHAPTER VII

IN HIS GENUINE DISTRESS at finding himself sixteen hundred dollars in debt, Fitzgerald determined to work very hard; he planned to write a novel and a play within the next nine months. Before this new dedication to work could take effect, however, they decided, during the summer of 1920, to drive to Montgomery in their unreliable second-hand Marmon. Between mechanical disasters, bad hotels, and the natives' responses to their matching linen knickerbocker suits, they had enough trouble on the trip to make an hilarious three-part article when Fitzgerald came to write it up.[1] Parties in Montgomery delayed them, but by the middle of August they were back in Westport and Fitzgerald was started on his new novel. He was full of optimism about it and, having sold the serial rights to *The Metropolitan* for seven thousand dollars, he assured Perkins it would be ready for serialization by the middle of September and available for book publication in the spring.[2] "Scott's hot in the midst of a new novel," Zelda wrote, "and West Port is unendurably dull," but as Fitzgerald told Perkins, "the duller Westport becomes, the more work I do."[3]

By November, however, they were finding that "late autumn made the country dreary" and moved into an apartment at 38 West 59th Street. Through the fall Fitzgerald alternated parties with spurts of strenuous work on the novel. ("Done 15,000 words in last three days which is very fast writing even

for me who write very fast," he told Perkins.) [4] By January
enough hard work — and it took a great deal — had been done
so that Part I of *The Beautiful and Damned* had been finished;
a month later Wilson was reading and criticizing Part II and
Fitzgerald was hoping to have the rest completed by the end
of the month. Actually the book was not finished until just
before they sailed for Europe at the beginning of May.[5]

In March Zelda had discovered she was pregnant, which
meant that if they were to take the trip to Europe which they
had planned they would have to do so quickly, and amid a
good deal of confusion they managed to get away on May 3
on the *Aquitania*. They began the trip with enthusiasm, Fitzgerald going carefully through the first-class passenger list
and marking the names of all the important people, including
"Mr. Francis S. Fitzgerald" ("Disguise! Sh!" he noted), but
they quickly became depressed. They landed in England and
then went on almost immediately to France, which was, Fitzgerald wrote Leslie, "a bore and a dissapointment, chiefly, I
imagine, because we know no one here." [6] They sat for an
hour outside Anatole France's house hoping he would go in
or out, but he did not oblige them.[7] They went on to Florence
and Rome, where they were similarly disappointed, and by
the end of June they were back in London. There they dined
with Galsworthy and, as he reported to Edmund Wilson, Fitzgerald said to him: "Mr. Galsworthy, you are one of the
three living writers that I admire most in the world: you and
Joseph Conrad and Anatole France!" When Wilson asked
Fitzgerald what Galsworthy had said to that, Fitzgerald said:
"I don't think he liked it much. He knew he wasn't that
good." [8] But if that second observation represents accurately
Fitzgerald's cool, professional judgment of Galsworthy, there
is a kind of truth in his first remark, too, the truth of his great
admiration for writers and his desire to express it dramatically,
with some sort of emotional truth. An even more extravagant
display of this second impulse occurred when he met Joyce in

Paris. Addressing Joyce as "Sir" he asked him if he were not very proud of his achievement. Then he announced that, to show his abasement before Joyce's genius, he was going to jump out of the window. Joyce prevented the paying of this tribute and said afterwards in obvious puzzlement: "That young man must be mad — I'm afraid he'll do himself some injury." [9]

Fitzgerald had begun his visit in England by announcing that he planned to settle there; then, after ten days in London, decided from one day to the next to go home. He called Charles Kingsley, Scribner's London representative, at seven-thirty one morning to say he needed money; one hour later he was on Kingsley's doorstep in Richmond where he announced that he had had a rotten time, clutched the twenty pounds Kingsley had managed to scrape together for him, and shot off in a cab to catch the nine-thirty train for Liverpool.[10] Not even Edmund Wilson's appeal from Paris — "Cancel your passage and come to Paris for the summer!" — could stop them. "What an overestimated place Europe is!" Fitzgerald concluded.[11] Zelda summed up the whole phantasmagoric period from their marriage to their return from Europe in her exuberant and ungrammatical prose: "Lustily splashing their dreams in the dark pool of gratification, their fifty thousand dollars bought a cardboard baby-nurse for Bonnie, a second-hand Marmon, a Picasso etching, a white satin dress . . . a yellow chiffon dress . . . a dress as green as fresh wet paint, two white knickerbocker suits exactly alike, a broker's suit . . . and two first-class tickets for Europe." [12]

By the end of July they were back in Montgomery considering the possibility of taking a house there, for they were determined to get away from New York and the parties, at least until their child was born. But eventually Scott's home town won out, and in the middle of August they arrived in St. Paul, where Scott's old friend Sandra Kalman had rented them a house at Delwood for the summer. It was a triumphant return for the young man who had left eight months before with just enough money to keep him going in New Orleans. Between the continued popularity of *This Side of Paradise* and the first serial rights of *The Beautiful and Damned* he was making more money than ever. Moreover he was a famous man. He and Zelda were paragraphed in the papers when they arrived and Fitzgerald was quoted as saying that he "had got tired of New York and had decided to come to a nice quiet town to write." He also informed the press that he had three novels mapped out in his mind and that he would run off a dozen stories for a weekly magazine, presumably the *Post*, before he tackled them. The papers referred to him as "St. Paul's first successful novelist" and he was obviously doing his best to look the part. He even addressed the Woman's Club of St. Paul, informing them that he was the inventor of bobbed knees.[13] "And all the while," as one sympathetic observer remarked, "he is a somewhat wistful, very sensitive, impulsive and attractive young man, not half as spoiled as it would be reasonable to expect."[14]

It was a brave show, and publicly Fitzgerald did his best to make it appear that they had their lives under control; privately, however, he was discouraged about the way they were living and its effect on his work. Out of one of those states of depression in which he was inclined to exaggerate the disorder of their lives, he wrote Perkins: "I'm having a hell of a time because I've loafed for 5 months and I want to get to work. Loafing puts me in this particularly obnoxious and abominable gloom. My 3rd novel, if I ever write another, will I am sure be black as death with gloom. I should like to sit down with ½ a dozen chosen companions and drink myself to death but I am sick alike of life, liquor and literature. If it wasn't for Zelda I think I'd disappear out of sight for three years. Ship as a sailor or something and get hard — I'm sick of the flabby semi-intellectual softness in which I flounder with my generation."[15] For the moment the man who wanted to achieve had the upper hand of the man who wanted to enjoy. As a result he got through an enormous amount of work that fall and winter. He had hired an office downtown, a bare affair with nothing but a desk and two chairs; its location was known only to a few of his most intimate friends. Here he went daily to work. He got *The Beautiful and Damned* ready for book publication in March, he produced two very long short stories — "The Popular Girl" and "The Diamond as Big as the Ritz" — and he completed the first draft of the play which was to occupy him more and more for the next two years.

Nor was their personal life unhappy, for all the gloom of Fitzgerald's letter to Perkins. He and Zelda were happy together and there were long summer days of consultations over his work, to which Zelda made very real contributions; they golfed and swam and dined with the Kalmans. Their talent for giving excitement and charm to an occasion made it a gay time. Fitzgerald planned and carried off by his enthusiasm all sorts of jokes. On the occasion of the Cotillion in January, for instance, he wrote a parody society-page description of the party and had it printed up as a newspaper. COTILLION IS A SAD FAILURE, said the headline, and the subhead, FRIGHTFUL ORGY AT UNIVERSITY CLUB. "The benedict's cotillion given Friday the 13th," said the description, "was the worst social failure of the year. In a sordid fist fight started by Mr. William Motter four noses were broken and one removable bridge was bent out of recognition. The fight was said to have started because some remark derogatory to Yale was made before Mr. Motter [Mr. Motter had gone to Princeton]. . . . It is to be hoped that these vain frivolous peacocks who strut through the gorgeous vistas of the exclusive and corrupt St. Paul clubs will learn to conduct themselves in a more normal, wholesome way." [16]

As always, the people who really knew Fitzgerald felt most his infectious enthusiasm and the charm of his childlike curiosity and love of play-acting. His friend Tom Boyd described how Fitzgerald saw a blind man tapping along the street and immediately wanted to know what it felt like to be blind. He closed his eyes and began to tap his way along the street too. "He had almost experienced the sensations of a blind man for an entire block on a crowded street when unluckily, two middle aged women passed us by and passing, one said to the other: 'Oh look at that.' And Fitzgerald opened his eyes." When he discovered they were speaking, not about him, but about a bargain in a store window he was furious. He insisted, however, that he had walked as well as the blind man and was indignant when Boyd denied it firmly and said that in fact he walked like a man with the blind staggers. But a minute later something else caught his fancy and he was once more cheerful and enthusiastic.[17] His childhood friend, Tubby Washington, remembers with similar amusement how he went one day to Fitzgerald's office to borrow fifty dollars from him for the most innocent of purposes, only to encounter Fitzgerald The Man of the World. "Well, well, Tubby," he said, leaning back in his chair, "now what's this all about? Got some girl knocked up in Chicago, eh?" When Tubby insisted the matter was nothing so conventionally melodramatic as that, Fitzgerald began by assuring him he could not lend the money and ended by talking himself around to lending forty-nine dollars, the odd dollar being a fairly accurate measure of Fitzgerald's respect for the mythology of laissez-faire.[18] He loved nothing better than to expose this mythology. Tubby had, earlier, gone to apply for a job which his father had got for him by pulling wires and then had been forced to listen to a long harangue about the firm's "always having a place for bright young men, etc."; he hurried home to share this choice absurdity with Fitzgerald. They roared over it together, and Fitzgerald presently wrote a story about it called "Dalyrimple Goes Wrong."

Tom Boyd and his wife, Peggy, and Cornelius Van Ness

and one or two others formed a congenial literary group around the Kilmarnock Book Shop at Fourth and Minnesota, and Fitzgerald spent long hours there arguing and drinking with them. When Joseph Hergesheimer, then at the peak of his fame, came through in January to dazzle St. Paul with his coonskin coat, shell-rimmed spectacles, and cane, it was this group which entertained him.[19]

In October the Fitzgeralds moved back to the city, first to a hotel and then, after their daughter was born on October 26, to a house at 646 Goodrich Avenue which Mrs. Kalman again found for them. Discovering at the last moment that in their casual way they had made no arrangements whatever for the baby, Mrs. Kalman also found herself purchasing supplies and providing a nurse for the baby. It was she, too, who supported an incredibly nervous father through the ordeal of waiting at the hospital. In his excitement at the baby's birth Fitzgerald sent telegrams broadcast announcing that a second Mary Pickford had arrived. His New York friends wired back: CONGRATULATIONS FEARED TWINS HAVE YOU BOBBED HER HAIR and Mencken advised that they NAME HER CHARLOTTE AFTER CHARLES EVANS HUGHES.[20]

But if the Fitzgeralds were usually happy and attractive they were also occasionally unhappy and difficult. They disliked St. Paul, particularly in winter. "We are both simply mad to get back to New York," Zelda wrote. ". . . This damned place is 18 below zero and I go around thanking God that, anatomically and proverbially speaking, I am safe from the awful fate of the monkey."[21] Zelda revenged herself on St. Paul by offending against its mores. She stood on the back platforms of trolleys smoking, and made a business of shocking the young men who danced with her ("My hips are going wild; you don't mind, do you?"). At the movies she commented loudly. "I think Gilda Gray is the most beautiful girl in the world, don't you? If I were a man I'd give a year of my life to live with her a week. She has rather thick ankles, don't you think? I wouldn't give five minutes to live with her a week if I were a man."

After the baby was born and Zelda was tied down, St. Paul became exasperatingly dull. Fitzgerald's impulse was to have more parties, and he used to fall into embarrassing public arguments with Zelda about inviting people to the house. "You won't come, will you?" Zelda would say to people Fitzgerald had invited to come for a drink. "The baby wakes up and yells and the place is too small. We don't want you." Then Scott would draw them aside to say confidentially: "Zelda's got this silly notion that we can't have anyone in the place; she ought to have it knocked out of her head; you'll come up, won't you, and help me cure her of this idea." Back of it all somewhere was the ceaseless battle of the mind; one of Fitzgerald's St. Paul acquaintances remembers overhearing him muttering to himself as they drove past a church one night: "God damn the Catholic Church; God damn the Church; God damn God." [22]

In February Fitzgerald was down with flu and beginning to work himself into his customary pre-publication frame of mind.

My deadly fear now is — he wrote the long-suffering Perkins — not the critics but the public. Will they buy — will you and the bookstores be stuck with forty thousand copies on your hands? Have you overestimated my public and will this sell up to within seven thousand of what *Paradise* has done in two years? My God! Suppose it fell flat! [23]

On March 3 *The Beautiful and Damned* was published.

It is, compared to *This Side of Paradise*, a painstakingly thought-out book, and for that reason a much less effective one; its real purpose is constantly being obscured by its "literary" purpose, Fitzgerald's conscious effort to be ironic and superior in the fashionable manner of George Jean Nathan (on whom he drew heavily for Maury Noble). What Fitzgerald the literary man believed he was doing is quite clear from the blurb on the dust jacket (in which he almost certainly had a hand). ". . . it reveals with devastating satire a section of American society which has been recognized as an entity — that wealthy, floating population which throngs the restaurants, cabarets, theatres, and hotels of our great cities" — a description that fits the famous chapter about the floating newly rich in Wells' *Tono-Bungay* far better than it fits *The Beautiful and Damned*. But this intention is at odds with the real story Fitzgerald had to tell, the story of what he had known and felt in the incredible years since the success of *This Side of Paradise*. The consequences of these mixed purposes were clear to the best of the reviewers. ". . . Mr. Fitzgerald," said Mary Colum, "has not the faculty [needed by a satirist] of standing away from his principal characters"; and Carl van Doren said that "what hurts 'The Beautiful and Damned' is deliberate seriousness — or rather, seriousness not deliberated quite enough. . . . Fitzgerald has trusted . . . his doctrine rather more than his gusto." "'The Beautiful and Damned,'" said H. W. Boynton, "is a real story, but a story greatly damaged by wit . . . the bane, not the making, of a true story-teller." [24]

The result of this mixture is a confusion of the novel's purpose, and this confusion is increased by Fitzgerald's disregard for form. In this last respect he had learned a good deal since *This Side of Paradise*, but he still seemed to think there was some special virtue in passages written in play form; there are three of these, including an embarrassing scene in the manner of *Man and Superman* between Beauty and The Voice. He also allowed himself to go haring off in any direction which promised a little smart satire or talk about the meaninglessness of it all. Gloria's entrance is delayed in order that he may do a satiric portrait of her parents, who never appear again; Gloria is made to evince a most implausible fellow feeling for the lower-middle classes in order that the rabble who patronize second-rate cabarets may be looked down on at length; Anthony, the least likely of all people to do so, answers an ad for salesmen in order that go-getters may be satirized.

The book also contains a great deal of witty cynical dialogue and lecturing on Life.

MAURY: . . . I shall go on shining as a brilliantly meaningless figure in a meaningless world.

DICK: (pompously) Art isn't meaningless.

MAURY: It is in itself. It isn't in that it tries to make life less so . . .

ANTHONY: (to Maury) On the contrary, I'd feel that it being a meaningless world, why write? The very attempt to give it purpose is purposeless.[25]

Perhaps the worst offense of this kind is the long harangue delivered by Maury Noble from the roof of the Marietta station, a passage of which *The Dial*'s reviewer observed that it sounds "like a résumé of *The Education of Henry Adams* filtered through a particularly thick page of *The Smart Set*."[26]

Some of these things Fitzgerald half suspected. "If you think my 'Flash Back in Paradise' in Chap I is like the elevated moments of D. W. Griffith say so," he wrote Bishop of the scene between Beauty and The Voice.[27] And to Wilson, who had criticized severely the ideas in the original version of Maury Noble's speech, he said, "I've almost completely rewritten my book. . . . I've interpolated [in the Symposium scene] some recent ideas of my own and (possibly) of others." At the same time he could say: "I devoted so much more care myself to the *detail* of the book than I did to thinking out the *general* scheme. . . ."[28]

The worst effect of this mixed purpose was the way it muddled the characters of Anthony and Gloria. Fitzgerald never made up his mind whether he wanted to stand apart from them and treat them satirically or to enter into their experience with sympathy and understanding. "As you first see him," the fashionable satirist says of Anthony, "he wonders frequently whether he is not without honor and slightly mad . . . these occasions being varied, of course, with those in which he thinks himself rather an exceptional young man, thoroughly sophisticated. . . ." [29] But when he comes to describe the courtship and honeymoon of Gloria and Anthony, this cool, man-of-the-world air deserts him and he is carried away by the poignancy and delight of their love. About this muddle his friend Edmund Wilson was very severe: ". . . since his advent into the literary world, [Fitzgerald] has discovered that there is another genre in favor: the kind which makes much of the tragedy and 'the meaninglessness of life.' Hitherto, he had supposed that the thing to do was to discover a meaning in life; but he now set bravely about to produce a distressing tragedy which should be, also, 100 per cent. meaningless." [30]

But this description is not fair to *The Beautiful and Damned*, for there is more than the fashionable Fitzgerald in it; there is also the novel he would have written straight had he not made his advent into the literary world. About this novel there are still some of the defects of *This Side of Paradise*. There is still for example, the curious shocked immaturity about sex: Anthony's prep-school philandering with Geraldine and the lovers who push about menus on which they have written "you know I do" and describe each other as "sort of blowy clean," Gloria's smart dictum that "a woman should be able to kiss a man beautifully and romantically without any desire to be either his wife or his mistress." Like the lovers of *This Side of Paradise*, these lovers are embarrassingly real (they are real; Fitzgerald and Zelda said these things to one another).

Nonetheless, *The Beautiful and Damned* has a central purpose and meaning. Fitzgerald got into it his acute sense of disaster and his ability to realize the minutiae of humiliation and suffering. "It is," as William Troy put it, "not so much a study in failure as in the *atmosphere* of failure." [31] It would be difficult, for example, to match the scene in which Anthony, penniless and drunk, tries to borrow money from Maury Noble and Bloeckman. Fitzgerald's difficulty is in finding a cause for this suffering sufficient to justify the importance he asks us to give it and characters of sufficient dignity to make their suffering and defeat tragic rather than merely pathetic. It is not that he did not try; amid the confusion of other purposes there is a fairly consistent effort to make Anthony the sensitive and intelligent man who, deprived of a conventional career by his refusal to compromise with a brutal and stupid world, finds his weaknesses too strong to allow him the special career he imagines for himself. He is tempted to cowardice by his imagination; he cannot blame others for his failures and fight them because of "that old quality of understanding too well to blame — that quality which was the best of him and had worked swiftly and ceaselessly toward his ruin." Over against Anthony, Fitzgerald sets Richard Carmel, too stupid to know he is compromising or to see that the success he has won by compromising is not worth having, and Maury Noble, cynical enough to compromise even though he knows the worthlessness of what he gets.

The trouble with this story is that Anthony is not convincing as the intelligent and sensitive man; what is convincing is the Anthony who is weak, drifting, and full of self-pity — perhaps because Fitzgerald was exaggeratedly aware of these qualities in himself. You are convinced by the Anthony who drifts into the affair with Dorothy Raycroft under a momentary flicker of his romantic imagination, though he knows perfectly well that he does not believe in the affair; you are convinced by the Anthony who is continually drunk because only thus can he sustain "the old illusion that truth and beauty [are] in some way intertwined"; you are convinced by the partly intolerable, partly absurd, partly pathetic Anthony who tries to sustain his dignity and honor even after he has deteriorated — against Maury who tells him to sober up, against Bloeckman who has unintentionally humiliated Gloria, against Gloria herself. This Anthony is fully realized. But the thing that would justify this pathos, the quality of character which would make Anthony a man more sinned against than sinning, is almost wholly lacking. In her way Gloria is a more successful character in spite of the gap between what she is at the beginning of the book and what she is at the end. What she believes in — the rights and privileges of her beauty — is more trivial even than what Anthony believes in — the rights and privileges of his own undemonstrated intellectual superiority. But she believes in it with courage, and when she is forced, in brutal circumstances, to recognize it is fading, she takes her defeat with something like dignity.

The story of Gloria and Anthony is full of precisely observed life, and Fitzgerald makes us feel the grief they suffer; but he is able to provide neither an adequate cause for their suffering nor adequate grounds in their characters for the importance he gives it. In the end you do not believe they ever were people capable of using well the opportunities for grace and mobility that wealth provides; you believe them only people who wanted luxury and stimulation. They are pitiful, and their pathos is often overwelmingly convincing; but they are not tragic and damned as Fitzgerald meant them to be. At the time he wrote *The Beautiful and Damned* he had mastered the quality but not the reason of his moral judgment of his experience; had he not muddied his book with smartness, he might, even at this stage in his career, have written a definitive novel of sentiment. His attempt to make *The Beautiful and Damned* a kind of American *Madame Bovary* defeated him; he could not yet, as he could when he got to *The Great Gatsby*, separate his sympathy from his judgment, because he could not really define his judgment.

CHAPTER VIII

BECAUSE OF the tension of the winter in St. Paul, they decided to visit New York as soon as Zelda could leave the baby. "I never knew," Fitzgerald wrote Perkins, "how I [y]earned for New York." [1] In the middle of March they arrived at the Plaza and plunged into a party which did not end until they got back to St. Paul at the beginning of April. "I was sorry our meetings in New York were so fragmentary," Fitzgerald wrote Wilson afterwards. "My original plan was to contrive to have long discourses with you but that interminable party began and I couldn't seem to get sober enough to be able to tolerate being sober. In fact the whole trip was largely a failure." [2]

At the same time *The Beautiful and Damned* was getting a mixed reception from the critics and a reception from the public which, if excellent by most people's standards, was not up to what Fitzgerald had anticipated. By the time the book was published he had borrowed from Scribner's $5643, the amount he would make from the sale of 18,810 copies (the figures are his own, for it was part of his ceaseless anxiety at the mysterious way his debt piled up that he kept minute track of it). An advance of $5600 to an author so popular as Fitzgerald was not extravagant, but to the writer who had pressed hard to finish a second novel quickly and had driven himself since he returned from Europe to produce enough short stories to keep out of debt, it seemed a defeat. "It is not," he wrote Perkins, "that I have not been working. The situation is due to the Metropolitan. A finished story is being held up by Reynold's [the literary agent's] office until they pay for the one before." [3] This is more a confession of bewilderment than an explanation. What was the man who had already had, with the sale of the serial rights and the advance from Scribner's, two thirds of the profits from a book which was not yet even published doing in a position where he needed $1000 at once because payment for a story was delayed a week or ten days? Even if he could maintain his rate of production without damaging his development as a writer, he could hardly assume that his popularity would remain at its peak or that he would never write anything which did not sell beyond expectations. Yet he seemed unable to reduce his expenses. "My play," he concludes a little hopelessly in the letter I have been quoting from, "left here yesterday and I feel, as I usually do that I'll soon be out of the woods. . . ."

The disappointing sales of *The Beautiful and Damned* convinced him that it had been "a dire mistake to serialize it," and if any number of the critics were working from the serial version rather than the book, it was, for as Fitzgerald wrote Perkins, "Hovey [the editor of *Metropolitan Magazine*] has clipped and cut it up abominably." [4] Everything in the ending, for example, which emphasizes the deterioration of Anthony and Gloria has been cut in order to reduce, as far as possible, the irony of the "happy" ending.[5] Fitzgerald had apparently suspected the worst when he sold the serial rights, for when Boyd was shown the manuscript of the book in September and exclaimed over its superiority to the first installment he had read in the *Metropolitan Magazine*, Fitzgerald looked at him "in rather a funny way" and said: "Well, they bought the rights to do anything they liked with it when they paid for it." [6] He was convinced enough of the evils of serialization by this experience that, when he asked $15,000 for the serial rights to *Gatsby* and was offered only $10,000 (by *College Humor*), he turned the offer down.[7] Scribner's optimistically printed a third edition of *The Beautiful and Damned* of 10,000 copies a month after publication when the sale was only 33,000 and Perkins was saying that he "doubted if we can hope that it will be an overwhelming success now. . . ." A year after publication the sales had barely exceeded—by 3000-odd copies—the original printing of 40,000 "not," in Fitzgerald's judgment, "an inspiring sale."[8]

When he got back to St. Paul he settled down at once to selecting and revising the stories for his next book of short stories. In his spare time he wrote and directed the St. Paul Junior League show. His piece, called "The Midnight Flappers," presented a carbaret scene in which there appeared "a southern flapper [played by Zelda], a society flapper, a very tough flapper and a regular flapper—with a background of Yale 'rowboat-men,' prohibition agents, well-bred inebriates and cake-walkers."[9]

His book of stories, *Tales of the Jazz Age*, was published in September. As with *Flappers and Philosophers*, which had followed *This Side of Paradise*, he had to dig deep to find enough stories to fill the book. He put in everything he had written since the previous volume except "Popular Girl" and "Two for a Cent" and reached back further for three pieces he had rejected when *Flappers and Philosophers* was collected, "The Camel's Back," "Porcelain and Pink," and "Mr. Icky." Thus there was some grounds for *The Dial*'s severe assertion that in the collection Fitzgerald was exploiting "the dross in his first book"; with his queer honesty he said as much himself, remarking of "Jemina" that "it seems to me worth preserving a few years" and of "The Camel's Back" that he liked "it least of all the stories in this volume." Of the book as a whole, he said it was for "those who read as they run and run as they read."[10] But he was not to be persuaded by the argument that sales would be injured when Perkins, in an unexpected outburst, suddenly launched an attack on "Tarquin of Cheapside"; "the crime," Perkins said, "is a repugnant one for it involves violence, generally requires unconsciousness, is associated with negroes." [11] On the other hand, Fitzgerald's feelings about the quality of some of these stories, though frankly enough expressed, did not prevent his publishing them and observing that "[*Tales of the Jazz Age*] will be bought by *my own personal public*, that is by the countless flappers and college kids who think I am a sort of oracle. . . . The splash of the flapper movement was too big to have quite died down — the outer rings are still moving." [12] About this he was quite right, for while *The Beautiful and Damned* was doing worse than *This Side of Paradise* had, *Tales of the Jazz Age* did slightly better than *Flappers and Philosophers*.[13]

If *Tales of the Jazz Age* was a badly watered book it was still a better one than *Flappers and Philosophers*. The latter had not contained more than one or two stories worth looking at twice, "The Ice Palace" with its fine climactic scene, and "The Cut-Glass Bowl," which, in spite of its tendency to overdramatize, has what Fitzgerald himself called "that touch of disaster" common to his best stories. "Dalyrimple Goes Wrong" has the genuineness of all the stories he based on his own inner experience. But the rest are popular stories which are not the worst of their kind only because of Fitzgerald's verve.

There are more good stories in *Tales of the Jazz Age*; there is "The Lees of Happiness" with its haunted, tragic version of a possible Fitzgerald life — and its ironic description of his own short stories as "passably amusing stories, a bit out of date now, but doubtless the sort that would then have whiled away a dreary half hour in a dental office"; there are "May Day" and "The Diamond as Big as the Ritz," where Fitzgerald's beautifully defined feeling about limitless wealth is only slightly marred by smart writing; there is "The Jelly

Bean" with its delicate sense of social position; and there are the two fantasies, "O Russet Witch" and "The Curious Case of Benjamin Button," both slight in idea but full of life. The strength of these stories is the precision and genuineness of their feeling. Their weakness is that Fitzgerald was seldom able, at this point in his career, to reason out what he felt. The controlling idea is never clearly enough defined to provide a meaningful structure, nor has it, usually, any close relation to the story's sentiments. His habit was to vamp passages of generalization here and there in a story and round it off with a piece of popular philosophizing, as he does in "The Diamond as Big as the Ritz," or simply to let a mechanical plot serve as a framework for the sentiments. About this time Edmund Wilson, with his usual penetrating understanding of Fitzgerald's work, wrote him of the first version of his play, *The Vegetable*: "I think you have a much better grasp on your subject than you usually have — you know what end and point you are working for as isn't always the case with you." [14]

Since the previous fall Fitzgerald had been working on the play he had first projected two years before. In January he had written Perkins that he was in the midst of "an awfully funny play that's going to make me rich forever. It really is. I'm so damned tired of the feeling that I'm living up to my income." [15] In February he finished the play and began trying it on various producers; they were uninterested. By the end of May he had revised it and tried several places, again without success. In July he did another revision of it and found a tentative name for it, *Gabriel's Trombone*. In August Sam Harris was considering this new version. [16]

They had moved out to the lake in June, this time to the White Bear Yacht Club; living at the club spared Zelda the uncongenial task of housekeeping and Scott's irritating fidgets about household noises; and at the club they were conveniently at the location of the summer's parties. Meanwhile Fitzgerald loafed; he had temporarily exhausted his material. In the spring he played with the idea of a novel about the Middle West and New York in 1885; "it will concern less superlative beauties than I run to usually," he wrote Perkins, "and will be centered on a smaller period of time. It will have a catholic element." [17] But he soon lost interest in this idea and began to dicker "with 2 men who want to do *Paradise* as a movie with Zelda and I in the leading rolls." Perkins was horrified at the idea, and Fitzgerald tried to reassure him by promising that it would be his "first and last appearance positively." [18] That scheme too came to nothing. He talked so much about his lack of material that one day Heywood Broun, in New York, came around to see John Bishop to suggest Fitzgerald might like to do a part-time column for *The World* at $125 a week if he wanted a chance to look for material; Broun estimated the job would take half Fitzgerald's time. [19] That Broun should have supposed Fitzgerald could afford to sell half his working time at this price is evidence of the sincerity of his conviction that the life portrayed in Fitzgerald's books did not exist.

If Fitzgerald loafed partly because he had exhausted his material, he did so partly, too, because of the belief he and Zelda shared that if you were good enough you not only could live according to the hedonistic code of the twenties but would probably turn out all the better for doing so. Zelda stated their belief without qualification:

I should think that fully airing the desire for unadulterated gaiety, for romance that she knows will not last, and for dramatizing herself would make [a woman] more inclined to favor the "back to the fireside" movement than if she were repressed until age gives her those rights that only youth has the right to give.

I refer to the right to experiment with herself as a transient, poignant figure who will be dead tomorrow. . . . I see no reason for keeping the young illusioned. Certainly disil-

lusionment comes easier at twenty than at forty — the fundamental and inevitable disillusionments, I mean.[20]

Fitzgerald's less assured version of this belief was, as he put it
in a newspaper article:

"What kind of a wife will the girl make who has had
numerous petting parties?"

The answer is that nobody knows what kind of a wife
any girl will make.

"But," they continue, "won't she be inclined to have petting
parties after she's married?"

In one sense she will. The girl who is a veteran of
many petting parties was probably amorously inclined from
birth. . . .

But it may even be true that petting parties tend to lessen
a roving tendency after marriage. A girl who knows before
she marries that there is more than one man in the world
but that all men know very much the same names for love
is perhaps less liable after marriage to cruise here and there
seeking a lover more romantic than her husband.[21]

This was the code of the twenties; the Fitzgeralds believed in
it sincerely and conducted their lives according to its precepts.
No doubt it has faults of moral naïveté and sentimentality.
But neither these faults nor the fact that experimenting with
themselves led the Fitzgeralds to habits of self-indulgence and
disorder rather than back to the fireside should make one forget the circumstances which led them to adopt it. The hypocrisy, the ignorance, and the cant about "experiments noble in
purpose" of the moralists the twenties objected to were something worse than what the rebels believed in as an alternative.
To that alternative the Fitzgeralds committed themselves.
They were going to "air the desire for unadulterated gaiety"
on the conviction that "youth's a stuff will not endure" and
then, duly disillusioned, settle into a resigned old age. Fitz-

gerald was even inclined for a while to think that he would commit suicide at thirty, though he gradually advanced the date until — sadly enough for he never saw it — he settled on fifty. " 'Up to forty-nine it'll be all right,' I said. 'I can count on that. For a man who's lived as I have, that's all you could ask.' " [22]

In October, because of the play and because they longed for New York again, they decided to move back there. They went on at the beginning of October, but were so involved in going to see the Greenwich Village Follies — where the curtain by Reginald Marsh included a view of Zelda diving into a fountain — and otherwise catching up that it was the middle of the month before they finally settled on a $300-a-month house on Gateway Drive in Great Neck and Zelda went back to St. Paul to bring the baby and her nurse east. They bought a secondhand Rolls-Royce (their cars were always romantic but secondhand) and settled down to New York. ". . . with the impunity of their years," as Ernest Boyd said, "they can realize to the full all that the Jazz Age has to offer, yet appear as fresh and innocent and unspoiled as characters in the idyllic world of pure romance. The wicked uncle, Success, has tried to lead these Babes in the Wood away and lose them, but they are always found peacefully sleeping in each other's arms. The kind fairies have watched over them, as they wandered in the city underwoods, from Palais Royal to Plantation, from Rendezvous to Club Gallant, with many a *détour* before the delayed and ever-miraculous departure for Great Neck, and safe arrival there in the most autonomous automobile on Long Island." [23]

There is some exaggeration in Boyd's account, yet it is substantially true. If they were more worldly people than they had been two years before in New York, they were still eager and enthusiastic and Fitzgerald's combination of brashness and honesty was disarming.[24] It shows clearly in the portrait Edmund Wilson did of him in "The Delegate from Great

Neck." When Van Wyck Brooks in that dialogue points out the characteristic American impoverishment he thinks he sees in Henry James' career, Fitzgerald is made to say: "The Puritan thing, you mean. I suppose you're probably right. I don't know anything about James myself. I've never read a word of him." A moment later he is explaining to Brooks that "I find that I can't live at Great Neck on anything under thirty-six thousand a year and I have to write a lot of rotten stuff that bores me and makes me depressed." But when Brooks protests that no writer needs to live on such a scale, he says, "Well, don't you think, though, that the American millionaires must have had a certain amount of fun out of their money? . . . Think of being able to give a stupendous house party that would go on for days and days, with everything that anybody could want to drink and a medical staff in attendance and the biggest jazz orchestras in the city alternating night and day! I must confess that I get a big kick out of all the glittering expensive things." This outburst is followed by an invitation to Brooks to attend a party at Great Neck which will include Gloria Swanson, Sherwood Anderson, Dos Passos, Marc Connelly, Dorothy Parker, Rube Goldberg, Ring Lardner, and "a man who sings a song called, Who'll Bite your Neck, When my Teeth are Gone?" "Neither my wife nor I knows his name," he adds, "but his song is one of the funniest things we've ever heard!" [25] "I wonder," Hemingway wrote him a little later, "what your idea of heaven would be — A beautiful vacuum filled with wealthy monogamists all powerful and members of the best families all drinking themselves to death." [26]

They gave many parties, for as Fitzgerald remarked ruefully, "it became a habit with many world-weary New Yorkers to pass their week-ends at the Fitzgerald house in the country." [27] He and Zelda wrote a set of Rules for Guests at the Fitzgerald House. "Visitors," it said, "are requested not to break down doors in search of liquor, even when authorized to do so by the host and hostess"; and, "Week-end guests are respectfully notified that the invitations to stay over Monday, issued by the host and hostess during the small hours of Sunday morning, must not be taken seriously." [28] These rules were only partly a joke, for a Fitzgerald party was likely to go on indefinitely. It might begin at some night club. There would be, perhaps, a bootlegger, "some probably intimidated and indignant friends from the hinterland," a mixed collection of literary and theatrical people, and a few unaccountable strays like the man who sang "Who'll Bite your Neck, When my Teeth are Gone?" Burton Rascoe once described the course of such an evening:

> Fitzgerald showed us some card tricks he had learned from Edmund Wilson, Jr., told us the plot of "the great American novel" which he is just writing (and asked me not to give it away), and the plots, too, of some new scenarios, and made a speech, and sang a pathetic ballad of his own composition, "Dog, Dog, Dog." Mencken kept calling him Mr. Fitzheimer and Nathan made him as dispirited as words very well can by kidding him about one of the plots he was relating. . . .[29]

By the time they were ready to pick up the second-hand Rolls somewhere near the Plaza and go home, they would have attracted a crowd of friends for the confused drive to Great Neck.

The journey to and from Great Neck was always an adventure, for a car was not a safe instrument in the hands of either of them. Once Fitzgerald drove Max Perkins straight into a pond instead of following the curve of the road "because it seemed more fun"; Zelda got herself arrested as "the Bob-haired Bandit," and once she drove slowly out of a side road in front of a car which missed her only by a heroic effort. When her passenger asked breathlessly if she had not seen it, she said, Oh yes, that she had.[30] Yet somehow, in spite of their driving and in spite of the law, they always managed the return to Gateway Drive, where it was customary for their man to find them sleeping quietly on the front lawn when he got up in the morning.

This life made the proper operation of a household difficult at best, and, as Fitzgerald said of himself, ". . . I have [never] been able to fire a bad servant, and I am astonished and impressed by people who can." [31] They had three such servants at Great Neck. It was an expensive domestic arrangement. Nor were the parties cheap, nor the liquor, nor what Ernest Boyd called Fitzgerald's "embarrassing habit of using his check book for the writing of inexplicable autographs in the tragic moments immediately preceding his flight through the weary wastes of Long Island." [32] They spent $36,000 during their first year at Great Neck.

Yet at the center of all this confusion, there persisted in Fitzgerald the hard core of his dead earnestness about being a good writer. It showed itself, perhaps a little incongruously, on the occasion of Dreiser's literary party. Dreiser, who seldom entertained or went out, appears to have had no idea how to go about giving such a party. He had his guests — Mencken, Van Vechten, Ernest Boyd, Sherwood Anderson, Llewelyn Powys, and a good many others — seated in straight-back chairs lined along the wall like chairs in a ballroom. Evidence as to the refreshment provided is mixed, but there appears to have been little or nothing to drink. Dreiser seems to have neither introduced his guests to one another nor attempted in any way to draw them together, and the party was dying a lingering death when Fitzgerald arrived. With his deep admiration for anyone who had talent and integrity as a writer, Fitzgerald looked up to Dreiser with awe. "I consider H. L. Mencken and Theodore Dreiser," he said, "the greatest men living in the country today." [33] He had determined, therefore, to make a fitting gesture for the occasion of his first meeting with so great a writer and had spent considerable time obtaining a really good bottle of champagne for Dreiser. Its purchase had involved some judicious sampling. Nonetheless, when he reached Dreiser's, he managed to struggle up to his host and deliver a formal expression of his admiration. He then handed over the bottle of wine. Dreiser put it carefully in the icebox and the party sank back into its previous torpor. After an hour or so everyone gave up hoping that Dreiser would ever get the champagne out again, and so, one by one, the guests dragged themselves away.[34]

Similarly, on another occasion, he insisted on paying tribute to Edith Wharton. Finding himself at Scribner's while she was there and able to persuade no one to intrude on Mrs. Wharton to the extent of introducing him, he burst in on a conference in Mr. Scribner's own office and introduced himself to her. Indeed, he is reported to have thrown himself at her feet and said: "Could I let the author of 'Ethan Frome' pass through New York without paying my respects?"[35]

Episodes like these have a ludicrous aspect which Fitzgerald sometimes half consciously cultivated, but his admiration for real literary achievement was dead earnest. Admiring serious writers as he did, he never ceased to want to emulate them, "to pit himself," as Edmund Wilson put it, "against the best in his own line that he knew." He was presently to show his seriousness about being a good writer with *The Great Gatsby*, and to demonstrate his almost pathetic admiration for real literary distinction in his response to its reception. Even his play, *The Vegetable*, though clearly written with an eye on the Big Money, was written with care and literary ambition.

In September, 1922, *The Vegetable* had been rejected again and as soon as they were settled in Great Neck Fitzgerald sat down to rewrite it completely for the third time. Late in April it was finally accepted by Sam Harris and scheduled to go into rehearsal in October. Meanwhile Fitzgerald had begun to work rather casually on a new novel. In March he had sold the movie rights to *This Side of Paradise* for what was then the considerable sum of $10,000, so that there was no immediate financial pressure on him; his notes through this period consist mainly of "Dec. [1922] A series of parties. . . . Jan. [1923] Still drunk. . . . April. Third Anniversary. On the wagon. . . . July. Intermittent work on novel. Constant drinking. . . . Aug. More drinking." At the end of the summer he tried to settle down and got some steady work done on his novel. But in October *The Vegetable* went into rehearsal and, like many authors, Fitzgerald became fascinated by the process of production, spending his days at the theater watching and arguing and his nights revising what seemed not to be going well in rehearsals. His excitement rose to fever pitch through November; he was delighted with Ernest Truex in the lead and sure the play was going to be a great success. In the middle of November they opened at the Apollo Theater in Atlantic City and *The Vegetable* flopped dismally. "It was," wrote Fitzgerald, "a colossal frost. People left their seats and walked out, people rustled their programs and talked audibly in bored impatient whispers. After the second act I wanted to stop the show and say it was all a mistake but the actors struggled heroically on. There was a fruitless week of patching and revising, and then we gave up and came home."[36]

The Vegetable is not nearly so bad as this history suggests. The political fantasy in the second act is more inventive than anything in *Of Thee I Sing*, which is based on a similar idea and was to be a hit a few years later.[37] Perhaps both plays suffer from the fact that they have nothing to say on the subject of politics except that politics are hopelessly absurd. This was the conventional attitude of the period, but it is too inclusive and undefined an attitude to make for pointed satire. Fitzgerald's play also suffers because in writing political satire at all he was working at something which did not draw on any of his deeper resources. He had a vein of light comedy

which served him for popular stories and he shared superficially his period's feelings about politics. But these feelings
were not among the ones he had really made a part of himself,
and his expression of them never had the intensity and precision he achieved when his feelings were deeply involved.
Moreover, he was always in danger when he was writing
fantasy, for he was inclined to use material which was more
extravagant than its point justified and to make so much fantastic that nothing seemed remarkable. There are, of course,
exceptions to this general statement, but even in Fitzgerald's
partially successful fantasies — such as "The Diamond as Big
as the Ritz," or "A Short Trip Home," or "The Adjuster" —
the fantasy itself is often the weakest thing. These stories
succeed by virtue of the intensity of their feeling, usually of
human evil, rather than because of their fantasy, which is
likely to hover uneasily between symbolism and allegory, as
it does in "The Adjuster." Between the tendency of his
fantasy to overreach itself and the vagueness of the satire's
assertion about politics, *The Vegetable*'s second act is never
more than mildly amusing.

But political satire is not the main point of Fitzgerald's play;
his main point is that the American dream of rising from news-
boy to President is ridiculous and that the Jerry Frosts of this
world are far happier being the postmen nature made them
than being presidents. "The spirit [of the play is]," as one reviewer remarked, "an obvious act of deference to Mencken's
virulent contempt for the American people." [38] It was a curious point for Fitzgerald to be making, and his assertion of
Jerry's triumph as a postman in the last act is unconvincing
because he is so successful in making Jerry a hopeless cipher
in the first act. This first act is the strongest in the play; it
contains a good deal of sharp observation of Jerry and
"Charlit" Frost's domestic life. After all the deficiencies of the
play have been considered it remains a good deal more shrewd
and amusing than most things of its kind. Perhaps the worst

that can be said about it is that it fatally compromised its hopes of Broadway success by its seriousness and originality and at the same time weakened the point it wanted to make about the middle-class civilization of America by its concessions to the Broadway conventions for successful farce.

When Fitzgerald got back to Great Neck after the failure of *The Vegetable* he found himself, to his profound astonishment, $5000 in debt. He did the only thing he knew to do in these circumstances; he went on the wagon, retired to the large bare room with the oil stove over their garage, and set to work to write himself out of his financial plight. The task was made no easier by the fact that the previous January he had, for $1500, sold *Hearst's International* an option on all his stories. This contract had been the result of a considerable struggle on the part of Carl Hovey, who greatly admired Fitzgerald's stories, against the opposition of everyone "from W. R. down." When Fitzgerald submitted "Rags Martin-Jones and the Pr—nce of W—les," there was such an outcry "upstairs" that Hovey had to give up the fight. Fitzgerald then had what he called "a grand fight" with the Hearst organization and the contract was cancelled.[39]

Between November and April, when he got out of debt and enough ahead so that he felt he could go back to his novel, Fitzgerald produced eleven stories and earned over $17,000.[40] It had been a nerve-racking drive of working for long stretches at twelve hours a day and, often, producing a story at one sitting. "But I was," said Fitzgerald with restraint, "far from satisfied with the whole affair. A young man can work at excessive speed with no ill effects, but youth is unfortunately not a permanent condition of life."[41] It was six months before he was able to say: "I have got my health back—I no longer cough and itch and roll from one side of the bed to the other all night and have a hollow ache in my stomach after two cups of black coffee. I really worked hard as hell last winter—but it was all trash and it nearly broke my heart as well as my iron constitution." [42] This account is exaggerated, for Fitzgerald was, like so many writers, always something of a hypochondriac, and he was inclined to become more so whenever his work went badly. Yet the winter did put a severe strain on him, and it was in January of 1923 that he first began to suffer from insomnia and to put himself to sleep with the daydream about being a football player or a general which he describes in "Sleeping and Waking." [43] At the same time he took a sort of pride in his remarkable burst of energy and its financial rewards and in what he thought was Zelda's inability to appreciate what he was doing. These feelings come out in "Gretchen's Forty Winks," written in the middle of his big push.

While they were living at Great Neck Fitzgerald and Ring Lardner became intimate friends. Their friendship was an odd but very close one; they drank and argued together till dawn again and again and got into some epic scrapes. One night in May, 1923, for example, they decided they wanted to meet Conrad and express to him their admiration. Conrad had come to this country on a much publicized visit at the height of his fame and was staying with his publisher, Doubleday, at Oyster Bay. But he was shy and suffering from gout and he went nowhere and saw almost nobody. Fitzgerald and Lardner devised a typical Fitzgerald scheme for breaking through this barrier. They would go to the Doubledays and perform a dance on the lawn. Their notion was that this dance would make Conrad see he was dealing with men who knew how to turn an amusing, yet delicate and sincere, compliment and that from there everything would be clear sailing. But before Conrad could be properly charmed they found themselves thrown off the Doubleday estate for creating a drunken disturbance.

It would be difficult to say just what there was about Fitzgerald which appealed to the bitterness and despair which show clearly in Lardner's best stories and which Fitzgerald himself tried to define. What appealed to Fitzgerald in Lardner, though not simple, can be partly understood because Fitzgerald wrote about it carefully. He saw Lardner, as he said after Lardner had died, as "proud, shy, solemn, shrewd, polite, brave, kind, merciful, honorable — with the affection these qualities aroused he created in addition a certain awe in people. . . . Under any conditions a noble dignity flowed from him, so that time in his company always seemed well spent." [44] There is no doubt about Lardner's possession of these qualities or about his talent for friendship; it shows in everything he said and did, in the marvelous letters he wrote and in the funny things he printed about his friends. In the parody he did of the "intimate glimpses" of famous writers, "In Regards to Genius," he wrote of Fitzgerald, for example:

Another prominent writer of the younger set is F. Scott Fitzgerald. Mr. Fitzgerald sprung into fame with his novel This Side of Paradise which he turned out when only three years old and wrote the entire book with one hand. Mr. Fitzgerald never shaves while at work on his novels and looks very funny along towards the last five or six chapters. His hobby is leashing high bred dogs and when not engaged on a book or story, can be seen most any day on the streets of Great Neck leashing high bred dogs of which there is a great number. He cannot bear to see any of them untied.[45]

That a man with these personal qualities and undoubted gifts should, out of obscure despair, destroy himself, and, because he was proud, destroy himself so quietly that he never admitted he was doing it — this was a situation bound to fascinate Fitzgerald. With all his ebullience and self-dramatization Fitzgerald had a deep respect for the kind of pride and restraint he felt in Lardner. Moreover, his fear of emotional bankruptcy in his own life, of a state in which he could care for nothing enough any more to go on with it, was growing rapidly at this time. "Being in the town where the emo-

tions of my youth culminated in one emotion," he wrote
Perkins from Montgomery, "makes me feel old and tired. I
doubt if, after all, I'll ever write anything again worth putting
in print." [46]

The more he felt he was deteriorating — and the deliberate
drive to make money during the winter of 1923-24 seemed to
him as destructive as the dissipation which preceded it — the
more he was fascinated by a man who seemed able to preserve
his pride and dignity in complete emotional bankruptcy. This
achievement represented a heroism which Fitzgerald respected
all the more because he realized how impossible it would be
for him.

While he knew Lardner he alternated between efforts to
shake him out of indifference toward his gifts and a kind of
baffled admiration for Lardner's stoicism. After struggling
unsuccessfully to get Lardner to tackle a big subject, he finally
persuaded him to take an interest in a collection of stories.
"My God!" he wrote ten years later in undiminished astonishment, "he hadn't even saved them — the material of 'How to
Write Short Stories' was obtained by photographing old issues
of magazines in the public library!" [47] Into looking up these
stories, persuading Max Perkins to publish them, finding a
title for the book, and getting Lardner to take a mild interest
in the whole business Fitzgerald threw himself with all the
generous enthusiasm he always had for a writer he admired.[48]
Lardner's contemporary reputation as a serious writer was
largely Fitzgerald's work, though even he could not keep
Lardner at it after he had left for Europe, and Perkins gradually gave up pressing Lardner for material.

Much later, when Fitzgerald came to write the story of his
own emotional bankruptcy in *Tender Is the Night*, he used
what he understood of Lardner's attitude for Abe North, and
all through *Tender Is the Night* there runs a persistent but un-
emphatic suggestion of the resemblance between Dick Diver,
whose destruction is Fitzgerald's self-judgment, and Abe

North; they are secret sharers. In the earlier versions of *Tender Is the Night* the portrait of Abe North is much more detailed than in the printed book and one passage from a description of this character in the earlier version is worth quoting because a key phrase from it remained in Fitzgerald's mind to reappear again more than a decade later in the passage I have quoted above from his tribute to Lardner: "In spite of the amount of liquor he was carrying a great, solemn dignity flowed from him — a dignity that would have been heavy had he been less modest. But Francis guessed that behind the face that was like a cathedral there was something in him that was bitter and bored."

By April, 1924, Fitzgerald found himself at last out of the woods financially and able to return to the novel he had put aside in the middle of the previous October. But before he could get much work done on it, he and Zelda suddenly decided that their life in Great Neck was impossible, financially and socially, and that they would go to France and "live on practically nothing a year." [49] They were escaping, Fitzgerald thought, "from extravagence and clamor and from all the wild extremes among which we had dwelt for five hectic years, from the tradesmen who laid for us and the nurse who bullied us and the couple who kept our house for us and knew us all too well. We were going to the Old World to find a new rhythm for our lives, with a true conviction that we had left our old selves behind forever — and with a capital of just over seven thousand dollars." [50] They would find, as Fitzgerald knew all too well by the time he wrote that, that they could not so easily leave their old selves behind, but for the moment they were full of optimism. Like Gatsby, Fitzgerald "wanted to recover something, some idea of himself perhaps, that had gone into loving [Zelda]. His life had been confused and disordered since then, but if he could once return to a certain starting place and go over it all slowly, he could find out what that thing was." [51]

Lardner sent them off with a farewell poem to Zelda which concluded:

> *So dearie when your tender heart*
> *Of all his coarseness tires*
> *Just cable me and I will start*
> *Immediately for Hyères.*
> *To hell with Scott Fitzgerald then!*
> *To hell with Scott his daughter!*
> *It's you and I back home again*
> *To Great Neck where the men are men*
> *And booze is ¾ water.*[52]

After a couple of weeks of great confusion they got settled temporarily in the Grimm's Park Hotel at Hyères and set about finding a villa. "This is a strange hotel," Zelda wrote Perkins, " — we are surrounded by invalids of every variety and all the native Hyèresans have goiter." It was, Fitzgerald noticed in the guidebook a little too late, "the very oldest and warmest of the Riviera winter resorts" and there appeared to be nothing on the menu but goat's meat.[53] But by June they had found a satisfactory place to live at St. Raphaël, a large and handsome place with extensive gardens called the Villa Marie. There they settled for the summer. "Oh, we are going to be so happy away from all the things that almost got us but couldn't quite because we were too smart for them!"[54] says the hero of *Save Me the Waltz* when he and his wife move into a villa at St. Raphaël. They bought a Renault "à six chevaux," Fitzgerald grew a mustache and gradually surrendered to the French barber's idea of how his hair ought to be cut, and they soaked in the sun long hours on the beach. For a while things went along so well that Fitzgerald wrote Perkins optimistically, "We are idyllicly settled here and the novel is going fine — it ought to be done in a month. . . ." They were planning to go home in the autumn when the book was finished.[55]

But in July there was a serious crisis in their lives. When they had first come to St. Raphaël they had met a French aviator by the name of Edouard Josanne. He was a dark, romantic fellow with a classically handsome profile and curly black hair and he almost immediately fell deeply and openly in love with Zelda. This was a familiar experience for Fitzgerald though he never altogether accustomed himself to it. But when Zelda in her turn began to show an interest in Josanne it was another matter. "The head of the gold of a Christmas coin," Zelda wrote of the character in *Save Me the Waltz* who is based on Josanne, ". . . broad bronze hands . . . convex shoulders . . . slim and strong and rigid. . . ." [56] The affair came to quick and violent climax by the middle of the month and, apparently after one or two noisy and undignified scenes set off by Fitzgerald, Edouard departed from St. Raphaël, leaving Zelda a long letter in French and his photograph. "It was the most beautiful thing she'd ever owned in her life, that photograph," Zelda wrote in *Save Me the Waltz*. "What was the use of keeping it? . . . There wasn't a way to hold on to the summer, no French phrase to preserve its rising broken harmonies, no hopes to be salvaged from a cheap French photograph. What ever it was that she wanted from [him], [he] took with him. . . . You took what you wanted from life, if you could get it, and you did without the rest." [57] There is a courage about this assessment of the experience which is typical of Zelda; there is also a disregard for its effect on anyone else which helps to explain Fitzgerald's later feeling that "never in her whole life did she have a sense of guilt, even when she put other lives in danger — it was always people and circumstances that oppressed her." [58]

The effect of this experience on Fitzgerald was enormous. He had given himself completely to his feelings about Zelda, and if those feelings changed during the course of their marriage, he never imagined that he loved her less or she him. He had never acquired the twenties' habit of tolerating casual affairs. He remained all his life essentially the boy who was shocked as an undergraduate by his classmates' casual sex life; if he came to tolerate this kind of thing intellectually later, he never reconciled his feelings to it. Sexual matters were always deadly serious to him, a final commitment to the elaborate structure of personal sentiments he built around anyone he loved, above all around Zelda. His attitude was the attitude of Gatsby toward Daisy, who was for him, after he had taken her, as Zelda was for Fitzgerald, a kind of incarnation.[59] "The emotions of my youth," as he said, "culminated in one emotion," his feeling for Zelda. It was the damage done to this structure of sentiments which was most disturbing in the Josanne affair. ". . . no one, I think," as Lionel Trilling said in a review of The Crack-Up, "has remarked how innocent of mere 'sex,' how charged with sentiment is Fitzgerald's description of love in the jazz age";[60] the descriptions of love in Fitzgerald's books are all descriptions of his own love.

Thus, his capacity for being hurt by Zelda was always very great. A month after the crisis he noted that they were "close together" again and in September that the "trouble [was] clearing away." But long afterwards he wrote in his Notebooks: "That September 1924 I knew something had happened that could never be repaired."[61]

By some odd quirk Fitzgerald found that this crisis scarcely affected his ability to work. "It's been a fair summer," he wrote Max Perkins. "I've been unhappy but my work hasn't suffered from it. I am grown at last."[62] That last sentence was one he was to repeat half hopefully and half ironically for the rest of his life. In August he had gone on the wagon and begun to get a great deal of good work done on his novel. Early in November he sent it off to Scribner's, though he was anxiously revising almost up to the day of publication; he was particularly dissatisfied with chapters six and seven. "I can't quite place Daisy's reaction," he wrote Perkins.[63] As late as February 18, 1925, he cabled Perkins, HOLD UP GALLEY FORTY FOR BIG CHANGE. This change involved cutting five or six pages from the heart of the quarrel between Gatsby and Tom and rewriting the whole passage.[64]

Meanwhile Zelda had been reading *Roderick Hudson* and as a result they decided to spend the winter in Rome. Fitzgerald wrote a *Post* story as quickly as he could after dispatching the novel, in order to provide ready money, and they got away about the middle of the month.[65] It was not a happy winter. Fitzgerald was in a state of tension after three months of hard work on his novel and there were unresolved difficulties in their relation left over from the previous summer. It was not until after Christmas, when Fitzgerald went on the wagon, that they were at peace again. "Zelda and I," Fitzgerald wrote John Bishop, "sometimes indulge in terrible four day rows that always start with a drinking party but we're still enormously in love and about the only truly happily married people I know." [66] They clung hard to this conviction and made it true for themselves.

They spent much of their time with the film company which was in Italy making *Ben Hur* in what they remembered as "bigger and grander papier-maché arenas than the real ones." [67] They made a good friend of Carmel Myers, who was staring in the picture, and years later she helped Fitzgerald with one of his many protégés in Hollywood.[68] From this time forward the movies fascinated Fitzgerald. Later he was to say, "I saw that novel . . . was becoming subordinated to a mechanical . . . art. . . . I had a hunch that the talkies would make even the best selling novelist as archaic as silent pictures." [69] That "best selling" is an important part of the complex which made the movies fascinating to him: even in 1923 he had got almost as much for the movie rights to *This Side of Paradise* as he had made from *The Beautiful and*

Damned as a book. But the movies fascinated him too, as they must fascinate any artist, because, as a visual dramatic art, they have such exciting possibilities of greatness, for all their actual shoddiness, and because they offered Fitzgerald what always drew him, a Diamond-as-Big-as-the-Ritz scale of operation, a world "bigger and grander" than the ordinary world.

But they hated Rome. They were always cold and they never could habituate themselves to the petty thievery which they found was a standard part of all relations with landlords, waiters, and taxi drivers in Italy. Once they were ordered from their table in a hotel to make room for some Roman aristocrat, and Fitzgerald never forgot his rage, as is shown by a note, apparently written about 1929 for his Notebooks but never included: "I've lain awake whole nights practicing murders. After I — after a thing that happened to me in Rome I used to imagine whole auditoriums filled with the flower of Italy, and me with a machine gun concealed on the stage. All ready. Curtain up. Tap-tap-tap-tap-tap." [70]

At one point Fitzgerald, in drunken exasperation, got in a fight with a group of taxi drivers when, at a late hour, they refused to take him to his hotel except for an extravagant fare. After one of his few successful blows struck a plain-clothes policeman who tried to interfere, Fitzgerald was hauled roughly off to jail. Zelda and a friend were able to rescue him only with some difficulty and a considerable distribution of largesse. The beating had been a severe one and Fitzgerald suffered from it physically for some time. But its effect on his pride and conscience was even more important. His immediate motives, he knew, had been good: the taxi drivers had been extortionate and insulting; if he had lost control of himself, he had had some reason, and his first impulse was to assert indignantly his outraged innocence. But gradually, as he thought about the experience, he came more and more to blame himself; what had happened to him that he got into drunken brawls with taxi drivers? Thus bit by bit the humiliation of this experience came to seem to him a measure of his own deterioration, and he made out of the episode a symbol. Ten years later he spoke of it as "just about the rottenest thing that ever happened in my life" and by retelling it with a careful but persistent emphasis on his drunken loss of control he made it one of the most revealing instances of Dick Diver's deterioration in *Tender Is the Night*. His deepest feelings about the experience are even more clearly revealed by the fact that this episode originally constituted the opening chapter of *Our Type*, where it was intended to give dramatic emphasis to Francis Melarky's outbursts of murderous rage, a quality of character on which the whole novel was to turn.[71]

In January both Fitzgeralds were sick and they decided to go to Capri to recover. Scott merely had grippe and was soon better but Zelda had a painful attack of colitis which she could not shake off. She was, with periods of temporary improvement, ill for a full year with it.[72] It was while they were at Capri that Zelda began to paint, an interest which endured, with one long interruption for her ballet work, for the rest of her life. Fitzgerald met Compton Mackenzie, whose *Sinister Street* had meant so much to him ten years earlier, and liked him, though he no longer admired Mackenzie's work. "I asked him," Fitzgerald told Edmund Wilson later, "why he had petered out and never written anything that was any good since *Sinister Street* and those early novels." [73] The question is very much in character; poor Mackenzie could only reply that it was not true, as, indeed, it was not.

Fitzgerald himself was full of optimistic talk about starting a new novel, especially to Perkins, whom he always imagined he deceived more than he did about his periods of idleness; he did almost nothing during this spring except to worry about Zelda's illness and about the reception of *Gatsby* and, in his anxiety, to drink more heavily than, as he knew, he should.[74] One of his wonderfully funny letters written to Bishop from Capri concludes: "I am quite drunk again and enclose a postage stamp." [75] He was behind financially, as he always was after a spell of working on a book; he had borrowed to the limit against the expected royalties on *Gatsby* and owed Reynolds three stories, only one of which he actually got written during the spring.[76]

The reception of his novel worried him most; he had committed all his forces in it and he realized that he was now old enough to be judged without qualification for his youth. His desire to put his talent to some serious use had flared up strongly after his experience of the previous winter and he had made a supreme effort with *Gatsby*. It was for him a test case of whether, in spite of his popularity and the critics' hesitations about his earlier work, he could develop into a good novelist. As he waited, therefore, for its publication he became more and more nervous, not simply over whether it would be a financial success — he always had to worry about that — but over whether it would be considered good by the people whose judgments he respected.

Write me — he said to Bishop — the opinion you may be pleased to form of my chef d'oevre and others opinion. *Please!* I think its great. . . . Is Lewis' book any good. I imagine that mine is infinitely better — what else is well-reviewed this spring? Maybe my book is rotten but I don't think so.[77]

There were remarks like this in nearly every letter he wrote, and beneath the joking there was more and more anxiety as publication date approached. Just before *Gatsby* was to appear — publication date was April 10 — they decided to return to Paris, driving north from Marseilles in their car (the car, as usual, broke down, at Lyons, and they went the rest of the way by train). April 10 caught them in the south of France and Fitzgerald, his anxiety now beyond all reason, cabled Perkins on April 11, less than twenty-four hours after publication, ANY NEWS.

CHAPTER IX

THE GREAT GATSBY is usually considered Fitzgerald's finest novel. Established opinion is represented by Lionel Trilling: "Except once, Fitzgerald did not fully realize his powers. . . . But [his] quality was a great one and on one occasion, in *The Great Gatsby*, it was as finely crystallized in art as it deserved to be." [1] Perhaps people are so sure of this judgment, despite *Tender Is the Night*'s claim to consideration, because it was quickly reached when the book was published and became a commonplace during the late twenties as time passed and Fitzgerald published no new novel. *The Dial* called *Gatsby* "one of the finest of contemporary novels," the *Saturday Review* said it revealed "thoroughly matured craftsmanship" and had "high occasions of felicitous, almost magic craftsmanship." Even Mencken, though he thought that it was "in form no more than a glorified anecdote" and that Fitzgerald did not get "under the skin of its people," was deeply impressed by "the charm and beauty of the writing." [2]

Fitzgerald thought he knew what bothered Mencken. "I gave no account (and had no feeling about or knowledge of) the emotional relations between Gatsby and Daisy from the time of their reunion to the catastrophe. However the lack is so astutely concealed by the retrospect of Gatsby's past and by blankets of excellent prose that no one has noticed it. . . . I felt that what [Mencken] really missed was the lack of any emotional backbone at the very height of it." [3] He was also capable of sharp detailed criticism of the book: "I thought that the whole episode (2 paragraphs) about their playing the Jazz History of the world at Gatsby's first party [Chapter III] was rotten," he wrote Perkins. "Did you? Tell me frank *reaction* — PERSONAL. Don't THINK. We can all think!" [4]

But whatever its limitations, *The Great Gatsby* was a leap forward for him. He had found a story which allowed him to exploit much more of his feeling about experience, and he had committed himself to an adequate and workable form which he never betrayed. "I want to write something *new*," he told Perkins, " — something extraordinary and beautiful and simple and intricately patterned." Where he learned how to make that pattern is not easy to say. He was never very conscious of his literary debts. What he did know was that integrity of imagination was nearly everything. As he wrote his daughter when she began to think of being a writer, "What you have felt and thought will, by itself, invent a new style, so that when people talk about style they are always a little astonished at the newness of it, because they think it is only a *style* that they are talking about, when what they are talking about is the attempt to express a new idea with such force that it will have the originality of the thought." [5] It is typical of his intuitive way of working that one of the best symbols in *Gatsby*, the grotesque eyes of Doctor T. J. Eckleburg's billboard, was an accident. Perkins had had a dust jacket designed for the book before Fitzgerald went abroad; it is a very bad picture intended to suggest — by two enormous eyes — Daisy brooding over an amusement-park version of New York. In August, 1924, as soon as Fitzgerald got back to the book, he wrote Perkins: "For Christ's sake don't give anyone that jacket you're saving for me. I've written it into the book."

The dust jacket was not, of course, the real source of that image, but it was the only source Fitzgerald consciously understood, and he was hardly more aware of his literary sources. Gilbert Seldes said that the book was written in "a series of scenes, a method which Fitzgerald derived from Henry James through Mrs. Wharton"; and Seldes had talked to Fitzgerald about the book. Moreover, Wilson had been urging James on him. He had also been reading Conrad. His use of a narrator and the constant and not always fortunate echoes of Conrad's phrasing — e.g., "the abortive sorrows and short-winded elations of men" — show the extent of this influence. Yet when a correspondent of *Hound & Horn* ventured the guess that Thackeray had been an important influence on the book, Fitzgerald replied, "I never read a French author, except the usual prep-school classics, until I was twenty, but Thackeray I had read over and over by the time I was sixteen, so as far as I am concerned you guessed right." [6]

His use of a narrator allowed Fitzgerald to keep clearly separated for the first time in his career the two sides of his nature, the middle-western Trimalchio and the spoiled priest who disapproved of but grudgingly admired him. Fitzgerald shuffled back and forth between their attitudes in his attempt to find a title for the book. His first suggestion, *Among Ash Heaps and Millionaires,* soon gave way to *The Great Gatsby;* but he kept experimenting with others which would suggest a more satiric attitude toward Gatsby, such as *Trimalchio in West Egg.* "The only other titles that seem to fit it are *Trimalchio* and *On the Road to West Egg.* I had two others *Gold-Hatted Gatsby* and *The High-Bouncing Lover* but they seemed too light," he wrote Perkins. A month later he had returned to *The Great Gatsby,* but by January he was saying, "My heart tells me I should have named it *Trimalchio*"; and on March 25, two weeks before publication, he cabled: CRAZY ABOUT TITLE UNDER THE RED WHITE AND BLUE WHAT WOULD DELAY BE.[7]

Perhaps the formal ordering of the Gatsby material was

easier for him because, at least in its externals, it was not so close to him as his material usually was. Wolfsheim, for instance, was based on Arnold Rothstein; Fitzgerald had met Rothstein once but knew nothing about him beyond the ordinary rumors.[8] Gatsby himself — once again in externals — was based on a Long Island bootlegger whom Fitzgerald knew only slightly. After one visit at his place Fitzgerald told Edmund Wilson all about this man and Wilson put his description into "The Crime in the Whistler Room." (Opposite Wilson's description, in his own copy of *This Room and This Gin and These Sandwiches*, Fitzgerald wrote: "I had told Bunny my plan for Gatsby.")

> He's a gentleman bootlegger: his name is Max Fleischman. He lives like a millionaire. Gosh, I haven't seen so much to drink since Prohibition. . . . Well, Fleischman was making a damn ass of himself bragging about how much his tapestries were worth and how much his bath-room was worth and how he never wore a shirt twice — and he had a revolver studded with diamonds. . . . And he finally got on my nerves — I was a little bit stewed — and I told him I wasn't impressed by his ermine-lined revolver: I told him he was nothing but a bootlegger, no matter how much money he made. . . . I told him I never would have come into his damn house if it hadn't been to be polite and that it was a torture to stay in a place where everything was in such terrible taste.[9]

Again, however, these details account only for the externals of Gatsby; the vulgar and romantic young man Fitzgerald found somewhere inside himself to fill this outline of a character is what matters. About this young man he could only say, "He was perhaps created in the image of some forgotten farm type of Minnesota that I have known and forgotten, and associated at the same moment with some sense of romance . . . a story of mine, called "Absolution" . . . was intended to be a picture of his early life, but . . . I cut it because I preferred to preserve the sense of mystery." [10] Because the form of *Gatsby* keeps Fitzgerald's assertions of the romance and of the vulgarity clearly separated, he was able to make out of those unworn shirts of Max Fleischman the fine episode of Gatsby's many shirts, to blend without confusion the elements of bad taste and idealism implied by that pile of material with "stripes and scrolls and plaids in coral and apple green and lavender and faint orange, with monograms of Indian blue" on which Daisy suddenly bowed her head and cried.[11]

Nick Carraway, Fitzgerald's narrator, is, for the book's structure, the most important character. Quite apart from his power to concentrate the story and its theme into a few crucial scenes and thus increase its impact, a great deal of the book's color and subtlety comes from the constant play of Nick's judgment and feelings over the events. Fitzgerald had struggled awkwardly with all sorts of devices in his earlier books to find a way to get these things in without intervening in his own person and destroying our dramatic perception of them. Nick, as one of the characters in the story, not only allows but requires him to imply feelings everywhere.

> [Daisy] turned her head as there was a light dignified knocking at the front door. I went out and opened it. Gatsby, pale as death, with his hands plunged like weights in his coat pockets, was standing in a puddle of water glaring tragically into my eyes.
>
> With his hands still in his coat pockets he stalked by me into the hall, turned sharply as if he were on a wire, and disappeared into the living-room. It wasn't a bit funny.[12]

Nick has come east after the war to be a real Easterner, but his moral roots are in the Middle West. He is prepared, in the book's very first scene, to respond to the beauty and charm

of Daisy, adrift like some informal goddess in that "bright,
rosy-colored space" which is the Buchanans' drawing room.
But he is humorously aware of their difference: " 'You make
me feel uncivilized, Daisy,' I confessed. . . . 'Can't you talk
about crops or something?' " A moment later, when Daisy
has confessed her unhappiness with Tom, he has an uncomfortable glimpse of what is really involved in this difference.
"The instant her voice broke off, ceasing to compel my attention, my belief, I felt the basic insincerity of what she had
said. It made me uneasy, as though the whole evening had
been a trick of some sort to exact a contributary emotion
from me. I waited, and sure enough in a moment she looked
at me with an absolute smirk on her lovely face, as if she had
asserted her membership in a rather distinguished secret society to which she and Tom belonged." [13]

It is a secret society distinguished by more than he had
supposed, for Nick is learning that the rich are different from
you and me in more than their habituation to the appurtenances of wealth which give their lives such a charmed air
for the outsider like Gatsby. What astonished Gatsby was
the way Daisy's beautiful house in Louisville "was as casual
a thing to her as his tent out at camp was to him." For Gatsby
"there was a ripe mystery about it, a hint of bedrooms upstairs more beautiful and cool than other bedrooms, of gay
and radiant activities taking place through its corridors, and
of romances that were not musty and laid away already in
lavender but fresh and breathing and redolent of this year's
shining motor-cars and of dances whose flowers were scarcely
withered." [14]

But while Nick is humorously aware of this charm, he is a
Carraway and he has grown up "in the Carraway house in a
city where dwellings are still called through decades by a
family's name." When at the end of the book he unexpectedly
runs into Tom in front of a jewelry store on Fifth Avenue, he
thinks:

I couldn't forgive him or like him, but I saw what he had done was, to him, entirely justified. It was all very careless and confused. They were careless people, Tom and Daisy — they smashed up things and creatures and then retreated back into their money or their vast carelessness, or whatever it was that kept them together, and let other people clean up the mess they had made. . . .

I shook hands with him; it seemed silly not to, for I felt suddenly as if I were talking to a child. Then he went into the jewelry store to buy a pearl necklace — or perhaps only a pair of cuff buttons — rid of my provincial squeamishness forever.[15]

It is characteristic of Fitzgerald's control of his material that he can sum up all he wants to say about Tom in that last sentence with Nick's ironic glance at the "string of pearls valued at three hundred and fifty thousand dollars" which had been the symbol of Daisy's surrender to Tom's world. "A pearl necklace — or perhaps only a pair of cuff buttons." "I see you're looking at my cuff buttons," Meyer Wolfsheim says to Nick. "I hadn't been looking at them, but I did now. They were composed of oddly familiar pieces of ivory. 'Finest specimens of human molars,' he informed me." This kind of control is everywhere in the book. Gatsby, giving Nick his cheap-magazine version of his life, says that he "lived like a young rajah in all the capitals of Europe — Paris, Venice, Rome — collecting jewels, chiefly rubies, hunting big game, painting a little. . . ." Nick is disgusted by this image "of a turbaned 'character' leaking sawdust at every pore as he pursued a tiger through the Bois de Boulogne." But when Gatsby is showing Daisy his house and Nick sees the pictures of Dan Cody and Gatsby in yachting costume, he is on the verge of seriously "[asking] Gatsby to see the rubies." In the same way Nick makes a little joke about Daisy's chauffeur, Ferdie, when he brings Daisy to tea. "Does the gasoline affect his nose?" he asks. "I don't think so," Daisy answers innocently.

"Why?" But her innocence is only assumed, for it was her own joke; she had told Nick in the book's first scene about her butler whose nose had been permanently injured because he had to polish silver from morning till night.[16]

So Nick, having learned just how much brutal stupidity and carelessness exist beneath the charm and even the pathos of Tom and Daisy, goes back to the West, to the country he remembers from the Christmas vacations of his boyhood, to "the thrilling returning trains of my youth, and the street lamps and the sleigh bells in the frosty dark and the shadows of holly wreaths thrown by lighted windows on the snow. I am part of that. . . ." The East remains for him "a night scene from El Greco" in which "in the foreground four solemn men in dress suits are walking along the sidewalk with a stretcher on which lies a drunken woman in a white evening dress. Her hand, which dangles over the side, sparkles cold with jewels. Gravely the men turn in at a house — the wrong house. But no one knows the woman's name, and no one cares." [17]

Thus, though Fitzgerald would be the last to have reasoned it out in such terms, *The Great Gatsby* becomes a kind of tragic pastoral, with the East exemplifying urban sophistication and culture and corruption, and the Middle West, "the bored, sprawling, swollen towns beyond the Ohio," the simple virtues. This contrast is summed up in the title to which Fitzgerald came with such reluctance. In so far as Gatsby represents the simplicity of heart Fitzgerald associated with the Middle West, he is really a great man; in so far as he achieves the kind of notoriety the East accords success of his kind and imagines innocently that because his place is right across from the Buchanans' he lives in Daisy's world, he is great about as Barnum was. Out of Gatsby's ignorance of his real greatness and his misunderstanding of his notoriety, Fitzgerald gets most of the book's direct irony.

Gatsby himself is a romantic who, as his creator nearly did, has lost his girl because he had no money. On her he had focused all his "heightened sensitivity to the promises of life." For him money is only the means for the fulfillment of "his incorruptible dream." "I wouldn't ask too much of her. You can't repeat the past," Nick says to him of Daisy. " 'Can't repeat the past?' he cried incredulously. 'Why of course you can!' " For Gatsby the habits of wealth have preserved and heightened Daisy's charm. No one understood that better than he.

> "She's got an indiscreet voice," I remarked. "It's full of — " I hesitated.
> "Her voice is full of money," [Gatsby] said suddenly.
> That was it. I'd never understood before. It was full of money — that was the inexhaustible charm that rose and fell in it, the jingle of it, the cymbals' song of it. . . . High in a white palace the king's daughter, the golden girl. . . .[18]

But if a lifetime of wealth colors Daisy's charm in a way that Gatsby's new wealth cannot imitate, it has also given her the habit of retreating with Tom "into their money or their vast carelessness" whenever she has to face responsibility. So, as Gatsby watches anxiously outside their house after the accident in order to protect Daisy, she sits with Tom over a plate of cold fried chicken and two bottles of ale in the kitchen. "There was an unmistakable air of natural intimacy about the picture, and anybody would have said they were conspiring together." After looking through the window at them, Nick returns to Gatsby. "He put his hands in his coat pockets and turned back eagerly to his scrutiny of the house, as though my presence marred the sacredness of the vigil. So I walked away and left him standing there in the moonlight — watching over nothing." [19] The next day, waiting for a telephone message from Daisy which never comes, he is shot by Wilson.

In contrast to the grace of Daisy's world Gatsby's fantastic mansion, his incredible car, his absurd clothes, "his elaborate formality of speech [which] just missed being absurd" all appear ludicrous. But in contrast to the corruption which underlies Daisy's world, Gatsby's essential incorruptibility is heroic. Because of the skilful construction of *The Great Gatsby* the eloquence and invention with which Fitzgerald gradually reveals this heroism are given a concentration and therefore a power he was never able to achieve again. The art of the book is nearly perfect.

Its limitation is the limitation of Fitzgerald's own nearly complete commitment to Gatsby's romantic attitude. "That's the whole burden of this novel," he wrote a friend, " — the loss of those illusions that give such color to the world so that you don't care whether things are true or false as long as they partake of the magical glory." [20] Fitzgerald's irony touches only the surface of Gatsby and the book never suggests a point of view which might bring seriously into question the adequacy to experience of "a heightened sensitivity to the promises of life." The world of Tom and Daisy, which is set over against Gatsby's dream of a world, is superficially beautiful and appealing but indefensible: Tom's muddled attempts to defend it, his "impassioned gibberish" about " 'The Rise of the Colored Empires' by this man Goddard," prove how indefensible it is.[21]

"They're a rotten bunch," Nick shouts back to Gatsby as he leaves him for the last time. "You're worth the whole damn bunch put together." Then he thinks: "I've always been glad I said that. It was the only compliment I ever gave him, because I disapproved of him from beginning to end. First he nodded politely, and then his face broke into that radiant and understanding smile, as if we'd been in ecstatic cahoots on that fact all the time. His gorgeous pink rag of a suit made a bright spot of color. . . ." But though the tone of this passage is perfect, even down to the irony of the colloquial "*rag* of a suit," it does not seriously qualify Nick's

— and Fitzgerald's — commitment to Gatsby, to the romantic "capacity for wonder" and its belief "in the green light, the orgiastic future," which justifies by its innocent faith Gatsby's corruption.

The last two pages of the book make overt Gatsby's embodiment of the American dream as a whole by identifying his attitude with the awe of the Dutch sailors when, "for a transitory enchanted moment," they found "something commensurate to [their] capacity for wonder" in the "fresh, green breast of the new world." Though this commitment to the wonder and the enchantment of a dream is qualified by the dream's unreality, by its "year by year reced[ing] before us," the dream is still the book's only positive good; the rest is a world of "foul dust," like the "valley of ashes — a fantastic farm where ashes grow like wheat in ridges and hills and gardens" — through which one passed every evening on his way to the night world of East and West Egg.[22]

2

Early in May 1925 the Fitzgeralds reached Paris from the south of France and there they rented an apartment at 14 rue de Tilsitt for the rest of the year. "It represented to some degree," as Louis Bromfield observed, "the old aspirations and a yearning for stability, but somehow it got only halfway and was neither one thing nor the other. . . . The furniture was gilt Louis XVI but a suite from the Galeries Lafayette. The wall paper was the usual striped stuff in dull colors that went with that sort of flat. It was all rather like a furniture shop window and I always had the impression that the Fitzgeralds were camping out there between two worlds." SALES SITUATION DOUBTFUL, Perkins cabled about *Gatsby*. EXCELLENT REVIEWS.[23] The sales continued to be, by Fitzgerald's standards, mediocre, though the reviews were the best he had ever had. By the time *Gatsby* was published, his debt to Scribner's was something over $6200; by October the sales were just short of twenty thousand copies, slightly below what would have covered this debt. By February a few thousand more copies had been sold and the book was dead.

As Fitzgerald had written Bishop, "We want to come back but we want to come back with money saved and so far we haven't saved any." [24] He had hoped *Gatsby* would make him the kind of money he wanted. This was to hope for a miracle, but Fitzgerald was an optimistic young man and events had conspired, by producing a series of brilliant successes for him, to convince him that if he did his best he would attain fame and fortune. Such expectations were a part of the pattern he had been brought up on, and if he had outgrown much of his upbringing, he had not lost his conviction that money in large quantities was the proper reward of virtue. He showed his usual mixture of naïveté and insight about this attitude. From the day he announced he would be satisfied with a sale of twenty thousand copies of *This Side of Paradise* he had continued to assume that a novelist should get very large returns for his work. "If," he wrote Perkins about *Gatsby*, "[my next novel] will support me with no more intervals of trash I'll go on as a novelist. If not I'm going to quit, come home, go to Hollywood and learn the movie business. . . . there's no point in trying to be an artist if you can't do your best." [25] This is a sensible statement — Fitzgerald knew what he could command in Hollywood — except that Fitzgerald's idea of "support" is fantastic. His writing, even without the "trash," had supported him more than adequately up to this time. Omitting what he got from everything that might be thought trash and including only his novels and the six best short stories he had so far written, he had averaged between $16,000 and $17,000 a year during his career as a writer (his total income from 1920 to 1924 inclusive was $113,000, a little better than $22,500 a year).[26] This income ought to have

Childhood in Buffalo: Aged 2½

b) Christmas 1899. Aged 3, with his father, whom he admired all his life.

c) Aged 5, when he described himself "by occupation actor, athlete, scholar, philatelist and collector of cigar bands."

Scott Fitzgerald shortly after he left Princeton. A passport photograph. His old friends say it shows exactly what he looked like at that time.

Fitzgerald just before he was married, on the front steps of the Sayre
house, Montgomery, Alabama, 1919.

The three Fitzgeralds in France, Christmas, 1925. The pose is characteristic of the half gay, half ironic attitude with which Fitzgerald faced the world.

Zelda and Scott Fitzgerald on the Riviera, 1926. "Just a real place to rough it."

Zelda and Scott arriving at a performance of *Dinner At Eight* in Baltimore, 1932. *(Baltimore Sun)*

La Paix, 1932. Fitzgerald in his study, where he wrote most of *Tender is the Night*.

1937. This is the Fitzgerald of the last years, the author of *Tender is the Night* and *The Last Tycoon*.   *Photo by Carl Van Vechten*

supported them, and Fitzgerald knew it. "I can't reduce our scale of living," he continued in his letter to Perkins, "and I can't stand this financial insecurity. . . . I had my chance back in 1920 to start my life on a sensible scale and lost it and so I'll have to pay the penalty. . . . Yours in great depression." But why did he feel his chance had been lost at the start? A man who intends to be a serious writer in the twentieth century knows that he will be lucky to average a quarter of Fitzgerald's income over a lifetime; and it is hard to believe anyone could be so subject to extravagance that he would have to sacrifice his whole career to it, especially when he is a man — as Fitzgerald was — powerfully driven to succeed in that career and at the same time tortured — as again Fitzgerald was — by debt.

The answer to these questions lies in Fitzgerald's imaginative involvement with wealth and in the way its effect was reinforced by the belief in "airing the desire for unadulterated gaiety" which he and Zelda shared. It was difficult enough that Fitzgerald's imagination drove him to try to live like a man of inherited wealth and that their extravagance and inefficiency always made that life cost more than it needed to. It was worse that, until tragedy struck them, they sought innocently and sincerely for that "orgiastic future" that haunted Gatsby. Fitzgerald's imagination saw the meaning of their experience. No one will ever improve on Gatsby's attempt to imitate the life of inherited wealth or his devotion to the "orgiastic future" as a commentary on Fitzgerald's life. He also saw their inefficiency as the newly rich and made a joke of it in "How to Live on $36,000 a Year." But his imagination could realize and evaluate this attitude because he was committed to it in practice. His financial dilemma was more than the penalty he paid for having failed to start his life on a sensible scale; it was what he paid for the theme of his finest work.

Fitzgerald later described this summer of 1925 in Paris as

one of "1000 parties and no work";[27] he was worried about his drinking. It was easy to make a joke of it, as Hemingway, of whom they were beginning to see a great deal, did in *The Torrents of Spring*: "It was at this point in the story, reader, that Mr. F. Scott Fitzgerald came to our home one afternoon, and after remaining for quite a while suddenly sat down in the fireplace and would not (or was it could not, reader?) get up and let the fire burn something else so as to keep the room warm." [28] But he was beginning to be drunk for periods of a week or ten days and to sober up in places like Brussels without any notion of how he had got there or where he had been.[29]

Perhaps, like most of us, Fitzgerald had always given himself the benefit of the doubt about his behavior when he was drunk, but about this time he began describing much that he did as more orderly and rational than it was. In *A Moveable Feast* there is a scene that, despite its exaggerated stylization, shows what was happening to him. One night at the Dingo, he had gone through the startling transformation that alcohol now and then caused in him all his life.

> As he sat there at the bar holding the glass of champagne the skin seemed to tighten over his face until all the puffiness was gone and then it drew tighter until the face was like a death's head. The eyes sank and began to look dead and the lips were drawn tight and the color left the face so that it was the color of used candle wax.

A few days later Hemingway said to him he was sorry the stuff had hit him so hard.

> "What do you mean you are sorry? What stuff hit me what way? What are you talking about, Ernest?"
> "I meant the other night at the Dingo."
> "There was nothing wrong with me at the Dingo. I simply got tired of those absolutely bloody British you were with and went home." . . .

"Yes," I said. "Of course."

"That girl with the phoney title who was so rude and that silly drunk with her. They said they were friends of yours."

"They are. And she *is* very rude sometimes."

"You see. There's no use to make mysteries simply because one has drunk a few glasses of wine. Why did you want to make the mysteries? It isn't the sort of thing I thought you would do." [30]

More and more often during these years alcohol affected Fitzgerald in this way; as Hemingway remarked on another occasion in his brutally precise way, "Fitzgerald was soft. He dissolved at the least touch of alcohol." [31] For his account of his conduct at the Dingo, Fitzgerald probably had some complicated motive derived from his conception of the personal relations between himself and Hemingway, for in his novelist's way he always had a half-shrewd, half-fantastic theory of such relations in terms of which he maneuvered with the care of a general responsible for whole armies. Not, as Callaghan shows, that Fitzgerald was systematically devious in personal relations in the way Hemingway was, for he was much less self-protective. But they were both complex men.

Still, making every allowance for motives of this kind, Fitzgerald's conception of that night at the Dingo is dangerously remote from what he actually did as Hemingway describes it, and his conceptions of other situations, where there were no complicated personal relations, were often equally remote from the facts. Perhaps he improved his accounts of these more trivial occasions for the benefit of his listeners without himself losing track of the facts — all his life he had tried to entertain people by making good stories out of his experience — but it is difficult not to suspect that at this time he was beginning to lose track of the second of the two rules he says in his Notebooks he made for himself in order that he might be "both an intellectual and a man of honor simultaneously," namely, "that *I do not tell . . . lies that will be of value to myself*, and secondly, *I do not lie to myself.*[32]

For example, in December of this year he told Perkins that "I called on Chatto & Windus in London last month and had a nice talk with Swinnerton, their reader." Swinnerton's version of that "nice talk" is different.

I went from my office to the waiting-room, where a young man sat, with his hat on, at a small table. He did not rise or remove his hat, and he did not answer my greeting, so I took another chair, expressing regret that no partner was available, and asking if there was anything I could do. Assuming, I suppose, that I was some base hirling, he continued brusque to the point of truculence; but we spoke of the purpose of his visit, and after a few moments he silently removed his hat. Two minutes later, looking rather puzzled, he rose. I did the same. I spoke warmly of *The Great Gatsby*; and his manner softened. He became an agreeable boy, quite ingenuous and inoffensive, and finally asked my name. I told him. If I had said 'The Devil' he could not have been more horrified. Snatching up his hat in consternation, he cried: 'Oh, my God! *Nocturne*'s one of my favorite books!' and dashed out of the premises.[33]

A very similar Fitzgerald appears in Hemingway's story about going to Lyons with Fitzgerald that spring of 1925 to pick up the car they had left there on their way north. To be sure, Hemingway represents himself in this story as the skilful man of the world handling the impossible drunk with a perfection of ingenuity and patience it is not quite possible to believe in. Nonetheless, Fitzgerald's insistence that he was suffering from "congestion of the lungs" is characteristic of him in this state, and it must have been particularly maddening to Hemingway with his conviction that the ability to hold one's liquor is an important manifestation of manliness and his feeling that people like Fitzgerald who could not were "soft." "You could not," he said, "be angry with Scott any more than you could be angry with someone who was crazy," a conclusion which damns Fitzgerald very thoroughly with faint affection. In any event, it is difficult to know how much Fitzgerald was putting a good face on things and how much he was deceiving himself — his ordinary self; the writer in him understood completely even his most drunken moments and used them in stories — when he wrote Gertrude Stein a little later that "Hemingway and I went to Lyon shortly after to get my car and had a slick drive through Burgundy. He's a peach of a fellow and absolutely first-rate." [34]

But though it is not possible to determine how much Fitzgerald understood what was happening to him, it is clear he felt himself to be living in a nightmare. Something of what he felt during these years he put into "Babylon Revisited," and in *The World's Fair* he described one of its evenings in detail.

> . . . then six of us, oh, the best the noblest relicts of the evening . . . were riding on top of thousands of carrots in a market wagon, the carrots smelling fragrant and sweet with earth in their beards — riding through the darkness to the Ritz Hotel and in and through the lobby — no, that couldn't have happened but we were in the lobby and the bought concierge had gone [f]or a waiter for breakfast and champagne. We were making a waiter trap — what was it, something about a waiter trap, made of — I have forgotten, but I remember with almost the vividness and violence of his native plains, Mr. George T. Horseprotection.
>
> He was a large brown splendidly-dressed oil-Indian — with many faults; he had been out all night and was coming home to bed but presently he was sitting with us, wide awake and trying to pay for the champagne. I was a little ashamed of him before Major Hengest but to my surprise Major Hengest was very impressed so I began, weakly, to like him too. It was quarter of five and Napoleon looked a little formidable on top of his column but we went on to the Grand Duc with him.
>
> The Grand Duc had just begun its slow rattling gasp for

life in the inertness of the weakest hour. Discernible near us through the yellow smoke of dawn were Josephine Baker, the Grand Duc Boris, Eskimo, Pepy, a manufacturer of dolls voices from Newark, Albert McKiscoe happily unable to walk and the King of Sweden. In the corner a huge American negro, with his arms around a lovely French tart, roared a song to her in a rich beautiful voice and suddenly Melarky's Tennessee instincts remembered and were aroused. . . . he began looking at everyone disagreeably and truculently. Dinah glanced at him and then suddenly got up to go.

She was a minute too late. As we were going another colored man was coming in — he had just finished playing in some night club orchestra for he carried a horn case, and was coming to meet his friends — the case swung against Francis' knee.

"God damn it, get out of my way!" said Francis savagely, "Or I'll push your black face in."

"You're not behaving like a gentleman should behave," said the colored man indignantly, "I cern'ly intended — "

"Put down that case!"

Then, before we could intervene it had happened — Francis hit him a smashing blow in the jaw and he crashed up against the door and down into the café — his legs disappearing slowly down [the] steps.

. . . At that moment Mr. John B. Horseprotection came rushing out and in a moment we were in a cab with him. Major Hengest with great presence of mind had gotten the two women into another taxi and called to me that he was taking them home.

"Now then," said John T. Horseprotection in character, "Ah'll take you gentlemen to the best place on the reservation."

Francis sat there with a haunted face, "God, what a son-of-a-bitch I am. He was a nice-looking fellow." Tears began to run out of his eyes, "Sort of dignified — just finished his work. Was Dinah gone?"

"Nobody saw. We're all sons-of-bitches sometimes," I assured him generously. . . .

"Here we are," interrupted Mr. Horseprotection. "Now you see something — something really funny. They have to know you, but I guess they know me."

And then suddenly we were in a world of fairies — I never saw so many or such a variety together. There were tall gangling ones and little pert ones with round thin shoulders, and great broad ones with the faces of Nero and Oscar Wilde, and fat ones with sly smiles that twisted into horrible leers, and nervous ones who hitched and jerked opening their eyes very wide. There were handsome, passive dumb ones who turned their profiles this way and that, noble-faced ones with the countenances of senators that dissolved suddenly into girlish fatuity; pimply studgy ones with the most delicate gestures of all; raw ones with red lips and frail curly bodies . . . self-conscious ones who looked with eager politeness toward every noise; English ones with great racial self-control, Balkan ones — a small cooing Japanese.

The others must have been looking around simultaneously, for we all said "Let's get out" together. After that we rode in the Bois I think. Then Francis and Abe and I, the last survivors went in to drink coffee in the Ritz Bar.[35]

"But don't get up close," as Father Schwartz, the mad priest of "Absolution" who also longed for the world's fair, says, "because if you do you'll only feel the heat and the sweat and the life." [36]

But the time was not all spent like that. There was a scheme according to which Fitzgerald and Hemingway and Dean Gauss met once a week for lunch and discussed some serious topic, setting the topic for the next meeting at the end of each session so that they could prepare themselves. Fitzgerald also had the satisfaction of *Gatsby*'s critical reception. In addition to the handsome reviews, he got many personal letters of great enthusiasm. "It is just four o'clock in the morning," Deems Taylor wrote him, "and I've got to be up at seven, and I've just finished 'The Great Gatsby', and it can't possibly be as good as I think it is." [37] Similar letters came from Woollcott and Nathan, from Cabell and Seldes, from Van Wyck Brooks and Paul Rosenfeld. Even better were the letters from Willa Cather and Mrs. Wharton and T. S. Eliot; these overwhelmed the Fitzgerald who stood in awe of distinguished writers: he got the Gausses out of bed at one in the morning to come over and celebrate Willa Cather's letter. The letter from Mrs. Wharton, with its modesty and its informed comments on the book, meant more to him than all the others, for Mrs. Wharton was a remote and awful figure to the young rebels of Paris.[38]

When it turned out that Mrs. Wharton wanted them to come to the Pavillon Colombe for tea, Fitzgerald was flattered and ready to throw himself once more at the feet of the author of *Ethan Frome*. When the day arrived, Zelda said she was damned if she would go forty or fifty miles from Paris just to let an exceedingly proper and curious old lady stare at her and Scott and make them feel provincial. Fitzgerald therefore went alone, full of trepidation and secretly, perhaps, suspecting Zelda might be right. All the way out he kept stopping to fortify himself, and bit by bit became more determined not to be put down. No doubt all his feelings of inferiority as a Middle-Westerner, as a product of the lower-middle class, and as a member of the younger generation were aroused. He was scarcely settled for tea with Mrs. Wharton and the few guests she had gathered to meet him than he set out to show them all he was not cowed. The conversation went something like this.

"Mrs. Wharton," Fitzgerald demanded, "do you know what's the matter with you?"

"No, Mr. Fitzgerald, I've often wondered about that. What is it?"

"You don't know anything about life," Fitzgerald roared, and then — determined to shock and impress them — "Why, when my wife and I first came to Paris, we took a room in a bordello! And we lived there for two weeks!"

After a moment he realized that, instead of being horrified, Mrs. Wharton and her guests were looking at him with sincere and quite unfeigned interest. The bombshell had fizzled; he had lied outrageously, shocked himself, and succeeded only in bringing his audience to an alert and friendly attention. After a moment's pause Mrs. Wharton, seeming to realize from his expression how baffled Fitzgerald was, tried to help him.

"But Mr. Fitzgerald," she said, "you haven't told us what they did in the bordello."

At this Fitzgerald fled, making his way back to Paris, where he was to meet Zelda, as best he could. At first when Zelda asked him how it had gone he assured her that it had been a great success, they had liked him, he had bowled them over. But gradually the truth came out, until — after several drinks — Fitzgerald put his head on his arms and began to pound the table with his fists.

"They beat me," he said. "They beat me! They beat me! They *beat* me!" [39]

In August they went to Antibes for the month. "There was no one at Antibes this summer," Fitzgerald wrote Bishop, "except me, Zelda, the Valentinos, the Murphy's, Mistinguet, Rex Ingram, Dos Passos, Alice Terry, the MacLeishes, Charles Bracket, Maude Kahn, Esther Murphy, Marguerite Namara, E. Phillips Openheim, Mannes the violinist, Floyd Dell, Max and Chrystal Eastman, ex-Premier Orlando, Etienne de Beaumont — just a real place to rough it and escape from all the world. But we had a great time." [40] This year was the beginning of that brief period when a group of Americans were to make on the summer Riviera a brilliant social life. "The gay elements of society," said Fitzgerald, "had divided into two main streams, one flowing toward Palm Beach and Deauville, and the other, much smaller, toward the summer Riviera. One could get away with more on the summer Riviera, and whatever happened seemed to have something to do with art. From 1926 to 1929, the great years of the Cap d'Antibes, this corner of France was dominated by a group quite distinct from that American society which is dominated by Europeans." [41] The Cap d'Antibes was remote enough to seem safe from the tourists; it was an uncomfortable overnight trip from Paris; it was also primitive enough to seem very French: the movie house operated only once a week; the telephone service was shut down for two hours at noon and completely after seven at night. This happy situation did not of course last; already in 1925, as Fitzgerald's letter to Bishop shows, things were getting out of hand, and by 1927 the half-mile of glorious beach was jammed with Americans, an apartment house was going up, and there were two American bars doing a flourishing business.[42] By 1929 no one swam off Eden Roc any more, except for a hangover dip at noon; people spent their time, as Fitzgerald said, in the bar discussing each other.[43]

But for a few years after the Gerald Murphys had made it the style of a special few, it was a gay, casual, informal place. The men wore French workmen's shirts, striped bathing trunks, and jockey caps; they lived an easy, relaxed life between beach and villa and the blue shuttered Hôtel du Cap d'Antibes. The whole feeling of the place is in the opening chapters of *Tender Is the Night,* how remarkably you see when you compare Fitzgerald's account of it with some other description such as that in Charles Brackett's *American Colony*. Gerald and Sara Murphy, with their charm, their social skill, and their wealth, were the heart of the original group. Fitzgerald drew on Gerald Murphy for these characteristics in Dick Diver. Murphy was always inventing amusing games for everyone, including the children: he once arranged an elaborate mock wedding between himself and Fitzgerald's daughter, which was carried out with perfect gravity. Mrs. Murphy shared her husband's social gifts; "Picasso always said of her (even if she'd prepared a basket lunch for the beach) 'Sara est très festin.'" This gift baffled and fascinated Fitzgerald; as one of their friends remarked, "he thought it was something you did with money." [44] Imaginatively the Fitzgeralds were more than equal to the demands of a society like this. Once, for instance, Fitzgerald got up a children's-party game about the Crusades involving complicated maneuvers with a famous set of lead soldiers. Nearly a decade later Robert Benchley wrote him, after reading *Tender Is the Night*: "Anyone who gets down on his stomach and crawls all afternoon around a yard playing tin-soldiers with a lot of kids, shouldn't be made unhappy. I cry a little every time I think of you that afternoon in Antibes." [45]

But, like all skilful hosts, the Murphys ruled firmly: people were expected to fall in with their schemes. Their parties were carefully planned and as beautifully managed as the Divers' party. Occasionally people failed to accept the place assigned them. Fitzgerald is said to have got drunk once when he was omitted from a Murphy party, and to have stood outside the garden where the guests were having cocktails and thrown the contents of a garbage can over the wall into their midst. [46] But with the Fitzgeralds such gestures were something more than social rebellion. They had reached a stage which was difficult for themselves as well as others, and, like Dick Diver, Fitzgerald began to find himself excluded not only from parties but from hotels and other public places. They still believed that life ought to provide them something wonderful and exciting to do. "We grew up," Zelda said ironically later, "founding our dreams on the infinite promise of American advertising. I *still* believe that one can learn to play the piano by mail and that mud will give you a perfect complexion." [47] To do what you wanted to was a matter of your honor, of your "sincerity." The Fitzgeralds had been committed to this conception of sincerity from the start. But as time went on and they satisfied the accumulated and organized desires of their early years, doing what they wanted to became doing whatever momentary impulse suggested. Less and less did they find any long-term desires to which they wanted to sacrifice their momentary inclinations; more and more they lived at the edge of consciousness, where all the obscure and confused impulses of their natures hovered. They were at the mercy of these impulses because they were still striving to reach a kind of activity which would seem unusual and exciting.

Impulse led them to act extravagantly and incalculably. One night at the Casino at Juan-les-Pins, very late in the evening, Zelda suddenly rose from the table and, holding her skirt high, danced around the empty ball room, seriously, with great dignity, appallingly alone with her impulse to express herself. On another occasion, in Nice, as they were going down the steps into a night club, they encountered an old woman "with a tray of all sorts of little paper cornucopias of nuts and candies, rather prettily laid out." When some of the party stopped to admire it, Fitzgerald "gave it a sort of gay nineties kick and sent everything flying." It was, as one of his friends remarked, "an ugly little scene," very like the scene between Francis Melarky and the Negro, and like Francis, Fitzgerald was full of remorse the minute his friends remonstrated with him — "You know," said one of them long afterwards about the episode, "how sore you get with a small child you are fond of who acts up?"

Under the pressure of such disorganized desires the Fitzgeralds became more and more unpredictable. One evening, with the Murphys, they found themselves at a table next to Isadora Duncan at a small inn in the mountains. It quickly became apparent that Fitzgerald was the man she had, according to her custom, selected to spend that night with. He went over to her table and sat at her feet while she ran her hands through his hair and called him "my centurion." Presently she arose to go, telling Fitzgerald where she was staying in a loud, clear voice. At this Zelda, who out of some pride or principle never remonstrated with Fitzgerald and had been ignoring the whole episode, stood up, leapt across the table, and plunged down a long flight of stone steps. When the Murphys reached her she was cut and bleeding but not seriously hurt. She offered no explanation. By now both Fitzgeralds felt they must go on to something exciting. Scott proposed that they put all the chickens they could find at the inn, some sixteen, on the spit in the great fireplace and cook them. But the Murphys insisted on going home. Within a short time the Fitzgeralds followed them, but at a point on the road where it crossed a trolley line, they turned up the track onto a trestle instead of following the road. Their car bumped over the open ties a few yards and stalled. They settled back in their seats and fell asleep, though they had been told that the trolley came around a blind curve and onto this trestle at high speed so that even the crossing was very dangerous. They were found the next morning by a peasant, up early to take his vegetables to market, and carried to safety by him less than twenty minutes before the morning trolley crashed into their car and smashed it to pieces.[48]

CHAPTER X

WHILE THIS "great time" at Antibes was going on Fitzgerald conceived the plan for *The World's Fair*, a novel on which he was to work for three years before giving up the plot and most of what he had written and starting afresh. *The World's Fair* — it was also called at one time or another *The Boy Who Killed His Mother* and *Our Type* — is the story of a talented boy, Francis Melarky, who makes a success in Hollywood as a technician and then is brought to the Riviera by his mother for a vacation. His father is serving a long prison term, apparently for some crime of violence; there is a suggestion that Francis has inherited a murderous temper. Francis' mother is a commonplace woman distinguished only by her unscrupulous determination to retain possession of Francis; there is bad feeling between them from the beginning. Fitzgerald intended to have Francis kill his mother — "Will you ask somebody," he wrote Perkins, "what is done if one American murders another in France. . . . In a certain sense my plot is not unlike Dreiser's in the American Tragedy." [1] The murder had been central to the plot from the moment of the novel's conception at Antibes: "*Our Type*," he had written Perkins when he first got the idea for it, "is about several things, one of which is an intellectual murder on the Leopold-Loeb idea. Incidentally it is about Zelda and me and the hysteria of last May and June in Paris." [2] As Fitzgerald worked on the novel during the next three years and studied the Murphys and Antibes, he began to shift the background from Paris to the Riviera; this change can be seen taking place between the versions of a given passage (for some parts of the story there are three versions). Altogether Fitzgerald completed four long chapters — about twenty thousand words — before he gave up this story of matricide in 1929.

The book originally began with a chapter describing Francis' getting in a fight with the Italian police and being beaten up, as Fitzgerald had been, but this chapter was presently made the seventh and the second chapter made the beginning. This chapter describes the arrival of Francis and his mother on the Riviera and — except for the relation of Francis and his mother and a fine scene with Mary and Abe Grant (North) — is like the opening chapter of *Tender Is the Night*. It is followed by the Pipers' (Divers') dinner party and the duel and, finally, a long chapter in which Francis accompanies the Pipers to Paris to see Abe Grant off to America. This is the chapter which uses "the hysteria of last May and June in Paris," most of which was eliminated in *Tender Is the Night* to make way for the love affair between Dick and Rosemary.[3]

But though Fitzgerald sent Perkins an optimistic report of progress in September and was still trying to put a good face on things a month later (". . . progresses slowly and carefully with much destroying and revision"), he was getting little work done.[4] There were many parties, in Paris with the Murphys and the Hemingways and the MacLeishes, and in London. "[We] went," wrote Fitzgerald, with his characteristic ambivalence about such things, "on some very high tone parties with Mountbattens and all that sort of thing. Very impressed, but not very, as I furnished most of the amusement myself."[5] It was an unhappy winter. They were tired of parties without seeming able to stop going to them, and things had gone stale. ". . . if somebody would come along,"

says the heroine of *Save Me the Waltz* of this time, "to remind us about how we felt about things when we felt the
way they remind us of, maybe it would refresh us." [6] They
quarreled with the Murphys and Fitzgerald had a nasty argument with Robert McAlmon, one of the expatriates. Their
apartment in the rue de Tilsitt, like nearly every place they
ever lived, was uncomfortable; it "smelled of a church chan-
cery because it was impossible to ventilate" and turned out
to be "a perfect breeding place for the germs of bitterness
they brought with them from the Riviera." [7] When Zelda
became ill in January they departed with relief for Salies de
Béarn in the Pyrenees.

During that fall Owen Davis had made a dramatic version
of *The Great Gatsby* and on February 2, 1926, it opened at
the Ambassador Theatre in New York, with James Rennie as
Gatsby and Florence Eldridge as Daisy. Davis' version begins
with a prologue which deals with the meeting of Daisy and
Gatsby in Louisville, goes directly to Nick Carraway's cottage
for their first post-war meeting, and runs the plot out with
two acts in Gatsby's library. Wilson becomes Tom Buchanan's
chauffeur and so moves into the play, as Alexander Woollcott
put it, "bag and, as you might say, baggage." Daisy begins
the final sequence of events by offering to become Gatsby's
mistress, and her offer is rejected. Thus Davis answers the
question which Fitzgerald could not.

Rennie was well cast as Gatsby, and there was little doubt
after the first few nights that Brady had a success. Percy
Hammond summed up the general impression when he wrote:
"Mr. Davis's deft shifting of the book's essential episodes is a
marvel of rearrangement and dovetailing. . . . The speech of
the characters is retained in much of its clear-cut veracity, and
the 'atmosphere' of Long Island's more rakish sectors is pretty
well preserved. . . . 'The Great Gatsby' in the theater is at
least half as satisfactory an entertainment as it is in the book." [8]
One newspaper noticed that coincident with the opening of

the play three speakeasies also opened in West 49th Street. The play ran into the summer and had a considerable career on the road.

". . . as it was something of a *succès d'estime*," Fitzgerald wrote Harold Ober of the play, "and put in my pocket seventeen or eighteen thousand . . . I should be, and am, well contented." The play's success also made possible the sale of *Gatsby* to the movies, from which Fitzgerald received $15,-000 or $20,000 more. These windfalls were welcome, for during 1925 and 1926 his total production was seven short stories and a couple of articles.[9] The three main parts in the movie were taken by Warner Baxter, Lois Wilson, and Neil Hamilton; a new actor named William Powell was thought to be very effective as Wilson, the garage man. The picture ended with a subtitle to the effect that some people — meaning Gatsby — live and die for others, followed by a shot of Tom and Daisy and the wee one carefully posed on the porch of their happy home. It is probably best summed up by a review which remarks that it was "a racy, raw, and sentimental concoction which Mr. Fitzgerald will not relish but most of the movie fans will." [10]

According to Scribner's regular custom, *The Great Gatsby* was followed in February, 1926, by a volume of short stories. Fitzgerald had not made a collection of stories since *Tales of the Jazz Age* in the fall of 1922, and he was confident he could put together a book with "no junk in it." [11] He certainly included in *All the Sad Young Men* nothing he knew to be junk and it is a far better book than his previous collections. The enforced production of short stories after the failure of *The Vegetable* in the winter of 1924 gave him an accumulation of twenty-one stories to choose from, and despite what he said of the 1924 stories at the time they were written, they were not all bad. Six of the nine stories he chose for *All the Sad Young Men* came from this group, though two of the remaining three — "Winter Dreams" (written in

September, 1922) and "The Rich Boy" (written between April and August, 1925) — are the best stories in the volume.[12] These two stories also show the difference between Fitzgerald's early short stories and those of the middle period of his career.

Into "Winter Dreams" he got all the acute sense of the destructiveness of time which was his strongest feeling as a young writer — the sadness of Judy Jones' loss of beauty, the greater sadness of Dexter Green's discovery that he has lost the ability to feel this loss. When Dexter Green, having given up Judy Jones, discovers that "so soon, with so little done, so much of ecstasy had gone from him," he welcomes the chance to return to her and to be "unconsciously dictated to by his winter dreams again." It was, though he did not quite understand it, a great relief to him to discover he was still capable of ecstasy. When, after seven years of not seeing her, he is told that she has faded, he feels sad that her magic is gone, but he feels overwhelming grief that he cannot care very much that it has. This loss of the ability to feel deeply is the story's theme, and Fitzgerald realizes it in a narrative which is full of good, honest things. But the theme has certain limitations. These limitations are clear in Dexter Green's final judgment, where the discrepancy between his overwhelming grief and its occasion creates a faint air of false rhetoric: " 'Long ago,' he said, 'long ago, there was something in me, but now that thing is gone. Now that thing is gone, that thing is gone. I cannot cry. I cannot care. That thing will come back no more.' " [13] This slightly disturbing effect reaches out into the story's structure too. It makes something Fitzgerald knew was important to his sense of experience — Dexter's business career, his place in the world — appear irrelevant and thus gives to what is really a carefully constructed story an air of looseness. At one point Fitzgerald himself says half apologetically that "things creep into [this story] which have nothing to do with those dreams [Dexter] had when he was young." They do have something to do with the dreams Fitzgerald wanted to tell, but not with those he clearly understood he was telling.

"The Rich Boy" is a finer story than "Winter Dreams" because Fitzgerald understood his own intention better when he wrote it. Now he was so aware of how much Anson Hunter's place in the world mattered that he made the story primarily one of how Anson's queer, rich-boy's pride deprived him of what he wanted most, a home and an ordered life. Hating not to dominate, Anson cannot love those he does dominate, cannot commit himself to the human muddle as he must if he is to have the life he wants. All the cross currents of his nature are displayed in the understated climactic scene when Anson spends a night with Paula and her husband just before Paula's baby is born.

> She rested her head against [her husband's] coat.
> "He's sweet, isn't he, Anson?" she demanded.
> "Absolutely," said Anson, laughing.
> She raised her face to her husband.
> "Well, I'm ready," she said. She turned to Anson: "Do you want to see our family gymnastic stunt?"
> "Yes," he said in an interested voice.
> "All right. Here we go!"
> Hagerty picked her up easily in his arms.
> "This is called the family acrobatic stunt," said Paula. "He carries me up-stairs. Isn't it sweet of him?"
> "Yes," said Anson.
> Hagerty bent his head slightly until his face touched Paula's.
> "And I love him," she said. "I've just been telling you, haven't I, Anson?"
> "Yes," he said.
> "He's the dearest thing that ever lived in this world; aren't you, darling? . . . Well, good night. Here we go. Isn't he strong?"

"Yes," Anson said.

"You'll find a pair of Pete's pajamas laid out for you. Sweet dreams — see you at breakfast."

"Yes," Anson said.[14]

The very rich *are* different from you and me. So precise is Fitzgerald's awareness of how Anson Hunter differs that he gets all his climaxes with quiet moments like this one and never has to resort to rhetoric. Because every paragraph implies much more than it says, the story appears much more tightly constructed than "Winter Dreams," though the two stories are planned in much the same way. "Anson's first sense of his superiority came to him when he realized the half-grudging American deference that was paid to him in the Connecticut village [where the Hunters had their summer home]. . . ." "He was convivial, bawdy, robustly avid for pleasure, and we were all surprised when he fell in love with a conservative and rather proper girl." "There were so many friends in Anson's life — scarcely one for whom he had not done some unusual kindness and scarcely one whom he did not occasionally embarrass by his bursts of rough conversation or his habit of getting drunk whenever and however he liked."

There are other good stories in *All the Sad Young Men.* There is "Absolution," which contrasts a romantic young man, who has a bad conscience and dreams of himself as a worldly hero named Blatchford Sarnemington, with a spoiled priest, who is filled with piety and a maddening dream of a life like an eternal amusement park. There is "The Adjuster," where only the handling of Doctor Moon spoils a fine account of suffering and maturity. There is " 'The Sensible Thing' " with its moving description of Fitzgerald's own wooing. It was a good book and it fully deserves its favorable critical reception and its sale of fourteen thousand copies.

During this winter of 1924-25 Fitzgerald devoted himself

to getting Hemingway recognized. At least a year earlier he had recommended Hemingway to Perkins' attention;[15] now he started to work on all his friends. Glenway Wescott has recalled how Fitzgerald drew him aside at Antibes and urged him to do something to help Hemingway's career.

> He thought I would agree that *The Apple of the Eye* and *The Great Gatsby* were rather inflated market values just then. What could I do to help launch Hemingway? Why didn't I write a laudatory essay on him? With this questioning, Fitzgerald now and then impatiently grasped and shook my elbow. There was something more than ordinary art-admiration about it, but on the other hand it was no mere matter of affection for Hemingway. . . . I was touched and flattered by Fitzgerald's taking so much for granted. It simply had not occurred to him that unfriendliness or pettiness on my part might inhibit my enthusiasm about the art of a new colleague and rival.[16]

It did not inhibit Fitzgerald, who hastened to write his own laudatory essay, "How to Waste Material," for *The Bookman*.[17]

Hemingway had just finished *The Torrents of Spring* and had completed the first draft of *The Sun Also Rises* (the final draft was ready in April). His publishers, Boni & Liveright, were embarrassed by *The Torrents of Spring:* Sherwood Anderson was one of their most valuable authors, and *The Torrents of Spring* is a parody of Anderson. But they did not want to lose *The Sun Also Rises*, and Hemingway would be legally free to take it elsewhere if they rejected *The Torrents of Spring*. It is hardly surprising that Boni & Liveright were convinced Hemingway deliberately wrote *The Torrents of Spring* as part of a plot, devised by him and Fitzgerald, to free him from them.[18] In the end, however, they decided to reject Hemingway's parody. Fitzgerald had certainly hoped the matter would work out this way, but there is no reason to suppose

Hemingway wrote the book for this purpose. "[Ernest's] book," Fitzgerald wrote Perkins, "is almost a vicious parody on Anderson. You see I agree with Ernest that Anderson's last two books have let everybody down who believed in him — I think they're cheap, faked, obscurantic and awful." [19] This was Hemingway's motive. "I have known all along," he wrote Fitzgerald, "that they could not and would not be able to publish it as it makes a bum out of their present ace and best seller Anderson. Now in 10th printing. I did not, however, have that in mind in any way when I wrote it." [20] When Boni & Liveright finally rejected *The Torrents of Spring*, Hemingway turned down offers from several other publishers and signed with Scribner's.

> As you see — he wrote Fitzgerald — I am jeopardizing my chances with Harcourt by first sending the Ms to Scribner and if Scribner turned it down It would be very bad as Harcourt have practically offered to take me unsight [sic] unseen. Am turning down a sure thing for delay and a chance but feel no regret because of the impression I have formed of Maxwell Perkins through his letters and what you have told me of him. Also confidence in Scribners and would like to be lined up with you. . . . Well, so long. I'm certainly relying on your good nature in a lousy brutal way.

Though the feeling between them later became less friendly, Fitzgerald never lost his deep admiration for Hemingway's talent; he paid generous tribute to it in "Handle with Care": ". . . a third contemporary had been an artistic conscience to me — I had not imitated his infectious style, because my own style, such as it is, was formed before he published anything, but there was an awful pull toward him when I was on a spot." [21] As soon as Hemingway had signed with Scribner's Fitzgerald began to fuss over his work like a maiden aunt. He was particularly worried about *The Sun Also Rises*, and Hemingway took to teasing him about his own plans for *The World's Fair:*

> If you are worried [*The Sun Also Rises*] is *not* a series of anecdotes — nor is it written very much like either Manhattan Transfer nor Dark Laughter. . . . The hero, like Gatsby, is a Lake Superior Salmon Fisherman. (There are no salmon in Lake Superior) The action all takes place in Newport, R. I. and the heroine is a girl named Sophie Irene Loeb who kills her mother. The scene in which Sophie gives birth to twins in the death house at Sing Sing where she is waiting to be electrocuted for the murder of the father and sister of her, as then, unborn children I got from Dreiser but practically everything else in the book is either my own or yours. I know you'll be glad to see it. The Sun Also Rises comes from Sophie's statement as she is strapped into the chair as the current mounts.[22]

He came down to visit the Fitzgeralds at Juan-les-Pins in August, much depressed by his marital difficulties. He brought with him a carbon of *The Sun Also Rises*, and he and Fitzgerald discussed it at great length. When he got back to Paris he wrote: "I cut The Sun to start with Cohn — cut all that first part. made a number of minor cuts and did quite a lot of re-writing and tightening up. Cut and . . . in proof it read[s] like a good book. . . . I hope to hell you'll like it and I think maybe you will. Have a swell hunch for a new novel. I'm calling it the World's Fair. You'll like the title." In the final analysis Fitzgerald, almost as ambitious for Hemingway as for himself, decided that the fiesta, the fishing trip, and the minor characters were wonderful, but that in Jake Hemingway had bitten off "more than can yet be chewn between the covers of a book." He disliked Lady Brett but was not sure his judgment of the character was not colored by his knowledge of the person it was based on.[23]

The Fitzgeralds had been in Juan-les-Pins since May, when

they had taken a handsome house there called the Villa St. Louis. In a moment of enthusiasm Fitzgerald had told Perkins that they were "wonderfully situated in a big house on the shore with a beach and the Casino not 100 yds. away and every prospect of a marvelous summer." Apart from a quick trip to Paris in June to have "Zelda's appendix neatly removed," they remained there into the autumn.[24] Except that Zelda was ill for the rest of the year, they had a good time. The Murphys were there to give their fine parties, and sooner or later nearly everyone interesting seemed to turn up, from Grace Moore and Alexander Woollcott to Bishop and Donald Ogden Stewart. They dined with Grace Moore in Monte Carlo and were fascinated by the odd gentleman who was there for dinner in a leopard skin; not even Fitzgerald and Charles MacArthur had thought of that trick, though they spent much of the summer inventing similar ones. Once they planned to saw a waiter in two (with a musical saw to "eliminate any sordidness") to see what was inside him, but Zelda told them it was not worth it, that they would only find old menus and tips and pencil stubs and broken china. Another time they lured the orchestra from the Hôtel Provençal to the Villa St. Louis, locked them in a room with a bottle of whiskey, and settled down outside the door for an evening of listening to their old favorites. The orchestra grew weaker and weaker, but Fitzgerald and MacArthur did not, and the poor musicians did not escape till dawn.

Adding Ben Finney to their staff they wrote and photographed, on the grounds of the Hôtel du Cap, a movie about a Princess Alluria, the wickedest woman in Europe. MacArthur wrote in an "incest theme" with the Japanese Ambassador as "the incestor," and they spent a good deal of time thinking up unprintable titles to write on the walls of Grace Moore's villa so that they could be photographed. "I complained and scrubbed once or twice," she said, "but the new captions that then appeared were so much worse than the old that it seemed better to do with the four-letter words one knew than those one knew not of." [25]

These practical jokes, though in retrospect entertaining, were sometimes ominously destructive. On one occasion they raided a small restaurant in Cannes, carried off all its silverware, and kidnaped the proprietor and waiters. These victims they tied up and carried to the edge of a cliff, full of dire threats of murder. They did not stop until they had exhausted every device of terrorization they could imagine. The impulse to destroy visible behind this practical joking shows also in Fitzgerald's social disturbances, as when, at a formal dinner in the Murphys' garden, he suddenly rose and threw a ripe fig at the bare back of one of the guests. All the guests — including his victim — ignored him completely; he was left standing, alone and invisible, like a man in a nightmare. It defeated him completely, so that he appeared to be almost comforted later when Gerald Murphy remonstrated with him and he could be crestfallen and repentant. His dislike of the English must have been partly the result of their habit of suavely ignoring him when he tried to apologize for his bad behavior; they simply refused to admit that he had existed on such occasions. Perhaps he was compelled to such bad behavior by the conviction that it was innocent fun, and felt that it misfired because he did not belong and understand, as Gatsby's efforts to give "interesting" parties misfired and, inexplicably, alienated Daisy.

There was little of the practical joker and none of the repentant in Zelda. She was even more striking in appearance now than she had been as a girl. Her hair had darkened to a "glossy dark gold"; Fitzgerald compared its color to a chow's. Her whole face had matured, until even her mouth — "the cupid's bow of a magazine cover" — only intensified the almost hawklike upper part of her face with its firm brow and nose and its remarkable eyes. She was always immaculate — "a fresh little cotton dress every day." She talked very little.

"I don't believe," Sara Murphy wrote of her long afterwards, "she liked very many people, although her manners to everyone were *perfect.* . . . Her dignity was *never* lost in the midst of the wildest escapades. Even that time at the Casino she was cool and aloof, and unconscious of onlookers. No one ever took a liberty with Zelda, as far as I know. It did upset her to hear Scott scolded or criticized — she flew to his defense and backed him up in everything." [26]

A good deal of injustice has certainly been done the Zelda of the twenties because she later went insane and it is difficult not to let the knowledge that she did so affect one's view of what she was like before 1930. Many of their friends thought at the time that she saw more clearly than Fitzgerald how seriously their lives were getting out of hand and had greater strength of character in resisting dissipation than he did. There is much to support this view. To a friend who helped her get Fitzgerald home late one night during these years she said as she got out of the taxi, "Now I'll have to start all over again," and to his insistence on going out one night with the Callaghans, though he was drunk and exhausted, "Zelda said wearily, 'You'd better let him go with with you. I'm going to bed.'" Of their life at this time, Louis Bromfield said:

> Of the two Zelda drank better and had, I think, the stronger character, and I have sometimes thought that she could have given it up without any great difficulty and that she was led on to a tragic end only because he could not stop and in despair she followed him. I have sometimes suspected that Scott was aware of this and that it caused remorse which did nothing to help his situation as it grew more tragic.[27]

On the other hand, it could be maintained, as Hemingway maintained all his life, that Zelda was jealous of Fitzgerald's achievement and used her ability to outdrink him to keep him from working. "Scott," as Hemingway put it, "was afraid for her to pass out in the company they kept that spring and the places they went to. ["This spring she was making him jealous with other women."] Scott . . . had to drink more than he could drink and be in control of himself. . . . Finally he had few intervals of work at all." [28]

There is no doubt that Zelda often resented Fitzgerald's concentration on work. Often enough she simply complained that it deprived them of fun and parties, but from the beginning she seems to have wanted also to compete with Fitzgerald by making a success as a writer or — later on — as a dancer or a painter: perhaps for people as attractive as they were at their best even the parties were occasions for competition. At the same time Zelda to some extent depended on Fitzgerald to provide the security for which, as a girl, she had depended on her father. People like the Callaghans were astonished when, at a moment of what appeared to them innocent gaiety for Zelda, Fitzgerald peremptorily ordered her home to bed: "her whole manner changed; it was as if she knew he had command over her; she agreed meekly. . . ." [29]

Where the relation between two people was as complicated as this one, perhaps all one can safely say is that at one time or another all these things were true of their marriage. In any event, during the middle years of the twenties, Zelda's customary social demeanor was a brooding and fiery silence from which she would occasionally emerge to make some sudden gesture which, if often disturbing, was usually serious and symbolic. When Alexander Woollcott and Grace Moore's fiancé, "Chato" Elizaga, were leaving for Paris at the end of the summer, there was a farewell dinner for them on the terrace at Eden Roc. After a considerable number of toasts, Zelda got up and said: "I have been so touched by all these kind words. But what are words? Nobody has offered our departing heroes any gifts to take with them. I'll start off." And she stepped out of her black lace panties and threw them toward Woollcott and Elizaga. Elizaga caught them and, announcing that he must perform an adequately heroic act in return for his lady's favor, leapt from the rocks into the

Mediterranean. Everyone dashed down after him, and when order had been re-established, they suddenly became aware of Woollcott, completely naked, carefully donning his straw hat, lighting a cigarette, and walking slowly up the path to the hotel. They learned later that he had walked with great dignity but still naked into the lobby, up to the desk for his key, and on upstairs to his room.[30] On another occasion, after she and Fitzgerald had been quarreling all evening, Zelda, instead of getting into the car when they were leaving, lay down in front of it and told Fitzgerald to run over her. Fitzgerald got into the car, apparently angry enough to do so, but it failed to start and their friends intervened.[31]

With all these diversions, Fitzgerald naturally got little work done. When they had first reached the Riviera he had had a moment of optimism. "My book is *wonderful*," he wrote Perkins. "I don't think it'll be interrupted again. I expect to reach New York about Dec. 10th with the ms. under my arm." Two weeks later he was still going strong: "The novel . . . now goes on apace. This is confidential but *Liberty*, with certain conditions, has offered me $35,000 sight unseen. I hope to have it done in January." [32] But there is no further mention of the novel until December, when he answered a direct question from Perkins by saying, "My book [is] not nearly finished." He did not write a single story between February, 1926 (when he wrote "Your Way and Mine" for *The Women's Home Companion*), and June, 1927 (when he wrote "Jacob's Ladder" for the *Post*). This failure, together with his failure to complete the novel, effectively canceled the profitable arrangement with *Liberty*. As always when he was not working, he was depressed, now, however, not simply because of his failure to write serious fiction, or indeed, to write at all; he also felt that he was steadily deteriorating. "I wish I were twenty-two again," he said, "with only my dramatic and feverishly enjoyed miseries. You remember I used to say I wanted to die at thirty — well, I'm twenty-nine and the prospect is still welcome. My work is the only thing that makes me happy — except to be a little tight — and for these two indulgences I pay a big price in mental and physical hangovers." As if to demonstrate how persistent this mood was, he wrote Perkins two months later: "If you see anyone I know tell 'em I hate 'em all, him especially. Never want to see 'em again. Why shouldn't I go crazy? My father is a moron and my mother is a neurotic, half insane with pathological nervous worry. Between them they haven't and never have had the brains of Calvin Coolidge. If I knew anything I'd be the best writer in America" — "which isn't saying a lot," he added when he recurred to this subject in another letter.[33]

But if coming home, as he said, revolted him as much as the thought of remaining in France, they nonetheless made up their minds to return to America. Zelda was ill, their morale was badly shaken, and their money was running out, for "that was a period," as one of their friends said, "when [Scott's] pockets were always full of damp little wads of hundred franc notes that he dribbled out behind him wherever he went the way some women do Kleenex." [34] Fitzgerald saw nothing to do but flee, and they sailed for America from Genoa on the *Conte Biancamano* on December 10. It was an unhappy return. They did not have the money they had planned, three years earlier, to save before they came home; the manuscript of Fitzgerald's novel was not under his arm. If he still appeared, at thirty, to be a "stocky, muscular, clear-skinned [young man] with wide, fresh, green-blue eyes" and blond hair, who announced boldly to the press on his arrival in New York that "he [had] nearly completed a novel . . . which deal[t] with Americans in Europe," he felt himself to be a man who for over two years had done no serious work and very little work of any kind, who was leading a self-indulgent life, a man in whom as in Dick Diver, "The change came a long way back — but at first it didn't show. The manner remains intact for some time after the morale cracks." [35]

CHAPTER XI

THEY CAME BACK to America with the intention of settling down and living a more orderly life, so they started off by visiting Fitzgerald's parents, who were now living in Washington, and Zelda's family in Montgomery. Just after Christmas, however, Fitzgerald got a chance to fulfill his old threat to go to Hollywood and learn the movie business; John Considine of United Artists asked him to come out to do a "fine modern college story for Constance Talmadge" ("one of the hectic flapper comedies, in which Constance Talmadge has specialized for years," the newspapers called it.)[1] After some jockeying Fitzgerald agreed to go for $3500 down and $8500 on the acceptance of the story, for they needed the money too much to refuse an offer of this kind even if it was likely to interrupt their program of orderly living.[2]

After a delay at El Paso (Fitzgerald was convinced he had appendicitis and insisted on leaving the train for a hospital), they reached Los Angeles and settled at the Ambassador. They were given a big welcome, receiving the royal recognition of lunch at Pickfair, making friends with Lillian Gish, and renewing their friendship with Carmel Myers, to whom Fitzgerald inscribed a copy of *The Great Gatsby* with his old gaiety: "For Carmel Myers from her Corrupter F. Scott Fitzgerald. 'Don't cry, little girl, maybe some day someone will come along who'll make you a dishonest woman' Los Angeles." Almost immediately they found themselves part of a congenial group which included Carl Van Vechten, John Barrymore, Richard Barthelmess, and Lois Moran. Fitzgerald was fascinated by Lois Moran and she by him. She even persuaded him to have a screen test made in the hope that he might get a part as her leading man. By the time he came to write *Tender Is the Night*, Fitzgerald had decided to take a superior attitude toward this little scheme.[3]

But she was important to his imagination and he put what she represented for him into the portrait of Rosemary Hoyt in *Tender Is the Night*. For a long time after this Hollywood visit she had his attention; he cut pictures of her from the newspapers at the time of her marriage, and among the notes of events he thought dramatic enough for stories is one about a visit she paid him in Baltimore. Like Dick Diver with Rosemary, he was charmed by her youth and beauty and innocence: he was thirty, and hated it, and she was twenty. It made him feel young again to be so extravagantly admired, but of course there is no evidence that his feeling for her was ever so mixed up with personal exhaustion as was Dick's for Rosemary. This part of Dick's story was the spoiled priest's version of what was potential rather than actual in the relation.

There was a whirl of parties, night clubs, and practical jokes. At a tea of Carmel Myer's Fitzgerald made himself what one gossip columnist described as "conspicuous by [his] presence" by collecting watches and jewelry from the guests and boiling the whole collection in a couple of cans of tomato soup on the kitchen stove.[4] James Montgomery Flagg, who ended by being disgusted with the Fitzgeralds, spent the evening with them after the tea. They wound up, he remembered, sitting on the coping of the Ambassador's parking place listening to Zelda sing a bawdy comic ballad. Fitzgerald, with a fifty-dollar tip, persuaded the Ambassador's night starter to cash him a check for several hundred dollars; he wanted the money to hire a car because he and Zelda had become obsessed with the idea that they must see John Monk Saunders, who, they asserted, was much too successful with women and ought to be altered; for that purpose they supplied themselves with scissors, bandages, and gauze at the hotel drugstore. They then routed Saunders out of bed and insisted on pulling open his bathrobe and urging everyone to observe how lovely his chest smelled. Saunders finally got rid of them, but all the way home Fitzgerald kept turning around to squint at Flagg and say "God! But you look old!" and Zelda told him about how, by signing Scott's name to things she had written, she had got large prices for them.[5] "These charming young people," Flagg said.[6] To many people like Flagg they no longer seemed the Babes in the Woods they had been in New York five years before, who "simply got tight and pulled a lot of sophomoric pranks" that "never were mean or cruel or unkind." [7]

When Fitzgerald finally completed his story for Constance Talmadge it was rejected. "At that time," he said years later, "I had been generally acknowledged for several years as the top American writer both seriously and, as far as prices went, popularly. I . . . was confidant to the point of conciet. Hollywood made a big fuss over us and the ladies all looked very beautiful to a man of thirty. I honestly believed that *with no effort on my part* I was a sort of magician with words. . . . Total result — a great time and no work. I was to be paid only a small amount unless they made my picture — they didn't." [8]

But this account implies less of an effort on his part than he actually made. *Lipstick* is a competently plotted if conventional Cinderella story about a girl at a prom. Though Fitzgerald did not name Princeton, he drew on its geography and customs for background and there is an authenticity about the prom scenes, the proctors, the Nassau Club, and the undergraduates which is rare in the movies at any time; "the young men are dressed in knickerbockers that are not too big, flannels not too wide or in 'business' suits that have no collegiate smack about them . . . for this is one of the oldest and most conservative of eastern universities . . . and its manners are simply the good manners of the world outside." [9]

As soon as the script was finished the Fitzgeralds left Hollywood. It was reported that they stacked all the furniture in the center of their room at the Ambassador, put their unpaid bills on top of it, and departed; when they got on the train they crawled on their hands and knees the length of the car to reach their compartment, to escape inconspicuously.[10] . . . BOOTLEGGERS GONE OUT OF BUSINESS COTTON CLUB CLOSED ALL FLAGS AT HALF MAST . . . BOTTLES OF LOVE TO YOU BOTH, Lois Moran wired them.[11]

The orderly life, which had been in abeyance during these months, was now revived. With the help of Fitzgerald's college friend, John Biggs, they found a beautiful old Greek-revival mansion outside Wilmington called Ellerslie. "The squareness of the rooms and the sweep of the columns," wrote Zelda, "were to bring us a judicious tranquility." [12] Fitzgerald addressed himself to the world situation and gave an interview in which he announced that he was very disturbed about it, that the mushiness and ineffectuality of liberalism compelled people to turn toward "The Mussolini-Ludendorff idea," that he deplored Mussolini in particular but that his hope for the nation lay "in the birth of a hero who will be of age when America's testing comes." [13] He also settled down to an honest struggle to complete his novel. He was realistic enough to warn Perkins against any publicity about it, but wired him that he EXPECT[ED] TO DELIVER NOVEL TO LIBERTY IN JUNE.[14] They made an effort to become a part of the social life in Wilmington and, as they always did when they tried, they charmed everyone and were soon firmly established there.

But like all their homes, Ellerslie did not work out very well. It was, as one of their friends remarked, a big house with not enough rooms, and tranquillity was not easily won, for under the stress of the accumulated disorder of their lives their own personal relations were gradually deteriorating into what Fitzgerald later called an "organized cat and dog fight." Their social success in Wilmington was the signal for that destructive impulse which was the product of Fitzgerald's unhappiness to assert itself, and he began to be rude to people. At the same time his complementary impulse to take upon himself the responsibility for making a group of people happy showed itself at the many week-end house parties they gave. For one such party he invented an elaborate game of polo played on farm horses with croquet mallets. Like much that he did, this game was symbolic, an ironic imitation of the lives of the Tom Buchanans of the world and their strings of polo ponies. He exerted himself endlessly in this way to make his guests happy, for "like most people who love a good time," as Zelda wrote after his death, "he kept happiness constantly in mind except toward the end when he grew embittered." [15]

As a part of their struggle for tranquillity they had their parents come for visits. Zelda spent two busy months building a marvelous dollhouse for Scottie; she made a set of charming lampshades decorated with *découpages* of all the houses they had ever lived in and of members of the family and the servants riding on the various animals they had owned; she painted the garden furniture with decorative and ingenious maps of France. They celebrated Christmas with an elaborate tree. Fitzgerald put himself on a drinking schedule, though there were occasions like the one where, having made a friend a cocktail and asserted he was not drinking, he idly poured himself a glass of gin and drank it off and then said with evident surprise: "Did I just drink a glass of gin? — I believe I did." [16]

Being near Princeton he went back there for the first time in several years to find that he "really loved the place." [17] This affection for Princeton led him to think of himself as a football expert again and to attend the games assiduously. This compensatory interest in football endured for the rest of his life. He liked to advise the Princeton authorities, and he once called Asa Bushnell at four in the morning to pass along an idea for a two-platoon system (one was to be a "pony" team, which shows the source of this idea in Fitzgerald's own day-dream of football heroism). Bushnell passed this Old Grad problem along to Crisler, who wrote Fitzgerald: ". . . your new Princeton System has . . . many virtues. I will use it on one condition. Namely, that you will . . . take full credit for its success and full blame for its failure, if any." Fitzgerald replied: "I guess we'd better hold the . . . System in reserve." [18] His revived interest in Princeton also led him to accept when Cottage Club asked him to come to the club and make a speech on a program of lectures by distinguished alumni of the club. When he got up to speak he found himself, in spite of having taken a fair number of relaxing drinks, badly frightened by a Princeton audience. He stumbled through a few sentences and then, muttering to himself in an audible whisper, "God, I'm a rotten speaker!" gave up altogether and sat down. [19]

He also got in a good deal of work on his book during this summer of 1927, the first for some time. He was full of optimism and talked confidently of how what he was now calling *The World's Fair* would "before so very long begin to appear in Liberty." [20] The work, however, petered out during the fall, and when Perkins inquired in February — he thought he needed to know about spring publication — Fitzgerald wrote in despair: "Novel not yet finished. Christ I wish it were!" [21] Work came to a complete stop when they decided to spend the summer of 1928 abroad.

This decision seems to have been reached because of a restlessness which no squareness of rooms or sweep of columns could subdue. But their immediate reason for going was Zelda's dancing. She had determined suddenly to become a ballet dancer and, almost from one day to the next, had taken to dancing with an intensity which, as one of their friends said, was like the dancing madness of the middle ages. [22] She began to go to Philadelphia two or three times a week to study with Catherine Littlefield and would come home to practice several hours a day in the living room, which was cleared for the purpose. There was something peculiar about this extreme concentration on dancing and Fitzgerald afterwards said that looking back he thought he could trace evidences of her insanity at least as early as 1927, when she had begun to show a number of disturbing signs, such as going through long periods of unbroken silence. Her effort to make a career for herself was touching, too, for as Alabama Knight had said to her child, "I believe I could be a whole world to myself if I didn't like living in Daddy's better";[23] there was getting to be less and less of his world for her to live in, and this as well as her ambition must have carried her along, "lost and driven now," as she said, "like the rest." [24]

From the time she was a girl — when a Montgomery paper said with Southern gallantry that "she might dance like Pavlova if her nimble feet were not so busy keeping up with the pace a string of young but ardent admirers set for her" — she had wanted to be a dancer.[25] This ambition had dissipated itself, like so much else in their lives, in parties. Now, when it was too late — good dancers start training as children and Zelda was approaching twenty-eight — she was concentrating feverishly on dancing. She was still very beautiful. "Her once fair hair [which] had darkened" by this time to a "thick, dark, gold" framed a face which was, Sara Murphy said, "rather like a young Indian's face, except for the smouldering eyes. At night, I remember, if she was excited, they turned black — & impenetrable — but always full of impatience — at *something* —, the world I think." [26] But the only effect of this beauty on her career as a dancer was to get her offers from the Folies Bergère.

They arrived in Paris in a haze of alcohol, without reservations or plans. A friend who met them finally got them a place to stay — it was not easy in Paris the summer of 1928. Scottie, who was excited by Paris, kept pointing out the sights as they drove through the city but neither of them was capable of responding. The summer was like that. Twice Fitzgerald wound up in jail. Zelda was starting to take lessons with Egarova and they quarreled over her dancing, for there was some drive in Fitzgerald to destroy her concentration. He appeared unable to endure Zelda's successful — if neurotic — display of will when he felt that self-indulgence and dissipation were ruining him. "It is the loose-ends," as Zelda said long after, "with which men hang themselves." [27]

Just before they returned to America they had a bitter quarrel during which unbelievable charges were made by both of them. This quarrel led to a break between them which was never really repaired. Late in September, "in a blaze," as Fitzgerald said, "of work & liquor" (he was trying to finish up "The Captured Shadow" for the *Post*) they came home to Ellerslie. "Thirty two years old," Fitzgerald wrote in his Ledger, "and sore as hell about it." [28] They were broke, though Fitzgerald's income — including a $6000 advance on his novel — had been $29,737 in 1927 and was running close to that in 1928. [29]

Back at Ellerslie Fitzgerald tried to settle down to his book. In November he wrote Perkins that he was going to send him two chapters a month of the final version until, by February, he would have sent it all. "I think this will help me get it straight in my own mind," he said, " — I've been alone with it too long." The November chapters were sent, and probably the December ones; but that was all. Four years later he asked Perkins to return "that discarded beginning that I gave you. . . ." [30]

He had brought back from France a kind of handyman — butler, chauffeur, and valet — named Philippe. Philippe had been a professional boxer, and he and Fitzgerald used to go out on the town together; friends spent a good deal of time late at night getting them home from the police station. As his frustration and bitterness increased, Fitzgerald became more difficult and his tendency to strike out at other people when he had been drinking grew on him. Gradually he became aware that an important change in his understanding of things — and perhaps in the things themselves — was taking place.

By this time contemporaries of mine had begun to dissappear into the dark maw of violence. A classmate killed his wife and himself on Long Island, another tumbled "accidentally" from a skyscraper in Philadelphia, another purposefully from a skyscraper in New York. One was killed in a speak-easy in Chicago; another was beaten to death in a speak-easy in New York and crawled home to the Princeton Club to die; still another had his skull crushed by a maniac's ax in an insane asylum where he was confined. These are not catastrophes that I went out of my way to look for — these were my friends; moreover, these things happened not during the depression but during the boom.[31]

In the spring of 1929 their two-year lease on Ellerslie ended and, writing the whole thing off as a bad investment, they set off for Europe once more. Fitzgerald explained to Perkins that he could not work in Delaware but that, once abroad, he would finish the novel by October.[32] They had observed, the previous summer, the flood of "fantastic neanderthals who believed something, something vague, that you remembered from a very cheap novel" who were pouring into Paris, so they took an Italian boat to Genoa, heading for the Riviera. It was a rough trip, during which they both got involved in idle flirtations over which they quarreled.[33] They were soon back in Paris, where Zelda continued to work hard on her dancing — "dancing & sweating," as Fitzgerald noted with rising irritation. Their lives were drawing further and further apart as Zelda gave all of her waking hours to her dancing; but, like the heroine of *Save Me the Waltz*, she kept remembering that if "the careless happy passages of their first married life could [not] be repeated — or relished if they were, drained as they had been of the experiences they held — still, the highest points of concrete enjoyment that [she] visualized when she thought of happiness, lay in the memories they held." [34]

Fitzgerald became more difficult when he was drinking as he became more unhappy over his inability not to do so, and it only made matters worse for him that, when he was sober, he saw clearly what was happening and could describe it to others perfectly objectively.

My latest tendency is to collapse about 11:00 and, with tears flowing from my eyes or the gin rising to their level and leaking over, tell interested friends or acquaintances that I haven't a friend in the world and likewise care for nobody, generally including Zelda, and often implying current company — after which the current company tend to become less current and I wake up in strange [places] . . . when drunk I make them all pay and pay and pay.

It was in fact even worse for him than that suggests, since even when he was drunk, if he thought about it, he understood what he was doing, as when he wrote John Bishop about "the sensuality that is your bête noire to such an extent that you can no longer see it black, like me in my drunkenness" — and then added in a P.S., "Excuse Christ-like tone of letter. Began tippling at page 2 and am now positively holy (like Dostoevsky's non-stinking monk)." [35] But this knowledge only made his predicament more painful to him. He fancied that people were beginning to avoid him and that there was even in Hemingway's attitude a certain coldness.[36] He took to brooding darkly over compliments until he had persuaded himself they were ironic and insulting. On the strength of a remark of Gertrude Stein's comparing "his flame" with Hemingway's, he wrote Hemingway a belligerent letter about his air of superiority. Hemingway replied with painstaking care. But late in the year there was more trouble.

During the spring and summer of 1929 Hemingway had been boxing regularly with Morley Callaghan, and once Fitzgerald persuaded them to let him come along and keep time for them. During the second round that day, Hemingway for some reason began to fight with considerable seriousness and Callaghan, much the lighter man, had to hit faster and harder to keep clear of Hemingway's now weightier punches. As the fighting became fiercer, Fitzgerald was so fascinated that he forgot to keep track of the time, and it was only when Callaghan stepped inside one of Hemingway's wild swings, caught him squarely on the jaw, and dropped him that Fitzgerald came to. Instead of concealing his error, he said in his characteristically impulsive way, "Oh, my God! I let the round go four minutes." Hemingway propped himself on his elbow and looked at Fitzgerald. "Christ!" he said, and then, after a pause, "All right, Scott. If you want to see me getting the shit knocked out of me, just say so. Only don't say you made a mistake." Fitzgerald was appalled by this; his face ashen, he drew Callaghan aside and said, "He thinks I did it on purpose. Why would I do it on purpose?" Then everyone began making an effort to put a good face on things and, as Callaghan concludes, "we all behaved splendidly. We struck up a graceful camaraderie. . . . And no one watching us sitting at the bar [later] could have imagined that Scott's pride had been shattered." [37]

Sometime later a lively but inaccurate account of this episode was picked up by a gossip columnist for the Denver *Post*. According to this account, Hemingway had spoken slightingly of a fight story of Callaghan's, saying Callaghan knew nothing about boxing (he had), and Callaghan had challenged him to fight and knocked him out. This story was repeated by Isabel Paterson in the *Herald Tribune*. Hemingway took the whole affair with the utmost seriousness; "something within him drove him to want to be expert at every occupation he touched," as Callaghan observed, and his vanity was particularly tender when his athletic prowess was in question. He persuaded Fitzgerald, against Fitzgerald's better judgment, to cable Callaghan (collect): HAVE SEEN STORY IN HERALD TRIBUNE. ERNEST AND I AWAIT YOUR CORRECTION. Callaghan had in fact already sent the *Herald Tribune* a good-humored correction:

Nor did I ever challenge Hemingway. Eight or nine times we went boxing last summer trying to work up a sweat and an increased eagerness for an extra glass of beer afterwards. We never had an audience. Nor did I ever knock out Hemingway. Once we had a timekeeper. If there was any kind of remarkable performance that afternoon the timekeeper deserves the applause. . . . I do wish you'd correct that story or I'll never be able to go to New York again for fear of being knocked out.

Fitzgerald's cable, however, made him really angry. He was in no way responsible for the story; what was Fitzgerald doing cabling him as if he had spread it, had now been caught out, and owed everyone an apology? He spoke so bitterly about the whole affair that word of his feelings eventually got back to Hemingway and he wrote to say he had made Fitzgerald send the cable.[38]

But the tensions that underlay the real affection Fitzgerald and Hemingway felt for one another could not be concealed when Fitzgerald was drinking. One night not long after this episode he began to reiterate monotonously that he was going to quarrel with Hemingway, that he felt a need to smash him. Eventually Hemingway was goaded into making a resentful reference to Fitzgerald's timekeeping, and Fitzgerald then asserted that Hemingway had accused him of dishonorable conduct. Again a painstaking letter of explanation from Hemingway smoothed things over after a fashion. Fitzgerald was probably right in his feeling that Hemingway, in a different way, was as complicated and emotionally disturbed a man as he was. But Hemingway, with his disciplined concealment of every attitude that did not belong to his carefully designed public self, had far more self-control.

But even such self-control as Fitzgerald had was breaking down badly, and in his suffering he struck out, blindly and unreasonably, at the people and things that mattered most to him. He was, as he knew, striking at himself. He was most sensitive about his failure to finish his book and once said to a newly introduced young writer who paid him a conventional compliment on *This Side of Paradise*: "You mention that book again and I'll slug you." [39]

They went as usual that summer to the Riviera and took a villa at Cannes, but everything at the Cap d'Antibes seemed changed for the worse. Zelda had one or two small engagements at Nice and Cannes and was working harder than ever at her dancing, and that led to more "rows and indifference" between them. In June Fitzgerald had a new idea for his novel and told Perkins that he was "working night and day" on it. [40] His new plan was to drop the matricide story he had been working on for such a long time and to write a story much like that of *Tender Is the Night*. The new novel was to be called *The Drunkard's Holiday*. This new idea involved him in a fresh effort to analyze Gerald Murphy, who, combined with Fitzgerald, was to be the hero of the new book. This analysis got to be too much for the Murphys, for when Fitzgerald was drinking he did not hesitate to give them the benefit of it. "You can't," Sara Murphy wrote him, "expect anyone to like or stand a *Continual* feeling of analysis & sub-analysis, & criticism — on the whole unfriendly — such as we have felt for quite awhile. It is definitely in the air, — & quite unpleasant. . . . If Gerald was 'rude' in getting up & leaving a party that had gotten *quite bad*, — then he was rude to the Hemingways and MacLeishes too. No, it is hardly likely that you would stick at a thing like *manners* — it is more probably some theory you have — (it *may* be something to do with the book). . . ." [41] However hard on the Murphys this new conception of his subject was, it did get him started again on his book; during most of September he was hard at work and much encouraged.

In October they started north for Paris, spending the night of the stock market crash at the Beau Rivage in St. Raphaël, "in the room Ring Lardner had occupied another year [when he visited them there in 1924]."

> We got out as soon as we could because we had been there so many times before — it is sadder to find the past again and find it inadequate to the present than it is to have it elude you and remain forever a harmonious conception of memory. [42]

Back in Paris they found an apartment at 10 rue Pergolèse and life went on much as it had the previous winter. It was a heart-breaking time for Zelda; she had been encouraged about her dancing that summer and she had reached the time when she ought to have been getting some professional offers. It was the moment of success or failure. All winter she kept hoping the people who came to the studio were emissaries of Diaghilev ready to offer her at least bit parts in one of his ballets; and each time they turned out to be people from the Folies Bergère "who thought they might make her into an American shimmy dancer." [43] In February, "because it was a trying winter and to forget bad times," they took a sight-seeing trip to Algiers.

Fitzgerald used this trip as part of the background for a story he wrote five months later and called "One Trip Abroad." [44] The story summarized their lives up to the time of Zelda's breakdown. It deals with two attractive young Americans, Nicole and Nelson Kelly, who have inherited money and come to Europe to live the good life, he to paint and she to sing. They start going about on the Riviera with a group of people one character describes as a "crowd of drunks . . . [who have] shifted down through Europe like nails in a sack of wheat, till they stick out of it a little into the Mediterranean Sea," people who are "somewhat worn away inside by fifteen years of a particular set in Paris." The Kellys break away from this set to join another which is intellectually superior but fundamentally quite as frivolous. As they gradually harden Nelson takes to drink. Eventually they both break down physically and go to Switzerland, "a country where very few things begin, but many things end," to recuperate. There they try to take stock of themselves and, "worn away inside," to regain their old self-contained world. But they find themselves without peace, often wanting company desperately; and Nelson sees his face in a bar mirror "weak and self-indulgent . . . the kind of face that needs half a dozen drinks really to open the eyes and stiffen the mouth up to normal."

Nicole expresses their bewilderment:

> It's just that we don't understand what's the matter. Why did we lose peace and love and health, one after the other? If we knew, if there was anybody to tell us, I believe we could try. I'd try so hard.

They had set out to fulfill their vision of the good life, a life essentially passive and dependent on outside stimuli, a confused and pathetic vision of beautiful, "civilized" places, "interesting," well-to-do people, and some pleasant way of being serious artists. They ended in emotional bankruptcy. This is Fitzgerald's personal and compassionate version of the story D. H. Lawrence told angrily in "Things" and Hemingway satirically in "Mr. and Mrs. Elliot." It is the spoiled priest's preliminary evaluation of their lives during the decade since the success of *This Side of Paradise*, an evaluation Fitzgerald was to work out carefully during the next three years in the story of Nicole and Dick Diver.

When they got back from their trip, Zelda, fighting off the knowledge of failure, went back to dancing harder than ever. She appeared frighteningly tensed up. Early in April, at a large luncheon at their apartment in the rue Pergolèse, she became so nervous for fear she would be late for her dancing lesson that an old friend offered, in the middle of luncheon, to take her to it. In the cab she was badly overwrought, shook uncontrollably, and tried to change into her ballet costume as they drove along. When they got into a traffic jam, she leapt out and started running. This episode was so disturbing that Zelda was persuaded to stop her lessons for a rest. But she soon returned to them, and, on April 23, she broke down completely.

At first in her illness she would not see Fitzgerald at all, carrying over into her hallucinations many of the fantastic suspicions which had been a growing part of their quarrels from as far back as the fall of 1928. This suspicion of him gradually faded out. But her general condition did not improve; there were long periods of madness interspersed with periods of relative lucidity throughout the summer. During the calmer times she painted a little and wrote a great deal, producing a libretto for a ballet and three short stories. There is something at once pathetic and frightening about the persistence of her will to produce during this period. Fitzgerald realized how important the stories were to her and wrote Perkins a note about them when they were submitted to *Scribner's Magazine*. "I think you'll see," he said, "that apart from the beauty and richness of the writing they have a strange haunting and evocative quality that is absolutely new. I think too that there is a certain unity apparent in them — their actual unity is a fact because each of them is the story of her life when things for a while seemed to have brought

her to the edge of madness and despair." [45] When *Scribner's*
rejected the stories, Fitzgerald tried to get Perkins to make a
book of them and the "series of eight portraits that attracted
so much attention in *College Humor*" during the previous
year.[46] But this scheme failed too.

When Zelda did not improve, Fitzgerald decided to take
her to Switzerland, where, he was told, the finest psychiatric
care in Europe was to be had. They went to Montreux, where
a number of specialists were called in; they agreed on the
diagnosis of schizophrenia. Fitzgerald was told that out of
every four such cases one made a complete recovery, and two
made partial ones. But there followed a summer and fall of
dreadful anxiety; with no let-up except for a single hour in
September, the terrible hallucinations and the violent eczema
which characterized Zelda's case continued through 1930, and
Fitzgerald remembered with special horror "that Christmas in
Switzerland" when Scottie came on from Paris and he tried
to make it gay for her. There is a faint echo of what Zelda
must have gone through in her description of Alabama's
delirium in *Save Me the Waltz*.[47]

Fitzgerald had his moments of respite from the strain of
watching Zelda suffer. He met Thomas Wolfe in Lausanne,
where he was staying, and liked and admired him; they drank
and talked endlessly together. Fitzgerald was specially charmed
by Wolfe's ability to keep things in an uproar. One night
when he and Wolfe were arguing in the street, Wolfe gesticu-
lated so vehemently that he struck a power line far above
Fitzgerald's head, snapped it, and plunged the whole community into darkness. They had to flee across the border to
escape the police.[48] There was a trip to Munich with Gerald
Murphy and some skiing at Gstaad. When his father died in
January he went home for the funeral at Rockville, Maryland,
and paid a flying visit to the Sayres in Montgomery. Under
other circumstances, his father's death would have disturbed
him as much as he was to feel several years later that it had.

But for the moment, as he wrote his cousin Ceci, "all those days in America seem sort of blurred and dream-like now." [49] His visit to Montgomery was not pleasant, for though Mrs. Sayre stood up for him staunchly, as she always did, Judge Sayre was far from trusting his ability to take proper care of Zelda.

Apart from fortnightly trips to see Scottie, who had been left in Paris with a governess in order that her education might not be interrupted, he stayed close to Zelda in Switzerland most of the time. "[Nervous trouble]," said Zelda with that simple courage which characterized her attitude toward her illness, "is worse always on the people who care than on the person who's ill." [50] It was Fitzgerald's nature to feel deeply the suffering of the person he most loved; something of what he felt during these months must have gone into his description of Doctor Diver's anonymous patient who, suffering from "nervous eczema" like a person "imprisoned in the Iron Maiden," was yet "coherent, even brilliant, within the limits of her special hallucinations." [51] Moreover, despite the doctors' assurances that Zelda's trouble went back a long way and that nothing he could have done would have prevented it, Fitzgerald had a deep feeling of guilt about it. He knew how much he was to blame for the irregularity of their lives; he knew what he had contributed to that "complete and never entirely renewed break of confidence" which had occurred in Paris in 1928; he knew — however unreasonable Zelda may have been about her dancing — how much harder he had made it for her. When the doctors told him that he "must not drink anything, not even wine, for a year, because drinking in the past was one of the things that haunted [Zelda] in her delirium," they were the voice of his own conscience. [52]

He put all his feelings of guilt and pity, as well as his determination to make what restitution he could, into Charles Wales in "Babylon Revisited." The situations differ, but Wales' feelings are Fitzgerald's:

. . . back in his room he couldn't sleep. The image of Helen haunted him. Helen whom he had loved so until they had senselessly begun to abuse each other's love, tear it into shreds. On that terrible February night . . . a slow quarrel had gone on for hours. There was a scene at the Florida, and then he attempted to take her home, and then she kissed young Webb at a table; after that there was what she had hysterically said. . . . They were "reconciled," but that was the beginning of the end. . . .[53]

Late in January, 1931, Zelda got well enough to spend whole days out skiing, and Fitzgerald's hopes that she was "almost well — really well" rose. She continued to improve until by spring she was able to travel a little. "Zelda is *so* much better," Fitzgerald wrote Perkins, ". . . she's herself again now, tho' not yet strong." [54] They went to Annecy and Menton, swam and played tennis and danced. "It was like the good gone times," Zelda said, "when we still believed in summer hotels and the philosophies of popular songs. . . . we danced a Wiener waltz, and just simply swep' around." Later, when she knew what a temporary respite it had been, she called this with bitter humor her "vacation from the nut-farm last summer [at] Annecy." [55] Toward the end of the summer they ventured farther, to Munich and Vienna. By September Zelda was well enough to go home, and they motored — "that is, we sat nervously in our six horse-power Renault" — to Paris and sailed for America, where they went to Montgomery with some idea of settling down quietly there. For a month or so they played golf and tennis and house-hunted, and Fitzgerald, as on all such homely occasions, found life dull.

When Metro-Goldwyn-Mayer asked him to do a revision on a script of Katherine Brush's *Red-Headed Woman*, he was glad to go to Hollywood. There he saw friends like Carmel Myers, talked nostalgically with his old rival Dorothy Speare, the author of *Dancers in the Dark,* and, arriving at a party one night at Carmel Myers', went straight upstairs for a bath.[56] His old feeling of excitement about the movies came back to him and he got his beautifully defined feelings about Hollywood — its color and scale, its fantasy, the sadness of the occasional fine mind caught in all this falseness and shoddy — into "Crazy Sunday," the story he wrote when he got back to Montgomery in January.[57]

But he remembered this as a time of failure.

. . . while all was serene on top, with [Zelda] apparently recovered in Montgomery, I was jittery underneath and beginning to drink more than I ought to. . . . I ran afoul of a bastard named ——, since a suicide, and let myself be gyped out of command. I wrote the picture & he changed as I wrote. . . . Result — a bad script. I left with the money . . . but disillusioned and disgusted, vowing never to go back, tho they said it wasn't my fault & asked me to stay. I wanted to get east . . . to see how [Zelda] was. This was later interpreted as "running out on them" & held against me.[58]

While Fitzgerald had been in Hollywood, Judge Sayre had died. At first Zelda seemed to take the shock well, but her father was important to her and his death was bound to affect her gravely. The first sign of trouble was an attack of asthma. Fitzgerald took her to St. Petersburg hoping the climate might help her, but she grew worse, and then, at the end of January, she broke down mentally again. This breakdown was a stunning blow to them. They had fought hard to believe Zelda was really well and their personal relations had recently been much happier. "The nine months before her second breakdown," Fitzgerald said shortly after, "were the happiest of my life and I think, save for the agonies of her father's death, the happiest of hers." [59] By this time he had read enough about schizophrenia to know that each attack made a final recovery less likely. He was a long way from giving up, but he was frightened and depressed.

He took Zelda to Baltimore for treatment and returned to Montgomery to await word from the doctors. A little more than a month later — it was written in six weeks, mostly while she was in the hospital — Zelda sent Perkins the manuscript of her novel, *Save Me the Waltz* ("we danced a Wiener waltz, and just simply swep' around"). Like everything else she wrote, it was a brilliant piece of amateur work written at remarkable and disturbing speed. As Fitzgerald said years later, "She was a great original in her way, with perhaps a more intense flame at its highest than I ever had, but she tried and is still trying to solve all ethical and moral problems on her own, without benefit of the thousands dead." [60] A suspicion of Scott — the result of that fierce desire to succeed on her own and outdo him which haunted their devotion — made her send the book directly to Perkins. Its central section was an attack on Fitzgerald. Perkins and Fitzgerald worked together to get her to make the revision of this section which was published.

Fitzgerald's main concern was for the effect of the book on Zelda's mental state. "If she has a success coming," he wrote Perkins, "she must associate it with work done in a workmanlike manner for its own sake, and part of it done fatigued and uninspired, and part of it done when even to remember the original inspiration and impetus is a psychological trick. She must not try to follow the pattern of my trail which is of course blazed distinctly on her mind." [61]

Zelda did not improve, and that spring Fitzgerald moved himself and Scottie from Montgomery to Baltimore and began to house-hunt. He found before long what was to be their home for the next year and a half, and for all the unhappiness they knew there, it was a lucky find. A large rambling brown Victorian house called La Paix on the Bayard Turnbulls' estate at Rodgers Forge, it had been built by Mr.

Turnbull's father as a summer home in the nineteenth century. The Turnbulls themselves, whom Fitzgerald came to admire greatly, lived within sight in a house they had recently built for themselves. Here he and Scottie settled down as near Zelda as possible. Gradually she improved enough to be at La Paix more and more of the time. In June Fitzgerald was able to take her to Virginia Beach, and they returned to settle at La Paix. "We have a soft shady place here," Zelda wrote Perkins, "that's like a paintless playhouse abandoned when the family grew up. It's surrounded by apologetic trees and warning meadows and creaking insects and is gutted of its aura by many comfortable bedrooms." [62]

CHAPTER XII

ALL THIS DISAPPOINTMENT and suffering had their effect on Fitzgerald. His drinking increased, and it made him subject to fits of nervous temper and depression and less capable of providing the regular life Zelda needed. It also affected his work, for in spite of his attempts to persuade himself then, and later, that he could work only with the help of gin, he was as inefficient as most people when he had been drinking. A part of his mind understood what he was doing. "Just when somebody's taken him up," he wrote in his Notebooks, "and is making a big fuss over him he pours the soup down his hostess' back, kisses the serving maid and passes out in the dog kennel. But he's done it too often. He's run through about everybody, until there's no one left." [1]

Yet in spite of these handicaps, he managed to make a home and a life for the three of them. He was fighting to save Zelda and to save himself, for the two things seemed to him inextricable. His conception of what he was trying to do is reflected in Dick Diver's struggle, especially when Dick says: "Nicole and I have to go on together. In a way that's more important than just wanting to go on." [2] Over and above his love for Zelda and his desire to save her, he had invested too much of his emotional capital in the relation he and Zelda had built together to be anything but an emotional bankrupt if that relation failed. "I should," said one of the people who knew him best at this time, "have felt he was much more to blame [about Zelda] if he had grown a little bored by, or indifferent to, her tragedy . . . than if he had grappled with it daily, and failed, as he did. No one could watch that struggle and not be convinced of the reality of his concern and suffering. He was, of course, a man in conflict with two terrible demons,— insanity and drink . . . but he appeared to be giving blow for blow; there was hope in him and flashes of confidence." [3]

It was a dogged fight, with many lost battles, a last stand of the Fitzgerald who had believed that "life is something you dominated if you were any good." In the end he lost both his objectives, and he knew for all his "flashes of confidence" how desperate the battle was. To a friend who wanted to draw Zelda back into the old life he wrote:

> . . . [you] insist on a world which we will willingly let die, in which Zelda can't live, which damn near ruined us both, which neither you nor any of our more gifted friends are yet sure of surviving; you insisted on its value, as if you were in some way holding a battle front and challenged us to join you. If you could have seen Zelda, as the most typical end-product of that battle during any day from the spring of '31 to the spring of '32 you would have felt about as much enthusiasm for the battle as a doctor at the end of a day in a dressing station behind a blood[y] battle. . . . We have a good way of living, basically, for us; we got through a lot and have some way to go; our united front is less a romance than a categorical imperative and when you criticize it in terms of a bum world . . . [it] seems to negate on purpose both past effort and future hope. . . . [4]

It was a strange life for the fabulous Fitzgeralds to have arrived at, a life so quiet, at least on the surface, that Fitzgerald was able to say in the fall of 1933 that they had "dined out exactly four times in two years." [5] Because of his awareness of its irony, he was always fond of remembering an occasion about this time when "a young man phoned from a city far off, then from a city near by, then from downtown informing me that he was coming to call, though he had never seen me. He arrived eventually with a great ripping up of garden borders, a four ply rip in a new lawn, a watch pointing accurately and unforgivably at three a.m. But he was prepared to disarm me with the force of his compliment, the intensity of the impulse that had brought him to my door. 'Here I am at last,' he said teetering triumphantly. 'I had to see you. I feel I owe you more than I can say. I feel that you formed my life.'" [6]

There were many good times. Afterwards Fitzgerald treasured the memory of sitting "at La Paix watching thru my iron grill [the bow window of his study was leaded] one of your tribe moving about the garden, & wondering if Zelda had yet thrown the tennis raquet at Mr. Crossby [the tennis coach]." [7] Sometimes he escaped from his prison to join the tennis game with Scottie and Zelda and the Turnbull children. "He played a sensational if somewhat unsteady game," Andrew Turnbull remembered. "He was best at the net where he could hit the ball hardest and where it had the shortest distance to go. His cry was 'I'll perforate you, Andrew!' which he never did, but his tone of voice always gave you the idea that he was going to do so."

He loved the children and was always successful with them because he met them quite seriously on their own grounds. He spent hours teaching them to dive, to shoot (with a .22 at Scottie's dolls); he made up elaborate historical games to be played with the beautiful Greek and Roman lead soldiers they had bought Scottie in France and awarded prizes for the best Roman city built for them on the dining-room table; he wrote a children's play which was performed at the Turnbulls' at Christmas; he helped the children build an igloo when there was a rare heavy snow. He did card tricks for them —

"though his hands were white and quivering, he did marvels with the cards." He talked, especially to Andrew, about football ("quantities of this," Andrew remembered), about courage and how to handle men and how to treat girls.

When T. S. Eliot came to Hopkins in the fall to give the Turnbull lectures, Fitzgerald dined with him at the Turnbulls' house on the hill and, in a flash of impudent courage, read a section of *The Waste Land* aloud to Eliot to show how it should be done. He was also full of curiosity about the Communists who were beginning to appear on all sides. He spoke out of his old twenties feeling about war to a liberal group at Hopkins and for a while the house was full of CPers. "The community Communist," Zelda wrote Perkins, "comes and tells us about a kind of Luna Park Eutopia. . . . I have taken, somewhat eccentricly at my age, to horseback riding which I do as non-committally as possible so as not to annoy the horse. Also very apologetically since we've had so much communism lately that I'm not sure it's not the horse who should be riding me." [8] After a good deal of excitement — and one man who camped with them for weeks and weeks — Fitzgerald gave it up. "To bring on the revolution," he noted, "it may be necessary to work inside the communist party." [9] His considered feelings about Marxism — at once naïve and penetrating — appear in the Brimmer episode in *The Last Tycoon*.

He also got down at last to steady work on his novel. The evidence suggests that the version of the novel he had projected about 1929 and had got some work done on was now drastically revised again. The minute he got back from Hollywood in January, 1932, he began to replan it, and the undated "Sketch" for *Tender Is the Night* was probably made at this time.* "I am exactly six thousand dollars ahead," he wrote Perkins in January. "I am replanning [my novel] to include what's good in what I have, adding 41,000 new words and

* See Appendix B.

publishing. Don't tell Ernest or anyone — let them think what they want." That supercilious Hemingway ghost who spent all his time thinking Fitzgerald would never write seriously again was a projection of his own conscience with which he haunted himself; it was one of his sharpest spurs. "Am going on the water wagon from the first of February to the first of April," he wrote Perkins a little later, "but don't tell Ernest because he has long convinced himself that I am an incurable alcoholic. . . . I am *his* alcoholic just like Ring is mine and I do not want to disillusion him, tho' even Post stories must be done in a state of sobriety." [10] Like this one, many of Fitzgerald's fantasies began to get nearer the surface at this time and to threaten to intrude on his daily life. In a moment of anger at Zelda in June he wrote his lawyer to ask about the legal requirements for divorce and in August made — as if from his deathbed — a witnessed statement that "I would like my novel in its unfinished form to be sent to John Peale Bishop . . . who I appoint as my literary executor in case of misfortune. . . ."

But his book was going so well that in momentary enthusiasm he wired Perkins: THINK NOVEL CAN SAFELY BE PLACED ON YOUR LIST FOR SPRING.[11] Zelda's second breakdown ended this hope, but of that August at La Paix he noted later that "the Novel [is] plotted and planned, never more to be permanently interrupted." [12] In October Zelda was writing that "Scott's novel is nearing completion. He's been working like a streak," and with one of his old outbursts of fun Fitzgerald wrote Perkins: "I now figure this [first installment for serialization in *Scribner's Magazine*] can be achieved by about the 25th of October. I will appear in person carrying the manuscript and wearing a spiked helmet. . . . *Please do not have a brass band as I do not care for music*." [13]

But all this time the deadly battle went on. All night long, night after night, the light burned behind the leaded bow window of his study, where Fitzgerald, if he was not working, was fighting his demons and often being defeated; "alone," as he said, "in the privacy of my faded blue room with my sick cat, the bare February branches waving at the window, an ironic paper weight that says Business is Good, a New England conscience — developed in Minnesota. . . ." [14] There were, said one of his closest friends, three things he loved at this time; they were his work, Zelda and Scottie, drink — in that order. The decline in his morale had increased his hypochondria, so that when he caught intestinal flu and was in the hospital for two weeks in September, he made much of it. Once again he began to suffer from insomnia. Whether he imagined it was worse than it was, as many people thought, or not, he suffered.

. . . so I get up and walk — he wrote in an essay on insomnia — I walk from my bedroom through the hall to my study, and then back again, and if it's summer out to my back porch. There is a mist over Baltimore; I cannot count a single steeple. . . . I could have acted thus, refrained from this, been bold where I was timid, cautious where I was rash.

I need not have hurt her like that.

Nor said this to him.

Nor broken myself trying to break what was unbreakable.

. . . what if all [after death] was an eternal quivering on the edge of an abyss, with everything base and vicious in oneself urging one forward and the baseness and viciousness of the world just ahead. No choice, no road, no hope — only the endless repetition of the sordid and the semi-tragic. . . . I am a ghost now as the clock strikes four. [15]

No wonder that, about this time, writing to Edmund Wilson, he headed one of his letters "La Paix (My God!)."

He continued to work hard on his book through December, though he noted that "drinking increased things go not so well." [16] In February he made a disastrous trip to New York. "I came to New York to get drunk," he wrote Wilson when he got back, ". . . and I shouldn't have looked up you and Ernest in such a humor of impotent desperation. I assume full responsibility for all unpleasantness — with Ernest I seem to have reached a state where when we drink together I half bait, half truckle to him. . . ." ("I talk with the authority of failure," as he put it elsewhere, " — Ernest with the authority of success. We could never sit across the table again.")[17]

Throughout the spring and early summer he was in and out of Hopkins with various ailments. He lost his driver's license. But he was still fighting. During the spring the Vagabond Players put on a piece of Zelda's called "Scandalabra" and Fitzgerald helped rewrite it, and when a friend did what he called "A Revusical" for the same company, Fitzgerald wrote a lyric for it. He was still working steadily on his book.

Besides writing Zelda was now painting, often in a disturbing vein; there were many crucifixions with faces hauntingly like her own and ballet dancers with enormous, swollen limbs.[18] She was not improving. "All through the year and a half that we lived in the country . . ." Fitzgerald wrote later, "there would be episodes of great gravity that seemed to have no 'build-up,' outbursts of temper, violence, rashness, etc. that could neither be foreseen or forestalled." [19] Sometime during this summer she and Fitzgerald sat down, in the presence of a psychiatrist and a secretary, to thrash out their difficulties. The strongest impression the psychiatrist retained from this discussion was of the intimacy of their two natures. At one point, Fitzgerald, trying to convince Zelda that she was "just an old schizophrenic," instanced an odd act of hers when she had been out riding. She denied the oddity hotly and Fitzgerald said, "Maybe it was a schizophrenic horse," and Zelda suddenly roared with laughter, saying, "O Scott, that's really good; that's priceless." Fitzgerald laughed, and everybody was for a moment good-humored. They were so close that they moved together from anger to amusement, without pride, as one does in the privacy of his own mind.

But because they were so intimate, their quarrels were destructive. "Family quarrels are bitter things," said Fitzgerald. ". . . they're not like aches or wounds; they're more like splits in the skin that won't heal because there's not enough material." [20] Under the strain of trying to carry through his program of building up Zelda's ego by encouraging her writing and painting, Fitzgerald often grew angry at the sacrifice of his own work it entailed. ". . . my writing was more important than hers by a large margin," he wrote at one of these times, "because of the years of preparation for it, and the professional experience, and because my writing kept the mare going. . . ." [21] Perhaps this assertion was partly justified; it is remarkable how often people felt, against their better judgments, that Zelda's view of things was more trustworthy than Scott's and let themselves be persuaded to accept it. What the doctor Fitzgerald was writing did understand was the way Fitzgerald often sacrificed what meant a great deal to Zelda, not to the legitimate demands of his work, but to his drinking and his nervous irritability. At such times, too, he probably hurt Zelda by allowing her to see his real opinion of her work, an opinion which was influenced by the competitive feeling which had always been a part of their relation. Sometime in 1934 he made a note for a story which runs:

Andrew Fulton, a facile character who can do anything is married to a girl who can't express herself. She has a growing jealousy of his talents. The night of her musical show for the Junior League [this is Zelda's *Scandalabra*] comes and is a great failure. He takes hold and saves the pieces and can't understand why she hates him for it. She has interested a dealer secretly in her pictures . . . and plans to make [an] independent living. But the dealer has only been sold on one specimen. When he sees the rest he shakes his head. Andrew in a few minutes turned out something in putty and the dealer perks up and says "That's what we want." She is furious.[22]

Nonetheless, it was basically true that their "united front [was] less a romance than a categorical imperative" — for them both. When their session with the psychiatrist was finished the psychiatrist asked the secretary, "Now who do you think ought to be in a sanitarium?" "All three of you," she said.[23]

Fitzgerald's mental state contributed to making Zelda's recovery more difficult. But much of his trouble in dealing with her came from his refusal to admit he could not reason with her; to do so would be to admit that part of himself was gone for good. When she went into her spells of silence and locked herself in the room for whole days at a time, he would slip notes under her door begging her to consider what a bad impression such conduct would make on the doctors. At bottom Zelda's trouble was something that was happening to them both.

In June Zelda accidentally set La Paix on fire by trying to burn something in a long-disused fireplace. The chimney caught and before the fire was under control the third floor had been burned out. Fitzgerald entered into the excitement of the occasion with gusto, directing the firemen and serving drinks all around when it was over. But it was a turning point for him. He would never have the house repaired because, he said, he could not endure the noise, and the macabre disorder of the place with its burnt-out and blackened upper story was a kind of symbol of the increased disarray of his own life. His dependence on alcohol for the energy to work had increased and he began to have less control over his tendency to get helplessly drunk; on one occasion he took Andrew Turnbull to Princeton for a football game and Andrew had to find his own way back to Baltimore. Fitzgerald suffered more from such episodes than anyone.

He also had sporadic bursts of anxiety about the effect of his drinking on Perkins and others whose confidence he was dependent on. He therefore made pathetically transparent attempts to pass himself off as a man who went on an occasional bust; he would write Perkins that "I was in New York last week on a terrible bust. I was about to call you up when I completely collapsed and laid in bed for twenty-four hours groaning. Without doubt the boy is getting too old for such tricks." [24] Nor did he succeed much better with his trick of bribing waiters to fill his tumbler with gin instead of water when he dined out. The pretense that all this was merely a healthy man's casual dissipation when his hands shook so that he could hardly light a cigarette deceived no one.

About this time a doctor in New York, perhaps hoping to frighten him into facing his situation, told him he would die if he did not stop drinking and put him on an allowance of one gill of gin a day. He gave Fitzgerald a gill measuring glass and Fitzgerald started home with the glass in one pocket and a quart of gin in the other. On the way home he stopped off in Wilmington to see his old friend John Biggs, now a distinguished judge. He was so obviously ill that Judge Biggs took him out to his home in the country. Sitting on the lawn Fitzgerald began to talk, and carefully, gill by gill, finished the quart of gin.[25] As his secretary said, he did not really want to get well.

In spite of illness and alcohol, he got the manuscript of *Doctor Diver's Holiday* to Perkins in October. He distrusted a title with the word *doctor* in it because he thought it might frighten readers off, but he did not think of *Tender Is the Night* until just before the novel began to run in *Scribner's Magazine*, and even then its adoption was delayed because Perkins thought it had no connection with the story. But Perkins was enthusiastic about the book and it was scheduled for serialization in four installments beginning in December.[26] He was pushing Fitzgerald hard for the final revisions, so that Fitzgerald was working very close to the magazine's deadlines. "The third installment," Perkins wrote November 10, 1933, "we shall need by December 14. . . . I hope it will give you a chance to lay off for a day or two." This was not tyranny. Perkins knew — for all Fitzgerald's efforts to deceive him — how easily Fitzgerald could slide from drinking just enough to keep going into a completely unproductive condition. As always, a part of Fitzgerald knew it too, and when the whole nightmare business of revising *Tender Is the Night* was over he wrote Perkins a shrewd clinical note about the effects of alcohol on composition.

It has been increasingly plain to me that the very excellent organization of a long book or the finest perceptions and judgment in time of revision do not go well with liquor. A short story can be written on a bottle, but for a novel you need mental speed that enables you to keep the whole pattern in your head and ruthlessly sacrifice the sideshows as Ernest did in "A Farewell to Arms." If a mind is slowed up ever so little it lives in the individual part of a book rather than in a book as a whole; memory is dulled. I would give anything if I hadn't had to write Part III of "Tender Is the Night" entirely on stimulant. If I had [had] one more crack at it cold sober I believe it might have made a great difference. . . . Ernest commented on sections that were needlessly included and as an artist he is as near as I know for a final reference.[27]

By now serious financial difficulties were beginning to accumulate for him. With his decline in popularity as the proletarian decade got under way and with his concentration on the writing of *Tender Is the Night*, he turned out only nine stories in 1932 and 1933 — six in the first year and three in the second. As the depression became more serious, the prices for his *Post* stories began to fall from the old $4000 to $3500 or $3000 and, occasionally, to $2500. His royalties in these years totaled $50. The result was an income less than half what it had been in 1931, and this includes over $5000 in advances on *Tender Is the Night*. He was even driven to borrowing from his mother, remembering bitterly how he had written her only three years before that "all big men have spent money freely."

Up to now he had met financial crises by a burst of story-writing or a trip to Hollywood, but he had made a failure of his last trip to Hollywood and he did not have the energy for the stories any more. ". . . after a good day's work," he said about this time, "I am so exhausted that I drag out work on a story to two hours when it should be done in one and go to bed so tired and wrought up, toss around sleepless, and am good for nothing next morning. . . . to work up a crea-tive mood there is nothing doing until four o'clock in the afternoon. Part of this is because of ill health. . . . I have drunk too much and that is certainly slowing me up. On the other hand, without drink I do not know whether I could have survived this time." He could still work all night when he got well started, but he paid a big price for it in spells when he could do nothing. Nor could these financial dif-ficulties be met by economies. His secretary, who tried vainly to put them on a budget, found at the month's end that there were always large checks to cash which no one could account for. "Their idea of economy," she remarked, "was to cut the laundress's wages $2.50." From this time until he went to Hollywood in 1937 Fitzgerald continued to fall behind financially.[28]

With most of *Tender Is the Night* off his hands he felt he owed himself a vacation and decided to take Zelda to Bermuda for Christmas. Before they went, they moved from La Paix to a smaller house at 1307 Park Avenue in Baltimore. This move was made partly for financial reasons, partly because Fitzgerald sensed that another period of his life had ended and did not want to stay at La Paix. Before they sailed he had lunch with Wilson in New York and there was a quarrel. Rightly or wrongly Fitzgerald blamed himself for this quarrel, for with the loss of his self-confidence ("Last of real self-confidence," he noted in February), he was inclined to blame himself for all failures in his personal relations and to feel he could not do anything right, just as, in his old self-confident days, he had found it easy to think he could not do anything wrong. He was still "haunted by [the] Wilson quarrel" a month later.[29] Not until March, when he went out of his way to call on Wilson, was he able "to think that our squabble, or whatever it was, is ironed out" and to cease blaming himself for it.[30] The Bermuda trip was a failure; he was down with pleurisy all the time they were there. They got back in time for their first Christmas at 1307 Park Avenue and Fitzgerald went back to work on the last installment of *Tender Is the Night* and on the proofs for the book. This work was interrupted abruptly by Zelda's third breakdown.

Between the after-effects of her previous breakdown and the effort it cost her — and she made a great effort — to keep Fitzgerald going, she had often been near the end of her rope while they were living at La Paix.

We are more alone than ever before while the psychiatres patch up my nervous system — she wrote John Peale Bishop. "This," they say "is the way you really are — or no, wasn't it the other way round?"

Then they present you with a piece of bric-a-brac of their own forging which falls to the pavement on your way out of the clinic and luckily smashes to bits, and the patient is glad to be rid of their award.

Don't *ever* fall into the hands of brain and nerve specialists unless you are feeling very Faustian.

Scott reads Marx — I read the cosmological philosophers. The brightest moments of our day are when we get them mixed up.[31]

Sometimes, when she was less certain than at others of which way round she really was, this tragic wit became frighteningly bitter. One of their friends remembers being at La Paix for dinner when Zelda came downstairs late. She stood for a perceptible moment in the doorway, a beautiful figure in a lovely evening dress. Then she stepped carefully out of her evening slippers, looked at their guest, and said in a sepulchral voice: "John, aren't you sorry you weren't killed in the war?" [32]

In January, as a result of these accumulated pressures, she broke down completely and returned to the sanitarium. Fitzgerald was still trying to help her and whenever he could would take her from the sanitarium for long walks about the Turnbulls' grounds next door. But one warm spring day, as they were sitting under the trees in what Zelda once called a "nice Mozartian hollow disciplined to elegance by imported shrubbery, of the kind which looks very out of place anywhere," Zelda, hearing a train approaching on a near-by branch line, leapt up and started to run toward it to throw herself under it.[33] Fitzgerald caught her just short of the embankment as the train passed. With the increase of such dangerous impulses they tried, on the advice of the doctors, a sanitarium in up-state New York. But Zelda only grew worse there and in May had to be brought back to Baltimore in a catatonic state.

For the next six years, except for brief periods of relative stability, she was confined to various hospitals and gradually, along with his other hopes, Fitzgerald began to give up his belief in her eventual recovery. "I left my capacity for hoping," he said, "on the little roads that led to Zelda's sanitarium." [34] Little by little he evolved an attitude which would protect him against the terrible temptation to believe in her reasonableness and to try to persuade her to be well. "Zelda," he kept telling himself, "is a case, not a person." [35] For the rest of his life, however, he kept having to fight this battle over again, for the psychological wrench involved in writing off the investment of love and happiness and effort they had both made in their relation was more than he could ever quite manage. "Do you remember," he wrote, trying as always to preserve the past, with all its enormous investment of feelings, that he would never know again,

> *Do you remember before keys turned in the locks,*
> *When life was a closeup, and not an occasional letter,*
> *That I hated to swim naked from the rocks*
> *While you liked absolutely nothing better?*
>
> *Do you remember many hotel bureaus that had*
> *Only three drawers? But the only bother*
> *Was that each of us got holy, then got mad*
> *Trying to give the third one to the other. . . .*
>
> *And, though the end was desolate and unkind:*
> *To turn the Calendar at June and find December*
> *On the next leaf; still, stupid-got with grief, I find*
> *These are the only quarrels that I can remember.*[36]

He knew so well that all this would gradually fade if they were separated. "As you probably know," he wrote one of the doctors in August, "I saw my wife yesterday and spent an hour and a half with her. It was much better than any of the nine or ten times that I have seen her since she broke down again last January. She seemed in every way like the girl I used to know. But, perhaps for that reason, it seemed to both of us very sad and she cried in my arms and we felt that the summer slipping by was typical of the way life is slipping by for both of us." [37] Life went on slipping by; they lived in different worlds, until bit by bit the common ground decreased and their letters became more and more sadly impersonal.

But the tragedy, with all its loss and remembrance, was always there for them both, almost too terrible to contemplate steadily. Sometime in 1938 or 1939, after one of their meetings, Zelda wrote:

Dearest and always Dearest Scott:

I am sorry too that there should be nothing to greet you but an empty shell. The thought of the effort you have made over me, the suffering this *nothing* has cost would be unendurable to any save a completely vacuous mechanism. Had I any feelings they would all be bent in gratitude to you and in sorrow that of all my life there should not even be the smallest relic of the love and beauty that we started with to offer you at the end. . . .

Now that there isn't any more happiness and home is gone and there isn't even any past and no emotions but those that were yours where there could be my comfort — it is a shame that we should have met in harshness and coldness where there was once so much tenderness and so many dreams. Your song.

I wish you had a little house with hollyhocks and a sycamore tree and the afternoon sun imbedding itself in a silver tea-pot. Scottie would be running about somewhere in white, in Renoir, and you will be writing books in dozens of volumes. And there will be honey still for tea, though the house should not be in Granchester.

I want you to be happy — if there were any justice you would be happy — maybe you will be anyway.

Oh, Do-Do Do Do —

I love you anyway — even if there isn't any me or any love or even any life —

I love you.

Nor, though he had another life, as Zelda did not, could Fitzgerald ever relinquish the burden of the past. When Zelda showed signs of increased stability in 1936 he wrote a friend that "there is a chance which I go to sleep hoping for, that she may be out into the world again . . . by April or May." [38] And when he came to write *The Last Tycoon* and to think about his feelings for Zelda in order to conceive Stahr's feelings for Minna, he found he had to work out the "case" position all over again. "How strange," he wrote in one of the notes for the book, "to have failed as a social creature — even criminals do not fail that way — they are the law's Loyal Opposition, so to speak. But the insane are always mere guests on earth, eternal strangers carrying around broken decalogues that they cannot read." [39] And in a moment of revulsion at this betrayal of the past, he spoke bitterly of "the voices fainter and fainter — How is Zelda, how is Zelda — tell us — how is Zelda." [40] Though she was ignorant of much of Fitzgerald's life after 1934, Zelda was substantially right when she wrote, a few days after his death, "Scott was courageous and faithful to myself and Scottie and he was so devoted a friend that I am sure that he will be rewarded; and will be well remembered." [41]

Through all this, he was struggling with the proofs of *Tender Is the Night*. Sick — he was more and more in the hospital now for two or three days at a stretch getting himself straightened out — and tired as he was, they seemed to him endless. But he finally fought his way through them and *Tender Is the Night* was published on April 12, 1934.

CHAPTER XIII

FITZGERALD awaited the publication of *Tender Is the Night* with all his customary intensity of expectation. Now he was worrying, not simply over sales and money, but over his morale, his ability to go on as a writer: "my Testament of Faith," he called *Tender Is the Night*. To the end of his life he clung stubbornly to the conviction that *Tender Is the Night* was his best book, a judgment that a good many critics have since come around to.

Considering how much in the way of a renewed belief in himself depended for Fitzgerald on the success of *Tender Is the Night*, he had remarkably bad luck with its reception. The reviewers, with one ear cocked for the dialectic and the other for further evidences of the literary gossip about Fitzgerald's disintegration, were mostly superficial and unfriendly. They judged the book "a rather irritating type of *chic*"; they said it had a "clever and brilliant surface but . . . [was] not . . . wise and mature"; they thought that "Fitzgerald's contemporary, Stephen Vincent Benét in 'James Shore's Daughter' . . . is more happy in maintaining the level of his achievement." [1]

Moreover the book struck Hemingway as an indication of how Fitzgerald was going wrong as a writer, and he tried to draw the moral for Fitzgerald in a strong letter ("Don't you know," says Dick Diver, "you can't do anything about people?"). [2] He was disturbed by the mixture of fact and invention about the Murphys; the importation into the character of Dick Diver, who had Gerald Murphy's exterior, of Fitzgerald's feelings about his own decline seemed to him a dangerous self-indulgence:

> Forget your personal tragedy — he wrote. We are all bitched from the start. . . . But when you get the damned hurt use it — don't cheat with it. . . . About this time I wouldn't blame you if you gave me a burst. Jesus its marvellous to tell other people how to write, live, die etc. . . . You see, Bo, you're not a tragic character. Neither am I. All we are is writers and what we should do is write. Of all people on earth you need discipline in your work and instead you marry someone who is jealous of your work, wants to compete with you and ruins you. It's not as simple as that and I thought Zelda was crazy the first time I met her and you complicated it even more by being in love with her and, of course you're a rummy. But you're no more of a rummy than Joyce is and most good writers are. . . . You are twice as good now as you were at the time you think you were so marvellous. . . . All you need to do is write truly and not care about what the fate of it is.[3]

This letter hurt Fitzgerald, but he answered it cheerfully and humbly: ". . . you may be entirely right [about the Murphys] because I suppose you were applying the idea particularly to the handling of the creative faculty in one's mind rather than to the effect upon the stranger reading it." [4] But Fitzgerald was so constituted that he never wrote well except when he identified himself with someone he admired, and so far as the representation of the Murphys (for those who would recognize them) goes, Gerald Murphy himself wrote Fitzgerald later, "I know now that what you said in 'Tender Is the Night' is true. Only the invented part of our life, — the unrealistic part [of *Tender Is the Night*] — had any scheme any beauty." [5]

Hemingway, in his anxiety to help Fitzgerald, did his evaluation of the book less than justice, for a year later he went out of his way to write Perkins: "A strange thing is that in retrospect his Tender is the Night gets better and better." [6] He also began to write Fitzgerald again in their old joking, friendly way about his gloom:

If you really feel blue enough get yourself heavily insured and I'll see you can get killed . . . and I'll write you a fine obituary . . . and we can take your liver out and give it to the Princeton Museum, your heart to the Plaza Hotel, one lung to Max Perkins and the other to George Horace Lorimer . . . and we will get MacLeish to write a Mystic Poem to be read at that Catholic School (Newman?) you went to. Would you like me to write the mystic poem now. Let's see. [7]

It was, however, unfortunate that when Fitzgerald needed encouragement as much as he ever had in his life, both the reviewers and the contemporary writer he admired most spoke harshly of the book. [8]

Not that Tender Is the Night has not its faults or that Fitzgerald did not see at least some of them for himself. He had had his reasons for putting a great deal of material into it: "[Tender Is the Night]," he wrote Bishop, "was shooting at something like Vanity Fair. The dramatic novel has cannons quite different from the philosophical, now called psychological novel." But he knew that, in trying to write the philosophical rather than the dramatic novel, he had made mistakes of selection. [9] He also knew that the frequent shifts in point of view were confusing and that the emphasis put on Rosemary Hoyt's point of view by Book I might easily mislead readers into believing she was the central character. This last difficulty disturbed him so much that he eventually became convinced the story should be arranged in straight chronological order, rather than starting with Rosemary's impression of the Divers, so that the reader would not meet Rosemary and her opinions until Dick and Nicole were firmly established in his mind. As early as 1936, when the Modern Library contemplated re-issuing the book, he had considered this rearrangement, and among his books when he died was a revised copy of *Tender Is the Night* inscribed: "This is the *final version* of the book as I would like it," in which he has carried it out.[10]

But this change clears up the confusion caused by the book's starting with Rosemary by sacrificing suspense, by telling us too soon what lies beneath the brilliant surface life Dick more and more desperately contrives.[11] Moreover, if the shifts in point of view are sometimes confusing, they are also sometimes very effective, as when Fitzgerald bridges the gap in time and character between the Nicole who marries Dick in September, 1917, and the Nicole of six years later whom Rosemary sees on the beach at the beginning of the novel, by suddenly shifting to Nicole's first-person summary.[12] The book needs more of this kind of thing than it has. The failure to impress on the reader the passage of time and the change of character in the last part is one of the worst consequences of Fitzgerald's living "in the individual part of the book rather than in . . . the whole" while he was writing it.[13]

He was also aware that he had failed to make Dick's character clear. "I did not manage, I think in retrospect, to give Dick the cohesion I aimed at. . . . I wonder what the hell the first actor who played Hamlet thought of the part? I can hear him say, 'The guy's a nut, isn't he?' (We can always find great consolation in Shakespeare.)"[14]

But if *Tender Is the Night* fails to make its central character completely coherent, and if its structure is damaged by a failure to solve the problem of point of view and by inadequate selection, these faults are at least in part the result of Fitzgerald's attempting to write a very ambitious novel. The book's defects are insignificant compared to its sustained richness of texture, its sureness of language, the depth and penetration of its understanding — not merely of a small class of people, as so many reviewers thought, but of the bases of all human disaster. With all its faults, it is Fitzgerald's finest and most serious novel.

It is evident from what we know about the book's writing that he began, as he always did, with an interest in particular people in particular places. As always too, he seems to have felt rather than reasoned his way to an appreciation of what their experience meant, to an understanding of how, for them in particular, and for an age in general, "things were getting thinner and thinner as the eternal necessary human values tried to spread over all that expansion." [15] In order to write a philosophical novel on this subject, as he desired to, Fitzgerald needed a logical ordering of this felt experience, a careful arrangement of it into a structure which would indicate how each of the elements of experience presses on Dick Diver and contributes to his destruction. He never quite achieved that ordering of his material except in Book I.

There, detail by detail, the sterility and deadness of his chosen world is established — dramatically, because Rosemary hardly ever grasps its full implications. Campion shakes his monocle at Royal Dumphry, saying: "Now, Royal, don't be too ghastly for words"; Violet McKisco explains that McKisco's novel is "on the idea of Ulysses. Only instead of taking twenty-four hours my husband takes a hundred years. He takes a decayed old French aristocrat and puts him in contrast with the mechanical age — " Out of this corruption and affectation flowers the little group which Dick holds together and at its best by his apparently effortless social gift, his "trick of the heart." And through Rosemary's dazzled love of the intelligence and grace of these people, we catch an occasional glimpse of the desperation just under the surface. "Do you know what time it is?" Rosemary asks. "It's about half-past one," Dick says. "They faced the seascape together momentarily. 'It's not a bad time,' said Dick Diver. 'It's not one of the worst times of the day.'" Or Mary North says, "I used to think until you're eighteen nothing matters." "'That's right,' Abe agreed. 'And afterwards it's the same way.'" All these elements are represented by a wealth of detail so fully ordered that the smallest demonstration of manners is a revelation of Fitzgerald's evaluation of his society: "The two young men are reading the Book of Etiquette together," says Dick after passing Campion and Dumphry on the beach; "Planning to mix wit de quality," Abe remarks. Thus we come to know concretely the ducal perversion and ingrown virginity of the Chicago aristocracy of the Warrens, which is more terrible because stronger than its English counterpart in the Campions and Lady Caroline Sibley-Biers; the Mama Abrams, "preserved by imperviousness to experience and a good digestion into another generation"; the pathetic, belligerent anxiety of the McKiscos to keep up with what "everybody intelligent knows"; the cultivated, anarchic nihilism of Tommy Barban, to which Nicole turns when she becomes her whole self again; the controlled despair and self-destruction of Abe North, which forms a quiet anticipatory parallel to Dick Diver's destruction. This is the representation of a world which is free to be anything it chooses, and chooses to honor lack of moral imagination until it reduces all but the perverted and the stupid to despair.[16]

If the varied insights which constitute Fitzgerald's awareness of this world are not so well ordered throughout the rest of the book, they are almost always beautifully realized, until, in the end, he has created for us a whole society's disintegration:

See that little stream — says Dick as he stands on one of the battlefields of the first World War — we could walk to it in two minutes. It took the British a month to walk to it — a whole empire walking very slowly, dying in front and pushing forward behind. And another empire walked very slowly backward a few inches a day, leaving the dead like a million bloody rugs. No Europeans will ever do that again in this generation. . . . This kind of battle was invented by Lewis Carroll and Jules Verne and whoever wrote Undine, and country deacons bowling and marraines in Marseilles and girls seduced in the back lanes of Wurtemburg and Westphalia. . . . There was a century of middle-class love spent here.[17]

At the heart of this description of a society's collapse is Dick Diver, alive — as the society is not — with the inheritance of the past his father has transmitted to him, " 'good instincts,' honor, courtesy, and courage." This, Fitzgerald thought, was his inheritance as his description of his own father shows. However often he failed, he always tried again to live up to this inheritance; Dick Diver's manners that are "a trick of the heart" are his. How important a part of Fitzgerald they were has been too little stressed.

The essential Fitzgerald was a man of great pride and a strong sense of personal dignity who believed deeply in the manners that express a man's own self-respect as well as his respect for others. The too-well remembered escapades make us forget how much of the time he practiced these manners, often, even, when he was drinking. Of the evening James Thurber spent with Fitzgerald in April, 1934 — not a happy moment in Fitzgerald's life — Thurber observed, "The Scott Fitzgerald I met was quiet and pleasant too, and not difficult. . . . of the four or five eminent writers of the Crazy Decade with whom I have spent the night hours drinking, Scott was the best behaved, the least menacing, and the quietest. . . ."[18] Perhaps he was sometimes too ready to assume people would regard destructive pranks as merely high-spirited gaiety, but he was quick to apologize, with difficult honesty, when he understood he had behaved badly. Moreover, the older he became (and the more, perhaps, he came to distrust his immediate responses to experience), the more important he came to feel good manners were. By 1929 there was an almost old-fashioned formality about him. "His manner was correctly courteous. All the little gentlemanly amenities seemed to be important to him. There was nothing lazy or slovenly about his speech or his movements." [19]

These manners were not just an act or even a habit; they were the expression of a deeply felt attitude. "My generation of radicals and breakers-down," as he wrote his daughter, "never found anything to take the place of the old virtues of work and courage and the old graces of courtesy and politeness." "A great social success," as he wrote her on another occasion, translating his own intentions into her terms, "is a pretty girl who plays her cards as carefully as if she were plain." [20] To the end of his life his sense of his own dignity and his consideration for others expressed themselves in this formal courtesy of manner, which, when it was illuminated by his vivid sympathy, as it so often was, gave him great distinction, a realized understanding and sympathy for others that seemed to them unique in their experience: Sheilah Graham's description of the impression he made on her is representative of the way he affected people at such times. [21]

More and more, however, throughout the thirties he began to feel that the exercise of such understanding was useless, perhaps meaningless in the world he found himself in after 1930, an enormous expenditure of emotional energy for which he had nothing to show. "Once I believed in friendship," he said near the end of his life, "believed I *could* (if I didn't always) make people happy and it was more fun than anything. Now even that seems like a vaudevillian's cheap dream of heaven, a vast minstrel show in which one is the perpetual Bones." [22] In exactly the same way Dick Diver feels that in this society he is living off inherited moral capital — when he senses instinctively "all the maturity of an older America" in the gold-star mothers and "almost with an effort . . . turned back to his two women [Nicole and Rosemary] at the table and faced the whole new world in which he believed"; when, at Gstaad, "he relaxed and pretended that the world was all put together again by the gray-haired men of the golden nineties" and "for a moment . . . felt that they were in a ship with a landfall just ahead"; when above all, he remembered "his father [who] had been sure of what he was." [23]

It is his possession of the kindness, the understanding, the manners of his inheritance which makes Dick give himself to the task of revivifying this dying society; "It was themselves he gave back to them, blurred by the compromises of how many years." A harder, less sensitive man could have resisted, but Dick, "wanting to be brave and kind . . . wanted, even more, to be loved."

There are many pressures on him — the corrupting force of Nicole's money; the inclination, because he loved Nicole till she was "the drought in the marrow of his bones," to let husband and psychiatrist get confused; the weight of the whole society's habitual disorder. But none of these pressures is the primary cause of his defeat; what really destroys Dick is emotional bankruptcy. As the society had exhausted its power on the western front, as Abe, precisely because he is kind and understanding, has been reduced to despair, so Dick uses up the emotional energy which is the source of his personal discipline and of his power to feed other people. "I thought of him," said Fitzgerald, ". . . as an 'homme epuisé,' not only an 'homme manqué.' " [24]

Because he thought of Dick as an homme epuisé, *Tender Is the Night* becomes Fitzgerald's first full exploitation of the most important of all his convictions about experience. He was a man for whom nothing existed at all if he did not feel strongly about it. Like the Troilus of Shakespeare's play, therefore, he was committed by his nature to the doctrine that value dwells rather in the particular will than in a thing's being precious of itself. Like Troilus, he risked sentimentality, absurdity, and in the end tragedy for this conviction, because he was incapable of existing at all except according to its terms.

This characteristic gave the past a special value for him; "that terrible door into the past," he called it, "through which we all must go." [25] It was terrible to him because the past was himself, was what he had invested his vitality in irrevocably. "He had come to realize recently," as he says of the hero of one of the stories written while he was at work on *Tender Is the Night*, "that life was not always a progress, nor a search for new horizons, nor a going away. The Gunthers were part of him; he would not be able to bring to new friends the exact things that he had brought to the Gunthers. If the memory of them became extinct, then something in himself became extinct also." [26]

He also began to fear the exhaustion of his emotional, his spiritual, energy, a final "lesion of vitality." This idea may have been suggested to him by Zelda's tragedy, for his first use of it occurs in a story he wrote for the Josephine series just when he was beginning to grasp what had happened to Zelda; the story is called "Emotional Bankruptcy." [27] It is the story of how Josephine meets "the love of her life" and discovers that, because she has spent her emotions so prodigally in her early youth, she can now "feel nothing at all." "When you kissed me," she tells him, "I wanted to laugh." "It made her sick to say this, but a desperate, interior honesty drove her on." The occasion provided by this Josephine story for the definition of Fitzgerald's feeling is trivial; but the feeling itself is not. It is the same one that dominates Dick Diver when, at the end of *Tender Is the Night*, he makes a last effort to be his old, sensitive self for Mary North: "But the old interior laughter had begun inside him and he knew he couldn't keep it up much longer." [28]

This possibility of vitality's exhaustion led Fitzgerald gradually to think of vitality as if it were a fixed sum, like money in the bank. Against this account you drew until, piece by piece, the sum was spent and you found yourself emotionally bankrupt. "I am not a great man," he wrote his daughter late in his life, "but sometimes I think the impersonal and objective quality of my talent and the sacrifices of it, in pieces, to preserve its essential value has some sort of epic grandeur. Anyhow after hours I nurse myself with delusions of that sort." 29 It became habitual with him to consider people's lives in the light of this feeling. The post-war Robert E. Lee was, he thought, an emotional bankrupt. His own father seemed to him a clear case:

One afternoon — I was ten or eleven — the phone rang and my mother answered it. I didn't understand what she said but I felt that disaster had come to us. My mother, a little while before, had given me a quarter to go swimming. I gave the money back to her. I knew something terrible had happened and I thought she could not spare the money now.

Then I began to pray. "Dear God," I prayed, "please don't let us go to the poorhouse; please don't let us go to the poorhouse." A little while later my father came home. I had been right. He had lost his job.

That morning he had gone out a comparatively young man, a man full of strength, full of confidence. He came home that evening a broken man. He had lost his essential drive, his immaculateness of purpose. He was a failure the rest of his days.30

But above all he saw himself, at the time of his own most severe crisis of morale, as a case of emotional bankruptcy.

I began to realize — he wrote in *The Crack-Up* — that for two years my life had been drawing on resources that I did not possess, that I had been mortgaging myself physically and spiritually up to the hilt. What was the small gift of [physical] life given back in comparison to that? — when there had once been a pride of direction and a confidence in enduring independence.

I realized that in those two years . . . I had weaned myself from all the things I used to love — that every act of life from the morning tooth-brush to the friend at dinner had become an effort. I saw that for a long time I had not liked people and things, but only followed the rickety old pretense of liking. I saw that even my love for those closest to me was becoming only an attempt to love, that my casual relations — with an editor, a tobacco seller, the child of a friend, were only what I remembered I *should* do, from other days.[31]

He then goes on to give the specific illustrations of that

deprivation
And destitution of all property,
Desiccation of the world of sense,
Evacuation of the world of fancy,
Inoperancy of the world of spirit[32]

which constitute this state, and remarks: "All rather inhuman and undernourished, isn't it? Well, that, children, is the true sign of cracking up." "At three o'clock in the morning," he concluded, remembering St. John of the Cross too (or perhaps remembering that Eliot had remembered him) and thinking ironically of what he called in *The Great Gatsby* that "neat, sad little waltz" which was popular the year Gatsby gave all his parties — "At three o'clock in the morning, a forgotten package has the same tragic importance as a death sentence, and the cure doesn't work — and in a really dark night of the soul it is always three o'clock in the morning, day after day." [33]

The importance to him of this conviction is indicated by his metaphor, that monetary image which is consistently elaborated in his remarks about vitality. What, for instance, except as a symbol, is that quarter doing in his memory of his father's loss of "immaculateness of purpose"; why, if he did not understand his mother's telephone conversation, did the eleven-year-old boy pray that they might not have to go to the poorhouse? Somewhere very deep in his imagination that complicated tangle of feelings he had about the rich interlocked with his feelings about the delight of vitality and the horror of its exhaustion.

If his talent was dependent on his vitality, then his popular writing had been a waste of something more precious than time. "What little I've accomplished," he wrote his daughter, "has been by the most laborious and uphill work, and I wish now I'd *never* relaxed or looked back — but said at the end of *The Great Gatsby*: 'I've found my line — from now on this comes first. This is my immediate duty — without this I am nothing.' " [34] There was nothing he did not know about his failure to stick to this line; the knowledge haunted the darkness of his sleepless nights: "In the dead of the night . . . I see the real horror develop over the roof-tops, and in the strident horns of night-owl taxis and the shrill monody of revelers' arrival over the way. Horror and waste — Waste and horror — what I might have been and done that is lost, spent, gone, dissipated, unrecapturable. . . . The horror has come now like a storm. . . ." [35]

Thus, by the time he came to write *Tender Is the Night*, he was haunted by the idea of emotional bankruptcy and made it the central meaning of Dick Diver's history. Dick yields to the other pressures that his world puts on him only after the slow, unavoidable devitalization that takes place inside him has done its work. That "lesion of vitality" is the heart of his mystery, and Fitzgerald traces it minutely in the book. At its beginning Dick is actually near exhaustion, hanging on to his self-discipline and his charm only by an effort of the will. "Did you hear I'd gone into a process of deterioration?" he says to Rosemary later. "Oh, no," Rosemary says. But he contradicts her. "It is true. The change came a long way back — but at first it didn't show. The manner remains intact for some time after the morale cracks." As his emotional energy

wanes the cracks in the order he has imposed on himself begin
to show. The first is his falling in love with Rosemary. His
yielding to this anarchic impulse is followed almost immediately by a period of terrifying, uncontrollable, childish jealousy — "Do you mind if I pull down the curtain? Please do.
It's too light in here" — and he is helpless.

> He knew that what he was now doing marked a turning
> point in his life — it was out of line with everything that had
> preceded it. . . . But . . . behaving as he did was a projec-
> tion of some submerged reality: he was compelled to walk
> there, or stand there, his shirt-sleeve fitting his wrist and his
> coat sleeve encasing his shirt-sleeve like a sleeve valve, his
> collar molded plastically to his neck, his red hair cut exactly,
> his hand holding his small brief-case like a dandy. . . . Dick
> was paying some tribute to things unforgotten, unshriven,
> unexpurgated.[36]

He was facing the truth that ". . . if you spend your life
sparing people's feelings and feeding their vanity, you get so
you can't distinguish what *should* be respected in them." "He
had lost himself — he could not tell the hour when, or the day
or the week, the month or the year. . . . Between the time
he found Nicole flowering under a stone on the Zürichsee and
the moment of his meeting with Rosemary the spear had been
blunted." After that his self-discipline slowly fissures and
crumbles until he is completely ruined. At first this breakdown shows as little, random wanderings of feeling; he no-
tices a pretty girl at Gstaad and plays to her; he is appealed to
by an unknown woman at Innsbruck — "He was in love with
every pretty woman he saw now." He lets his submerged
judgments of the world come to the surface in bitterness, to
the young Englishman at Gstaad, to Mary North — "But
you've gotten so damned dull, Mary" — to Lady Caroline.
He begins to drink, now not in a controlled way but as a kind
of fumbling gesture of protest.[37]

This loss of discipline is a loss of pride, because the emotional energy which gave him a meaning in terms of which he could discipline himself is exhausted. He is a hollow man, like Abe North who says with bitterness at the end, "Tired of friends. The thing is to have sycophants." [38] So it has become with Dick. Fitzgerald described the state from his personal experience with clinical minuteness in "Pasting It Together." ". . . the question," he wrote, "became one of finding why and where I had changed, where was the leak through which, unknown to myself, my enthusiasm and my vitality had been steadily and prematurely trickling away." And, like Dick, when he found out, he decided to cut his losses.

> The decision made me rather exuberant. . . .
> I felt like the beady-eyed men I used to see on the commuting train from Great Neck fifteen years back. . . . I was one with them now, one with the smooth articles who said:
> "I'm sorry but business is business." Or:
> "You ought to have thought of that before you got into this trouble." Or:
> "I'm not the person to see about that."
> And a smile — ah, I would get me a smile. I'm still working on that smile. It is to combine the best qualities of a hotel manager, an experienced old social weasel, a headmaster on visitors' day, a colored elevator man, a pansy pulling a profile, a producer getting stuff at half its market value, a trained nurse coming on a new job, a body-vendor in her first rotogravure . . . and of course the great beam of loving kindness common to all those from Washington to Beverly Hills who must exist by virtue of the contorted pan. . . .

"I have now," he concluded, perhaps remembering Hemingway's admonition ("All we are is writers"), "at last become a writer only." In exactly the same way Dick Diver at last becomes a doctor only.[39]

For years he has poured out his energy and imagination

making a world for people to live in, above all for Nicole. For six long years when she "roared in a voice so abandoned that its louder tones wavered and cracked, 'And sit and think that we're all rotting and the children's ashes are rotting in every box I open? That filth!' " and then begged him to help her, he had answered her by "restating the universe for her." Nicole lived in that universe until her whole personality grew solid again, even the part of it Dick had never known, the Warren part of it which "welcomed the anarchy of her lover," Tommy Barban, and taught her how to stare at Rosemary deliberately and then speak "in her grandfather's voice," slowly, distinctly, insultingly. At the moment when Nicole has recovered and can move out of Dick's world, Dick has reached the end of his power. For an instant he is tempted to take Nicole with him to destruction. Then he deliberately turns her over to Tommy.

> His face, wan in the light that the white spray caught and tossed back to the brilliant sky had none of the lines of annoyance she had expected. It was even detached; his eyes focussed upon her gradually as upon a chessman to be moved; in the same slow manner he caught her wrist and drew her near.
> "You ruined me, did you?" he inquired blandly. "Then we're both ruined. So — "

But as Nicole thinks, "all right, then" she will die with him, "she was unexpectedly free and Dick turned his back sighing. 'Tch! tch!' " He deliberately breaks his hold over her and then watches while she struggles to free herself from "the old hypnosis of his intelligence." When she succeeds and walks away, "Dick waited until she was out of sight. Then he leaned his head forward on the parapet. The case was finished. Doctor Diver was at liberty." By a terrible irony it has turned out that what he had refused to treat as a merely professional situation is just that; the case was finished. Baby Warren, who had from the start thought that the Warren millions were simply buying a doctor for Nicole, speaks Dick's epitaph for them all. "That's what he was educated for." [40]

The scope of *Tender Is the Night* is such that, for all the book's faults, its "philosophical" impact is unforgettable. It makes *The Great Gatsby*, which in structure so perfectly satisfies "the cannons" of the dramatic novel, seem neat and simple.

CHAPTER XIV

FITZGERALD waited anxiously for the reviews of *Tender Is the Night*. It was not just a matter of being taken seriously or even of making money now. It was a question of his ability to believe in himself. When the character of the reviews and the sales — *Tender Is the Night* sold around thirteen thousand copies — became clear, his morale dropped lower than it ever had before. This was the biggest battle he had lost yet.

In April he had started on a project which was to occupy him off and on for a year or more and, sporadically, for the rest of his life. This was a novel about medieval life which was to take a young man called Phillipe from about 880 to about 950; he was to participate in the founding of France as a nation and, in his old age, to watch the consolidation of the feudal system. It was to be called *The Count of Darkness*. Fitzgerald's plan was that "it shall be the story of Ernest" and his hope that "just as Stendahl's portrait of a Byronic man made *Le Rouge et Noir* so couldn't *my* portrait of Ernest as Phillipe make the real modern man." In the end, he got four long installments of this story written.[1] They are as bad as anything Fitzgerald ever wrote, and there is good reason to believe that *Red Book* bought the four installments partly in an effort to help him.[2] They are the clearest example there is of what Fitzgerald's work could be when he was not writing out of personal experience.

He was working now in a nightmare of discouragement about his writing and of despair about Zelda — she grew worse rather than better all year — and of worry over finances. In June he spent what he called "a crazy week in New York" and collapsed when he got home. He was in the hospital for some time, got out in July, and then had to go back again. He was beginning to find himself in dangerous financial straits. "The bills really begin," he noted in his Ledger in July; in September it was "Finances now serious" and in November "Debt bad." [3]

In September he tried, very tentatively, a love affair. It was an effort to get started living again. It took him away from Baltimore into Virginia on frequent visits and he eventually made a story out of the places he visited and his feelings about this relation.[4] He tried to believe he was pulling himself together, too. "I behaved myself well on all occasions but one, when I did my usual act, which is — to seem perfectly all right up to five minutes before collapse and then to go completely black." [5] But the love affair was no good, and by January, 1935, he was noting that he was "tiring of ——," and in April, "Good-bye to ——" This failure he thought was his own fault and it discouraged him further. For sometime afterwards he kept trying tentative love affairs, from brief encounters on weekends to somewhat more permanent affairs. None of them was very successful. Much as Fitzgerald felt he was missing something in life — and he could never bear to miss anything — by not being able to enjoy its casual pleasures, the very intensity that made him hate to miss anything made it impossible for him to have a casual love affair. "Oh, I've had all the fun," he once said, "but in my heart I can't stand this casual business. With a woman, I have to be emotionally in it up to the eyebrows, or its nothing. With me it isn't an affair — it must be the real thing, absorbing me spiritually and emotionally. . . . Silly, isn't it? Look at the fun we miss!" [6]

By fall he was in a mood of deep depression. Perkins came to Baltimore to see him and he made an effort to rally. After Perkins had gone Fitzgerald wrote him, "The mood of terrible depression & despair is not going to become characteristic & I am ashamed and felt very yellow about it afterwards. But to deny that such moods come increasingly would be futile." A couple of weeks later he was saying, with one of his revealing non sequiturs, ". . . you might have taken literally what I said. I am, in point of fact, never really discouraged; nevertheless to *communicate* it were a crime." And the façade came down with a crash a month later: "When the hell did you and Ober get together on my physical habits? It seems to me I've had so many — " but before he sent the letter to Perkins he tore up the rest of it.[7] During this whole time his devoted friend Doctor Benjamin Baker was trying to help him. They had an agreement that Fitzgerald would call Doctor Baker whenever he felt tempted to drink. Once Fitzgerald called him from New York. "Ben," he said, "I'm going to take a drink." Doctor Baker begged him to hold off for half an hour, and Fitzgerald said he would try. During that half-hour Doctor Baker got hold of a friend in New York who gave Fitzgerald half a dozen secconal tablets and put him on the train for Baltimore, where Doctor Baker met him and took him to the hospital. But these methods were only stop-gap. That Christmas Eve Zelda was well enough to come home overnight and they had a little tree. But she soon grew worse again.

For the next month he was struggling with the proofs of *Taps at Reveille*.[8] It gave him more trouble than any of his other books of short stories. In the first place Perkins, who was a great admirer of the Basil stories, wanted him to make a separate book of them — there were nine of them, quite enough for a short volume. But he would not publish the stories without revision, and the best Perkins could do was to get him to revise five for *Taps*.[9]

In the second place, since Fitzgerald had not published a volume of short stories since 1926, he had an accumulation of sixty-one stories to select from. He finally chose ten, in addition to the Basil and the Josephine stories which fill half the book. They may not have been the ten best stories he could have chosen: Fitzgerald was a shrewd, even brutal critic of his own work, but not always a judicious one. He tended, like all writers, to overrate his most recent work. While *Taps at Reveille* was in hand — it was put in hand in October, 1934 — he dropped "A New Leaf" and added "Her Last Case" and "The Fiend." Then, when the book was in proof, he dropped "Her Last Case" in favor of "The Night of Chancellorsville." [10]

The stories in *Taps at Reveille* fall into two distinguishable groups chronologically, and this division is important because it represents a division in the character of his work. The first group — these are the dates of the writing of the stories, not necessarily of their publication — includes the Basil stories (1928) and the Josephine stories (1930), "A Short Trip Home" (1927), "The Last of the Belles" (1928), "Majesty" (1929), "Two Wrongs" (1929); the second includes "Babylon Revisited" (December, 1930), "Crazy Sunday," "Family in the Wind," "One Interne" (all 1932). The first group of stories are the work of the Fitzgerald who was clinging to his old attitudes and convictions; they are the work of the superficially ironic but fundamentally romantic young man. Their sadness is the sadness of the lost past, like that of the best stories in *All the Sad Young Men*; their irony is an acute awareness, an acceptance, of its distance and difference from the present. This irony is everywhere in the best of the stories, unobtrusive but perfectly in control of the evoked sentiment for the past. It may control the main intention of the story, as in "The Last of the Belles," when Andy, standing in the deserted camp, thinks of wartime Tarleton and the young Ailie Calhoun: "All I could be sure of was this place that had once been so full of life and effort was gone, as if it had never existed, and that in another month Ailie would be gone, and the South would be empty for me forever." It may control the smallest details, as when Basil, having ordered "a club sandwich, French fried potatoes and a chocolate parfait" at the Manhattan Hotel, watches "the nonchalant, debonair, blasé New Yorkers" and wanting another chocolate parfait, is "reluctant to bother the busy waiter any more." It is this balance which gives these stories their power and charm.[11]

The other, smaller group of stories differ from these in an important respect. They were all written after Zelda's collapse and Fitzgerald's confrontation of his own deterioration. In them the past has lost its importance. In the first group of stories the main feeling is the sadness of loss and remembrance; the things past had been in themselves happy. But in these stories the past is used only for exposition; they are about the grim present. The first, and perhaps the finest, is "Babylon Revisited," an attempt to come to grips with all he felt about Zelda's collapse and his considered love and responsibility for Scottie. A more representative one is "Family in the Wind." Characteristically Fitzgerald described it as "based on his experiences in the tornadoes that recently swept part of Alabama."[12] But the story's value is a result of his attempt to adjust to the wreckage of his own career and his present condition. These feelings are complicated. There is the feeling of injustice, of punishment over and above the crime (a difficult feeling to handle because it is so close to self-pity). There is the acceptance of what is his own doing, including the loss of his fellows' respect, which was very important to Fitzgerald, even though his destruction of it was sometimes wanton. There is the awareness of "his own moribund but still struggling will to power."[13] And there is the sense of the pity and irony of anyone's being in this position whatever the causes.

"Family in the Wind" thus provides an early version of the

state of mind which Fitzgerald was going to describe with grimly comic exaggeration three years later in "Pasting It Together," that "spiritual 'change of life'" which began as "a protest against a new set of conditions which I would have to face and a protest of my mind at having to make the psychological adjustments which would suit this new set of circumstances." [14] As always this understanding and acceptance came first as an act of the imagination, an effort to conceive as fiction this fundamentally different kind of experience and his role in it.

I'm very happy, or very miserable — says Forrest Janney in "Family in the Wind" — I chuckle or I weep alcoholically and, as I continue to slow up, life accommodatingly goes faster, so that the less there is of myself inside, the more diverting becomes the moving picture without. I have cut myself off from the respect of my fellow man, but I am aware of a compensatory cirrhosis of the emotions. And because my sensitivity, my pity, no longer has direction, but fixes itself on whatever is at hand, I have become an exceptionally good fellow — much more so than when I was a good doctor. [15]

In February, when the last decision about *Taps at Reveille* had been made and the final proofs read, Fitzgerald turned once more to his personal problem. It seemed to him so overwhelming that he suddenly decided to flee, not so much from himself as to the privacy in which he could confront himself. He went south, first to Tryon and, later in the year, to Hendersonville, North Carolina, a little resort town of about twelve thousand people near Asheville. Here he holed up in a cheap hotel and tried to put himself on the wagon — "on *Thursday 7th* (or Wed. 6th at 8:30 P.M.)" as he noted in his Ledger. For a month he hung on there suffering from cirrhosis of the liver and trying to stick to beer. "One harrassed and despairing night I packed a brief case and went off a thousand miles to think it over. I took a dollar room in a drab little town where I knew no one and sunk all the money I had with me in a stock of potted meat, crackers and apples." "I can still see his room," said Nora Flynn, a friend who lived in Tryon and tried to help him, "with collar buttons on the bureau, and neckties hanging from the light fixture, and dirty pajamas all over." [16] But Mr. and Mrs. Flynn did not know how desperate his situation was. While he was staying in Hendersonville he made a little note of exactly how he lived.

I am living very cheaply. Today I am in comparative affluence, but Monday and Tuesday I had two tins of potted meat, three oranges and a box of Uneedas and two cans of beer. . . . It was fun to be poor — especially if you haven't enough liver power for an appetite. But the air is fine here and I liked what I had — and there was nothing to do about it anyhow because I was afraid to cash any checks and I had to save enough for postage for the story. But it was funny coming into the hotel and the very deferential clerk not knowing that I was not only thousands, nay tens of thousands in debt, but had less than 40 cents cash in the world and probably a $13. deficit at my bank. . . . I haven't told you the half of it, i.e. My underwear I started with was a pair of pajama pants — *just that*. . . . I washed my two handkerchiefs and my shirt every night, but the pajama trousers I had to wear all the time and I am presenting it to the Hendersonville Museum. . . .[17]

Both Mrs. Flynn and her husband were kind and gentle with him. He never forgot their generosity and always remembered "Nora's gay, brave, stimulating, 'tighten up your belt, baby, let's get going. To any Pole.'" "I am astonished sometimes," he added, "By the fearlessness of women, the recklessness — like Nora, Zelda. . . . But it's heartening when it stays this side of recklessness." [18] She did her best to cheer Fitzgerald but, as he said, "of all natural forces, vitality is the incommunicable one. . . . You have it or you haven't it, like health or brown eyes or honor or a baritone voice. . . . I could [only] walk from her door, holding myself very carefully like cracked crockery, and go away into the world of bitterness, where I was making a home with such materials as are found there." [19] She told him her own story, "old woes of her own . . . and how she had met them, over-ridden them, beaten them." During March he succeeded in making a story, "The Intimate Strangers," out of those old woes, one of the last romantic love stories he attempted.[20]

By the end of the month he was back in Baltimore, still "very sick," to find Zelda much worse; and as always there were his "terrible debts." *Taps at Reveille* was not going well. Except for a brilliant review by William Troy in *The Nation*, the reviewers talked about "avowed pot-boilers," and a "subject matter that clings desperately to the knee-skirts of the jazz age." [21] The book sold only a few thousand copies. There was a month of struggling with Zelda's fresh breakdown, but by the middle of April the worst was over and he wrote Perkins: "Zelda, after a terrible crisis, is somewhat better." "I am, of course," he added pathetically, "on the wagon as always. . . ." [22] It was not until three years later that he could say of this time that "the things that were the matter with me were so apparent, however, that I did not even need a psychoanalyst to tell me that I was being stubborn about this (giving up drinking) or stupid about that (trying to do too many things). . . ." [23]

In May matters were brought to a crisis for him by an attack of tuberculosis. Tuberculosis had been half a disease and half an excuse with Fitzgerald for years; it had even been suspected in his childhood. He had probably had a mild attack when he went to New Orleans in 1919. In 1929, the medical records show, he had had a considerable hemorrhage; he did nothing about it, but the healed scar showed clearly in an X-ray taken in 1932. Now the pictures showed a real cavity and Doctor Baker sent Fitzgerald off to a top specialist, Doctor Paul Ringer, in Asheville.

> I had sat in the office of a great doctor — he wrote later — and listened to a grave sentence. With what, in retrospect, seems some equanimity, I had gone about my affairs in the city where I was then living, not caring much, not thinking how much had been left undone, or what would become of this and that responsibility, like people do in books; I was well insured and anyhow I had been a mediocre care-taker of most of the things left in my hands, even of my talent.[24]

Because he was frightened of the effect on his earning capacity if it were known he was tubercular, he persuaded Doctor Ringer to take care of him while he lived at the Grove Park Inn at Asheville.[25] He was vague to Perkins — "I am closing the house and going away somewhere for a couple of months," he wrote — and even told close friends only that he was leaving "for a protracted sojourn in the country . . . still seeking to get back the hours of sleep that I lost in '33 and '34. . . . I hate like the devil to leave [Zelda] but it is doctor's orders." [26]

"And then suddenly, surprisingly, I got better" — at least the tuberculosis subsided — "and cracked like an old plate as soon as I heard the news." He had suddenly reached that state which he called "emotional bankruptcy" — "an over-extension of the flank, a burning of the candle at both ends; a call upon physical resources that I did not command, like a man overdrawing at his bank." He could no longer believe in any of the things that had made him fight up to now, "a feeling," he called it, "that I was standing at twilight on a deserted range, with an empty rifle in my hands and the targets down. No problem set — simply a silence with only the sound of my own breathing" — watching "the disintegration of [my] own personality." [27]

For the rest of the summer he made his headquarters in

Asheville, going to Baltimore and New York occasionally. Late in the summer he was in a hospital in New York and a month later he had a more serious collapse back in Baltimore and spent a longer stretch in the hospital. After he got out he decided to give up the house on Park Avenue and take an apartment in the Cambridge Arms — "the attic, Cambridge Arms," he used to head his letters.

It was a time when his friends worried about his daughter's living with him. She was fourteen years old and it would be another year before she went away to school. His friends, especially his agent, Harold Ober, took over a large part of the responsibility for her during the next few years and she lived mostly with them when she was not at school or camp. Fitzgerald had curiously old-fashioned views of how children should be raised and a special feeling of responsibility for his daughter because she had no mother — a feeling which was only increased by his awareness of what he put her through when he was drinking. He was often ridiculously severe. His attitude shows in the stories he wrote about her, despite the gloss of liberality he gave his own conduct.[28] When it was not so adorned it was touching and — from Scottie's point of view — probably intolerable. "Don't," he would implore his cousin Ceci when Scottie was visiting in Norfolk —

> Don't let her go out with any sixteen year old boys who have managed to amass a charred keg and an automobile license as their Start-in-Life. Really I mean this. My great concern with Scottie for the next five years will be to keep her from being mashed up in an automobile accident. . . . P.S. I mean that, about any unreliable Virginia boys taking my pet around. . . . Scottie hasn't got three sisters — she has only got me. Watch her *please!* [29]

In addition to this intensified version of the usual parental anxieties, he suffered from continual fear that Scottie might, like him and like the Ginevra King he had imagined for the

Josephine stories, become emotionally bankrupt. "Our danger," he would write her, "is imagining that we have resources — material and moral — which we haven't got. . . . Do you know what bankruptcy exactly means? It means drawing on resources which one does not possess. . . . But I think that, like me, you will be something of a fool in that regard all your life, so I am wasting my words." Nevertheless he could not resist wasting them: a year and a half later he was telling her exactly the same thing: "The real handicap for a girl like you would have been to have worn herself out emotionally at sixteen." [30]

Then he would remember the way he had treated her when he was tired and overwrought or drunk and write penitently to her (age fifteen), "I think of you constantly and if I ever prayed it would be that the irritations, exasperations and blow ups of the past winter wouldn't spoil the old confidence we had in each other." [31] The severe father, the difficult alcoholic, and the man who loved his child intensely and wanted her confidence continued to alternate all through Scottie's adolescence.

He struggled through the old ritual of having Zelda at home for Christmas that winter but during February and March he was in the hospital several times. "Me caring for no one and nothing," he noted in his Ledger.[32] At the same time his work began to decline in quality. Except for the three crack-up articles he wrote at the end of 1935 in a serious attempt to get at his own state of mind ("The Crack-Up," "Handle with Care," and "Pasting It Together"), he had been turning out nothing but mediocre work for a year or more; it was remarkable that he turned out even printable work considering the circumstances. But now his fiction began, for the first time in years, to be rejected.[33] He grew anxious over the apparent failure of his creative power, for it fitted altogether too well with his theory of emotional bankruptcy to be taken lightly. As late as the middle of 1937, he wrote his friend and secretary, Martha Marie Shank: "Went to New York, wrote two stories on the spot and *sold them on the spot*. Can it be that the climate here [this letter was written from Tryon] isn't good for work?" [34] Some sense of what he had to do set him writing a series of autobiographical pieces during these early months of 1936, pieces which could exploit the new personality toward which he was moving and save him the hopeless struggle to fake the old optimistic excitement which had been the making of his popular fiction in the past. ("It grows harder to write now," he said wryly, "because there is so much less weather than when I was a boy and practically no men and women at all.") [35] They brought him, with the exception of the crack-up series, less fame and — at $250 apiece from *Esquire* — much less fortune than he had earned in the past. But they are beautifully written little sketches, and through them he gradually worked out fully the attitude which had first appeared in *Taps at Reveille* and was to dominate the stories he wrote during the rest of his life. [36]

Though he was convinced, as one close observer put it, that "his writing ability had left, or was leaving, him for good," Fitzgerald's crack-up was not so final as he supposed. But, as he remarked of a disaster earlier in his life, "A man does not recover from such jolts — he becomes a different person and, eventually, the new person finds new things to care about." [37] If Fitzgerald was not, as his father had been, "a failure the rest of his days," he was a scarred man whose success was of a very different order from what the man he had been before he went emotionally bankrupt had desired and, to a large extent, achieved. For the rest of his life he continued to think of himself as living on what he had saved out of a spiritual forced sale. "The price was high," he said, "right up with Kipling, because there was one little drop of something — not blood, not a tear, not my seed, but me more intimately than these, in every story, it was the extra I had. Now it is gone and I am just like you now." [38]

In April he decided to put Zelda in a sanitarium called Highlands, near Asheville; it was to be her permanent headquarters for the rest of his life. In July he gave up the apartment in Baltimore and moved temporarily to a hotel. Here Zelda was allowed to come for a weekend visit. His pity for her, when they were separate and he allowed himself to brood about it, was very deep. "I think I feel [the whole tragedy of Zelda] more now than at any time since it's inception. She seems so helpless and pitiful," he said about this time.[39] But he was himself in such a nervous condition that he could seldom endure for more than a few hours the strain of living in the limited world she inhabited. This time he got drunk and they quarreled. Zelda walked out of the hotel and when the friend Fitzgerald had called for help arrived he found Fitzgerald carefully emptying her suitcase and tearing up her clothes, slowly, piece by piece. He refused to discuss where Zelda might have gone. After a long search the friend found her at the station, exquisitely dressed, a thoroughly sophisticated woman, except that she was wearing a hat like a child's bonnet with the strings carefully knotted under her chin. She was reading the Bible. Though it was hours before train time, she insisted quietly that she had to remain there because she had to get back to Highlands. She was penniless, and their friend had to find Fitzgerald again, get Zelda's fare from him, and take it to Zelda at the station.

All too frequently their visits ended so. Fitzgerald would plot and plan endlessly in advance to make a little vacation from Highlands as perfect as possible for Zelda: he once interrupted Dean Gauss in the midst of Commencement exercises to have him look at a dress he had bought Zelda in New York and was taking to her. But when he was actually with her he would go to pieces. "I added to the confusion," he said of another trip, "by getting drunk, whereupon she adopted the course of telling all and sundry that I was a dangerous man and needed to be carefully watched. . . . On the boat coming up from Norfolk . . . I had some words with the idiotic trained nurse. . . . all this isn't pretty on my part, but if I had been left alone, would have amounted to a two day batt." [40]

Sometimes he would make a success of such a visit. Their best times were while he was living at Asheville in 1936 and 1937; living in comparative quiet there, he was better than he had been for some time, and Zelda improved after she got to Highlands to the point where he was much encouraged. "Your mother," he wrote his daughter, "looks five years younger and prettier. . . . Maybe she will still come all the way back. So things are not as blue-looking as they have been this past winter and spring." [41] This improvement was, of course, comparative. On several occasions Fitzgerald took Zelda back to Tryon with him to gatherings at the Flynns or the Bannings. Once, one of the guests reported, "She came in looking like Ophelia, with water lilies she'd bought. . . . Wine was served and she drank it in an eager gulp and right away it set her off." Fitzgerald drew her quietly into a corner and began a little fairy story in which she was a princess in a tower and he her prince; gradually she came to herself. Mrs. Flynn herself commented on another occasion when Zelda came in looking old and ill and, after walking about just touching things for a while, started to dance. "I shall never forget," she said, "the tragic, frightful look on [Scott's] face as he watched her. . . . They had loved each other. Now it was dead. But he still loved that love and hated to give it up — that was what he continued to nurse and cherish." [42]

On one such occasion in July he took Zelda swimming near Asheville. Feeling better than he had in a year and a half, "I thought I would be very smart and do some diving." It went all right for a little, but then, "trying to show off for Zelda," he ventured a dive from the fifteen-foot board and, while he was still in midair, tore the muscles of his shoulder so badly that he ended with his arm dangling an inch or two out of the socket.[43] The shoulder started to heal after a couple of weeks but then Fitzgerald, soaking with sweat on a very hot night, tripped over the raised platform of the bathroom. It was four o'clock in the morning and, nearly helpless in his cast, he took three quarters of an hour to crawl to the telephone and get help. He caught cold and developed "Miotosis" (a form of arthritis) in his shoulder and had to go back to bed for several weeks more. It was the middle of September before he could get around again.

The worst consequence of this accident was its effect on his morale. Putting it in the best light he could, Fitzgerald described this effect by saying: "I had been seriously sick for a year and just barely recovered and tried to set up a household in Baltimore which I was ill equipped to sustain. I was planning to spend a fairly leisurely summer, keeping my debt in abeyance on money I had borrowed on my life insurance. . . . To make a long story short, I was on my back for ten weeks, with whole days in which I was out of bed trying to write or dictate, and then a return to the impotency of the trouble." [44] What happened was that, out of pain and boredom and to get stimulation for his work, he began to drink again. Something of what he felt can be deduced from the story he wrote about this accident called "Design in Plaster," and something more from the fact that during this time he twice attempted to commit suicide. Once his secretary came in and found him lying on the bed in a darkened room and staring at the ceiling. She sat down on the chair beside the bed and said: "Scott, what is going to become of you?" He looked at her for a moment in a way she still remembers with terror and then said quietly, "God knows." [45] It was truly a time when, as he said, "it is always three o'clock in the morning, day after day."

On September 24, his fortieth birthday, an enterprising and inhuman reporter came to interview him. He found Fitzgerald in his room, up and about but still under nurse's care, and noted "his jittery jumping off and onto his bed, his rest-less pacing, his trembling hands . . . his frequent trips to a highboy, in a drawer of which lay a bottle." Each time Fitz-gerald poured a drink into the measuring glass on his bedside table, he would look appealingly at the nurse and ask, "Just one ounce?" As time went on ("Much against your better judgment, my dear," he was now saying to the nurse) he got franker. "A writer like me," he said, "must have an utter confidence, an utter faith in his star. . . . I once had it. But through a series of blows, many of them my own fault, some-thing happened to that sense of immunity and I lost my grip." When the reporter asked him about his own generation, he said, "Some became brokers and threw themselves out of windows. Others became bankers and shot themselves. . . . And a few became successful authors." His face twitched. "Successful authors!" he cried. "Oh, my God, successful authors!" [46]

When all this appeared in print Fitzgerald was frightened — for its effect on his market — and hurt; "Martha Marie," he said to his secretary, "it nearly broke my heart." "None of the remarks attributed to me did I make to him. They were taken word by word from the first 'crack-up' article . . ." he said. "I had a temperature of 103 with arthritis, after a ten weeks' siege in and out of bed. He was an s. o. b. and I should have guessed it." [47]

This interview shows Fitzgerald in the state of mind he used for his story "An Alcoholic Case," which he wrote in December. [48] But he was still capable of his old charm and excitement when properly appealed to. At Max Perkins' in-sistence Marjorie Kinnan Rawlings, who was spending the summer in the Carolina mountains working on *The Yearling*, came to see him. Her recollection of the occasion is vivid:

> He was exhilarated. He talked of his own work. He was modest, but he was *sure*. He said that he had made an ass of

himself, that his broken bone was the result of his having tried to "show off" in front of "debutantes" when he dived proudly into a swimming-pool, that he had gone astray with his writing, but was ready to go back to it in full force. . . . I remember being impressed by the affection with which he spoke of Hemingway. . . . He also spoke of Hemingway with a quality that puzzled me. It was not envy of the work or the man, it was not malice. I identified it as irony. . . . He was not interested in me as a writer or as a woman, but he turned on his charm as deliberately as a water-tap, taking obvious pleasure in it. The irony was here, too, as though he said, "This is my little trick. It is my defiance, my challenge to criticism, to being shut out." [49]

Not very long before this Fitzgerald and Perkins had been taken to see an old Southern house by a member of the family.

Scott and I — Perkins remembered — both being Yankees . . . took a kind of interest in all this, which Scott, who was very sensitive, perceived was not considerate of our companion's feelings. So he suddenly launched into an account of the surrender at Appomattox. "Well," he said, "it was all a great mistake, the surrender. The facts never got out. The camera men flashed the pictures at the wrong moment, and then it couldn't be changed to the truth. For the truth was that . . . Grant said, 'General Lee, there is no pen here. May I borrow your sword to sign with?' For Grant, of course, had no sidearms, as history records. And in the moment when Lee courteously handed him his sword for that purpose the press pictures were taken." [50]

"This," Perkins adds with his usual modesty, "doesn't sound like much when written, but Scott in all his high spirits made a fine thing of it." All the characteristic elements are here: Fitzgerald's comic nonsense about camera men, the joke about the strength of pens and swords, the high spirits, the desire to make others happy. This, like the Fitzgerald Mrs. Rawlings saw, is the old unbeaten Fitzgerald.

His shoulder gradually mended through the autumn and he got himself "an ancient Packard roadster" and began to get out again. In September his mother died. She left $42,000 and he tried hard to get his share of it at once; it would not have been much: he owed his mother's estate $5000 or $6000. ". . . it would be suicidal," he wrote his sister, "to keep on writing at this nervous tensity often with no help but what can be gotten out of a bottle of gin. . . . There is no use reproaching me for past extravagances nor for my failure to get control of the liquor situation under these conditions of strain. . . . [I] have used the liquor for purposes of work or of accomplishing some duty for which I no longer have the physical or nervous energy." [51]

When it became clear that there would be no money from the estate for six months or so, he turned, for the first time in his life, to a wealthy friend for help. "I do not know," he wrote, "very many rich people well, in spite of the fact that my life has been cast among rich people — certainly only two well enough to have called upon in this emergency. . . ." [52] In this way he got himself through the fall and in December he returned to Baltimore, partly at least because he wanted to give a tea dance for his daughter so that she could repay some of her social debts there. "Old dowager Fitzgerald," he called himself. The dance was not a success, because Fitzgerald drank too much in an attempt to rise to the occasion. Once more he had to go into a hospital.

As soon as he was out, he returned to Asheville and again, as he had before his accident, he began the long pull back. With the money he had borrowed and the now imminent inheritance from his mother he had ready cash and could take things a little easier. With the pressure eased, his old Irish stubbornness reasserted itself and he began honestly to face his tendency toward "unnecessary rages, glooms, nervous tensity, times of coma-like inertia. . . ." "I stopped drinking in January," he wrote his cousin, "and have been concentrating on other mischief, such as work. . . . Scottie must be educated & Zelda can't starve. As for me I'd had enough of the whole wretched mess some years ago & seen thru a sober eye find it more appalling than ever." To another friend he summed up the causes of his disaster: "A prejudiced enemy might say it was all drink, a fond mama might say it was not providing for the future in better days, a psychologist might say it was a nervous collapse — it was perhaps partly all these things. . . . My life looked like a hopeless mess there for awhile and the point was I didn't want it to be better. I had completely ceased to give a good Goddamn. . . . So much for me and I don't think it will ever happen again." [53]

But "when you once get to the point where you don't care whether you live or die — as I did — it's hard to come back to life," and he did not come all the way back.[54] Still he began to go about again. He took to eating in a place called Misseldine's in Tryon and invented all sorts of wonderfully absurd stories about it. By Easter he was well enough to have his daughter for her vacation and very nearly to make a success of the visit. "I loved having you here (except in the early morning)," he wrote her when she was back at Miss Walker's, "and I think we didn't get along so badly, did we? Glad you had a gay time in Baltimore and New York and have a friend at Groton. They are very democratic there — they have to sleep in gold cubicles and wash at old platinum pumps. This toughens them up so they can pay the poor starvation wages without weakening." [55]

CHAPTER XV

EVER SINCE he had got into financial straits, Fitzgerald had thought of trying to get to Hollywood again. During 1936 he had worked to find a job there. What was to be his last story for the *Post* was written in June ("Trouble"; it was not printed until March, 1937), and, apart from an occasional story for *Collier's* or *Liberty*, he was now pretty much committed to *Esquire*. The effect of this change of market was to cut the price of his work to a tenth of what it had been. His income reached a new low in 1936 ($10,180) and would have fallen to half of that in 1937 had he not gone to Hollywood. All this he could foresee.

But his attempts to get a foothold in Hollywood were "compromised" as he put it by the "Crack-Up" articles. "It seems to have implied to some people that I was a complete moral and artistic bankrupt," he wrote a friend.[1] His indignant conviction that his alcoholism was only a malicious delusion of Hemingway's made him blind to the wide public knowledge of his habits. Having his own rationalization of his case, he hardly understood how much "The Crack-Up" revealed and believed he was playing his cards cunningly when he was showing his hand most openly, as when he remarked in an aside that he had "not tasted so much as a glass of beer for six months."

His attitude — it was intensified because the writer was

Hemingway — showed in his response to the reference to him in "The Snows of Kilimanjaro." In the original version of the story Hemingway's hero thinks, "He remembered poor old Scott Fitzgerald and his romantic awe of [the rich] and how he had started a story once that began, 'The very rich are different from you and me.' And how someone had said to Scott, Yes they have more money. But that was not humorous to Scott." [2] Neither was this.

The most famous of all anecdotes about Fitzgerald derives from this passage — and perhaps from Hemingway's repetition of it in conversation. The story does not, as do most versions of the anecdote, claim Hemingway made this retort to Fitzgerald, though the implication is that he did. Perkins, however, wrote Fitzgerald that "I was present when that reference was made to the rich, and the retort given, and you were miles away." This public reference to him astonished and enraged Fitzgerald, and he wrote Hemingway, "Please lay off me in print. If I choose to write *de profundis* sometimes it doesn't mean I want friends praying aloud over my corpse. No doubt you meant it kindly but it cost me a night's sleep. And when you incorporate it (the story) in a book would you mind cutting my name?" "I wrote Ernest about that story of his," he told Perkins, "asking him in the most measured terms ["a somewhat indignant letter," he called it elsewhere] not to use my name in future pieces of fiction. He wrote me back a crazy letter, telling me about what a Great Writer he was and how much he loved his children, but yielding the point — 'If I should outlive him — ' which he doubted. To have answered it would have been like fooling with a lit firecracker. Somehow I love that man, no matter what he says or does, but just one more crack and I think I would have to throw my weight with the gang. . . ." [3] Hemingway's letter — unfortunately lost — was not so irrelevant as Fitzgerald suggests, for he also told Fitzgerald that "since I had chosen to expose my private life so 'shamelessly' in *Esquire*, he felt that it was sort of an open season for me. . . ." And though Fitzgerald ironically attributes his restraint in not replying to "approaching maturity on my part," it was his myth about Hemingway which saved him from sending the "hell of a letter" he wrote. "[Ernest] is quite as nervously broken down as I am," he said, "but it manifests itself in different ways. His inclination is toward megalomania and mine toward melancholy." [4] Hemingway quietly dropped Fitzgerald's name (it became "Julian") when "The Snows of Kilimanjaro" appeared in *The First Forty-Nine Stories*.

Just as he was astonished to discover that Hemingway would venture this reference and that " 'the poor old Scott' line . . . has been a standby of my dear friends for almost a decade," so he was surprised when Hollywood drew back after "The Crack-Up." [5] But he kept trying for a job and in August he got an offer to go out and do a story "of adolescents around seventeen." The contract was to be for four weeks at $1500. Because of his shoulder he had to refuse, but by the following April he had another feeler.[6] In June the arrangement was completed. He was to go to M-G-M for six months at $1000 a week with an option for twelve months more at $1250. This option was in due course picked up.

Since one of his main motives for going to Hollywood — though not the only one — was to pay his debts, the first thing he did was to make an arrangement with his agent, Harold Ober, to do so. His plan was to deposit his salary with Ober, who would then give him $400 a month, to support himself, keep Scottie in school and Zelda in Highlands. The rest was to be set aside for taxes and payments against his debts to Ober and Perkins and, later, Scribner's. These debts amounted, according to his own estimate, to something like $40,000 at the time.[7] He maintained substantially this arrangement until his debts were paid.

But though the clearing of these "terrible debts" was very

important to him, he also felt something of the old fascination of Hollywood and the old desire to conquer it. It was a place that he had never got the best of. To those who might think Hollywood a surrender he let his doubts have the upper hand. "It's a hell of a prospect in every other way except money," he wrote his cousin Ceci, "but for the present & for over 3 years the creative side of me has been dead as hell." [8] But at exactly the same time (both letters were written on the train on the way out) he was writing Scottie:

> I feel a certain excitement. The third Hollywood venture. Two failures behind me though one no fault of mine. . . .
>
> I want to profit by these two experiences — I must be very tactful but keep my hand on the wheel from the start — find out the key man among the bosses and the most malleable among the collaborators — then fight the rest tooth & nail until, in fact or in effect, I'm alone on the picture. That's the only way I can do my best work. Given a break I can make them double this contract in less than two years.[9]

It was this feeling of excitement that stayed with him, so that when he was making jottings for *The Last Tycoon* he reminded himself of "my own fears when I landed in Los Angeles with the feeling of new worlds to conquer in 1937. . . ." And it was with this ambition to conquer that he tackled his job. He spent much of his spare time having pictures run off for him and studying other writers' scripts, and he kept a file of notes on the pictures he had seen. As late as November, when he had finished a revision of *A Yank at Oxford* and was hard at work on *Three Comrades*, he called himself "a semi-amateur" at movie construction ("though I won't be that much longer").[10] He was determined, this time, to do a good job, to give everything he had. For a while he kept completely sober, and as long as he was under contract to M-G-M he only went on an occasional bust.[11]

In July he got Helen Hayes to bring Scottie out to spend

the rest of the summer with him and when she had returned to Miss Walker's he wrote her one of his oddly touching letters. "I think of you a lot," he concluded. "I was very proud of you all Summer and I do think that we had a good time together. Your life seems gaited with much more moderation and I'm not sorry that you had rather a taste of misfortune during my long sickness, but now we can do more things together — when we can't find anybody better. There — that will take you down! I do adore you and will see you Christmas. Your loving Daddy." [12]

All through the autumn he continued to write enthusiastically about what he called this "tense crossword puzzle game, creative only when you want it to be, a surprisingly interesting intellectual game." His good health and morale, "miraculously returned after three terrible years," were a continual surprise to him.[13] In the first week of September he came east and took Zelda on a trip to Charleston which went off without a hitch. Again at Christmas time, in spite of his being dead tired from a final rush of work on *Three Comrades*, he took Zelda to Miami and Montgomery and back to Asheville without incident.[14] He entered into the social life of Hollywood with a renewal of his old innocent delight in big names. "Had the questionable honor [of] meeting Walter Winchell, a shifty-eyed fellow surrounded by huge bodyguards," he wrote Scottie. "Norma Shearer invited me to dinner three times but I couldn't go, unfortunately as I like her. May be she will ask me again. . . . Took Beatrice Lily, Charley MacArthur . . . to the Tennis Club the other night, and Errol Flynn joined us — he seemed very nice though rather silly and fatuous." [15]

But in spite of his improved health and his genuine enthusiasm for his job he was neither a well man nor one with much in reserve. Moreover, it showed. "There seemed to be no colors in him. The proud, somewhat too handsome profile of his early dust-jackets was crumpled. . . . The fine forehead, the leading man's nose, the matinee-idol set of the gentle, quick-to-smile eyes, the good Scotch-Irish cheekbones, the delicate, almost feminine mouth, the tasteful, Eastern (in fact, Brooks Bros.) attire — he had lost none of these. But there seemed to be something physically or psychologically broken in him that had pitched him forward from scintillating youth to shaken old age." [16] He soon dropped out of the social life of Hollywood; it was too much for him, and he no longer liked parties anyhow. Insomnia continued to bother him, and he went on feeling uncertain about his own purpose and identity, feeling that he was watching "the disintegration of [his] own personality."

All his life he had depended on his belief that he could hold the part of himself that responded to experience without restraint and the morally responsible part of himself, the spoiled priest, in reasonable balance. This was a matter of the spoiled priest's understanding the responsive self, knowing the reasons for his outbursts, and, when necessary, bringing him to heel. He was thinking of his own failure to maintain this balance when he wrote his daughter, "Baby, you're going on blind faith . . . when you assume that a small gift for people will get you through the world. It all begins with keeping faith with something that grows and changes as you go on. You have got to make all the right changes at the main corners — the price for losing your way once is years of unhappiness." He put the point even more strongly to a girl who began to go to pieces when he broke off a love affair with her in 1935: "The luxuriance of your emotions under the strict discipline which you habitually impose on them makes that tensity in you that is the secret of all charm — when you let that balance become disturbed, don't you become just another victim of self-indulgence — breaking down the solid things around you and, moreover, making *yourself* terribly vulnerable?" [17]

When he began, in 1928 and 1929, to suspect that the spoiled priest had lost control, he was seriously worried; by 1932 he was saying even to Perkins, with whom he always tried to maintain the pretense that he was in better control of himself than he was, "Five years have rolled away from me and I can't decide exactly who I am, if anyone. . . ." After the terrible year of 1936, the spoiled priest no longer knew what his experiencing self had become, and he felt his personality had disintegrated. It was no longer a matter of keeping faith with something that had grown and changed; now he could not even find that something. Once during his early days in Hollywood he sent himself a postal card which he carefully preserved. "Dear Scott," it said, " — How are you? Have been meaning to come in and see you. I have [been] living at the Garden of Allah. Yours Scott Fitzgerald." Once during this time, in a moment of drunken despair, he tried to commit suicide, but that was not characteristic; he had far too much sense of responsibility for Scottie and Zelda, and too much courage too, not to go on doing the best he could however little meaning it had for him.

> He was, a good deal of the time, great fun to be with, he listened as well as he talked, he could be terribly funny, terribly serious, and sometimes, happily, both at once. Possibly half a dozen times I had seen him difficult and belligerent, and then he could be maddening, but it would be badly misleading to picture him as staggering through those last Hollywood years. . . . my most lasting impressions are not of his drinking and falling, but of his thinking and trying.[18]

But in an important sense Scott Fitzgerald was never, as a personality, wholly there again; to old friends like Edmund Wilson he seemed like a polite stranger when he and Sheilah stayed with the Wilsons in the fall of 1938. For brief moments sometimes, like Dick Diver, "he relaxed and pretended that the world was all put together again," but most of the time for the rest of his life he was a man mostly going through the motions, scarcely believing in the reality of anything he felt or did except when, drunk, his despair exploded into terrifying violence. Several such occasions are unforgettably described in *Beloved Infidel*.

Once, for example, when he was drunkenly annoyed with Sheilah for throwing out two bums he had been entertaining at Encino, he threw a bowl of soup across the dining room and, when the nurse tried to calm him down, kicked her viciously and then began trying to hurt Sheilah by reminding her of her most painful secret, her origins in the East End of London as Lily Sheil; finally he started looking for his gun, saying he was going to shoot her. Fortunately she and his secretary had hidden the gun and she escaped, but for days he went on threatening her. When he finally sobered up, he wrote her: "I loved you with everything I had, but something was terribly wrong. You don't have to look far for the reason — I was it. Not fit for any human relation. . . . I want to die, Sheilah, and in my own way." [19] All of him that remained intact — indeed, it grew stronger — was his gift, though the exercise of it was inhibited by his lack of physical energy. Nevertheless, when he was fully roused by a subject, as he would be once more by the subject of *The Last Tycoon*, he could write better than ever.

In October he got a wire from Ginevra King, who was visiting in Santa Barbara. It filled him with such excitement about the past that he considered what course to follow like a problem in high diplomacy. "She was the first girl I ever loved and I have faithfully avoided seeing her up to this moment to keep that illusion perfect, because she ended up by throwing me over with the most supreme boredom and indifference. I don't know whether I should go or not. It would be very, very strange. These great beauties are often something else at thirty-eight, but Genevra had a great deal beside beauty." But he went and they had lunch together. "[We] had a much better time than I had anticipated," Mrs. Pirie (Ginevra) remembered. "Afterwards . . . he suggested we go to the bar — I settled for a lemonade but he insisted on a series of double Tom Collins. I was heartsick as he had been behaving himself for some months before that. For the next few days I was besieged with calls, but as he was in love with someone in Hollywood, I believe, he soon gave up the pursuit." "She is still a charming woman and I'm sorry I didn't see more of her," Fitzgerald wrote.[20]

He was in love with Sheilah Graham, then just beginning her career as a columnist in Hollywood. Born Lily Sheil in London's East End and brought up in an orphanage, she had indomitably made her way in the world, first by a strange but successful marriage with a much older man, then as a chorus girl, and finally as a journalist. From the beginning she showed a determination to dominate the world that must have been part of her appeal to Fitzgerald. The very first time she came into the office of James Drawbell (then editor of the *Chronicle*), "a chorus girl with a strange idea in her head," she had her career all mapped out. "I want to get on to a newspaper, then I want to go to New York and work there, and after that — Hollywood," she told him, and, astonishingly enough, that is exactly what she did.[21]

Before she left London she even managed to move familiarly in what were quite elevated social circles. It does not seem likely that the Duchess of Devonshire and her friends were quite so deceived by Sheilah's imaginary account of her respectable social background as she believed they were; it must have been their appreciation of the naïveté of her belief in the value of such a background and the heroic energy with which she played her role that gave this very pretty girl her charm for them.[22] For all her drive and ambition, she was essentially young and innocent and touching — even more appealing because, not recognizing the real source of her charm, she had no vanity about it.

She and Fitzgerald first saw one another — just over a week after Fitzgerald had arrived in Hollywood — at a party of

Robert Benchley's, oddly enough a party to celebrate her engagement to a British gossip columnist, the Marquis of Donegall. Fitzgerald thought she was the European actress Tala Birrell. At a Writers' Guild dinner sometime later they were at nearby tables and spoke fleetingly, but another week passed before Fitzgerald made sure who she was and persuaded Jonah Ruddy to take them out to dinner together; that night Fitzgerald had all his old wonderful charm, and before it was over Sheilah was well on her way to loving him.[23]

The best account there will ever be of how Fitzgerald felt about Sheilah is the story of Stahr and Kathleen in *The Last Tycoon*. Almost every detail of their falling in love is there, reimagined to fit the circumstances of Stahr's story but unchanged in feeling. Fitzgerald's confusion over Sheilah's identity and his overwhelming sense of her resemblance to Zelda is in Stahr's mixing up Kathleen and her friend Edna and his haunted sense of her resemblance to his dead wife, Minna; his brief glimpse of Sheilah at the Writer's Guild dinner is in Stahr's glimpse of Kathleen at the screen-writers' ball at the Ambassador; his response to Sheilah's engagement to a lord and to her joking assertion that she had had eight lovers is in Kathleen's casual revelation that she had been a king's mistress; the drive to Malibu, when Sheilah told him the true story of her life, is in the drive to Stahr's unfinished house where he and Kathleen consummate their love. Above all Fitzgerald's devotion to Zelda and the past is in Stahr, who is "in love with Minna and death — with the world in which she looked so alone [when she was dying] that he wanted to go with her." [24]

Fitzgerald's portrait of Kathleen shows us a girl of great beauty with a past so strange that she can be wholly ignorant of the most commonplace facts of the world she is now living in — as Sheilah, living among the writers and intellectuals of Hollywood, had never heard of Willa Cather — and at the same time take for granted many hard facts of life that she had been facing undaunted for years, facts that few of these intellectuals had ever known at first hand. It makes her at once naïve and unshockable. The only thing Sheilah was really frightened of was that some one might discover the truth about her past. When she broke down under Fitzgerald's characteristically relentless cross-examination and told him the truth about herself, she was convinced he would cease to care for her: "he'll never want to see me again. I'm drab, drab, all the glamor is vanishing," she thought.

Apart from the strength of her feeling for him that that confession shows — she had never told these things to anyone before — there is the pathos of her thinking the truth about her would make her seem drab, when it was much more likely to appeal strongly to Fitzgerald's imagination and make them much closer than before. For much of his life Fitzgerald had seen himself as a man trying to play a role, a man who lived among the rich and successful without being one of them. The very fact that he now thought of himself as having failed in that role would only make Sheilah's success in hers the more appealing to him. No one understood better than he the needs of the imagination that could drive one to such a deception or the cost and heroism of living it. From the moment Fitzgerald understood the whole truth about Sheilah, he fought — not always wisely but always with everything he knew — to help her carry off her role. Her energy and courage must have been a constant pleasure to him, and her success — despite its constant, painful emphasis of his own obscurity — a compensation.

In the fall of 1937 Sheilah broke her engagement with Lord Donegall, and almost immediately, on a trip to Chicago he took to help Sheilah with a radio broadcast, Fitzgerald began to drink, and for the first time since she had known him Sheilah saw the other Fitzgerald. As usual, he told every-one on the plane who he was; he made ill-timed belligerent gestures that were meant to help Sheilah with the radio people; he led on a girl in the airport bus with compliments ("Isn't she pretty? Such lovely hair, such poise — a very lovely young woman") and then suddenly said to her, "You silly bitch." When Sheilah finally got him to the airport he was too drunk to be allowed on the plane and they had to wait over five hours for the next flight. To keep him out of bars, she drove him around in a cab for the whole time and finally got him sober enough to fly back to Hollywood.[25] When Sheilah stuck to him through all the awful time, she really made her decision, and despite the two times later when she left him, she was committed to him from then on.

Fitzgerald did not commit himself so quickly; perhaps he never wholly committed himself. It was not that he did not love Sheilah as much as he was capable of loving anyone new, but he worried about his capacity to live this new life and also to carry his obligations from the past. As late as January, when he went East, he talked the whole matter over doubtingly with Nora Flynn. Her letter to him about their conversation shows how he felt. "I am sure you are doing the right thing — about Zelda — I know you have been beyond words, wonderfull to her — I also know that the time has come for you to have a life of your own — to choose your own life, not for Zelda or for Scottie but just for *you* . . . I have a strange feeling that Sheilah is the right person for you. . . ."[26] So, within the limits of his nearly exhausted and already heavily committed emotional capital, Fitzgerald gave himself to this relation.

It was the luckiest thing that could have happened to him. It gave him someone he cared for very much to live with and to worry over and fight for, something he had not had since he and Zelda had begun to quarrel bitterly in the late twenties. His bouts of drinking were not something that could be stopped by anyone's care and good sense, however much he might love her, as Sheilah soon discovered, as perhaps Zelda in her different way had discovered before her. Fitzgerald had a pride that would not allow him to accept such help, and perhaps it could not have been enough even if he had accepted it, for deep down in him there seems to have lingered his old belief that the only way he could keep his feelings alive for his work over long stretches was by drinking, and for all anyone can tell he may have been right. Nevertheless, the peace and order and happiness Sheilah brought into his life drastically reduced the times when he felt he had to drink, and he went long spells — the last one over a year — without doing so.

By the end of January, 1938, he had completed the script of *Three Comrades* and had the characteristic Hollywood experience of having the producer, Joseph Mankiewicz, spoil all that he thought best in it by rewriting it. In rage and anguish he wrote Mankiewicz:

> Well, I read the last part and I feel like a good many writers must have felt in the past. . . .
> To say I'm disillusioned is putting it mildly. I had an entirely different conception of you. For nineteen years . . . I've written best selling entertainment, and my dialogue is supposedly right up at the top. But I learn from the script that you've suddenly decided that it isn't good dialogue and you can take a few hours off and do much better. . . .
> Oh, Joe, can't producers ever be wrong? I'm a good writer — honest. I thought you were going to play fair.[27]

But there was nothing to be done except to make an ironic portrait of Mankiewicz for *The Last Tycoon*. This was the end of any real hope Fitzgerald had of getting creative satisfaction from his work in Hollywood. He was now thinking of it as "a strange conglomeration of a few excellent over-tired men making the pictures, and as dismal a crowd of fakes and hacks at the bottom as you can imagine." But he went back to playing the crossword puzzle game on a new picture for Joan Crawford called *Infidelity*. He was not excited about it as he had been about *Three Comrades*, only tired and a little sardonic. "Writing for [Joan Crawford] is difficult," he wrote Gerald Murphy. "She can't change her emotions in the middle of a scene without going through a sort of Jekyll and Hyde contortion of the face, so that when one wants to indicate that she is going from joy to sorrow, one must cut away and then back. Also, you can never give her such a stage direction as 'telling a lie,' because if you did, she would practically give a representation of Benedict Arnold selling West Point to the British." In July he wrote Scottie quite seriously, "I don't think I will be writing letters many more years and I wish you would read this letter twice. . . . You don't realize that what I am doing here is the last tired effort of a man who once did something finer and better." [28]

In April they ran into censorship trouble over *Infidelity* and with most of a good and difficult script written, Fitzgerald had to drop it. It was never revived. For the duration of his contract with M-G-M he worked on *The Women* and *Madame Curie*. Because of his disappointment with movie work he began to think of writing again. "I don't write any more," he had said to Thornton Wilder. "Ernest has made all my writing unnecessary"; and in the fall of 1937 he had said without irony to Perkins, "All goes well — no writing at all except on pictures." But by April he was saying that "if I am to be out here two years longer, as seems probable, it certainly isn't advisable to let my name sink . . . out of sight . . ." and making anxious proposals for various reprints. This anxiety continued to mount as time went by until, by 1940, he was saying to Perkins: "I wish I was in print. . . . Would the 25 cent press keep *Gatsby* in the public eye — or *is the book unpopular?* Has it *had* its chance? . . . But to die, so completely and unjustly after having given so much. Even now there is little published in American fiction that doesn't slightly bare my stamp — in a *small* way I was an original." [29]

That April Sheilah found a house for them at Malibu and Fitzgerald moved out there from the Garden of Allah, where he had been living since his arrival in Hollywood. His anxiety over Scottie now became even more intense than usual, for she was about to go to college. At the last moment, after a harrowing though innocent episode during College Board examinations the previous spring, she had been accepted by Vassar. Fitzgerald's lifelong habit of identifying himself with those he loved — and he loved Scottie very much — combined with a flood of recollections of his own undergraduate days to make him even more than usually advisory. "[Vassar's] position," he wrote her delightedly, "is rather like Harvard's — you'd have to include it in any list of the big three, while you could name Harvard, Columbia, and Chicago, and leave out poor little Princeton altogether." He then redoubled his anxious, loving, exasperating efforts to help her manage her life wisely. "Poor Scott," one of his friends said. "He had to go through Princeton and Vassar too!" He tried to choose Scottie's courses and her friends for her; he spent hours making her outside reading lists and lists of questions about what he had told her to read; he harried and chivied her about the smallest detail of her life. When she went on too many weekends, or got poor marks, or ran into debt, he would write her violently angry letters. "I'm habituated to the string of little lies," he would write, ". . . but this sort of thing can lead into a hellish mess. . . . Friends! — we don't even speak the same language. I'll give you the same answer my father would have given to me. . . . Either you can decide to make concessions to what I want in the East or you can come out here Thanksgiving and try something else. . . . With dearest love, believe it or not, Daddy." Sometimes he would try irony, as when he scrawled at the bottom of a letter, "I have paid Peck & Peck & Peck & Peck & Peck." [30]

At one point Scottie's adviser intervened in her defense. "To tell you the honest truth," she wrote Fitzgerald, "I was horrified by your letter . . . because I can't see how an eighteen-year-old girl could have behaved badly enough to merit so much parental misgiving and despair — such dark bodings for the future." But Fitzgerald was quite unmoved; "I thought the letter from Miss Barber had a somewhat impertinent tone," he said stiffly.[31]

Most of the time, however, he was not angry, only inexhaustibly concerned. The letter he wrote her as she was starting for Poughkeepsie and her freshman year is typical:

Dearest Pie:

Here are a few ideas I didn't discuss with you and I'm sending this to reach you on your first day.

For heaven's sake don't make yourself conspicuous by rushing around inquiring which are the Farmington Girls, which are the Dobbs Girls, etc. You'll make an enemy of everyone who *isn't*. . . . I'd hate to see you branded among them the first week as a snob. . . .

If I hear of you taking a drink before you're twenty, I shall feel entitled to begin my last and greatest non-stop binge, and the world also will have an interest in the matter of your behavior. It would like to be able to say, and would say on the slightest provocation: "There she goes — just like her papa and mama." . . .

I think it would be wise to put on somewhat of an act in reference to your attitude to the upper classmen. In every college the class just ahead of you is of great importance. . . . It would pay dividends many times to treat them with an outward respect which you might not feel. . . .

Everything you are and do from fifteen to eighteen is what you are and will do through life. Two years are *gone* and half the indicators *already point down* — two years are left and you've got to pursue desperately the ones that point up!

I wish I were going to be with you the first day, and I hope the work has already started.

With dearest love —
DADDY

Underneath everything there was his pathetic desire to participate in her life: "These are such valuable years. Let me watch over the development a little longer. What are the courses you are taking? Please list them. Please cater to me. . . . What do the Obers say about me? So sad? . . . What play are you in? . . . What proms and games? Let me at least renew my youth! . . . As a papa — not the made [mad] child of a mad genius — what do you do? and how?" [32]

In October, because Malibu had become too cold and damp for Fitzgerald, Sheilah found a house on the estate of Edward Everett Horton at Encino in the San Fernando Valley; she gave up her own house, keeping only a small flat off Sunset Boulevard, and moved in with Fitzgerald. In November he took on what turned out to be a disastrous job for Walter Wanger. Budd Schulberg, then fresh out of Dartmouth and starting a career as a script writer, had been assigned by Wanger to a picture about the Dartmouth Winter Carnival. Wanger then decided there ought to be an older hand on the picture and hired Fitzgerald to collaborate with Schulberg. When he told Schulberg, he said, "My God, isn't Scott Fitzgerald dead?" "On the contrary," said Wanger, "he's in the next office reading your script."

It always raises doubts in a script writer's mind when he has a collaborator assigned to him, but Schulberg knew Fitzgerald's work and admired it and they got along fine during a series of long conferences that consisted mostly of discussions of literature. Schulberg remembers that he struggled unsuccessfully to bring together the world in which he had always imagined Scott Fitzgerald living and the world in which he himself wrote scripts. But though they seemed to make little progress with the script, Schulberg was not seriously worried; he supposed Fitzgerald, the experienced script writer, was quietly planning the picture and would presently say, "Here's what we're going to do." Fitzgerald was worrying about the script, pacing his room nights over it, but he was not making much progress. This was the perilous state

of their work when Wanger decided that they must see the
Winter Carnival itself and, despite Fitzgerald's protest that
he remembered undergraduate life very well, they found
themselves boarding a plane for the East to join the crew
already installed at Hanover waiting for the Winter Carnival
and the script.

At the airport Schulberg's father presented him with a
magnum of champagne — it was his first big assignment —
and after some hesitation Fitzgerald was persuaded to join
Schulberg in drinking it. Sheilah was actually on the same
plane, but she and Fitzgerald greeted each other as polite
acquaintances and went their separate ways so that she was
not aware of what was happening. In New York, Fitzgerald
went on to gin and by the time they were on the train for
White River Junction he was at the stage where he was telling
everyone who he was and how much he earned. It is characteristic of the way he, like Gatsby, could, even when he
was at his worst, get behind the conventional judgments and
the self-interest of intelligent people that Schulberg, when he
realized what was happening, put himself immediately and
unequivocally on Fitzgerald's side; he tried desperately to
keep Wanger, who was also on the train, unaware of Fitzgerald's condition. Then, despite his wretched condition — he
had added a bad cold to his drunkenness and lack of sleep —
suddenly at five in the morning Fitzgerald ad libbed a beautiful opening shot for the picture; it was like Gatsby's proving
to Tom Buchanan that he really was an Oxford man. With
his usual impetuousness Fitzgerald insisted on waking Wanger
up to tell him about his idea, thus alerting Wanger to his
condition. But that was all the script they had when they
arrived the next morning at Hanover to find the crew clamoring for something to shoot. Fortified by Wanger's now dangerous impatience, Schulberg improvised enough to get them
by for the moment.

Through some slip-up there was no reservation for the two

writers at the Inn and they were squeezed into an attic room with a double-decker bed. Fitzgerald insisted that this was a measure of Hollywood's respect for writers. They spent that night in their attic room talking of Fitzgerald's books; he was pathetically pleased to discover how well Schulberg knew them and began talking about himself with his characteristic, almost frightening detachment. "You know," he said, "I used to have a beautiful talent once, Baby. It used to be wonderful feeling it was there. . . ." Then for two days longer Fitzgerald wandered around Hanover with his cold and his four days' growth of beard amidst the gloss and gaiety of the Winter Carnival, a tactless ghost from another age of college pleasures.

On what turned out to be their last evening he had just settled himself, very disheveled, at the Alpha Delt party when Wanger came in and ordered Schulberg to get him out of sight. Fitzgerald was full of the spirit of the occasion, however, and insisted on Schulberg's taking him to the Psi U house. As they passed the Inn Schulberg tried to steer him to bed, but Fitzgerald heard in his voice the tone of a man handling a drunken friend and turned on him sharply. "You son of a bitch!" he said. "All right, I'll go there by myself." Schulberg finally got him into the coffee shop of the Inn, and there they dictated to one another a parody script. "We fade in on the thin clear cold slope of the ski slide," they would say, "and fade through to the thin clear cold mind of a Dartmouth undergraduate." After an hour or so they struggled out into the night again, and came face to face with Wanger. He took a good look at them and said: "You two are getting out of here, right away."

"Wanger will never forgive me for this," Fitzgerald said on the way to the Junction. "He sees himself as the intellectual producer and he was going to impress Dartmouth by showing them he used real writers, not vulgar hacks, and here I, his real writer, have disgraced him before the whole college." But what troubled him in the long run was the feeling that he had let Schulberg down, and until the script was finished he kept sending Schulberg apologetic little suggestions of things that might be done with it. They were so battered and dirty when they reached New York that no hotel would take them in. Finally Sheilah, who had been waiting for Fitzgerald in New York, got him into Doctors Hospital; it was two weeks before he was well enough to return to Hollywood.[33]

Fitzgerald had not got a screen credit for his work on *The Women* and he had been replaced on *Madame Curie* after two months; the only screen credit he had was therefore the one for *Three Comrades*. His contract was not renewed, and he had to face a new situation. His first tentative plan was that "at present, while it is possible I may be on the Coast another year, it is more likely the work will be from picture to picture with the prospect of taking off three or four months in the year, perhaps even more, for literary work."[34] In January he was hired to do some revision on *Gone With the Wind* but found himself in the midst of a complicated row and made little impression. A little later he worked for a month or so with Donald Ogden Stewart on *Air Raid*. When that was shelved (for something called *Honeymoon in Bali*) even the idea of working from picture to picture became impossible to arrange and he began to drink heavily again.

In April he made an effort to start his novel but, though he talked about it a good deal to Perkins and Ober, he got little done; at the same time he was quarreling seriously with Sheilah over his drinking and very abruptly one day he decided to go east and take Zelda on a trip to Cuba. He was exhausted, drunk, and in low spirits and the trip ended calamitously. In Cuba, in a moment of confused heroism, he attempted to put a stop to a cock fight and was badly beaten for his pains. At the end of April he arrived back in New York in very bad shape. There his old friends the Cases, who managed the Algonquin where he was staying, got a doctor and a nurse for him. Again he was in Doctors Hospital for

some time before he was able to return to California, and it
was July before he was able to get about as usual. "Almost
every time I have come to New York lately," he wrote Perkins, "I have just taken Zelda somewhere and have gone on
more or less of a binge, and [Ober] has formed the idea that
I am back in the mess of three years ago." [35] Ober was un-
comfortably close to the truth.

But it was a truth Fitzgerald was very anxious to conceal,
and he constructed an elaborate fiction about a recurrence of
tuberculosis, complete with temperature readings, X-ray reports, and details about cavities.[36] But though at that time he
did not have tuberculosis, he was always anxiously expecting
it to flare up (as it had briefly in December 1938). This anxiety was as persistent as his belief that whenever he went to
the movies the person behind him was kicking the back of his
chair. He even worried about Sheilah's using his cup or towel.
He had always been hypochondriacal when he was drinking
and it was easy for him now to imagine he was tubercular;
any steady drinking made him very ill, and any drinking at
all became steady drinking. His way of bringing himself out
of such bouts was drastic but perhaps necessary. He would
get a doctor and nurses and put himself through a three- or
four-day cure during which he was fed intravenously and
tossed sleeplessly through the nights in retching misery. He
emerged from such cures wan and shaken.[37]

He was also soon in fresh financial difficulties. As early as
the previous November he had borrowed from Perkins and
in February he had begun to borrow against his insurance
again. Even so he was in sore trouble by July. During May
and June, when he had been struggling with the aftereffects
of the Cuban trip, he had begun again to think of writing.
He asked Harold Ober for details of the contemporary short-
story market and took up once more his project for a novel.
On the strength of these new intentions, he tried to borrow
money from Ober, as he so frequently had in the past.[38]

It was never easy for Ober to find the kind of money Fitzgerald always needed; often in the past he had deprived himself in order to provide it. Now, hoping he might force Fitzgerald to work really hard, he said he could no longer make advances on unwritten stories. Fitzgerald responded to this decision with indignation. After years of having Ober advance him the expected price of a story, he had come to feel that this was almost the normal mode of conducting business; perhaps, too, he suspected Ober's motive and his pride was injured. The very fact that he did not wholly trust himself made him even more sensitive to such treatment. He had come very close to losing faith in himself with his failure at M-G-M and he desperately needed the encouragement of someone else's belief in him. It was the rage of guilt and despair that made him write Perkins, "[Ober] is a stupid hard-headed man and has a highly erroneous idea of how I live, moreover he has made it a noble duty to piously depress me at every possible opportunity." [39] If, on the contrary, Ober guessed all too accurately how Fitzgerald was living, the angry sarcasm of "noble" and "piously" shows how much Fitzgerald hated anyone's even suspecting his condition.

His answer to Ober combines a description of his inability to face what he believed to be Ober's loss of faith in him with a generous acknowledgment of what he owed Ober from the past.

As I said in my telegram, the shock wasn't so much at your refusal to lend me a specific sum . . . it was rather "the manner of the doing." . . .

I don't blame you. . . . my unwritten debt to you is terribly large and I shall always be terribly aware of it — your care and cherishing of Scottie during the intervals between school and camp in those awful sick years of '35 and '36. . . .

But Harold, I must never again let my morale become as shattered as it was in those black years. . . .

I have a neurosis about anyone's uncertainty about my ability that has been a principal handicap in the picture business. . . . One doesn't change at 42 though one can grow more tired and even more acquiescent — and I am very close to knowing how you feel about it all: I realize there is little place in this tortured world for any exhibition of shattered nerves or anything that illness makes people do.

So goodbye and I won't be ridiculous enough to thank you again.[40]

From this time on Fitzgerald dealt directly — and far from effectively — with the magazine editors, mostly with Arnold Gingrich of *Esquire* who treated him very, very generously. In July, 1939, he turned out two stories, "Design in Plaster" and "The Lost Decade," for Gingrich; they were his first stories since "Financing Finnegan," written in June, 1937. Of the twenty-three stories he wrote from this time until his death all but one were sold to *Esquire*. Seventeen of the twenty-three belong to the series about Pat Hobby, Fitzgerald's sardonic portrait of a broken-down script writer. "A complete rat" but not essentially a "sinister" character, he is what Fitzgerald in his worst moments saw himself becoming.

The six other stories of this period, together with the six he wrote in the spring of 1937 before going to Hollywood, constitute a distinct group; in them Fitzgerald faces the fact that he can no longer write the kind of popular love story he had made his short story reputation with and had to find a new subject and attitude. "It isn't particularly likely," he wrote one editor, "that I'll write a great many more stories about young love. I was tagged with that by my first writings up to 1925. Since then . . . they have been done with increasing difficulty and increasing insincerity. . . . I have a daughter. She is very smart; she is very pretty; she is very popular. Her problems seem to me to be utterly dull and her point of view completely uninteresting. . . . I once tried to write about her. I couldn't. So you see I've made a sort of turn." [41]

The stories in this group are not, of course, all equally good, but the vision projected in them is the vision of the late stories in *Taps at Reveille* and of the series of biographical sketches he had written in 1936 for *Esquire*. They are shorter than his earlier stories because of *Esquire*'s needs, with the result that Fitzgerald's quiet, humorous acceptance of suffering and disaster is disentangled from the plots of his earlier stories about such feelings, and the brilliant, subtle movement of his final prose gets its full effect. We do not need to be told what to feel about Mr. Trimble of "The Lost Decade"; knowing him is enough. We are ahead of the doctor in "The Long Way Out" in wanting to get back to the subject of oubliettes. The condemnation of the Paris of the twenties in "News of Paris —Fifteen Years After" need never be made explicit because the shuffling moral attitude of the twenties toward their own conduct is, for all the grace and sympathy with which that conduct is presented, so completely implied by the events themselves. These stories, because of their brevity, are purer in motive and written more delicately and economically than any of Fitzgerald's earlier stories.[42]

CHAPTER XVI

By the summer of 1939 he and Sheilah had made up
their quarrel and Fitzgerald was beginning to get control of
his drinking for considerable spells. But in the autumn, when
Sheilah was nastily attacked by *The Hollywood Reporter* for
something she had said on a lecture tour, he rushed violently
to her defense, got very drunk, and tried to challenge *The
Reporter*'s editor, W. R. Wilkinson, to a duel. In September
he got a brief week of work at United Artists on *Raffles*, but
he was still in great financial difficulties. Toward the end of
that month, however, Littauer at *Collier's* expressed a real interest in the novel Fitzgerald had had in the back of his mind
since he had first met Irving Thalberg in 1931. Littauer agreed
to pay $25,000 or $30,000 for the serial rights to this novel
if Fitzgerald would submit fifteen thousand words and an outline that they liked.[1]

The possibility that he might be released from the drudgery
of movie work and free to work on his novel for six months
or more seemed miraculous to Fitzgerald, and he went to
work with the old enthusiasm making notes and arranging the
impressions of Hollywood that had been slowly gathering in
his mind like the elements of a myth. He made hundreds of
pages of notes; they constitute a minutely detailed, wonderfully perceptive portrait of a place and time, far richer than
the small portion of these notes Fitzgerald got organized into

the six chapters of the novel he completed before he died. They show almost better than *The Last Tycoon* itself how intact his talent was despite his physical and nervous exhaustion.

As soon as he realized *Collier's* was seriously interested, Fitzgerald sat down and wrote Littauer a letter outlining the story in detail and telling him what he hoped to make of it. How strongly he felt about it, however, is clearest from his letter to Scottie:

> Scottina:
>
> (Do you know that isn't a nickname I invented but one that Gerald Murphy concocted on the Riviera years ago). Look! I have begun to write something that is maybe great, and I'm going to be absorbed in it for four or six months. It may not *make* us a cent but it will pay expenses and it is the first labor of love I've undertaken since the first part of "Infidelity." . . . Anyhow, I'm alive again. . . .[2]

He started to write with all the energy he could muster. "He didn't rise at a given hour and plan the day's work," his secretary has said. "Insomnia more or less prevented such a routine. . . . Some days he worked more than others; some days he worked not at all. . . . He wrote in bed, in longhand. He preferred to write out narrative and dictated and even enacted dialogue, pacing the floor rapidly. He tired easily and didn't have enough energy to devote a full day to writing, except under extreme pressure. . . . Once the plan for a story or idea was clear in his mind, he wrote rapidly. For instance, although it took him several years to accumulate and coordinate notes for *The Last Tycoon*, the actual writing time of the unfinished novel was only four months. He could do as many as a dozen pages in half a day." [3]

By the end of November he had completed six thousand words, probably the first chapter and the equivalent of one installment instead of the two Littauer had asked for. Nonetheless, he sent it off to Littauer and asked for a decision. Since the story has reached only the flood in the studio back lot by the end of the first chapter, it is hardly surprising that Littauer wanted to DEFER VERDICT UNTIL FURTHER DEVELOPMENT OF STORY. But Fitzgerald was uncontrollably impatient for encouragement and his financial difficulties were increasing — he had borrowed money to send Scottie back to Vassar. He abruptly cut off negotiations with *Collier's* and wired Perkins: PLEASE RUSH COPY AIR MAIL TO SATURDAY EVENING POST. . . . I GUESS THERE ARE NO GREAT MAGAZINE EDITORS LEFT. But, like *Collier's*, the *Post* wanted more to go on and there was no more, so that nothing came of this plan either.[4]

As was always true when he was drinking, he was tense and easily driven to despair. "I'm so tired of being sick and old," he wrote a friend when war broke out, " — would much rather be a scared young man peering out over a hunk of concrete or mud toward something I hate."[5] His decision to break off negotiations with *Collier's* when all they had done was to suggest he follow the original arrangement was not a wise one; when his efforts to interest the *Post* failed, he grew even more bitter and depressed, and, as if he had to take it out on some one, he precipitated a desperate drunken quarrel with Sheilah during which he struck her and then threatened to kill her. When he finally sobered up he tried to apologize, but Sheilah could not forget that terrible quarrel for months. They finally made their peace in January, 1940, and from then until his death Fitzgerald remained sober. In April they gave up the house at Encino and Fitzgerald moved into an apartment in town near Sheilah's.

Before he went back to work, he tried to make a quick profit from his idea and wrote a short story which is a simplified version of the love story of *The Last Tycoon* called, at first, "Pink and Silver Frost" and, later, "The Last Kiss." It gives a queer, unsympathetic portrait of Kathleen, of which there is almost nothing left in *The Last Tycoon*.[6] He could not sell this story so he went back to the novel, working on it as steadily as he could until April, when he took another movie job. By that time he had worked out in some detail nearly all of the six chapters which were completed at his death. He told his picture agent in May that he had written six chapters, but this statement can hardly be precise, since he spent a considerable part of November and December on the book, and during the last three weeks of his life he worked hard at it.

It had been a long time since he had had any picture work except the brief job on *Raffles*. At first he thought the reason was that he had stopped work for five months during 1939 and he wrote Scottie: "Sorry you got the impression that I'm quitting the movies — they are always there. . . . But I'm convinced that maybe they're not going to make me Czar of the Industry right away, as I thought 10 months ago. It's all right Baby — life has humbled me — Czar or not we'll survive. I am even willing to compromise for Assistant Czar!" [7] But by January he was frankly anxious. "Once Bud Schulberg told me that, while the story of an official blacklist is a legend, there is a kind of cabal that goes on between producers around a backgammon table, and I have an idea that some such sinister finger is upon me," he wrote his agent.[8]

In April, however, he found a picture job which, if it paid, according to his views, very little, was congenial and could be worked on outside the studio. In January Lester Cowan had bought the rights to "Babylon Revisited" for $800. "I sold 'Babylon Revisited' in which you are a character, to the pictures," Fitzgerald wrote Scottie, "(the sum received wasn't worthy of the magnificent story — neither of you nor of me — however, I am accepting it)." Cowan then offered Fitzgerald $5000 to make a script from it. Fitzgerald called the arrangement "a sort of half-pay, half 'spec' (speculation) business. . . . Columbia advances me living money while I work and if it goes over . . . I get an increasing sum. At bottom we eat — at top the deal is very promising." [9] He worked close to six hours a day getting the first draft out; this was an heroic effort in his condition, but he loved the story and called his work on it "more fun that I've ever had in pictures." [10] It appealed to him especially because he was now pretty well convinced that he "couldn't make the grade as a hack — that, like everything else, requires a certain practised excellence." What the excellence was he explained more carefully to his old friend Katherine Tighe: ". . . only in the last few months has life begun to level out again in any sensible way. The movies went to my head and I tried to lick the set up single handed and came out a sadder and wiser man. For a long time they will remain nothing more nor less than an industry to manufacture children's wet goods." [11] He finished the script, called *Cosmopolitan*, at the end of June; there was a month and a half of revising and dickering to see if Shirley Temple could be interested in the part of Victoria (the Honoria of the story), and then the script was shelved "for one that has been made for the brave Laurence Olivier who will defend his country in Hollywood (though summoned back by the British Government). This affects the patriotic and unselfish Scott Fitzgerald to the extent that I receive no more money from that source. . . ." [12] *Cosmopolitan* was, except for some minor doctoring jobs, the last picture Fitzgerald did.

But Fitzgerald's script is so good that its ghost keeps rising to haunt Mr. Cowan. In 1947 he asked a writer to revise it and when the writer said, "This is the most perfect motion-picture scenario I ever read. I don't see why you want to revise it," Mr. Cowan is reported to have said, "You're absolutely right. I'll pay you two thousand dollars a week to stay out here and keep me from changing one word of it." [13] During the summer of 1949 the script was again seriously considered for production.

Though Fitzgerald had been working steadily through the summer, he had not been well. "I can't exercise even a little any more, I'm best off in my room," he told Scottie.[14] In his notes for *The Last Tycoon* he wrote: "Do I look like death (in mirror at 6 p.m.)." He did. He was very thin and his face was gray and delicate-looking. Only his eyes seemed alive, though his wit was as brilliant as ever when he had the physical and nervous energy to exercise it. "Do you want a picture of me in my palmy days or have you got one?" he wrote Scottie with his queer objectivity. ("If you don't want this one send it back as thousands are clamoring for it," he said when he sent the picture.)[15]

With the money he collected from his picture work in September and October, he was able to devote himself to his novel and he determined to finish it. "I am trying desperately to finish my novel by the middle of December," he wrote Zelda, "and it's a little like working on *Tender Is the Night* at the end — I think of nothing else." A few days later he was saying, "I am deep in my novel, living in it, and it makes me happy. . . . Two thousand words today and all good." [16]

In November he had what his doctor called a "cardiac spasm" while he was buying cigarettes in Schwab's. How seriously he took it is shown by the fact that almost for the first time in his life he belittled instead of exaggerating an illness. "I'm still in bed but managing to write and feeling a good deal better. It was a regular heart attack this time and I will simply have to take better care of myself," he wrote Scottie.[17] Spending most of his time in bed, he got down to even harder work on *The Last Tycoon*. He knew exactly what he wanted to do: "I want to write scenes that are frightening and inimitable. I don't want to be as intelligible to my contemporaries as Ernest who as Gertrude Stein said, is bound for the Museums. I am sure I am far enough ahead to have some small immortality if I can keep well." [18] Much of the actual writing of the book must have been done at this time.

It is not easy to be just to an unfinished novel; everyone tends to read it according to his established bias about the author. The reviewers found, if they were inclined that way, that *The Last Tycoon* provided "no evidence that [Fitzgerald] could have adjusted its themes into a beautiful articulated piece of craftmanship. . . . It would have sprawled. . . ." Or they were convinced that "Had Fitzgerald been permitted to finish the book . . . there is no doubt that it would have added a major character and a major novel to American fiction." On the whole, however, the reviews were serious and sympathetic. Even Margaret Marshall, who had said at the time of Fitzgerald's death that *Tender Is the Night* was "a confused exercise in self-pity," thought that *The Last Tycoon* "would assuredly have been a brilliant novel about Hollywood." About the only representative of the old school of Fitzgerald reviewers was *Time*, which compared *The Last Tycoon* to *Citizen Kane* — though even this comparison may have been a compliment in *Time*'s judgment.[19]

So far as it goes, *The Last Tycoon* justifies this burden of favorable opinion. It is true that Fitzgerald had a more ambitious and complicated judgment of his material in mind than he had ever tried to manage before; possibly he could not have pulled the various strands of this judgment together in the end, or perhaps he would have had to sacrifice the dramatic material of the novel to do so. But as far as he got, the evidence is that he would have succeeded in retaining his complex theme and still have managed to control the structure.

As he always did, he started here from direct observation. Even the flood with which he begins the Hollywood part of the novel actually occurred while he was there. It is no secret that Fitzgerald drew freely on his conception of Irving Thalberg for Stahr.[20] It is possibly less obvious that, back of every other character in the book, from Kathleen and Brady to the director Red Ridingwood and the superannuated star Martha

Dodd, lay Fitzgerald's acute observation of a real person. No wonder he wrote his daughter, "And I think when you read this book, which will encompass the time when you knew me as an adult, you will understand how intensively I knew your world. . . ." [21] He could have said as much for his observation of the movie world in which he had worked for three years. Personally withdrawn from it and yet close to it every day, he was like Cecilia, who "accepted Hollywood with the resignation of a ghost assigned to a haunted house. I knew what you were supposed to think about it but I was obstinately unhorrified." [22] It was the perfect situation for a writer who simultaneously knew experience as a participant and judged it as an uninvolved observer. Only now, perhaps for the first time in his life with complete understanding, he undertook to cultivate and control this double view of his subject.

His respect for the concrete reality of the life he was describing and his obstinate inability to be horrified by it are what make his description of that life better than any other in print. He knew exactly what he had to do to make it, with all its queerness, real: "ACTRESS — introduced so slowly, so close, so real that you believe in her. Somehow she's first sitting next to you not an actress but with all the qualifications, loud and dissonant in your ear." It is by this means that the wonderful, ordered but confusing series of scenes in Chapters III and IV — they were to be matched by a similar series at the end of the book — get their effect. At the center of this world lives Stahr with his "face that was aging from within, so that there were no casual furrows of worry and vexation but a drawn asceticism. . . ." Stahr is the last of the great paternalistic entrepreneurs, in the last, the most complicated, and the most fantastic of nineteenth-century capitalism's empires. This was Fitzgerald's deliberate and achieved intention, and in the unfinished part of the book, as Mr. Wilson points out, Stahr was to be defeated primarily by the fact that in the modern kind of capitalist enterprise, with its mechanical structure and its split between the highly organized management of the industry and the highly organized employees, there was no function for the brilliant individual who controlled everything by intelligence and understanding and "held himself directly responsible to everyone with whom he has worked." "You're doing a costume part and you don't know it — the brilliant capitalist of the twenties," Wylie White says to Stahr.[23]

Yet, though Fitzgerald clearly felt this kind of man was doomed, and even rightly doomed, he admired his gifts more than any others; they were essentially gifts of humanity and imagination, and they were being used to organize, not a fictional world, but a real one. "I never thought," Stahr tells Brimmer, "that I had more brains than a writer has. But I always thought that his brain *belonged* to me — because I knew how to use them. Like the Romans — I've heard that they never invented things but they knew what to do with them. Do you see? I don't say it's right. But it's the way I've always felt — since I was a boy." [24] Fitzgerald, too, had felt it, since he was a boy. The dream of creating and managing a social enterprise had been part of his "great dream" since the days when he tried to take command of the games as a very small boy and had gone on to invent projects for the Gooserah Club and plays for the Elizabethan Dramatic Club.

A gift for organization and command had always been a characteristic of his heroes, though they had sometimes used that gift for trivial purposes. Amory Blaine had wanted "to pull strings, even for somebody else, or to be Princetonian chairman or Triangle president." [25] Gatsby had managed a great if illegal business enterprise, though it is far in the background of the novel (as when we hear Gatsby on the long-distance telephone: "I said a *small* town. . . . He must know what a small town is. . . . Well, he's no use to us if Detroit is his idea of a small town. . . .").[26] Dick Diver had used his gift to organize a social world for Nicole and her friends;

"The enthusiasm, the selflessness behind the whole performance ravished [Rosemary], the technic of moving many varied
types, each as immobile, as dependent on supplies of attention
as an infantry battalion is dependent on rations, appeared so
effortless. . . ." [27] But Stahr used this gift to manage a great
and complex industry and to try to improve it. "From where
he stood (and though he was not a tall man, it always seemed
high up) he watched the multitudinous practicalities of his
world like a proud young shepherd to whom night and day
had never mattered." [28] He is Fitzgerald's hero at his most
mature and serious, applying his gifts to the central activity
of American society.

Fitzgerald had not many illusions about business as such; it
"is a dull game," he said while he was writing the novel, "and
they pay a big price in human values for their money"; and
he suggested to Scottie that "Some time when you feel very
brave and defiant [about her conservatism] and haven't been
invited to one particular college function read the terrible
chapter in Das Kapital on *The Working Day*, and see if you
are ever quite the same." [29] It was the authority and responsibility that fascinated him. He believed very deeply that "We
can't just let our worlds crash around us like a lot of dropped
trays." [30]

> Suppose — Stahr tells the pilot in the first chapter — you
> were a railroad man. You have to send a train through there
> somewhere. Well, you get your surveyors' reports, and you
> find there's three or four or half a dozen gaps, and not one is
> better than the other. You've got to decide — on what basis?
> You can't test the best way — except by doing it. So you just
> do it.

"All leaders have felt that. Labor leaders, and certainly military leaders," Brimmer tells Stahr when Stahr repeats this idea
to him.[31]

Because Stahr was using his talent in a great and serious en-

terprise and because these similarities are evident to us as well
as to Brimmer, we gradually see that for Fitzgerald his story
is also a political fable. So far as he has gone he has handled
this part of his story with great subtlety. Andrew Jackson,
who like Stahr had faced a democratic crisis indomitably for
all his faults and his illness and his social disadvantage, is presented to us cynically by Wylie White in the Hermitage
scene in the first chapter. Wylie's cynicism half conceals the
difficult meaning of the past, its relevance to our present
dilemma, as something or other does everywhere in the novel.
There, at the Hermitage, Manny Schwartz, after telling Stahr
that "when you turn against me I know it's no use," commits
suicide. "He had come a long way from some Ghetto to present himself at that raw shrine. Manny Schwartz and Andrew
Jackson — it was hard to say them in the same sentence. It
was doubtful if he knew who Andrew Jackson was as he
wandered around, but perhaps he figured that if people had
preserved his house Andrew Jackson must have been someone
who was large and merciful, able to understand." "You sort
of wish that Andrew Jackson would come out and welcome
him in," one of Fitzgerald's notes adds. A little later, Prince
Agge, deeply puzzled by Stahr, sees an extra dressed as Lincoln
eating his lunch in the commissary. "This, then, he thought,
was what they all meant to be." "Stahr was an artist only, as
Mr. Lincoln was a general, perforce and as a layman." And in
his notes Fitzgerald kept reminding himself to "show Stahr
in Lincoln mood." In the last part of the book Stahr was to
go to Washington but to be ill and to see it clearly "only as he
leaves." [32]

Fitzgerald's writing is finer than any he had ever done before, and he had not made his final revision of any of it. All
his old gifts are in the book. Its scenes are sharp, clean, and
beautifully clear, as for instance when Stahr explains to Boxley what movies are.[33] Fitzgerald's essential, poetic gift for
getting at the quality and feel of a situation with muted figura-

tive language never worked more unremittingly or more tact-fully; in the scene on the plane with which the book opens, the stewardess "can always tell people are nice if they wrap their gum in paper"; the passengers make "the studied, un-ruffled exclamations of distaste that befitted the air-minded" when the plane dips; Schwartz stares at Stahr's back "with shameless economic lechery" and speaks of his daughter "as if she had been sold to creditors as a tangible asset." That gift places the startling, revealing, and touching detail just where it is needed:

> Martha Dodd was an agricultural girl, who had never quite understood what had happened to her and had nothing to show for it except a washed-out look about the eyes. . . .
>
> "I had a beautiful place in 1928," she told us, " — thirty acres, with a miniature golf course and a pool and a gorgeous view. All spring I was up to my ass in daisies."

And there is the wonderful dialogue:

> "Are you going to sing for Stahr?" Wylie said. "If you do, get in a line about my being a good supervisor."
>
> "Oh, this'll be only Stahr and me," I [Cecilia] said. "He's going to look at me and think, 'I've never really seen her before.' "
>
> "We don't use that line this year," he said.
>
> " — Then he'll say 'Little Cecilia,' like he did the night of the earthquake. He'll say he never noticed I have become a woman."
>
> "You won't have to do a thing."
>
> "I'll stand there and bloom. After he kisses me as you would a child — "
>
> "That's all in my script," complained Wylie, "and I've got to show it to him tomorrow."
>
> " — he'll sit down and put his face in his hands and say he never thought of me like that."
>
> "You mean you get in a little fast work during the kiss?"

"I bloom, I told you. How often do I have to tell you I
bloom."

"It's beginning to sound pretty randy to me," said Wylie.
"How about laying off — I've got to work this morning."

Throughout the book there is the quiet, powerful prose of
Fitzgerald's last period. There are no costume-jewelry com-
parisons or appeals to feelings outside the context of the narrative such as occasionally marred his earlier work. The feelings
always belong to the people and the events; they are never
forced on them, never asserted for their own sake.[34]

But whether he could have fulfilled the promise of this beginning we can never be sure. Like so much else in his life,
his heroic effort to finish his last novel came too late; and the
luck which might have kept him alive until he had finished
was not with him. He had predicted to Perkins in the middle
of December that he could complete a first draft by January
15, and at the rate he was going he might have done so; on
December 20 he had completed the first episode of Chapter
VI.[35] But that night — it was a Friday — as he and Sheilah
were leaving the Pantages Theatre after seeing *This Thing
Called Love*, he had another attack, so severe that he managed
to get out of the theatre only with Sheilah's help; that frightened her: he had never let her help him before. "I feel awful,"
he said, " — everything started to go as it did that night at
Schwab's." But he slept well that night and seemed himself
the next morning. After lunch, while they waited for the
regular visit of the doctor, Fitzgerald sat making notes on the
margin of an article about the Princeton football team. Suddenly he started up from his chair, clutched the mantel for a
moment, and then fell to the floor. In a few moments he was
dead.

He was buried with a flurry of ironies even thicker than he
had himself dared to devise for Gatsby. His body was laid out
in an undertaker's parlor on Washington Boulevard "which,"

as one observer remarked, " — to Beverly Hills — is on the other side of the tracks in downtown Los Angeles." He was not placed in the chapel but in a back room named the William Wordsworth room; no doubt it seemed to the undertaker the appropriate place for a literary man. Almost no one came to see him; one of the people who did said that

> he was laid out to look like a cross between a floor-walker and a wax dummy in the window of a two-pants tailor. But in technicolor. Not a line showed on his face. His hair was parted slightly to one side. None of it was gray.
>
> Until you reached his hands, this looked strictly like an *A* production in peace and security. Realism began at his extremities. His hands were horribly wrinkled and thin, the only proof left after death that for all the props of youth, he actually had suffered and died an old man.[36]

His old friend Dorothy Parker is said to have stood looking at his body for a long time and then, without taking her eyes off him, to have repeated quietly what "Owl-eyes" said at Gatsby's funeral: "The poor son of a bitch." [37]

His body was shipped to Baltimore for burial. He had always wanted to be buried with his father's family in the Catholic cemetery at Rockville, Maryland. But there were difficulties about this plan: his books were proscribed and he had not died a good Catholic. Despite the efforts of his friends to overcome these difficulties, the Bishop refused to allow him to be buried in hallowed ground. The funeral itself was a very simple one. When Fitzgerald had made his will in June, 1937, full of optimism about the fortune he was to make in Hollywood, he had written: "Part of my estate is first to provide for a funeral and burial in keeping with my station in life." But later he canceled "for a funeral" and inserted in pencil "the cheapest funeral." Then he added at the end of the paragraph: "The same to be without undue ostentation or unnecessary expense."

The services were held in a funeral parlor in Bethesda on December 27. Scottie was there, and Fitzgerald's cousins from Norfolk, the Abeles and the Taylors, and Zelda's brother-in-law, Newman Smith, from Atlanta. There were old friends like Max Perkins and Harold Ober and the Murphys from New York and college friends like Ludlow Fowler and Judge Biggs and a number of others who lived in Baltimore. One of those present estimated that there were all of thirty or forty people there. Miss Graham was not one of them. He was buried in the Rockville Union Cemetery. It was as near as he was allowed to be to his father, beside whose grave he had stood almost exactly ten years before thinking how "very friendly [it was] leaving him there with all his relations around him."

Not long before he died Fitzgerald scribbled on an odd scrap of paper a few imperfect lines for a poem he never got time to finish. As if conscious to the last of a need to tell his story, he was writing his own epitaph.

> *Your books were in your desk*
> *I guess and some unfinished*
> *Chaos in your head*
> *Was dumped to nothing by the great janitress*
> *Of destinies.*

The novel he wanted so desperately to complete was unfinished; the reputation in which he found his justification was only a faint echo (all his life he saved clippings about himself; at the end there were only a few scattered sentences from *The Hollywood Reporter* to be clipped); and he was, he knew, dying. Like Gatsby, who felt that if Daisy had loved Tom at all "it was just personal," Fitzgerald loved reputation, the public acknowledgment of genuine achievement, with the impersonal magnanimity of a Renaissance prince. He lived, finally, to give that chaos in his head shape in his books and to see the knowledge that he had done so reflected back to him from the world. He died believing he had failed.

Now we know better, and it is one of the final ironies of Fitzgerald's career that he did not live to enjoy our knowledge. "You can take off your hats, now, gentlemen," Stephen Vincent Benét wrote when *The Last Tycoon* appeared in 1941, "and I think perhaps you had better. This is not a legend, this is a reputation — and, seen in perspective, it may well be one of the most secure reputations of our time." [38]

On March 11, 1947, Highland Hospital burned down. Zelda Fitzgerald, who was on the top floor, was trapped and burned to death. She was buried beside Fitzgerald in the small-town quiet of the Rockville Cemetery. There is a common headstone.

APPENDIXES

NOTES AND REFERENCES

FITZGERALD'S PUBLISHED WORK

INDEX

APPENDIX A

A GOOD EXAMPLE of Fitzgerald's method of revision is provided by the passage in *The Last Tycoon* where the pilot tells the drunk in the Nashville airport that he is in no condition to fly and will have to wait for the next plane. There are three versions of the scene preserved in Fitzgerald's manuscripts, a pencil ms., a typed revision of this pencil ms., and a revision of this revision, which was used by Edmund Wilson for the printed text (*The Last Tycoon*, p. 14). The first version of the passage goes this way:

> The pilot was at the desk talking with the pursur and shaking his head as they both regarded a prospective passenger who lay alcoholicly on another bench fighting off sleep. He seemed to have used the three hours neither wisely nor well. The pilot shook his head definately at the purser and walked over to him.
>
> "Afraid we're not going to be able to carry you this time old man."
>
> "Wha?"
>
> The drunk sat up, very awful looking yet discernably handsome and I was sorry for him.
>
> "Go back to the hotel and get some sleep. There'll be another plane tonight."
>
> "Only going — te Dallas."
>
> "Not this time old man."

In his dissapointment the man fell off the bench, and the loudspeaker summoned us respectable people outside.

The passage is full of good things. There is the pilot's artificial friendliness, with its inoffensive professional condescension — how does one talk to drunks? There are the little touches which, without qualifying the drunk's awfulness or his humiliating, subhuman confusion, make him sympathetic — "his fighting off sleep," his "dissapointment" — all summed up and focused by Cecilia's irony about "respectable people." But the passage was not good enough for Fitzgerald. The next step was (I have italicized the places where changes occur):

The pilot was at the desk talking with the purser and shaking his head as they both regarded a prospective passenger who *had put two nickles in the electric phonograph* and lay alcoholically on *a* bench fighting off sleep. *The song, "Lost," thundered through the room, followed, after a slight interval, by his other choice, the equally dogmatic "Gone."* The pilot shook his head definitely at the purser and walked over to *the passenger.*

"Afraid we're not going to be able to carry you this *time, old* man."

"Wha?"

The drunk sat up, very awful looking, yet discernibly "*attractive*," and I was sorry for him *in spite of the music.*

"Go back to the hotel and get some sleep. There'll be another plane tonight."

"Only going *up in ee air.*"

"Not this time old man."

In his disappointment the man fell off the bench, and *above the phonograph*, a loudspeaker summoned us respectable people outside.

Much of this first revision is taken up with the introduction of the symbolic music, though Fitzgerald is also working on other elements in the scene. The third revision works with the whole scene (the italics mark the places where further changes occur):

The pilot was at the *desk with* the purser and *he shook* his head as *they regarded* a prospective passenger who had put two nickles in the electric phonograph and lay alcoholically on a bench fighting off sleep. *The first song he had chosen*, *Lost* [Fitzgerald's italics], *thundered through* the room, followed, after a slight interval, by his other *choice*, *Gone* [Fitzgerald's italics], *which was equally dogmatic and final*. The pilot shook his head *emphatically and* walked over to the passenger.

"Afraid we're not going to be able to carry you this time, old man."

"Wha?"

The drunk sat up, *awful-looking*, yet discernibly *attractive*, and I was sorry for him in spite of *his passionately ill-chosen* music.

"Go back to the hotel and get some sleep. There'll be another plane tonight."

"Only going up in ee *air*." [Fitzgerald's italics]

"Not this time, old man."

In his disappointment the *drunk* fell off the *bench* — *and* above the phonograph, a loudspeaker summoned us respectable people outside.

Much of this last revision is that unostentatious but careful suppression of unnecessary verbiage which is one of the familiar marks of Fitzgerald's best prose: the removal of "talking" and "both" in the first sentence, for example. Some of it is a sharpening, through tone and rhythm, of the characters: the drunk's (he has not been called that before) increased air of the eminently reasonable man, puzzled but polite in the face of official stupidity. Some of it — the new relative clause in the second sentence, the phrase "passionately ill-chosen music" — brings out more sharply the ironic, accidental symbolism of the songs. Some of it, like the dash in the last sentence, clarifies Cecilia's attitude, which is the controlling attitude of the whole passage. At the top of the final draft of the chapter from which this passage is taken, Fitzgerald wrote: "Rewrite for mood."

APPENDIX B

The following notes connected with the planning of Tender Is the Night *were together among Fitzgerald's papers. The evidence seems to suggest that all of them except the "Summary of Part III" were written at the same time and that this summary was made when Fitzerald got to the writing of the last section of the book. None of this material is dated, so that it is only a guess, based on internal evidence, that the main outline of the story and the character sketches were made at La Paix in 1932, when, for the last time, he started over again to write the book. The differences between this outline and the novel as Fitzgerald actually wrote it — particularly the book's failure to follow the outline's suggestions about Dick's sympathy with the Soviet Union — fit the changes in Fitzgerald's attitude during this period. The "Summary of Part III," on the other hand, fits the book fairly closely.*

GENERAL PLAN

Sketch

The novel should do this. Show a man who is a natural idealist, a spoiled priest, giving in for various causes to the ideas of the haute Burgeoise, and in his rise to the top of the social world losing his idealism, his talent and turning to drink and dissipation. Background one in which the liesure class is at their truly most brilliant & glamorous such as Murphys.

————————

The hero born in 1891 is a man like myself brought up in a family sunk from haute burgeoisie to petit burgeoisie, yet expensively educated. He has all the gifts, and goes through Yale almost succeeding but not quite but getting a Rhodes scholarship which he caps with a degree from Hopkins, & with a legacy goes abroad to study psychology in Zurich. At the age of 26 all seems bright. Then he falls in love with one of his patients who has a curious homicidal mania toward men caused by an event of her youth. Aside from this she is the legendary *promiscuous* woman. He "transfers" to himself & she falls in love with him, a love he returns.

After a year of non-active service in the war he returns and marries her & is madly in love with her & entirely consecrated to completing the cure. She is an aristocrat of half American, half European parentage, young, mysterious & lovely, *a new character*. He has cured her by pretending to a stability & belief in the current order he does not have, being in fact a communist — liberal — idealist, a moralist in revolt. But the years of living under patronage ect. & among the burgeoise have seriously spoiled him and he takes up the marriage as a man divided in himself. During the war he has taken to drink a little & it continues as secret drinking after his marriage. The difficulty of taking care of her is more than he has imagined and he goes more and more to pieces, always keeping up a wonderful face.

At the point when he is socially the most charming and inwardly corrupt he meets a young actress on the Rivierra who falls in love with him. With considerable difficulty he contains himself out of fear of all it would entail since his formal goodness is all that is holding his disintegration together. He knows too that he does not love her as he has loved his wife. Nevertheless the effect of the repression is to throw him toward all women during his secret drinking when he has another life of his own which his wife does not suspect, or at least he thinks she doesn't. On one of his absences during which he is in Rome with the actress having a disappointing love affair too late he is beaten up by the police. He returns to find that instead of taking a rest cure she has committed a murder and in a revulsion of spirit he tries to conceal it and succeeds. It shows him however that the game is up and he will have to perform some violent & Byronic act to save her for he is losing his hold on her & himself.

He has known slightly for some time a very strong & magnetic man and now he deliberately brings them together. When he finds under circumstances of jealous agony that it has succeeded he departs knowing that he has cured her. He sends his neglected son into Soviet Russia to educate him and comes back to America to be a quack thus having accomplished both his burgeoise sentimental idea in the case of his wife and his ideals in the case of his son, & now being himself only a shell to which nothing matters but survival as long as possible with the old order.

(Further sketch)   *Approach*

The Drunkard's Holiday will be a novel of our time showing the break up of a fine personality. Unlike *The Beautiful and Damned* the break-up will be caused not by flabbiness but really tragic forces such as the inner conflicts of the idealist and the compromises forced upon him by circumstances.

The novel will be a little over a hundred thousand words long, composed of fourteen chapters, each 7,500 words long, five chapters each in the first and second part, four in the third — one chapter or its equivalent to be composed of retrospect.

DICK

The hero was born in 1891. He is a well-formed rather athletic and fine looking fellow. Also he is very intelligent, widely read — in fact he has all the talents, including especially great personal charm. This is all planted in the beginning. He is a superman in possibilities, that is, he appears to be at first sight from a burgeoise point of view. However he lacks that tensile strength — none of the ruggedness of Brancusi, Leger, Picasso. For his external qualities use anything of Gerald, Ernest, Ben Finny Archie Mcliesh, Charley McArthur or myself. He looks, though, like me.

The faults — the weakness such as the social-climbing, the drinking, the desperate clinging to one woman, finally the neurosis, only come out gradually.

We follow him from age 34 to age 39.

The actress was born in 1908. Her career is like Lois or Mary Hag — that is, she differs from most actresses by being a lady, simply reeking of vitality, health, sensuality. Rather gross as compared to the heroine, or rather *will be* gross for at present her youth covers it. . . .

We see her first at the very beginning of her career. She's already made one big picture.

We follow her from age 17 to age 22.

The Friend was born in 1896. He is a wild man. He looks like Tunte and like that dark communist at the meeting. He is half Italian or French & half American. He is a type who hates all sham & pretense. (See the Lung type who was like Foss Wilson) He is one who would lead tribesmen or communists — utterly aristocratic, unbourgeoise king or nothing. He fought three years in the French foriegn legion in the war and then painted a little and then fought the Riff. He's just back from there on his first appearance in the novel and seeking a new outlet. He has money & this French training — otherwise he *would* be a revolutionist. He is a fine type, useful or destructive but his mind is not quite as good as the hero's. Touch of Percy Pyne, Denny Holden also.

We see him from age 28 to age 33.

ACTUAL AGE OF

DICK

September 1891 Born

" 1908 Entered Yale

June 1912 Graduated Yale   aged 20

June 1916 Graduated Hopkins. Left for Vienna (8 mo. there)

June 1917 Was in Zurich after 1 year and other work. Age 26

June 1918 Degree at Zurich. Aged 26

June 1919 Back in Zurich. Aged 27

September 1919 Married — aged 28 { after his refusing fellowship at University in neurology and pathologist to the clinic. Or does he accept? }

July 1925 After 5 years and 10 months of marriage is aged almost 34.

Story starts

July 1929 After 9 years and 10 months of marriage is aged almost 38.

NICOLE'S AGE

Always one year younger than century.

Born July 1901

courtship for two and one half years before that, since she was 13.

Catastrophe June 1917 Age almost 16

Clinic   February, 1918 Age 17

To middle October bad period

After armistice good period

He returns in April or May 1919

She discharged June 1, 1919. Almost 18

Married September 1919. Aged 18

Child born August 1920

Child born June 1922

2nd Pousse almost immediately to October 1922 and thereafter

Frenchman (or what have you in summer of 1923 after almost 4 years of marriage.

In July 1925 when the story opens she is just 24

One child almost 5 (Scotty in Juan les Pins)

One child 3 (Scotty in Pincio)

In July 1929 when the story ends she is just 28

The heroine was born in 1901. She is beautiful on the order of Marlene Dietrich or better still the Norah Gregor–Kiki Allen girl with those peculiar eyes. She is American with a streak of some foreign blood. At fifteen she was raped by her own father under peculiar circumstances — work out. She collapses, goes to the clinic and there at sixteen meets the young doctor hero who is ten years older. Only her transference to him saves her — when it is not working she reverts to homicidal mania and tries to kill men. She is an innocent, widely read but with no experience and no orientation except what he supplies her. Portrait of Zelda — that is, a part of Zelda.

We follow her from age 24 to age 29

Method of Dealing with Sickness Material

(1) Read books and decide the general type of case
(2) Prepare a clinical report covering the years 1916-1920
(3) Now examine the different classes of material selecting not too many things for copying.

> (1) From the sort of letter under E
> (2) " " " " " " F
>   (In this case using no factual stuff)
> (3) From the other headings for atmosphere, accuracy and material being careful not to reveal basic ignorance of psychiatric and medical training yet not being glib. Only suggest from the most remote facts. *Not* like doctor's stories.

Must avoid Faulkner attitude and not end with a novelized Kraft-Ebing — better Ophelia and her flowers.

Classification of the Material on Sickness

A. Accounts
B. Baltimore
C. Clinics and clipping
D. Dancing and 1st Diagnoses
E. Early Prangins — to February 1931
F. From Forel (include Eleuler Consultation)
H. Hollywood
L. Late Prangins
M. My own letters and comments . . . .

Both the content and the handwriting show that the following outline of Part Three was written later than the main sketch and at least some of the character sketches which are printed above.

11,000   Summary of Part III (1st half)

The Divers, *as a marriage* are at the end of their rescourses. Medically Nicole is nearly cured but Dick has given out & is sinking toward alcoholism and discouragement. It seems as if the completion of his ruination will be the fact that cures her — almost mystically. However this is merely hinted at. Dick is still in controll of the situation and thinks of the matter practically. They must separate for both thier sakes. In wild bitterness he thinks of one tragic idea but controlls himself and manages a saner one instead.

His hold is broken, the transference is broken. He goes away. He has been used by the rich family and cast aside.

Part III is as much as possible seen through Nicole's eyes. All Dick's stories such as are *absolutely necessary*: Edwardo, father, auto catastrophe (child's eyes perhaps), Struppen quarrel?, girls on Rivierra, must be told without putting in his reactions or feelings. From now on he is mystery man, at least to Nicole with her guessing at the mystery.

NOTES AND REFERENCES

THE FOLLOWING abbreviations are used in the notes.

AM	Arthur Mizener
ASYM	All the Sad Young Men, New York, 1926
B & D	The Beautiful and Damned, New York, 1922
CU	The Crack-Up, edited by Edmund Wilson, New Directions, 1945
EH	Ernest Hemingway
EW	Edmund Wilson
FFL	Frances Fitzgerald Lanahan
FSF	F. Scott Fitzgerald
Gatsby	The Great Gatsby, New York, 1925
JPB	John Peale Bishop
Letters	The Letters of F. Scott Fitzgerald, edited by Andrew Turnbull, New York, 1963
LT	The Last Tycoon, New York, 1941
MP	Maxwell Perkins
SEP	The Saturday Evening Post
SMTW	Zelda Fitzgerald, Save Me the Waltz, New York, 1932
TAR	Taps at Reveille, New York, 1935
TITN	Tender Is the Night, New York, 1934
TJA	Tales of the Jazz Age, New York, 1922
TSOP	This Side of Paradise, New York, 1920
ZSF	Zelda Sayre Fitzgerald

NOTEBOOKS. Fitzgerald left two large loose-leaf volumes of notes, some of which were printed by Edmund Wilson in *The Crack-Up*. They consist of passages selected from stories Fitzgerald planned not to reprint, general observations, and notes written on particular occasions or people which he thought might be useful in his work. These notes he arranged under such heads as "Conversations and Things Overheard," "Descriptions of Girls," etc. He then arranged these groups alphabetically.

LEDGER.   This is an old-fashioned record book of two hundred lined pages, in which, during the summer of 1922, Fitzgerald began to keep his personal records. It contains a "Record of Published Fiction," an annual statement of his earnings, and an "Outline Chart of My Life." Its record is precise, though often cryptic, up to 1936; after that it becomes irregular.

SCRAPBOOKS.   Both Zelda and Scott kept personal scrapbooks fairly carefully until the early twenties.

ALBUMS.   I have used this perhaps artificial term to distinguish from the scrapbooks the five volumes of clippings about his works which Fitzgerald collected during his life. I have numbered them in chronological order for convenience of reference.

INTRODUCTION

1. Notebooks, O; CU, p. 211. James Thurber, " 'Scott in Thorns,' " *The Reporter*, April 17, 1951, p. 35.
2. Morley Callaghan, *That Summer in Paris*, p. 159; EH, *A Moveable Feast*, p. 184.
3. To Margaret Case Harriman, August, 1935; *Letters*, p. 527.
4. "Pasting It Together," CU, p. 84.
5. JPB, "Books of the Month," *Vanity Fair*, October, 1921.
6. JPB in a review of *The Beautiful and Damned* in the New York *Herald*, clipping in Album II. Fitzgerald disliked this review; "one solid page of bull," he called it.
7. Notebooks, O; CU, p. 202.
8. Glenway Wescott, "The Moral of Scott Fitzgerald," CU, p. 326.
9. Allen Tate to AM, March 31, 1945.
10. "Handle with Care," CU, p. 75.
11. Thomas Boyd, "Literary Libels, II," the St. Paul *Daily News*, March 12, 1922. Fitzgerald's Ledger, p. 173, suggests that the novel was *Fortitude* and that he read it on his way west when he went home to write *This Side of Paradise* in 1919.
12. *The Autobiography of Alice B. Toklas*, p. 268; Burton Rascoe, *We Were Interrupted*, New York, 1947, p. 20. But Rascoe's recollections are not always to be trusted. He also says Fitzgerald told him he and Zelda were married the day TSOP was pub-

lished — a confusion of two different dates of which Fitzgerald
was certainly incapable — and that he wrote TSOP with Cabell's
Jurgen propped in front of him, when *Jurgen* was not published
till the fall of 1919, by which time TSOP was in Scribner's hands
(it was sent them September 3, 1919). Fitzgerald's own copy of
Jurgen is dated December 20, 1920. "Rascoe has accused him of
imitating James Branch Cabell. Fitzgerald laughs at this, for, as
he says, he never heard of Cabell or of any other modern novelists until after he graduated from Princeton." (Ward Greene, the
Atlanta Journal, 1922, Clipping in Album III.)

13. "My Lost City," CU, p. 27.
14. The *New Yorker*, January 4, 1941, p. 9.
15. The *Nation*, February 8, 1941, p. 159; *College English*, April, 1944,
    pp. 372f.
16. The New York *World Telegram*, December 26, 1940.
17. Introduction to *The Great Gatsby*, The Modern Library, 1934.
18. *A Moveable Feast*, p. 155.
19. Fitzgerald often revised his magazine stories when he put them
    in books. A comparison of the *Post* version of "Babylon Revisited"
    (February 21, 1931) and the version in *Taps at Reveille* illustrates
    the effect of a careful revision of a story; it is exactly like the
    effect of his revision of *Tender Is the Night* between the first,
    magazine version and the book.
20. Edmund Wilson, "Thoughts on Being Bibliographed," *Princeton
    University Library Chronicle*, February, 1944, p. 54.
21. To Mrs. Bayard Turnbull, June, 1933; *Letters*, p. 435.
22. To JPB, n.d., CU, p. 267. The Fitzgeralds went to Capri from
    Rome in February, 1925, made a quick visit to Rome in the mid-
    dle of the month, and returned to Capri. They were not in Rome
    again. Since this letter was written from Rome and mentions that
    they are just back from Capri, it must have been written between
    the middle and the end of February, 1925. At this time Fitzgerald
    was saying to Harold Ober about the prices of his short stories:
    "If the novel [*Gatsby*] is a big success I'm hoping my price will
    go up to $2000 regular. It's a neat sum and while I don't feel my
    stuff is worth anything like that it's as good as a lot that gets much
    more." (To Harold Ober, received January 23, 1925.)
23. To MP, May 20, 1940; *Letters*, p. 288.

CHAPTER I

1. *Doctor Diver's Holiday*, p. 453; TITN, p. 266.
2. Richard Washington.
3. Mrs. Philip McQuillan.
4. "An Author's Mother," *Esquire*, September, 1936.

5. To Mrs. Richard Taylor, August 14, 1940; *Letters*, p. 419.
6. To FFL, *ca*. August, 1935.
7. "The Crack-Up," CU, p. 69.
8. Mrs. Gerald Murphy to FSF, April 3, 1936.
9. To FFL, *ca*. March, 1939; *Letters*, p. 54.
10. *The Romantic Egotist*, chapter I, p. 5; B. F. Wilson, "Scott Fitzgerald," *The Smart Set*, April, 1924; Ledger.
11. *The Romantic Egotist*, chapter I, p. 30. The italics are mine.
12. *The Romantic Egotist*, chapter I, p. 13.
13. The reference to Sam White is in FSF's Scrapbook, the reference to Hobey Baker in TSOP, p. 46. The meeting with Buzz Law is described in "Princeton," *College Humor*, December, 1927, p. 28. Possibly Fitzgerald's memory played him slightly false here. There is a photograph of Law kicking from behind his own goal line with a bandage round his head in the Yale-Princeton game of 1913. But those were brave days when many backs played without helmets; Law was one of them and probably there were games in 1915 too in which he kicked from behind goal lines wearing a bloody bandage. The statement about seeing Law in Paris should be compared to Fitzgerald's remark on the same occasion in a letter to Ludlow Fowler: "Buzz Law, an old hero of mine, passed me on the street the other day looking by no means distinguished." (November 6, 1926.)
14. *The Romantic Egotist*, chapter II, p. 20.
15. "Basil at the Fair," SEP, July 21, 1928; Notebooks, S; CU, p. 226.
16. To FFL, July 5, 1937; *Letters*, p. 16.
17. To Beatrice Dance, September, 1936; CU, p. 280; *Letters*, p. 541.
18. *Gatsby*, p. 2.
19. TITN, p. 266; "Echoes of the Jazz Age," CU, p. 22.
20. This passage is from an unpublished ms. entitled "The Death of My Father." It appears to have been written immediately after the event, which occurred in 1931. Dick Diver's father is drawn directly from Fitzgerald's, and some of this material was used in TITN. This particular story also appears in the first chapter of *The Romantic Egotist*.
21. To Harold Ober, received June 3, 1926; *Letters*, p. 393. One of the stories Fitzgerald remembered was about how his father had as a small boy helped one of Moseby's guerrillas to escape. He tells this story in "The Death of My Father" and in *Doctor Diver's Holiday*, pp. 455-456. (Both of these are still in ms.) A much abbreviated version of the scene in *Doctor Diver's Holiday* appears in TITN, chapter XVIII. Fitzgerald also wrote an inferior story called "The End of Hate" based on this story of his father's; it appeared in *Collier's*, June 22, 1940.
22. *The Romantic Egotist*, chapter I, pp. 4 and 14; Ledger, p. 162; "That Kind of Party," the unpublished Basil story.

23. Notebooks, S; CU, p. 228. The passage is from "The Popular Girl," SEP, February 11 and 18, 1922.
24. To Alida Bigelow, September 22, 1919; *Letters*, p. 456.
25. Notebooks, U; CU, p. 233. On another occasion Fitzgerald ascribed St. Paul's "social complacency" to the fact that a considerable number of Easterners came there for their health in the 1850's (in a review of Grace Flandrau's *Being Respectable*, clipping in Album III).
26. Ledger, p. 165.
27. To John O'Hara, July 18, 1933; *Letters*, p. 505.
28. Ledger, p. 163.
29. C. N. B. Wheeler.
30. Basil is of course Fitzgerald himself, Ripley Buckner and Bill Kempf are Cecil Read and Paul Ballion. Like everything else in the story, this episode occurred, according to Fitzgerald's Ledger, in the spring of 1911.
31. TAR, pp. 6-7.
32. *The Romantic Egotist*, chapter I, p. 21.
33. Mr. Turnbull says, "Fitzgerald's sister told me that Aunt Annabel McQuillan sent her to Rosemary Hall but did *not* pay Fitzgerald's way at Newman, as was previously thought" (*Scott Fitzgerald*, p. 338). It was Miss Annabel McQuillan herself who told me she sent Fitzgerald to Newman, but she was a very old lady when I talked to her and may have been confused.
34. The episode is also described in *The Romantic Egotist*, chapter I, p. 32.
35. *The Romantic Egotist*, chapter I, p. 33.
36. TAR, pp. 27-29.
37. TAR, p. 34.
38. Charles W. Donahoe to AM, January 10, 1948. Fitzgerald did go out for Freshman football at Princeton; he was cut from the squad almost immediately.
39. Interview of Martin Amorous by Peggy Mitchell, the Atlanta *Journal*, 1924 (clipping in Album III).
40. "What I Think and Feel at Twenty-Five," the *American Magazine*, September, 1922, pp. 136-7.
41. Devereux C. Josephs to H. D. Piper, May 1, 1947.
42. TAR, p. 51.
43. TAR, p. 55.
44. TAR, p. 90. Of the five plays Fitzgerald wrote for the Elizabethan Dramatic Club, this is the only one that has been preserved. The original ms. — minus its final page — is at Princeton.
45. "Handle with Care," CU, p. 79.
46. "Who's Who," SEP, September 18, 1920, p. 42. The quotations in the footnote are from *The Romantic Egotist*, chapter I, p. 13 and *Gatsby*, p. 7. For "the romantic Buzz Law" see above, p. 6.

47. Ledger, p. 164.
48. The information comes from the St. Paul *Daily News*, FSF's Scrapbook, the poster which was used to advertise the play.
49. "The Invasion of the Sanctuary," Vanity Fair, November, 1923.

CHAPTER II

1. FSF Scrapbook.
2. V. Lansing Collins, *Princeton*, 1914, pp. 382-83.
3. Christian Gauss, "Edmund Wilson," *Princeton University Library Chronicle*, February, 1944, p. 41.
4. Edmund Wilson, "Thoughts on Being Bibliographed," *Princeton University Library Chronicle*, February, 1944, p. 58.
5. JPB, "Princeton," *The Smart Set*, November, 1921, pp. 57-58.
6. TSOP, p. 46.
7. TSOP, p. 47; *The Romantic Egotist*, chapter II, p. 22.
8. JPB, "Princeton," p. 58.
9. The *Daily Princetonian*, January 8 and 12, 1917.
10. JPB, "The Missing All," the *Virginia Quarterly Review*, Winter, 1937, p. 108.
11. TSOP, p. 56.
12. To ZSF, *ca.* August, 1940.
13. "Princeton," *College Humor*, December, 1927, p. 28.
14. EW, "Thoughts on Being Bibliographed," p. 54.
15. EW to FSF, August 28, 1915.
16. Gauss, "Edmund Wilson," p. 44.
17. "My Lost City," CU, p. 24. Wilson actually lived in Hamilton.
18. EW, "Dedication," CU, p. 8.
19. Notebooks, S; CU, p. 228.
20. "Princeton," p. 28.
21. TSOP, p. 27.
22. TSOP, p. 47.
23. "Winter Dreams," ASYM, pp. 62-3.
24. TSOP, p. 67.
25. Mrs. Maurice Flynn to H. D. Piper.
26. TSOP, p. 52.
27. Norris Jackson.
28. Note the reference in "Pasting It Together," CU, p. 84 to "the shoulder pads worn for one day on the Princeton freshman football field."
29. "Reade, Substitute Right Half," *Now and Then*, February, 1910.
30. "Sleeping and Waking," CU, p. 66.
31. JPB, "The Missing All," pp. 108-9.
32. FSF's review of *The Oppidan* (1922), clipping in Album II.

33. Fay was an albino and extraordinarily youthful in appearance.
34. When Fay died on January 10, 1919, Fitzgerald and Zelda imagined they had a premonition of disaster. As they sat together on the couch in the Sayres' living room, they were seized by uncontrollable fear. They learned of Fay's death the next day. (ZSF to H. D. Piper.) The description of Father Darcy's funeral in TSOP (pp. 286-87) is taken from the description of Fay's funeral Leslie sent Fitzgerald, January 16, 1919.
35. TSOP, pp. 26-7.
36. TSOP, p. 114.
37. Fay to FSF, October 19, 1918. The letter from Monsignor Darcy on pp. 115-16 of TSOP is a slightly adapted version of an undated letter from Fay written in Rome in the winter of 1917; the letter on pp. 171-74 is part of a letter from Fay of December 10, 1917; the poem quoted in it was also written by Fay. Monsignor Darcy's letter on p. 236 combines paragraphs from Fay's letters of June 6 and June 13, 1918.
38. Fay to FSF, August 17, 1918.
39. To Shane Leslie, September 17, 1920; Letters, p. 377.
40. "Who's Who," SEP, September 18, 1920, p. 61.
41. St. Paul Pioneer Press, September 10, 1914.
42. In his own copy of the program, Fitzgerald has pencilled in corrections which make the credits read: "Book and lyrics by F. Scott Fitzgerald, 1917. Revision by Walker M. Ellis, 1915." This description represents the facts.
43. "Chatter Trio," Fie! Fie! Fi-Fi!, The John Church Company, 1914.
44. "Babes in the Woods," the Nassau Literary Magazine May, 1917, p. 60. This story was incorporated into TSOP with only minor revisions (pp. 67-78).
45. Mrs. John Pirie to AM, November 7, 1947.
46. TSOP, p. 77.
47. "Winter Dreams," ASYM, p. 73.
48. Gatsby, p. 179.
49. TSOP, p. 90.
50. To Mrs. Bayard Turnbull, November 13, 1939; Letters, p. 445.
51. "My Lost City," CU, p. 24.
52. TSOP, pp. 80-88.
53. FSF's Scrapbook; the "Ode" was written by Marie Hersey.

CHAPTER III

1. His election to the editorial board of The Tiger was announced in the issue of June, 1915; his name appeared on the masthead in the September issue and then was dropped.

2. Christian Gauss to AM, October 17, 1944.
3. The letters are in FSF's Scrapbook.
4. "Who's Who," SEP, September 18, 1920.
5. To FFL, September 17, 1940; *Letters*, p. 94.
6. "Handle with Care," CU, p. 76.
7. To John O'Hara, July 18, 1933; *Letters*, p. 503.
8. The statement about Dick Diver is in the "Sketch Plan" for TITN (see Appendix B); James Drawbell, *The Sun Within Us*, p. 175.
9. Ledger, p. 170.
10. TSOP, pp. 109, 115.
11. The John Grier Hibben Papers, Princeton University Library. Fitzgerald's concentration on chemistry in this letter is not quite fair to Princeton. While he was there he failed a third of the courses he took and maintained a fourth-group (D–) average in the rest.
12. "The Missing All," The *Virginia Quarterly Review*, Winter, 1937.
13. To EH, November 8, 1940; CU, p. 285; *Letters*, p. 312.
14. To FFL, April 12, June 12, 1940; CU, pp. 292, 294; *Letters*, pp. 70, 79. It was President Walker Ellis, 1915, who took credit for Fitzgerald's book for *Fie! Fie! Fi-Fi!*; it was President C. L. Heyniger, 1916, who played football and left Fitzgerald to organize and direct *The Evil Eye*.
15. The *Nassau Literary Magazine*, January 1916, pp. 318-19. These lines appear in "Gossip," a department which, according to the index, was written for this issue by John Peale Bishop and Edmund Wilson, Jr. Five years later, Fitzgerald, obviously quoting from memory, ascribed ll. 3-6 of the poem to Wilson in an interview by Roy McCardell published in the *Morning Telegram* (Clipping in Album III). Mr. Wilson's own impression is "that John first wrote the vers libre piece in the *Gossip* and then I revised it and probably wrote the lines Scott quoted." (EW to AM, October 14, 1949.)
16. See "A Woman with a Past," TAR, which gives a fairly accurate account of the affair.
17. Ledger, p. 170.
18. Ginevra King to FSF, July 7, 1917.
19. The *Daily Princetonian*, January 11, 1917.
20. March, 1917.
21. The St. Paul *Daily News*, August 28, 1921.
22. To John Grier Hibben, June 3, 1920; *Letters*, p. 462.
23. "My Lost City," CU, pp. 24-5.
24. "Who's Who," SEP, September 18, 1920.
25. Malcolm Cowley, The *New Yorker*, June 30, 1945, p. 54.
26. Notebooks, O; CU, p. 200.
27. This quotation is from the version of *Tender Is the Night* on

which Fitzgerald worked up to about 1929. It was variously called *The World's Fair, Our Type,* and *The Boy Who Killed His Mother.* Its hero, Francis Melarky, is one of Fitzgerald's many versions of himself.

28. "Pasting It Together," CU, p. 74.
29. "The Crack-Up," CU, p. 69.
30. Notebooks, L; CU, p. 180.
31. Notebooks, O; CU, p. 183. This passage is from a story called "Six of One," *Red Book*, February, 1932.
32. EW.
33. The New York *Tribune*, April 11, 1920.
34. Ernest Boyd, *Portraits: Real and Imaginary*, pp. 220-21.
35. To FFL, November 4, 1939; CU, p. 305; *Letters*, p. 63.
36. Ledger, p. 171.
37. *Gatsby*, p. 21.
38. Glenway Wescott, "The Moral of Scott Fitzgerald," CU, p. 328.
39. To Francis Turnbull, November 3, 1938; *Letters*, pp. 577-578. He said much the same thing to James Boyd: "I have just emerged not totally unscathed, I'm afraid, from a short violent love affair. . . . maybe some day I'll get a chapter out of it. God, what a hell of a profession to be a writer. One is one simply because one can't help it" (to James Boyd, August, 1935; *Letters*, pp. 528-529).
40. They are "Babes in the Woods" and "The Debutante," both of which were later published in the *Smart Set* and still later incorporated into TSOP, and "The Pierian Spring and the Last Straw." All three stories appeared in the *Lit* between January and October, 1917.
41. To Mrs. Richard Taylor, June 10, 1917; *Letters*, p. 414.
42. To EW, January 10, 1918; CU, p. 250; *Letters*, pp. 321-322.
43. To EW, January 10, 1918; CU, p. 252; *Letters*, p. 323.
44. Fay to FSF, August 22, 1917.
45. To EW, September 26, 1917; CU, p. 245; *Letters*, p. 317.
46. *Poet Lore's* letter of acceptance is in FSF's Scrapbook; he had sent Wilson the poem earlier in the fall (see CU, p. 249), and he submitted it two years later to Professor Morris Croll for inclusion in *A Book of Princeton Verse II* (1919), where it was again not printed.
47. Fay to FSF, n.d.
48. To EW, Autumn, 1917; CU, p. 249; *Letters*, p. 321.
49. "Princeton," *College Humor*, December, 1927, p. 29. To EW, Autumn, 1917; CU, p. 248; *Letters*, p. 319.
50. To Mrs. Edward Fitzgerald, November 14, 1917; *Letters*, pp. 451-452.
51. To Mrs. Edward Fitzgerald, November 14, 1917; *Letters*, pp. 451-452.
52. Ledger, p. 171.

53. To Mrs. Richard Taylor, June 10, 1917; *Letters*, p. 414.
54. EW to AM, November 11, 1949. Compare the intense interest in the war in "Looking Back Eight Years," *College Humor*, June, 1928, written at just the time Wilson is speaking of.
55. "'I Didn't Get Over,'" *Esquire*, October, 1936; James Drawbell, *The Sun Within Us*, p. 176.
56. There was a barge sinking during a practice crossing of the Talapoosa River while Fitzgerald was in training. There was also an occasion when a propellant charge failed to go off and a fused shell stuck in a Stokes Mortar. The Director of the School of Arms, Major Dana Palmer, picked up the mortar and swung it so that the shell was thrown far enough away to explode without injuring anyone (Major Dana Palmer to AM, February 11, 1951).
57. To EW, January 10, 1918; CU, p. 252; *Letters*, p. 324.
58. To Mrs. Richard Taylor, June 10, 1917; *Letters*, p. 414.
59. EH to FSF, December 21, 1935.
60. "The Crack-Up," CU, p. 71.
61. The *Nassau Literary Magazine*, May, 1917. Printed as prose, this poem constitutes the epilogue to Book I of TSOP.
62. See the caption to the picture of the Fitzgeralds in *Hearst's International*, May, 1923.
63. TSOP, pp. 164-66.
64. To EW, January 10, 1918; CU, p. 252; *Letters*, p. 323.
65. "What I Think and Feel at Twenty-Five," the *American Magazine*, September, 1922, p. 137; see also "Who's Who," SEP, September 18, 1920.
66. Clipping in FSF's Scrapbook.
67. To EW, January 10, 1918; CU, p. 252; *Letters*, p. 323.
68. JPB to FSF, March, 1918.
69. Leslie to AM, November 5, 1947. Leslie's letter is still in Scribner's files. A section of ms., later incorporated into the TSOP ms. without change (it is the passage on p. 168 of TSOP) is inscribed "Completed at Cottage Club on leave, February, 1918." It was so inscribed when Cottage, in 1933, got up a committee to collect memorabilia of famous members. Fitzgerald eventually decided to send them, instead of this page, the ms. of "Good Morning Fool!" (TSOP, pp. 117-19). This piece of ms., also with an inscription stating that it was completed in Cottage in 1918, now hangs in the club library.
70. To EW, January 10, 1918; CU, p. 252; *Letters*, p. 324.
71. The episode of The Devil is in TSOP, Bk. I, chapter III, the Isabelle episode in Bk. I, chapter II, the Eleanor episode in Book II, chapter III. No complete ms. of *The Romantic Egotist* now exists but a ms. of five chapters — I, II, V, XII, and XIV — has been presented to the Princeton Library by Mr. Charles W.

Donahoe, and several sections of the existing ms. of TSOP are the revised typescript of *The Romantic Egotist*: the original names of the characters are still decipherable where they have been inked over. The statements in the text of what *The Romantic Egotist* contained are based on this evidence. The Isabelle episode of course existed even earlier than *The Romantic Egotist* (see p. 50 above).

72. Charles Scribner's Sons to FSF, August 19, 1918. This letter was almost certainly written by Maxwell Perkins.

73. Roger Burlingame, *Of Making Many Books*, p. 67; Shane Leslie to FSF, September 8, 1918.

74. Major Dana Palmer to AM, February 1, 1951; TSOP, p. 212.

CHAPTER IV

1. *Save Me the Waltz*, p. 65. I have assumed that Zelda's novel can be trusted to reveal her understanding of her own situation. It is clearly autobiographical, as Fitzgerald said publicly in 1932. His correspondence with Perkins shows that it was so literally autobiographical that even Fitzgerald balked and insisted on Zelda's rewriting the whole central passage. Innumerable small details indicate how much the book depends on fact: the room David and Alabama have for their honeymoon at the Biltmore is the one the Fitzgeralds had for theirs, 2109 (p. 54); the incident of the aviator's falling from his plane (pp. 42-43) occurred just as Zelda describes it (Fitzgerald used the same incident in "The Last of the Belles"); Bonnie's blue ski suit was Scottie's and the Kodak snaps still exist (p. 232).

2. SMTW, p. 73.

3. *Town Topics*, clipping in ZSF's Scrapbook.

4. "Tribute," the *New Yorker*, April 24, 1926.

5. *Metropolitan*, June 1922.

6. "What I Think and Feel at Twenty-Five," the *American Magazine*, September, 1922.

7. *Gatsby*, pp. 178-79.

8. "One Southern Girl," CU, pp. 157-58. Since the next-to-last line quoted here also appears in B & D (p. 329), this poem was written before the spring of 1921, probably just about then.

9. SMTW, p. 45.

10. SMTW, p. 47.

11. Major Dana Palmer to AM, February 11, 1951. *Flappers and Philosophers*, p. 54. Of the writing of "The Ice Palace," Fitzgerald once said: "The . . . idea grew out of a conversation with a girl in St. Paul. . . . We were riding home from a moving picture show late one November night [1919]. 'Here comes winter,' she

said, as a scattering of confetti-like snow blew along the street. I thought immediately of the winters I had known there, their bleakness and dreariness and seemingly endless length. . . . At the end of two weeks I was in Montgomery, Alabama, and while out walking with a girl I wandered into a graveyard. She told me I would never understand how she felt about the Confederate graves, and I told her I understood so well that I could put it on paper. Next day on my way back to St. Paul it came to me that it was all one story. . . ." ("Contemporary Writers and Their Work: F. Scott Fitzgerald," Clipping in Album I).

12. Notebooks, G.

13. Fitzgerald had an elaborate imaginary story about this occasion according to which he had gone into the Knickerbocker and got very drunk, and when he discovered his unit had left Camp Mills, had gone to the railroad people at Pennsylvania Station, told them he had confidential papers for President Wilson, and persuaded them to provide him a special locomotive to take him to Washington. He appears to have told this story first — for the sheer fun of it, without expecting to be believed — to his fellow officers when he rejoined his unit in Washington; he continued to tell it all his life (see, for example, Michael Mok, "The Other Side of Paradise," New York *Post*, September 25, 1936).

14. Major Dana Palmer to AM, February 11, 1951; Louis Bromfield to AM, December, 1950.

15. Ledger, p. 173; SMTW, pp. 50-51; ZSF's Scrapbook. Fitzgerald liked to say afterwards that he spent the war as "the army's worst aide-de-camp" ("Early Success," CU, p. 85). But the order appointing him General Ryan's aide-de-camp is dated December 6, 1918, so he served in that capacity only two months out of the fourteen he was in the army.

16. When Fitzgerald was writing *The Count of Darkness* he jotted down a note about the heroine: ". . . after yielding she holds Phillipe at bay like Zelda me in 1917 [sic: 1918]."

17. JPB to FSF, November 11, 1918.

18. Stanley Kunitz, *Living Authors*, p. 128; Mok, "The Other Side of Paradise."

19. Mok, "The Other Side of Paradise."

20. "Who's Who," SEP, September 18, 1920.

21. "Auction — Model 1934," CU, p. 59.

22. " 'The Sensible Thing,' " ASYM, p. 219.

23. Ledger, p. 173; ZSF to FSF, n.d.

24. "My Lost City," CU, pp. 25-26.

25. "Echoes of the Jazz Age," CU, p. 13.

26. Richard Washington.

27. See Andrew Turnbull, *Scott Fitzgerald*, p. 339; Ledger, p. 173; to FFL, September 21, 1940.

28. "'The Sensible Thing,'" ASYM, p. 227. We have Fitzgerald's own word for it that this is "a story about Zelda and me. All true" (to MP, June 1, 1925; *Letters*, p. 189). The Amory-Rosalind story in TSOP, another version of their story, was written before the engagement was renewed and thus omits what is told here.

29. John Mosher, "The Sad Young Man," the *New Yorker*, April 17, 1926, p. 20. Compare Gatsby's similar departure from Louisville (*Gatsby*, p. 183).

30. "The Bridal Party," SEP, August 9, 1930, p. 10. This story is not, in general, about Zelda but about the famous wedding of Powell Fowler in Paris in the summer of 1930; but this passage almost certainly derives from Fitzgerald's own feelings about Zelda.

31. TSOP, pp. 212-19.

32. Interview by Carleton R. Davis, the New York *Tribune*, May 7, 1920. Fitzgerald made the same remark a little later in a document which has some bibliographical interest. For the meeting of the American Booksellers Association that May Scribner's bound up a number of copies of TSOP for special presentation which contain an extra leaf. This leaf carries a photograph of Fitzgerald and three brief paragraphs addressed by him to the booksellers. Most of the copies I have seen are inscribed.

33. EW to FSF, August 9, 1919.

34. To EW, August 15 [1919]; CU, p. 253; *Letters*, p. 324. Wilson dates this letter "1920," but its reference to his own letter quoted above shows it belongs to 1919. Probably Fitzgerald's "August 15" is incorrect; at least Wilson's reply to this letter is dated "August 14, 1919."

35. Except, of course, the Eleanor episode (see pp. 46-47 above). Much of the new material was doubtless not written in these two months, however. Apart from "The Debutante" (TSOP, pp. 179-93), "Babes in the Woods" (TSOP, pp. 73-78), "On a Play Twice Seen" (TSOP, p. 147), and "Princeton, the Last Day" (TSOP, p. 168), which had appeared much earlier in the *Nassau Lit* and the *Smart Set* Fitzgerald himself noted as one of the sources of TSOP "destroyed stories of 1919" (Ledger, p. 3). These would be some of the stories that were written and rejected while he was a copywriter.

36. To MP, July 26, 1919; *Letters*, p. 137.

37. Richard Washington; to MP, September 4, 1919, *Letters*, p. 137.

38. To EW, August 15, 1919; CU, p. 254; *Letters*, p. 325.

39. C. O. Kalman.

40. To Shane Leslie, September 17, 1920; *Letters*, p. 377.

41. To John Grier Hibben, June 3, 1920; *Letters*, p. 462.

42. Mr. Milton Griggs clearly remembers the occasion of this offer but not the exact salary, but Fitzgerald's friends remember it as impressive.

43. Ledger, p. 174. See "Forging Ahead," SEP, March 30, 1929, pp. 12-3.
44. "Early Success," CU, p. 86.
45. To MP, September 18, 1919; *Letters*, p. 139. In July Fitzgerald had asked whether, if they got the book by August and liked it, Scribner's could have it published by October. These requests show how large a part his concern to impress Zelda played in his determination to succeed.
46. TSOP, pp. 209-10. Like much else in TSOP, Rosalind's assertion has its source in what Zelda had said. "All the material things are nothing," she had written him. "I'd just hate to live a sordid, colorless existence — because you'd soon love me less — and less. . . ." (ZSF to FSF, n.d.)
47. To FFL, April 27, 1938.
48. ASYM, pp. 189-90.
49. Samuel Butler, *Note Books*, p. 217.
50. To Alida Bigelow, September 22, 1919; *Letters*, pp. 456-457. In the third sentence Fitzgerald meant to write "one score and three years," I think. He was to be twenty-three years old on September 24, *two days* after the writing of this letter.
51. To MP, September 18, 1919; *Letters*, p. 139. *The Demon Lover* is the title of that stupid but impressive novel Richard Carmel writes in B & D.
52. The new stories were "Dalyrimple Goes Wrong" and "The Smilers," written in September; "Porcelain and Pink," "Benediction," and "The Cut-Glass Bowl," written in October; "Head and Shoulders" and "Mr. Icky," written in November; "Myra Meets His Family" and "The Ice Palace," written in December. The old story was "The Four Fists"; written in one evening, it was a story Fitzgerald had always particularly disliked: "I've always hated and been ashamed of that damned story 'The Four Fists,' " he wrote Perkins. "Not that it is any cheaper than *The Off Shore Pirate* because it isn't but simply because it's a plant, a moral tale and utterly lacks vitality" (to John Grier Hibben, June 3, 1920; *Letters*, p. 462; to MP, *ca.* December 1, 1921).
53. Ledger, p. 174; "Early Success," CU, p. 86.
54. "Early Success," CU, p. 86.
55. " 'The Sensible Thing,' " ASYM, pp. 232-38.
56. To MP, February 3, 1920; *Letters*, p. 144.
57. To MP, *ca.* January 10, 1920; *Letters*, p. 144.
58. In October he proposed to make a novelette to be called "The Diary of a Literary Failure" for *Scribner's Magazine* out of a journal he had been keeping for over three years; he was going to write this novelette concurrently with writing "The Demon Lover"; by the end of the year both these projects were defunct

(to Robert Bridges, October 25 and December 26, 1919; the first of these is in *Letters*, p. 140). The journal seems to have disappeared.

59. To MP, November 10, 1920.

60. To MP, *ca.* January 10, 1920; *Letters*, p. 141.

61. To MP, *ca.* January 10, 1920; *Letters*, p. 141. Just after his return from New York a month earlier he had written Bridges: "I'm in the most frightful literary slump — and I'm writing a movie to see if I can rest up my brain enough to start a new novel and also get the wherewithal to live until I finish it" (to Robert Bridges, December 26, 1919).

62. The novel, called "Darling Heart," turned on the seduction of the heroine. It was perhaps a first and torturously indirect effort to come to imaginative terms with his seduction of Zelda, an experience he finally dealt with wholly satisfactorily in Gatsby's seduction of Daisy. For a long time he found the subject impossible to leave alone and badly embarrassed Hemingway the first time they met by bringing it up at once (see *A Moveable Feast*, p. 151). "Darling Heart" was quickly dropped when there was an outburst of suppressions of daring novels and Fitzgerald told Perkins he planned to "break up the start of my novel and sell it as three little character stories to *Smart Set*" (to MP, February 3, 1920; *Letters*, p. 144). The only story he sold to *Smart Set* at this time was "May Day," which was certainly never part of "Darling Heart." Possibly he used some of "Darling Heart" for the story of Anthony Patch and Dorothy Raycroft (B & D, Book III, Chapter 1); that story is one of his many versions of himself and Zelda.

63. To MP, January 21, 1920; *Letters*, p. 143.

64. The telegrams are in ZSF's Scrapbook.

65. FSF to Harold Ober, *ca.* December 1919 and February 5, 1922.

66. T. B. Costain to Paul Reynolds, March 27, 1922; Harold Ober to FSF, February 25, 1932. "Crazy Sunday" was also turned down by *Cosmopolitan* and *Red Book*, and it was, because of its subject matter, out of the question for the women's magazines.

67. FSF to Harold Ober, received March 15, 1926; *Letters*, p. 392. "Good stories," as he had told Ober late in March, 1925, "write themselves — bad ones have to be written so this ["Not in the Guide-Book"] took up about three weeks. And look at it. I'd rather not offer it to the Post because everybody sees the *Post* but I know its saleable and I need the money."

68. "A Short Autobiography," the *New Yorker*, May 25, 1929.

69. "Auction — Model 1934," CU, p. 59, says the "blue feather fan [was] paid for out of a first *Saturday Evening Post* story; it was an engagement present — that together with a southern girl's first corsage of orchids"; and in "Early Success," CU, p. 86, Fitzgerald

says: "I spent the thirty dollars [which he received from *Smart Set* for "Babes in the Woods"] on a magenta feather fan for a girl in Alabama." Neither of these statements is quite accurate. Fitzgerald's first *Post* story was sold in November; the magenta fan was sent Zelda the following February; the orchids were sent her for the occasion of the formal announcement of their engagement in March. (See Ledger, p. 174, and ZSF's Scrapbook.) In November he had sent his sister Annabel a blue ostrich plume fan. (Mrs. Clifton Sprague to AM, March 23, 1959.)

70. "Handle with Care," CU, p. 77.
71. Compare Dexter Green's recollections of college, especially, "They had played [that tune] at a prom once when he could not afford the luxury of proms, and he had stood outside the gymnasium and listened." ("Winter Dreams," ASYM, p. 67.)
72. The Montgomery *Advertiser*, March 20, 1920. See note 69 above.

CHAPTER V

1. René Wellek and Austin Warren, *Theory of Literature*, p. 72.
2. Clipping, Album I.
3. Owen Johnson, *Stover at Yale*, New York, 1912, p. 258.
4. TSOP, p. 304.
5. "Carnegie Library Notes," *Atlanta Constitution*, February 13, 1921. I am indebted to Miss Carrie Williams of the Carnegie Library for a copy of this review. Frances Newman also wrote a cutting review of ASYM for the New York *Herald Tribune*, April 26, 1926.
6. EW to FSF, November 21, 1919. Four months later — perhaps unconsciously repeating what he had heard from Wilson — Bishop wrote: "We have read your delicate burlesque of Compton Mackenzie's 'Sinister Street,' and feel that you have a gift in this direction. . . ." (JPB to FSF, March 23, 1920.)
7. *Frances Newman's Letters*, New York, 1929, p. 42.
8. Clippings, Album I.
9. Burton Rascoe, *We Were Interrupted*, pp. 19-20.
10. Frederick Lewis Allen, *Only Yesterday*, Bantam Books, p. 109; "Echoes of the Jazz Age," CU, p. 14.
11. Notebooks, K; CU, p. 169.
12. To MP, June 1, 1925; *Letters*, p. 187.
13. "Thousand-and-First Ship," CU, p. 159.
14. The Allenby description (p. 46) and the Light-Horse Harry Lee reference (p. 167) illustrate how he could overdo the sentiments.
15. TSOP, pp. 90-91. "The meeting of Amory and Isabelle is certainly drawn from our own meeting . . . and the after references to the volumes of Part I & Part II letters that sped back & forth between

us." (Ginevra King Pirie to AM, December 4, 1947.) Mrs. Pirie's adult judgment of their relation is valuable: "I truly feel that my part in Scott's college life was a detriment to him . . . but I was too thoughtless in those days & too much in love with love to think of consequences. These things he has emphasized — and over-emphasized in the Josephine stories but it is only fair to say I asked for some of them." (Ginevra King Pirie to AM, November, 1947.)

16. "The Literary Spotlight: F. Scott Fitzgerald," *The Bookman*, March, 1922, pp. 20-21; reprinted in *The Literary Spotlight*, ed. John Farrar, New York, 1924. These essays were anonymous, but Fitzgerald knew that Wilson had written the one about him. Wilson spoke even more bluntly in the letter he wrote Fitzgerald when he first read the book: "I have just read your novel with more delight than I can well tell you. It ought to be a classic in a class with *The Young Visiters*. . . . Your hero is an unreal imitation of Michael Fane of Sinister Street who was himself unreal . . . as an intellectual Amory is a fake of the first water and I read his views on art, politics, religion and society with more riotous mirth than I should care to have you know. . . . in the latter part of the book, you make Amory the hero of a series of dramatic encounters with all the naïve and romantic gusto of a small boy imagining himself a brave hunter of Indians. . . . Cultivate a universal irony and do read something other than contemporary British novelists. . . ." (EW to FSF, November 21, 1919.)

17. "The Conning Tower," the New York *Tribune*, July 6 and 14, 1920. FPA seldom missed a chance for an unfriendly comment on Fitzgerald and when he finally said something kind about *The Great Gatsby*, Fitzgerald wrote Perkins an unprintable comment on him.

18. Glenway Wescott, "The Moral of Scott Fitzgerald," CU, p. 329.

19. "Financing Finnegan," *Esquire*, January, 1938.

20. To EW, February, 1928; CU, p. 273; *Letters*, p. 343.

21. To MP, July 7, 1920. Scribner's had ordered three printings of the book by April first, so that no corrections were possible until the fourth printing, as Perkins carefully explained to Fitzgerald (July 8, 1920). For the many errors in TSOP, Perkins was also somewhat to blame; he "would never, at any stage of its making, let it go out of his hands, and Perkins, but for the stern supervision of his secretary, Miss Wyckoff, would probably be something of an orthographic phenomenon himself." (Roger Burlingame, *Of Making Many Books*, p. 112.)

22. *The Times Literary Supplement*, June 23, 1921, p. 402; Heywood Broun, the New York *Tribune*; clipping in Album I.

23. Frederick Lewis Allen, *Only Yesterday*, Bantam Books, p. 128.
24. *Frances Newman's Letters*, New York, 1929, p. 39. When she sent Cabell Fitzgerald's letter about the review, she said: "Please send it back — first blood, you know." (*Letters*, p. 44.)
25. To MP, April 23, 1938; *Letters*, p. 277. He once proposed to Perkins "a glossary of absurdities and inaccuracies in *This Side of Paradise*" to go with a new edition (to MP, December 24, 1938; *Letters*, p. 281).
26. TSOP, p. 4.
27. *Frances Newman's Letters*, p. 41.
28. The reference to Wilson is in "Handle with Care," CU, p. 79; the reference to TSOP in "Early Success," CU, p. 88.
29. MP to FSF, March 26, 1920.
30. ZSF to FSF, n.d. The telegrams are in ZSF's Scrapbook.
31. Ludlow Fowler.
32. "Auction — Model 1934," CU, p. 60.
33. Ludlow Fowler.
34. "Auction — Model 1934," CU, p. 60.
35. "Early Success," CU, p. 88.
36. I have reconstructed this episode from the accounts of friends who were with Fitzgerald, largely from Edmund Wilson's account. The version of it given in "Early Success" (CU, p. 89) omits a good deal and is, in certain respects, demonstrably inaccurate. The date is fixed by *The Daily Princetonian*'s report (issue of May 3, 1920) of the *Lit* banquet.
37. Christian Gauss to FSF, November 14, 1930.
38. "Show Mr. and Mrs. F. to Number ——,'" CU, p. 41.
39. "Early Success," CU, p. 87.
40. Michael Arlen, *The Green Hat*, London, 1924, pp. 310-11.
41. *Some Do Not* shows Sylvia most clearly; "*The Great Gatsby*," said Gilbert Seldes, "is passionate as Some Do Not is passionate." (The *Dial*, August, 1925, p. 162.)
42. "Echoes of the Jazz Age," CU, p. 14.
43. Joseph Freeman, *An American Testament*, p. 246.
44. To EW, February, 1933; CU, p. 277; *Letters*, p. 345.
45. The St. Paul *Daily News*, September 25, 1921.
46. "Echoes of the Jazz Age," CU, p. 13.
47. B & D, p. 56.
48. "The Crack-Up," CU, p. 70.
49. Walter Lippmann, *A Preface to Morals*, New York, 1929, p. 16.
50. Margaret Case Harriman, *Take Them Up Tenderly*, p. 143.
51. Carl Van Vechten, *The Blind Bow-Boy*, pp. 160-66.
52. The New York *Times*, June 27, 1922, p. 14.
53. SMTW, p. 62.

CHAPTER VI

1. "My Lost City," CU, p. 27.
2. "The Moral of Scott Fitzgerald," CU, p. 323.
3. The phrases are from EW to AM, February 22, 1950. The latter he ascribes to JPB.
4. John Farrar, clipping in Album III.
5. "The Hours," CU, p. 345.
6. "Rags Martin-Jones and the Pr—nce of W—les," ASYM, pp. 140-41.
7. "Babylon Revisited," TAR, p. 406.
8. *Town Topics*, clipping in ZSF's Scrapbook. As Hemingway points out in *A Moveable Feast* (p. 181), falling asleep this way protected them. "They went to sleep on drinking an amount of liquor or champagne that would have little effect on a person accustomed to drinking . . . and when they woke they would be fresh and happy, not having taken enough alcohol to damage their bodies before it made them unconscious."
9. Zelda dove into the fountain at Union Square; the event was later celebrated in the Greenwich Village Follies (see p. 164 below). Fitzgerald jumped into the Pulitzer fountain; his account of his motives for doing so is incorporated into Wilson's "The Delegate from Great Neck," *Discordant Encounters*, p. 58. Fitzgerald's attempt to undress at the *Scandals* appears in B & D, p. 390.
10. Fitzgerald refers to the fight in "My Lost City," CU, p. 28 (the fight occurred that summer of 1920 and was written up in *The News*) and Edmund Wilson described it in "The Crime in the Whistler Room," *Discordant Encounters*, pp. 195-97.
11. This note occurs among the material for LT.
12. "Echoes of the Jazz Age," CU, p. 22.
13. "Early Success," CU, p. 90.
14. "My Lost City," CU, pp. 28-29.
15. The quoted phrases here are from *Gatsby*, p. 218 and the ms. of *Our Type* (the passage is quoted at length on p. 64 above). See also "My Lost City," CU, pp. 27-28.
16. "My Lost City," CU, p. 27.
17. Richard Washington.
18. Notebooks, O; CU, p. 199.
19. B & D, p. 142.
20. The New York *Tribune*, April 4, 1920.
21. The New York *Tribune*, April 11 and 16, 1920.
22. "Early Success," CU, p. 88.
23. "Early Success," CU, p. 88.
24. The New York *Tribune*, May 7, 1920. Richard Carmel also gave this interview, B & D, pp. 188-89. Fitzgerald answered Broun two

years later when he reviewed Broun's novel, *The Boy Grew Older*, for the St. Paul *Daily News*. "[Broun's] literary taste," he said, ". . . is pretty likely to be ill-considered, faintly philistine and often downright absurd." (Clipping in Album III.)

25. MP to FSF, April 16, 1920.

26. This list is in Album I.

27. "'Show Mr. and Mrs. F. to Number ——,'" CU, p. 41.

28. ZSF to Ludlow Fowler, May 19, 1920. "The Cruise of the Rolling Junk," *Motor*, February, 1924, pp. 24-25.

29. The gesture is sometimes ascribed to Fitzgerald (e.g., Thomas Boyd, "Literary Libels, II," the St. Paul *Daily News*, March 7, 1922). The local paper reported with ill-concealed anger that when "the chief and his assistants . . . went to the Fitzgerald house . . . investigation proved of little use, everyone of the occupants claiming they knew nothing about the alarm. Some member of the family suggested that possibly someone came into their house during their absence and sent in an alarm." "There is a statute," the local reporter concludes, "which deals severely with people who send in false alarms for the fun of it." When Fitzgerald was brought before the prosecutor the next week he said "that he did not feel he was to blame for the alarm being sent in but that he would take the responsibility and bear the costs of the department making the run." The newspaper clippings about this affair are in ZSF's Scrapbook.

30. SMTW, p. 70.

31. G. J. Nathan, *Intimate Notebooks*, p. 105; ZSF's Scrapbook. Tana turns up practically intact in B & D.

32. George Jean Nathan to ZSF, July 28, 1920.

33. P. 224.

34. To FFL, July 7, 1938; *Letters*, p. 32.

35. B & D, p. 156.

36. MP to H. D. Piper. Mr. Turnbull quotes some fascinating observations of the kind of pressure Zelda was putting on Fitzgerald at this time from the diary of Fitzgerald's college friend Alec McKaig, who was seeing a great deal of them during these months. For example: "Spent evening at Fitzgeralds. Fitz has been on wagon 8 days — talks as if it were a century. Zelda increasingly restless — says frankly she simply wants to be amused and is only good for useless, pleasure-giving pursuits; great problem — what is she to do?" (*Scott Fitzgerald*, p. 114.)

37. James Drawbell, *The Sun Within Us*, pp. 173-74.

38. To Charles Scribner, August 12, 1920; *Letters*, p. 145.

39. Grace Moore, *You're Only Human Once*, New York, 1944, p. 114.

40. The New York *Tribune*, April 2, 1922.

41. To MP, January 31, 1922; *Letters*, p. 153.

42. Ledger, p. 169.
43. To FFL, June 14, 1940.
44. SMTW, p. 75.
45. To Harold Ober, received February 4, 1926.
46. Harold Ober to FSF, January 5, 1934. For the occasion when Ober felt he must refuse Fitzgerald help see p. 320.
47. "How to Live on $36,000 a Year," SEP, April 5, 1924.
48. For the first three years of his career, Fitzgerald had a great success with the movies. He began by selling "Head and Shoulders" for $2500 to Metro in 1920; it was quickly produced, with Viola Dana and Gareth Hughes, under the impossibly conventional title, *The Chorus Girl's Romance*. He next sold the same company "The Off-Shore Pirate," which was also quickly produced with Viola Dana and Jack Mulhall in the leads. ("The Off-Shore Pirate" was written about a St. Paul girl, Ardita Ford; when the picture reached St. Paul she gave a locally celebrated theatre party so that everyone could "see what I am like in the movies.") A little later he sold "Myra Meets His Family" to Fox; it was produced under the title *The Husband Hunter* with Eileen Percy in the lead. In 1922 he sold the silent rights to B & D to Warner Brothers "for $2500.00 which seems a small price. . . . Please don't tell anyone what I got for it. . . ." (To MP, April 15, 1922.) Also quickly produced with Marie Prevost and Kenneth Harlan, it was, according to James Gray, "one of the most horrific motion pictures of memory." (St. Paul *Dispatch*, March 2, 1926.) The talking rights to B & D seem to have been sold in 1929. In 1923 he sold TSOP to Famous Players for $10,000, under an arrangement according to which he did a treatment for them. "[Famous Players]," he told an interviewer, "are going to produce 'This Side of Paradise,' with Glen Hunter in the leading rôle. I have written first of all a ten-thousand word condensation of my book. This is not a synopsis, but a variation of the story better suited for screening." (Interview by B. F. Wilson; clipping in Album III.) For some reason nothing ever came of this plan; in 1936 Fitzgerald wrote his daughter: "Paramount owns the old silent rights but never made it." (To FFL, July, 1936.) In 1923 he also wrote an original story, called "Grit," for the Film Guild, which cast Glen Hunter in the lead.
49. To Harold Ober, August 2, 1939; *Letters*, p. 406. To FFL, June 12, 1940; CU, p. 294; *Letters*, p. 79.
50. "Dalyrimple Goes Wrong," *Flappers and Philosophers*, p. 233.
51. "Handle with Care," CU, p. 77; to EH, August, 1936, *Letters*, p. 311.
52. MP to H. D. Piper.
53. "Handle with Care," CU, p. 77.

54. To FFL, Autumn, 1937; CU, p. 288.
55. Notebooks, M; CU, p. 182.
56. LT, pp. 156-58.

CHAPTER VII

1. "The Cruise of the Rolling Junk," *Motor*, February, March, April, 1924.
2. To MP, July 7, 1920.
3. ZSF to Ludlow Fowler, August 16, 1920. To MP, June 30, 1920.
4. To MP, November 10, 1920.
5. To MP, January 13, February 13 and 16, 1921; Ledger, p. 4.
6. To Shane Leslie, May 24, 1921; *Letters*, p. 379.
7. *Brentano's Book Chat*, October, 1921.
8. EW to AM, November 11, 1949.
9. This story comes from Edmund Wilson, who had it from Herbert Gorman.
10. Charles Kingsley to MP, June 21 and July 19, 1921.
11. EW to FSF, July 5, 1921. To MP, June 10, 1921.
12. SMTW, p. 75.
13. The St. Paul *Daily News*, August 16 and September 2, 1921.
14. John V. A. Weaver, "The Lion's Cage," The *Brooklyn Eagle*, March, 1922; clipping in Album II.
15. To MP, August 25, 1921; *Letters*, p. 148.
16. Clipping in ZSF's Scrapbook.
17. Thomas Boyd, "Literary Libels, II," The St. Paul *Daily News*, March 19, 1922.
18. Richard Washington. Fitzgerald, like most people who have known poverty, had too vivid a memory of what a few dollars can mean ever to put up much resistance to a borrower. Compare "Hot and Cold Blood" (1923), ASYM.
19. The St. Paul *Daily News*, February 4, 1922; Emily Clark, *Innocents Abroad*, p. 97; to MP, March 5, 1922, *Letters*, pp. 154-55; Ledger, p. 176.
20. These telegrams are in ZSF's Scrapbook.
21. ZSF to Ludlow Fowler, December 22, 1921.
22. Arthur Hartwell.
23. To MP, February 6, 1922. Scribner's printed two editions of 20,000 each before publication.
24. The reviewers quoted here are Mary Colum, the *Freeman*, April 26, 1922, Carl Van Doren, the *Nation*, March 15, 1922, and H. W. Boynton, the *Independent*, April 22, 1922.
25. B & D, pp. 23-24.
26. Vivian Shaw, the *Dial*, April, 1922.
27. To JPB, *ca.* March 7, 1922; CU, p. 258; *Letters*, p. 353.

28. To EW, November 25, 1921; *Letters*, pp. 327-28. To JPB, *ca.* March 7, 1922; CU, p. 258; *Letters*, p. 353.
29. B & D, p. 3.
30. Edmund Wilson, "Scott Fitzgerald," the *Bookman*, March, 1922, p. 24; reprinted in the *Literary Spotlight*, ed. by John Farrar, New York, 1924.
31. William Troy, "Scott Fitzgerald — The Authority of Failure," *Accent*, Autumn, 1945, p. 56.

CHAPTER VIII

1. To MP, *ca.* January 20, 1922.
2. To EW, n.d.: CU, p. 259; *Letters*, p. 334.
3. To MP, *ca.* February 28, 1922.
4. To EW, June 25, 1922; *Letters*, p. 336, to MP, August 17, 1921.
5. The following passages in the book do not appear in the serial version: pp. 405-14, 430-33, 441-42, 444 (from "Turning about from the window . . ." to "Well, things would be different"). The final paragraph of the serial version was cut by Fitzgerald at Zelda's suggestion.
6. "Literary Libels, II," the St. Paul *Daily News*, March 12, 1922. Fitzgerald had borrowed $3400 from Reynolds in May 1921, to pay for their trip abroad. At that time he had wanted to sell the serial rights to B & D to repay this loan and therefore granted *Metropolitan* the right to cut. (See FSF to Harold Ober, May 2, 1921.)
7. To MP, January 24 and February 15, 1924.
8. MP to FSF, April 6 and 17, 1922. To EW, June 25, 1922; *Letters*, p. 336.
9. The St. Paul *Daily News*, April 9, 1922.
10. The *Dial*, February, 1923, p. 311; TJA, pp. vii-xi.
11. MP to FSF, August 2, 1922. Fitzgerald appears to have been particularly fond of "Tarquin of Cheapside." As "Tarquin of Cheepside" it had appeared in the *Nassau Lit* in April, 1917, and later, only slightly revised, in the *Smart Set*, February, 1921.
12. To MP, May 11, 1922; *Letters*, p. 158.
13. TJA sold 12,829 copies in its first year, *Flappers and Philosophers* 11,878.
14. EW to FSF, May 26, 1922.
15. To MP, *ca.* January 1, 1922.
16. The story of the play's revisions and rejections runs through the Wilson-Fitzgerald and the Perkins-Fitzgerald correspondence all spring and summer.
17. To MP, June 20, 1922.
18. To MP, *ca.* July 15 and 18, 1922.
19. JPB to FSF, May 26, 1922.

20. "Eulogy of the Flapper," *Metropolitan*, June, 1922.

21. "Making Monogamy Work," syndicated by the Metropolitan Newspaper Service, February, 1924.

22. "The Crack-Up," CU, p. 70.

23. Ernest Boyd, *Portraits: Real and Imaginary*, New York, 1924, pp. 217-18.

24. In "The Crime in the Whistler Room" (*Discordant Encounters*, pp. 180-81), Edmund Wilson describes one of his characters as "an attractive young man with a good profile, who wears a clean soft shirt and a gay summer tie, but looks haggard and dissipated. . . . His manner . . . alternates between too much and too little assurance, but there is something disarmingly childlike about his egoism." Opposite this passage in the margin of his own copy of the play Fitzgerald wrote: "Bunny on Papa." But Mr. Wilson says: "My conception of the character was quite distinct from Scott. Scott, for example, though he sometimes looked pale, could not be described as *haggard*."

25. *Discordant Encounters*, pp. 49-59.

26. EH to FSF, July 1, 1925.

27. "How to Live on $36,000 a Year," SEP, April 5, 1924.

28. *Portraits: Real and Imaginary*, pp. 223-26.

29. Clipping in ZSF's Scrapbook.

30. Fitzgerald drove Perkins into the pond in July, 1923, according to his Ledger; the story is told in John Mosher's "That Sad Young Man" (the *New Yorker*, April 17, 1926), where Perkins is made a "publicity manager" and the pond a lake. A year later Perkins wrote Fitzgerald: "I thought that night a year ago that we ran down a steep place into a lake. There was no steep place and no lake. . . . Durant took his police dog down to the margin of that puddle of a lily pond, — the dog waded almost across it; — and I'd been calling it a lake all these months. But they've put up a fence to keep others from doing as we did." (MP to FSF, August 8, 1924.) The Bob-haired Bandit story is in "Echoes of the Jazz Age" (CU, p. 21); the other story I had from Edmund Wilson.

31. "Handle with Care," CU, p. 76.

32. *Portraits: Real and Imaginary*, pp. 222-23.

33. B. F. Wilson, "F. Scott Fitzgerald," the *Smart Set*, April, 1924, p. 33.

34. Like all literary anecdotes frequently repeated, this one has become badly confused. Sherwood Anderson says Fitzgerald never got past the door; Burton Rascoe says he came in and "teetering from one guest to another, inquiring which was Dreiser, he finally found his host. . . ." There are many other discrepancies. The party seems to have taken place in January, 1923. See Ernest Boyd, *Portraits: Real and Imaginary*, pp. 221-22; Llewelyn Powys,

The Verdict of Brindlegoose, pp. 131-32; Burton Rascoe, *We Were Interrupted,* pp. 229-302; Sherwood Anderson, *Memoirs,* pp. 335-37. Anderson's version, with its unique details, its suspiciously stylized dialogue, and its neat tie-up with a previous experience of Anderson's own with Dreiser appears the least trustworthy of any of these accounts.

35. James Gray, the St. Paul *Dispatch,* March 2, 1926. The speech is perhaps a little too good to be true, but the gesture is very like Fitzgerald. There is no doubt about his admiration for Mrs. Wharton.

36. "How to Live on $36,000 a Year," SEP, April 5, 1924. He remained firm in this opinion: ". . . the whole thing has already cost me about a year and a half of work so I'd rather let it drop. It's honestly no good." (To Harold Ober, received March 2, 1925.)

37. Fitzgerald believed to his dying day that Kaufman had stolen his idea.

38. John F. Carter in the New York *Post;* clipping in Album III.

39. Carl Hovey to AM, February 2, 1951.

40. The stories were: " 'The Sensible Thing' " and "Our Own Movie Queen" written in November (Zelda wrote a good deal of the latter); "Rags Martin-Jones and the Pr—nce of W—les" and "Diamond Dick" written in December; "Gretchen's Forty Winks" written in January; "The Baby Party" written in February; "The Third Casket," "One of My Oldest Friends," and "The Pusher-in-the-Face" written in March; and "The Unspeakable Egg" and "John Jackson's Arcady" written in April. "The Baby Party" was written in a single all-night session and one of the April stories was a one-day job.

41. "How to Live on $36,000 a Year," SEP, April 5, 1924.

42. To EW, October 7, 1924; CU, pp. 264-265; *Letters,* p. 341.

43. CU, pp. 66-7. See p. 42 above.

44. "Ring," the *New Republic,* October 11, 1933, p. 255.

45. *What of It?,* p. 115. Zelda had a prize-winning police dog named Fritzi at this time.

46. To MP, *ca.* March, 1923.

47. "Ring," p. 255.

48. When Fitzgerald admired a writer his generosity was unlimited. His advocacy of Hemingway (see pp. 215-217 below) is a case in point, and at about the same time he was pressing Lardner to publish, he succeeded, by nagging furiously at Perkins, in getting Scribner's to publish Thomas Boyd's *Through the Wheat,* though they had originally rejected it. Though he was disappointed in Boyd's later work, he always believed he had been right about *Through the Wheat.*

49. "I put aside the novel three weeks ago" (to MP, *ca.* November 6, 1923; *Letters*, p. 161).

50. "How to Live on Practically Nothing a Year," SEP, September 20, 1924.

51. *Gatsby*, p. 133.

52. These verses are in ZSF's Scrapbook.

53. ZSF to MP, May, 1924. "How to Live on Practically Nothing a Year," SEP, September 20, 1924.

54. SMTW, p. 105. Lardner took over the whole burden of their hastily deserted house and affairs in Great Neck and did an admirably efficient job of settling them.

55. To MP, June 18, 1924; *Letters*, p. 164. Burton Rascoe, "A Bookman's Daybook"; clipping in Album IV.

56. SMTW, pp. 109-10.

57. SMTW, pp. 130-31. In the proofs the final sentence of this passage runs: "Whatever it was that she wanted from [him], [he] took with him . . . and the blank in [her] heart was no blanker than before she had known him." Zelda's account of this affair appears to be the most reliable. Fitzgerald used his feelings about it in a story called "Image on the Heart," *McCall's*, April, 1936, and in describing the relation between Nicole and Tommy Barban in TITN.

58. To FFL, May, 1938; *Letters*, p. 31.

59. *Gatsby*, p. 134.

60. The *Nation*, August 25, 1945, p. 182.

61. Ledger, p. 178. Notebooks, I.

62. To MP, August 27, 1924; *Letters*, p. 166.

63. To MP, *ca.* December 20, 1924; *Letters*, p. 172.

64. The new material runs from " 'I've got something to tell *you*, old sport' . . ." (p. 156) to " 'I just remembered that to-day's my birthday.' " (p. 163.) He had already done extensive rewriting on the proofs. The episode about "Blocks" Biloxi (pp. 153-54), for example, was a last-minute inspiration, and he rewrote the last half of chapter six (from "Tom was evidently perturbed. . . ." on p. 125) at this time and relocated most of the material about Gatsby's past.

65. To MP, *ca.* November 7, 1924; *Letters*, p. 169. The story was "Love in the Night," SEP, March 14, 1925.

66. To JPB, April, 1925; CU, p. 269; *Letters* p. 357.

67. "Auction — Model 1934," CU, p. 58.

68. To Carmel Myers, November 21, 1934; Charles Warren to FSF, December 6, 1934.

69. "Handle with Care," CU, p. 78.

70. Notebooks, extra material.

71. The quoted remark is in a letter to Howard Coxe, April 15, 1934.

A humorous account of the actual experience is given in an essay called "The High Cost of Macaroni," that describes their winter in Rome and was intended as a third installment of the *Post* series that begins with "How to Live on $36,000 a Year"; the *Post* rejected it. The Dick Diver episode is in TITN, Chapters XXII and XXIII.

72. Reports of Zelda's illness run through the Perkins correspondence. "Auction — Model 1934," CU, pp. 45-46, shows it was colitis.

73. EW to AM, November 11, 1949.

74. To MP, December 20, 1924, and February 18, 1925; *Letters*, pp. 173 and 177.

75. CU, pp. 265-67.

76. To MP, February 18, 1925; *Letters*, p. 177. The story was "Not in the Guide Book," written in February.

77. To JPB, February, 1925; CU, p. 266; *Letters*, p. 355.

CHAPTER IX

1. *The Great Gatsby*, New Directions, n.d., p. xiv.

2. The reviews quoted are by Gilbert Seldes, *The Dial*, August, 1925; S. V. Benét, *The Saturday Review of Literature*, May 9, 1925; H. L. Mencken, *The Baltimore Sun*, May 3, 1925.

3. To EW; CU, p. 270; *Letters*, pp. 341-42. Mr. Wilson dates this letter "1925"; Mr. Turnbull dates it "Spring, 1925." It states that they have just moved into their apartment in the rue de Tilsitt. They moved into it May 12, 1925.

4. To MP, December 20, 1924; *Letters*, p. 174.

5. To MP, July, 1922. To FFL, October 20, 1936; *Letters*, p. 11.

6. John Jamieson, *Hound & Horn*, October-December, 1932. To John Jamieson, April 7, 1934; *Letters*, p. 509. Shortly after he had written B & D, Fitzgerald made a list of the ten most important novels for the Chicago *Tribune*; in it he called *Nostromo* "the greatest novel since 'Vanity Fair' (possibly excluding 'Madame Bovary')" (Clipping in Album III). In 1940 he told Perkins that "I read [Spengler] the same summer I was writing 'The Great Gatsby,' and I don't think I ever quite recovered from him." What Spengler meant to him he then makes clear: "Spengler prophesied gang rule, 'young people hungry for spoil,' and more particularly 'the world as spoil' as an idea, a dominant, supersessive idea" (to MP, June 6, 1940; *Letters*, p. 290).

7. To MP, April 7, October 11, December 16, 1924, January 24, March 25, 1925. Only the fourth of these letters is in *Letters*, p. 509.

8. Compare Fitzgerald's description with the summary of the rumors

about Rothstein given by Lloyd Morris, *A Postscript to Yesterday,* pp. 66-7 and 75.

9. *This Room and This Gin and These Sandwiches,* pp. 75-76. Zelda said late in her life that this was a Teutonic-featured man named von Guerlach. (ZSF to H. D. Piper.)

10. To John Jamieson, April 15, 1934; *Letters,* p. 509.

11. *Gatsby,* p. 112.

12. *Gatsby,* pp. 103-4.

13. The quotations in this paragraph are from *Gatsby,* pp. 15 and 21-2.

14. *Gatsby,* p. 178.

15. *Gatsby,* p. 216.

16. The quotations in this paragraph are from *Gatsby,* pp. 92-3, 87, 79, 113, 103, and 17.

17. *Gatsby,* pp. 211-13.

18. The quotations in this paragraph are from *Gatsby,* pp. 133 and 144.

19. *Gatsby,* p. 175.

20. To Ludlow Fowler, *ca.* August, 1924.

21. *Gatsby,* p. 16. Fitzgerald was thinking of Lothrop Stoddard's *The Rising Tide of Color,* Scribner's, 1921.

22. The phrases quoted in these two paragraphs are from *Gatsby,* pp. 185, 217-218, 3, 27. The first edition reads "orgastic future," and Fitzgerald meant it. " 'Orgastic' is the adjective for 'orgasm,' " he wrote Perkins (January 24, 1925; *Letters,* p. 175), "and it expresses exactly the intended ecstasy. It's not a bit dirty." Nonetheless, in his copy of the first edition in which he made a large number of pencilled corrections, he changed the adjective to "orgiastic." The only typographical error he corrects in this copy is the reading "eternal" for "external" on p. 58, and this mistake was caused by a confusing revision he made in the proofs. A few small changes were made in the second printing of the novel, but it was not until Scribner's reprint of the late fifties that an attempt was made to incorporate Fitzgerald's own corrections and revisions into the text; unfortunately they were not all correctly interpreted, and some new errors, such as dropped phrases, also crept into this edition. There is an interesting article on the text of *Gatsby* by Bruce Harkness, "Bibliography and the Novelistic Fallacy," *Studies in Bibliography,* 12 (1959), pp. 59-73. The best existing text of *Gatsby* is in *The Fitzgerald Reader,* Charles Scribner's Sons, New York, 1963, though even that text is not absolutely accurate (see the Foreword, p. xiii). There remain some unsolved puzzles. Did Fitzgerald mean "an urban distaste for the concrete" (*The Fitzgerald Reader,* p. 141) or "an urbane distaste"? Did he mean "with fire in the room" (p. 215) or "with

a fire in the room"? It seems almost certain he meant Myrtle Wilson to say, "you'd have thought she had my appendicitus out" (p. 127), not "you'd have thought she had my appendicitis out"; originally he wrote "had my appendix out," then corrected it in the galleys to "appendicitus," tracing over the last five letters of the word a second time to make them perfectly clear. The spelling "appendicitis" is a copyreader's. Michaelis's name creates an inexplicable puzzle. Originally he was named Mavromichaelis, and on p. 207, when he is spelling out his name for the policeman, he begins, "M-a-v-r-o." But then he adds "g". The galleys printed this "g" (it appears twice) as a capital and Fitzgerald carefully corrected it to lower case but did not change it. Where does it come from? There is no "g" in either Michaelis or Mavromichaelis. A simpler puzzle, since it is an explicable kind of oversight, is Fitzgerald's writing that Gatsby "was balancing himself on the dashboard" of his car (p. 151); this mistake for "running board" was missed by the original copyreader, by Fitzgerald, and by all subsequent copyreaders.

23. Louis Bromfield to AM, December, 1950. MP to FSF, April 18, 1925.
24. To JPB, February, 1925; CU, p. 267.
25. To MP, April 24, 1925; *Letters*, p. 180.
26. Ledger, pp. 52-57.
27. Ledger, p. 179.
28. *The Torrents of Spring*, p. 119.
29. Fitzgerald wrote Dean Gauss a card from Brussels that summer offering this explanation for his failure to make a luncheon engagement.
30. *A Moveable Feast*, pp. 152-53. The girl with the phoney title sounds like Lady Duff Twitchell, the model for Brett in *The Sun Also Rises*, whom Fitzgerald disliked so much he felt he could not fairly judge Brett as a character (see p. 217 below). If so, the silly drunk was presumably Pat Swazey.
31. For a description of Fitzgerald's drunken pallor even under ordinary drinking conditions, see James Drawbell, *The Sun Within Us*, p. 171; for another description of the death's-head effect see Morley Callaghan, *That Summer in Paris*, p. 194.
32. Notebooks, O; CU, p. 197. A little episode in *That Summer in Paris* illustrates the course Fitzgerald's ceaseless self-analysis was taking at this time. One night as he and Callaghan were walking toward the Deux Magots, when Fitzgerald was exhausted and a little drunk, "he linked his arm in mine. For about fifty paces he held on to my arm affectionately. I didn't notice him suddenly withdrawing his arm." Sometime later he said suddenly to Callaghan, "Remember the night I was in bad shape? I took your arm.

Well, I dropped it. It was like holding on to a cold fish. You thought I was a fairy, didn't you?" This particular fantasy is probably traceable to the accusations Zelda, in her disturbed state, was making at this time, accusations that appear in their turn to be developments of the complaints of his sexual inadequacy that Zelda made in earlier quarrels and that led Fitzgerald to make the anxious inquiries that elicited the grotesque advice Hemingway reports in *A Moveable Feast* (see *That Summer in Paris*, pp. 193 and 207 and *A Moveable Feast*, pp. 189-191). Hemingway took this problem very seriously; he brought it up again years later at a disastrous dinner with Fitzgerald and Wilson in New York, in 1933.

33. To MP, *ca.* December 27, 1925, *Letters*, p. 194; Frank Swinnerton, *Figures in the Foreground*, New York, 1964, p. 158. But Fitzgerald continued to suspect Chatto & Windus of snubbing him; "they answered a letter of mine on the publication of [*The Great Gatsby*] with the signature (*Chatto & Windus, per Q*), undoubtedly an English method of showing real interest in one's work" (to MP, January 21, 1930, *Letters*, p. 218).

34. *A Moveable Feast*, p. 166; to Gertrude Stein, June, 1925, *Letters*, p. 484.

35. *The World's Fair*, chapter IV. There are three stages of the ms. at this point in the story: a pencil version, a pencil revision and elaboration of this first version, a heavily revised typescript of the second version. So far as possible I have reproduced the final revised typescript, but it is imperfect (a whole page is missing from this passage); moreover, in the typescript Fitzgerald is beginning to cut the description of life in Paris in the interest of narrative; I have included some of the passages from the second version which the typescript cuts because the point of this quotation is the background of a typical Paris evening.

36. "Absolution," ASYM, p. 130.

37. Deems Taylor to FSF, July 21, [1925].

38. The letters from Mrs. Wharton and T. S. Eliot are in CU, pp. 309-10.

39. I owe this anecdote to Mr. Robert Chapman, who made a note of it immediately after hearing it from Richard Knight. A slightly different version of how Fitzgerald told the bordello story and what Mrs. Wharton said in reply appears in Andrew Turnbull's *Scott Fitzgerald*, p. 154. Mr. Turnbull's version comes from Theodore Chanler, who was at the Pavillon Colombe that day, and it may be the more accurate. Mr. Turnbull makes no reference at all to Fitzgerald's subsequent conversation with Zelda. It seems probable that Mr. Knight, who was a closer friend of Zelda than of Fitzgerald, got this detail as well as his version of the conversation at the Pavillon Colombe from Zelda. Probably no

recollection of an episode like this will be letter perfect, certainly not at the distance of time at which Mr. Knight and Mr. Chanler were reporting it.

40. To JPB, September 21, 1925; CU, p. 272; *Letters*, p. 359.
41. "Echoes of the Jazz Age," CU, pp. 18-19.
42. Gilbert Seldes, "Uneasy Chameleons," SEP, January 1, 1927.
43. "Echoes of the Jazz Age," CU, p. 19.
44. Both quotations about Mrs. Murphy are from Gerald Murphy to AM, January 19, 1950. "The greater part of the *originality* in our way of life has always been due to her. I helped to organize it."
45. Robert Benchley to FSF, April 29, 1934. Nicole bought a set of lead soldiers for her children when she and Rosemary went shopping in Paris; they cost over a thousand francs. (TITN, p. 127.)
46. Edmund Wilson.
47. SMTW, p. 283.
48. I am indebted to Mr. Gerald Murphy for these anecdotes. The quoted passages are from a letter of Mr. John Dos Passos about the incident, April 30, 1950. For the reference to Francis Melarky see p. 200 above.

CHAPTER X

1. To MP, February 8, 1926.
2. To MP, August 28, 1925.
3. This chapter was published under the title "The World's Fair" in *The Kenyon Review*, Autumn, 1948.
4. To MP, *ca.* September 10 and October 20, 1925; Ledger, p. 179.
5. To MP, December 27, 1925; *Letters*, pp. 194-95.
6. SMTW, p. 138.
7. SMTW, p. 131.
8. Clipping in Album IV.
9. 1925: "Not in the Guidebooks," "A Penny Spent," "The Rich Boy," "Presumption," "The Adolescent Marriage," "My Old New England Farm House on the Erie." 1926: "Your Way and Mine," "The Dance," "How to Waste Material." The quotation about the play is from FSF to Harold Ober, received June 3, 1926. The statement about Fitzgerald's profit from the movie is also based on the Ober correspondence.
10. Clippings in Album IV.
11. To MP, February 21, 1925.
12. If you ignore "Absolution," which was written, not as a short story, but as a prologue for *Gatsby*.
13. "Winter Dreams," ASYM, p. 90.
14. "The Rich Boy," ASYM, p. 53.
15. Roger Burlingame, *Of Making Many Books*, p. 47.

16. "The Moral of Scott Fitzgerald," CU, pp. 324-25.
17. The *Bookman*, May, 1926. "This won't make any money," he wrote Ober when he sent the essay to him, " — maybe $50 or a bit more but I'm awfully anxious to get it published. . . . Will you try *The American Mercury* — I especially want Mencken to see it first." (FSF to Harold Ober, received February 15, 1926.)
18. So at least Donald Friede, who was then a member of the firm, believed. (Donald Friede to AM, June 11, 1947.)
19. To MP, December 30, 1925; *Letters*, p. 195.
20. EH to FSF, December 31, 1925.
21. "Handle with Care," CU, p. 79.
22. EH to FSF, April, 1926.
23. EH to FSF, Spring, 1926; to MP, June 25, 1926, *Letters*, p. 205. In *A Moveable Feast* Hemingway goes to some pains to deny this account of Fitzgerald's association with the writing of *The Sun Also Rises*: "The fall of 1925 he was upset because I would not show him the manuscript of the first draft of *The Sun Also Rises*. . . . Scott did not see it until after the completed rewritten and cut manuscript had been sent to Scribner's at the end of April" (p. 184). This statement cannot be absolutely true, since Hemingway's letter quoted in the text says quite specifically that he "cut The Sun to start with Cohn — cut all that first part, etc." after his visit to Juan-les-Pins. Fitzgerald may have been referring to this occasion when he wrote O'Hara in 1936: "The only effect I ever had on Ernest was to get him into a receptive mood and say let's cut everything that goes before this" (to John O'Hara, July 25, 1936; *Letters*, p. 538).
24. To MP, May, June 25, 1926; the second of these letters is in *Letters*, p. 205.
25. Grace Moore, *You're Only Human Once*, pp. 108-9. Miss Moore's chronology is confusing, but these incidents probably occurred in 1926 rather than 1927. The Fitzgeralds were not on the Riviera in 1927.
26. The quoted phrases here are from Mrs. Gerald Murphy to AM, January 17, 1950.
27. Morley Callaghan, *That Summer in Paris*, p. 193; Louis Bromfield to AM, December, 1950.
28. *A Moveable Feast*, pp. 181-82.
29. *That Summer in Paris*, pp. 162-63.
30. *You're Only Human Once*, pp. 114-15.
31. Gerald Murphy.
32. To MP, June 10 and 25, 1926; *Letters*, pp. 205-6. There was only one condition, that Fitzgerald give all his stories, up to a maximum of ten, to *Liberty* for $3,500 apiece.
33. To MP, December 27, 1925, and February 20, 1926; *Letters*, pp. 193 and 199.

34. John Dos Passos to AM, April 30, 1950.
35. The description of Fitzgerald is from John Mosher's "The Sad Young Man" (the *New Yorker*, April 17, 1926), the quotation from TITN, p. 368.

CHAPTER XI

1. Clipping in Album IV.
2. There are wires from Considine to FSF, December 30, 1926, January 3 and 4, April 23, 1927.
3. TITN, p. 92; Clipping in Album IV; Mrs. Lois Moran Young to AM, April 22, 1948.
4. Mrs. Lois Moran Young to AM, April 22, 1948; clipping in Album IV. Arthur William Brown to AM, June 27, 1951.
5. Zelda wrote a number of pieces for *College Humor*, *McCall's*, and *Esquire* and signed them "Zelda and F. Scott Fitzgerald." The account Fitzgerald gave Perkins of " 'Show Mr. and Mrs. F. to Number ——' " and "Auction — Model 1934" (*Esquire*, May, June, July, 1934) is probably substantially true of all the joint pieces. "Zelda and I collaborated," he said, "— idea, editing and padding being mine and most of the writing being hers." (To MP, May 15, 1934.) There were, however, at least two stories, one wholly and the other largely by Zelda, which were printed as Fitzgerald's. They were "The Millionaire's Girl" (SEP, May 17, 1930) for which they got $4,000, and "Our Own Movie Queen" (*The Chicago Tribune*, June 7, 1925) for which they received $1,000. When Harold Ober, who had innocently sold "The Millionaire's Girl" to the *Post* as a Fitzgerald story, discovered his mistake, he informed the *Post* at once. But the story was already in type and the *Post* let it stand.
6. James Montgomery Flagg, *Roses and Buckshot*, pp. 210-11. Flagg's book is generally intemperate, and no man enjoys being told how old he looks but the details of his story are supported by Arthur William Brown to AM, June 27, 1951. Apart from the effect of the hostile tone, this story appears accurate.
7. The quoted remarks are from Mrs. Lois Moran Young to AM, April 22, 1948.
8. To FFL, July 5, 1937; *Letters*, p. 16.
9. This quotation is from the ms. of *Lipstick*, p. 2.
10. Flagg, p. 211.
11. March 14, 1927.
12. " 'Show Mr. and Mrs. F. to Number ——,' " CU, p. 47.
13. Interview by Harry Salpeter, New York *World*, April 3, 1927.
14. To MP, February 6, 1927.
15. ZSF to FFL, 1945.

16. Edmund Wilson.

17. "Early Success," CU, p. 89.

18. Fritz Crisler, "Old Grads: I Like 'Em," SEP, November 16, 1935. Crisler calls the subject of this anecdote "Hank O'Flaherty" in his article, but the correspondence itself shows it was Fitzgerald.

19. Whitney J. Oates. The occasion is dated by Fitzgerald's Ledger, p. 182.

20. To MP, January 20, 1927.

21. To MP, *ca.* February 1, 1928.

22. John Biggs.

23. SMTW, p. 109.

24. " 'Show Mr. and Mrs. F. to Number ———,' " CU, p. 48.

25. Clipping in ZSF's Scrapbook.

26. Sara Murphy to FSF, August 20, [1935]. "The face of a saint, a viking Madonna," Fitzgerald himself called it in TITN (p. 43).

27. To Mrs. Bayard Turnbull, n.d.

28. Ledger, p. 182.

29. Ledger, pp. 182 and 63.

30. To MP, November, 1928 and October 11, 1933.

31. "Echoes of the Jazz Age," CU, p. 20.

32. To MP, March 1, 1929.

33. "Echoes of the Jazz Age," CU, p. 20. Fitzgerald used the trip in "The Rough Crossing," (SEP, June 8, 1929), Zelda in SMTW, pp. 79-95.

34. Ledger, p. 183; SMTW, p. 167.

35. To EH, September 29, 1929, *Letters*, p. 306; to JPB, January or February, 1929, CU, pp. 273-74; *Letters*, p. 361.

36. Ledger, p. 183.

37. Morley Callaghan, *That Summer in Paris*, pp. 212-19, 241-43, 124; Callaghan to MP, December 6, 1929.

38. Isabel Paterson, "Turns with a Bookworm," New York *Herald Tribune*, November 24 and December 9, 1929; EH to Callaghan, January 4, 1929 [*sic:* 1930].

39. Allen Tate. The writer was Robert Penn Warren.

40. Ledger, p. 183. To MP, June, 1929; *Letters*, p. 215.

41. Sara Murphy to FSF, n.d. But it appears to belong to September, 1929.

42. " 'Show Mr. and Mrs. F. to Number ———,' " CU, p. 50.

43. To Harold Ober, [1936]; *Letters*, p. 402.

44. SEP, October 11, 1930.

45. To MP, *ca.* July 8, 1930; *Letters*, p. 223. In November, 1930, *Scribner's Magazine* bought a story that Perkins called "Miss Bessie" (a story called "Miss Ella" was printed in *Scribner's Magazine*, December, 1931). This story had been the rounds of the high-priced magazines. Zelda's "Millionaire's Girl" was printed

in SEP, May 17, 1930. The other stories were "A Workman,"
"The Drouth and the Flood," and "The House."

46. To MP, September 1, 1930; *Letters*, p. 224. There are only seven
such pieces in *College Humor*: "Looking Back Eight Years" (June,
1928), "Who Can Fall in Love After Thirty" (October, 1928),
"The Original Follies Girl" (July, 1929), "The Poor Working
Girl" (January, 1931, but written in 1929), "The Southern Girl"
(October, 1929), "The Girl the Prince Liked" (February, 1930),
"The Girl with Talent" (April, 1930). Zelda remarked much later
that these stories were potboilers written to pay for her ballet
lessons, but they are better than that (ZSF to H. D. Piper).

47. To FFL, October 20, 1936; *Letters*, p. 10. SMTW, pp. 258-62.

48. Mrs. Bayard Turnbull; Ledger, p. 184. "Some of our experiences
have become legendary to me and I am not sure even if they
happened at all. One story, (a lie or a truth), which I am in the
habit of telling, is how you put out the lights of Lake Geneva
with a Gargantuan gesture. . . ." FSF to Wolfe, April 2, 1934;
Letters, p. 508.

49. To Mrs. Richard Taylor, February 23, 1931; *Letters*, p. 416.

50. ZSF to MP, May 19, 1932.

51. TITN, pp. 240-43 and 313-14.

52. To MP, September 1, 1930; *Letters*, p. 224.

53. "Babylon Revisited," TAR, pp. 398-99. "Babylon Revisited" was
written in December, 1930, when Zelda was very ill.

54. To C. O. Kalman, March 11, 1931. To MP, May 21, 1931; *Letters*,
p. 225.

55. " 'Show Mr. and Mrs. F. to Number ——,' " CU, p. 53. ZSF to
MP, June 8, 1932.

56. Dorothy Speare, "Hollywood Madness," SEP, November 7, 1933.

57. Fitzgerald's original idea was to do an article to be called "Hollywood Revisited." He had some of it written when he decided to
do a story instead. The story was turned down by both the *Post*
and *Scribner's*; Fitzgerald's comment on its publication in *The
American Mercury* was: "Think Mencken bought it for financial
value of name." (To MP, *ca.* January 15, 1932; *Letters*, p. 226. To
Afred Dashiell, October, 1932.) "Crazy Sunday" is another case
of Fitzgerald's making a hero of a friend (in this case Dwight
Taylor) but "clinging to his own innards."

58. To FFL, July, 1937; *Letters*, pp. 16-17.

59. To Dr. Adolph Meyer, April 10, 1933.

60. To FFL, June 12, 1940; *Letters*, p. 78.

61. To MP, *ca.* May 1, 1932; *Letters*, p. 227.

62. ZSF to MP, June 8, 1932. Fitzgerald tried to use his early impressions of La Paix and of their handyman, Acquilla, in a story
called "On Schedule," SEP, March 18, 1933.

CHAPTER XII

1. Notebooks, K; CU, p. 171.
2. TITN, pp. 98-99.
3. Mrs. Bayard Turnbull to AM, May 15, 1948.
4. To Richard Knight, September 29, 1932; *Letters,* p. 500.
5. To Mrs. Bayard Turnbull, September 19, 1933; *Letters,* p. 436.
6. Notebooks, S; CU, p. 229.
7. To Mrs. Bayard Turnbull, June 1935; *Letters,* p. 440.
8. ZSF to MP, *ca.* October 6 and 22, 1932.
9. Notebooks, E; CU, p. 126.
10. To MP, *ca.* January 15, 1932, and January 19, 1933; the first of these is in *Letters,* p. 226.
11. To MP, March 25, 1932.
12. Ledger, p. 186.
13. ZSF to MP, *ca.* October 6, 1932. To MP, September 25, 1933; *Letters,* pp. 231-32.
14. "One Hundred False Starts," SEP, March 4, 1933.
15. "Sleeping and Waking," CU, pp. 66-67.
16. Ledger, p. 187.
17. To EW, February, 1933; CU, p. 277; *Letters,* p. 345. Notebooks, L; CU, p. 181.
18. In the spring of 1934 Cary Ross put on an exhibition of Zelda's work in New York. "Parfois la folie est la sagesse," said the motto on the little catalogue. "The work of a brilliant introvert, they were vividly painted, intensely rhythmic," said *Time* (April 9, 1934).
19. To Dr. Carroll, October 22, 1937.
20. "Babylon Revisited," TAR, p. 402; Notebooks, O; CU, p. 198.
21. To Dr. Murdock, August 28, 1934.
22. Notebooks, I.
23. Mrs. Allein Owens.
24. To MP, January 19, 1933; *Letters,* p. 229.
25. John Biggs.
26. The decision about the title came so late that some of the advertising actually uses *Doctor Diver's Holiday* and it was so called in *Who's Who* that year. Before TITN could be serialized in *Scribner's,* Fitzgerald had to arrange with *Liberty* about the agreement he had made with them in 1926 (see p. 222 above and note). This arrangement was made in October 1933, and *Scribner's* then undertook to pay Fitzgerald $10,000 for the serial rights, $6,000 of which was to be applied to his debt to Scribner's (MP to FSF, October 18, 1933).
27. To MP, March 11, 1935; *Letters,* pp. 259-60.

28. To MP, November 8, 1934; *Letters*, pp. 253-54. Mrs. Allein Owens.

29. Both quotations are from FSF's Ledger, extra material, 1934.

30. To EW, March 12, 1934; CU, p. 278; *Letters*, p. 342.

31. ZSF to JPB, Summer, 1932.

32. John Biggs.

33. ZSF to JPB, Summer, 1932.

34. Notebooks, O.

35. From a fragmentary draft of a letter, apparently to a relative, apparently never sent.

36. "Lamp in a Window," the *New Yorker*, March 23, 1935. But I have quoted FSF's manuscript, which has a few slight variations from the printed text.

37. To Dr. Murdock, August 28, 1934.

38. To C. O. Kalman, September 19, 1936.

39. This note was probably written in December, 1940; it is repeated almost word for word in a letter to FFL which belongs — on internal evidence — to that month.

40. Notebooks, F. What appears to be a first outline of Stahr's attitude appears in the Notebooks (C): "Cass thought. 'When I married Jill I didn't want to and I had every reason not to. But afterwards I had eight perfect years — eight perfect years with never a night of going to sleep in anger and never a morning when we didn't think first of each other.' He tried the usual specifics for sorrow — endless work, an expedition into drink, almost everything except women. And he said aloud a few times without striving for effect 'That's over — my heart's in the grave.' " Not only this note but many passages in "The Last Kiss" (*Collier's*, April 16, 1949) and LT are too close to the facts — or to Fitzgerald's version of the facts — to leave much doubt of the connection between Stahr's feelings for Minna and Fitzgerald's for Zelda.

41. ZSF to MP, *ca.* December 30, 1940.

CHAPTER XIII

1. The phrase about *Tender Is the Night* is quoted by James Thurber, " 'Scott in Thorns,' " *The Reporter*, April 15, 1951, p. 36; for his feeling about TITN, see *Beloved Infidel*, p. 239. The reviews quoted are: Peter Quennell, *New Statesman and Nation*, April 28, 1934; J. Donald Adams, the New York *Times*, April 15, 1934; and Amy Loveman, *Saturday Review of Literature*, April 7, 1934. There were serious and intelligent reviews by Malcolm Cowley, *New Republic*, June 6, 1934, John Chamberlain, New York *Times*, April 16, 1934, and C. Hartley Grattan, *Modern Monthly*, July, 1934.

2. TITN, p. 103.
3. EH to FSF, May 28, 1934. Hemingway was far from alone in this
   view; as early as 1917, during their courtship, people who thought
   Scott only "wild" were convinced Zelda was "a bit crazy" (Major
   Dana Palmer to AM, February 11, 1951). H. L. Mencken took
   much the same view of Zelda (Charles Angoff, *H. L. Mencken*,
   pp. 98-99). "I loved Scott very much," Hemingway said, "but he
   was extremely difficult with that situation he got himself into and
   Zelda constantly making him drink because she was jealous of his
   working well. . . . He had a very steep trajectory and was almost
   like a guided missile with no one guiding him" (EH to AM, July
   6, 1949). Fitzgerald once told Perkins that there had "always been
   a subtle struggle between Hem. & Zelda" (May 14, 1932; *Letters*,
   p. 229). The struggle was quite open. Hemingway thought Zelda
   crazy the first time he met her and told Fitzgerald so at once;
   Zelda said openly that she thought Hemingway "bogus."
4. To EH, June 1, 1934; *Letters*, p. 308. Philip Barry used the social
   life of the Murphy's house at Antibes in *Hotel Universe*; the contrast is interesting.
5. Gerald Murphy to FSF, December 31, 1935. This letter was written during the serious — eventually fatal — illness of one of the
   Murphy children.
6. Perkins repeated this remark in a letter to Fitzgerald of April 8,
   1935; Hemingway wrote it directly to Fitzgerald December 16,
   1935.
7. EH to FSF, December 21, 1935.
8. Many friends were generous in their praise. ". . . you have all
   your old power," Herbert Agar wrote him, "of making me feel
   the *temps perdu* as an interesting but pleasant pain. . . . You have
   an understanding and a thoughtfulness which you used to profess
   you would never acquire. I'm glad you have acquired it." (Herbert Agar to FSF, February 3, 1934.) Marjorie Kinnan Rawlings
   tried to explain to Perkins the book's "overpowering effect" on
   her by saying, "he visualizes people not in their immediate setting,
   from the human point of view — but in time and space. . . ."
   (Marjorie Kinnan Rawlings to MP, February 14, 1934.)
9. To JPB, April 7, 1934; *Letters*, p. 363. See also the letters to
   Perkins quoted on p. 231 and to EW, CU, p. 278, *Letters*, p. 346.
10. He did not complete this revision, getting only as far as Nicole's
    letters in Book II, chapter II. But besides making a number of
    minor revisions, he placed the whole of Book I after Book II,
    chapter X. This change is also described in the Notebooks (L),
    and on December 24, 1938, he wrote Perkins decisively: "It's great
    fault is that the *true* beginning — the young psychiatrist in Switz-
    erland — is tucked away in the middle of the book. If pages 151-

212 were taken from their present place and put at the start the improvement in appeal would be enormous."

11. Hartley Grattan made this point in his review, and Bishop wrote Fitzgerald: ". . . it was right — to see the Divers through Rosemary's romantic and naïve eyes." (JPB to FSF, April 4, 1934.)

12. TITN, pp. 208-12.

13. The quoted remark is from a letter to Perkins quoted on p. 256. There were other consequences of Fitzgerald's writing under these conditions — the disproportionate detail about minor elements, such as McKisco's reappearance (pp. 268-69) and Baby's rescue of Dick (pp. 296-303), the repetition of phrases ("lesions" of enthusiasm, vitality, and anxiety occur at pp. 271, 290, 352: the phrase was one he had first used in B & D, p. 284), inaccuracy (A and P for AP, p. 403). The difficulties caused by his failure to indicate the passage of time clearly are evident when the chronology is set forth. The book begins, chronologically, in 1917 (p. 151); Dick and Nicole are married in September, 1919 (p. 207); Nicole's soliloquy mentioned in the text covers the six years from their marriage to June, 1925 (p. 4), and indicates the course by which Dick has been driven to the edge of destruction. We follow the Divers closely from June, 1925, to December, 1925 (p. 224). But from this point on the slowness of Dick's disintegration and Nicole's return to her whole Warren self is unclear. We hardly notice that a year and a half passes between chapters XIII and XIV of Book II. The length of Nicole's third breakdown (p. 253) is not in itself important, but the length of Dick's exhausting struggle to save her is (it lasts somewhere between six and nine months), as is the additional year and a half before his final defeat in June, 1929 (p. 359). Perhaps Fitzgerald took the time scheme too much for granted because he was following his own "lesion of vitality" so exactly and knew it too well.

14. To Mrs. Edwin B. Jarrett, February 17, 1938; Letters, p. 567. Mrs. Jarrett had made a dramatization of the book. But Fitzgerald was quite clear about what he wanted to do. "It is absolutely necessary," he wrote Perkins, "for the unity of the book and the effectiveness of the finale to show Dick in the dignified and responsible aspect toward the world and his neighbors that was implied so strongly in the first half of the book. . . . It is legitimate to ruin Dick but it is by no means legitimate to make him ineffectual" (to MP, February 5, 1934; Letters, p. 240).

15. "Echoes of the Jazz Age," CU, p. 22.

16. The quotations in this paragraph are from TITN, pp. 9, 13, 14, 81, 25, 8. Abe's remark about mixing "wit de quality" was, Fitzgerald remembered, actually made by Robert Benchley, though Benchley did not recall it. (Benchley to FSF, April 29, 1934.)

17. TITN, pp. 74-75.
18. " 'Scott in Thorns,' " *The Reporter*, April 17, 1951, p. 36.
19. Morley Callaghan, *That Summer in Paris*, p. 150. For the description of Fitzgerald's father, see pp. 11-12 above. For a typical honest apology for bad behavior, see his letter to Thomas Lineaweaver, *ca.* 1928, *Letters*, pp. 492-93.
20. To FFL, July and November 18, 1938, *Letters*, pp. 36 and 43.
21. See *Beloved Infidel*, pp. 177-79.
22. To MP, May 20, 1940, *Letters*, p. 288.
23. The quotations in this paragraph are from TITN, pp. 131, 228, 266.
24. To EW, March 12, 1934; CU, p. 278; *Letters*, p. 346.
25. Notebooks, K.
26. "More than Just a House," SEP, June 24, 1933.
27. "Emotional Bankruptcy" was written in June, 1931, and published in SEP, August 15, 1931. As late as 1940 Fitzgerald was warning his daughter of the dangers of "an awful disease called emotional bankruptcy" (to FFL, January 25, 1940; *Letters*, p. 63).
28. TITN, p. 405.
29. To FFL, October 31, 1939; CU, p. 291; *Letters*, p. 62.
30. Michel Mok, "The Other Side of Paradise," the New York *Post*, September 25, 1936.
31. "The Crack-Up," CU, p. 72.
32. T. S. Eliot, "Burnt Norton."
33. "The Crack-Up," CU, pp. 73 and 75.
34. To FFL, June 12, 1940; CU, p. 294; *Letters*, p. 79.
35. "Sleeping and Waking," CU, p. 67.
36. The quotations in this paragraph are from TITN, pp. 368, 116, 119.
37. The quotations in this paragraph are from TITN, pp. 233, 262, 228-32, 263, 340, 351, 291-95, 351.
38. TITN, p. 107.
39. The quotations in this paragraph are all from "Pasting It Together," CU, pp. 80-84. The letter in which Hemingway admonished Fitzgerald is quoted on p. 264.
40. The quotations in this paragraph are from TITN, pp. 249, 250, 384, 372, 352, 390, and 404.

CHAPTER XIV

1. Notebooks, L. The four installments were published in *Red Book* in October, 1934, June and August, 1935, and November, 1941.
2. Arnold Gingrich. The delay in the publishing of the last installment bears out the story. Herbert Mayes bought two unpublished Gwen stories for *Good Housekeeping* in 1936 "when I knew he

was in financial difficulties. . . . They were poorly handled and I never had any intention of publishing them." (Herbert R. Mayes to AM, October 24, 1947.)

3. Ledger, p. 188.

4. "Her Last Case," SEP, November 3, 1934.

5. To MP, October 30, 1934.

6. Ledger, extra material; James Drawbell, *The Sun Within Us*, p. 177.

7. To MP, October 17 and 30, December 13, 1934; the first of these letters is in *Letters*, p. 252.

8. As usual he worried about the title; "women," he thought, "couldn't pronounce it." He tried to get Perkins to substitute one of several others, the best of which was *Last Night's Moon*. The book was once advertised as *Tales of the Golden Twenties* (New York *Times*, June 17, 1934). Fitzgerald as usual disliked the jacket: "Some one who can't draw as well as Scottie," he said (to MP, March 9, 1935; *Letters*, p. 258).

9. In the end Perkins' favorite, "Basil at the Fair," was omitted. Earlier Fitzgerald himself had wanted to make a book of the Basil stories. He suggested it to Perkins in 1928. By 1930, however, he was convinced that to do so would ruin him. But in 1933 he was again considering the idea (to MP, *ca.* July 21, 1928, *ca.* May 1, 1930, September 25, 1933; *Letters*, pp. 212, 221, 232).

10. "A New Leaf" and "Her Last Case" were in SEP, July 4, 1931 and November 3, 1934, "The Fiend" in *Esquire*, January, 1935, "The Night of Chancellorsville" in *Esquire*, February, 1935.

11. The quotations in this paragraph are from TAR, pp. 274 and 43. Possibly "Two Wrongs" is a partial exception to the generalization in the text. It is, of course, a history of Fitzgerald's own mental and emotional career done in terms of the theatre rather than the novel and it has some of the qualities of his later stories. It was probably written just after his attack of tuberculosis in 1929 (the story was written during October and November of that year) and out of his awareness of how orderly Zelda's life was compared to his own.

12. The Baltimore *Morning Sun*, May 8, 1932.

13. "Family in the Wind," TAR, p. 301.

14. To Mrs. Feley, July 20, 1939; *Letters*, p. 589.

15. "Family in the Wind," TAR, p. 299.

16. "Pasting It Together," CU, p. 80. Mrs. Maurice Flynn to H. D. Piper.

17. Notebooks, U.

18. Notebooks, G.

19. "The Crack-Up," CU, p. 74.

20. "The Intimate Strangers," *McCall's*, June, 1935.

21. The reviews referred to here are: William Troy, the *Nation*, April 17, 1935; T. S. Matthews, the *New Republic*, April 10, 1935; Elizabeth Hart, the *Herald-Tribune Books*, March 31, 1935.

22. To MP, April 15, 1935; *Letters*, p. 261.

23. To Roger Garis, February 22, 1938; *Letters*, p. 568.

24. "The Crack-Up," CU, p. 71. Fitzgerald is exaggerating the seriousness of his illness; according to Dr. Ringer's report, the tuberculosis was relatively mild. (Marie Shank to AM, October 26, 1949.)

25. The arrangement was not successful because Fitzgerald would not obey instructions, and it had to be discontinued. (Marie Shank to AM, October 26, 1949.)

26. To MP, May 11, 1935; *Letters*, p. 264. To Mrs. Bayard Turnbull, May 11, 1935; *Letters*, p. 438.

27. "The Crack-Up," CU, p. 72. "Handle with Care," CU, pp. 77-78 and 76. The dates given in CU for the "Crack-Up" pieces are the dates of publication. "The Crack-Up" itself was written in October 1935, "Handle with Care" and "Pasting It Together" in December 1935.

28. See "Too Cute for Words" and "Inside the House," SEP, April 18 and June 13, 1936. The first and better of these stories was written in December, 1935.

29. To Mrs. Richard Taylor, June 11, 1935; *Letters*, pp. 417-18.

30. To FFL, April 5, 1939, and November 29, 1940; *Letters*, pp. 55 and 98.

31. To FFL, July, 1936.

32. Ledger, extra material.

33. A Gwen story, called "Lo, the Poor Peacock," written in February, 1935, was rejected. It never has been published.

34. To Marie Shank, June 10, 1937. "Financing Finnegan" was written in June, 1937.

35. Notebooks, E; CU, p. 128.

36. During this period he did three sketches for *Esquire*, "Author's House," "Afternoon of an Author," "An Author's Mother," and, a little later, "Early Success" for *Cavalcade*.

37. Marie Shank to AM, October 26, 1949. "Handle with Care," CU, p. 76.

38. Notebooks, J; CU, p. 165.

39. To Mrs. Bayard Turnbull, June, 1935; *Letters*, p. 439.

40. To Dr. Carroll, April 7, 1938.

41. To FFL, July 16, 1936.

42. Mrs. Maurice Flynn to H. D. Piper.

43. Fitzgerald wrote dozens of accounts of this accident. I have quoted from letters to FFL, July 31, 1936, and to C. O. Kalman, September 19, 1936. The first of these letters is in *Letters*, p. 9.

44. To C. O. Kalman, October 10, 1936; *Letters*, p. 544.

45. "Design in Plaster," *Esquire*, November, 1939. This story probably also reflects the later occasion when Fitzgerald sprained his shoulder (see *Beloved Infidel*, pp. 226-27). Marie Shank to AM, October 26 and November 20, 1949.

46. Michel Mok, "The Other Side of Paradise," the New York *Post*, September 25, 1936.

47. Marie Shank to AM, October 26, 1949. To Mrs. William Hamm, October 28, 1936.

48. "An Alcoholic Case," *Esquire*, February, 1937.

49. Marjorie Kinnan Rawlings to AM, March 18, 1948.

50. MP to Maxwell Geismar, April 12, 1943; *Editor to Author: The Letters of Maxwell E. Perkins*, New York, 1950, pp. 222-23.

51. The quotations in this paragraph are from a letter to Mrs. Clifton Sprague, September 10, 1936.

52. To C. O. Kalman, October 10, 1936; *Letters*, p. 544.

53. To Roger Garis, February 22, 1938; *Letters*, p. 569. To Mrs. Richard Taylor [Spring, 1937]; *Letters*, p. 418. To C. O. Kalman [Spring, 1937]; *Letters*, pp. 549-50.

54. Notes for LT.

55. To FFL, [April, 1937]; *Letters*, p. 14.

CHAPTER XV

1. To Beatrice Dance, September, 1936; *Letters*, p. 542.

2. "The Snows of Kilimanjaro," *Esquire*, August, 1936.

3. MP to FSF, September 23, 1936. To EH, August, 1936; *Letters*, p. 311. To MP, September 19, 1936; *Letters*, p. 267. Fitzgerald's admiration for Hemingway endured to the end. Six months before he died he asked Perkins: "How does Ernest feel about things? . . . I would be interested in at least a clue to Ernest's attitude." Two months later he was again asking: "What about Ernest? What does he think?" (to MP, June 6 and August 15, 1940; the first of these letters is in *Letters*, p. 290).

4. The last two quotations in this paragraph are from Fitzgerald's letter to Beatrice Dance, September, 1936; *Letters*, p. 543.

5. To MP, October 14, 1940.

6. "Hollywood postponed but may come through," he wrote his daughter in a letter which, though undated, was written shortly after her Easter vacation that spring.

7. In March, 1940, Zelda left Highlands on the understanding that she would live quietly with her mother in Montgomery. For several years she spent most of her time there and this arrangement reduced Fitzgerald's expenses appreciably. The record of Fitzgerald's debts is incomplete, but $40,000 is certainly not an overestimation of them.

8. To Mrs. Richard Taylor, July 5, 1937; *Letters*, p. 419.

9. To FFL, July, 1937; *Letters*, p. 16.

10. To FFL, November 4, 1937; *Letters*, p. 20.

11. ". . . there were only three days while I was on salary in pictures that I ever touched a drop. One of those was in New York and two were on Sunday." (To Leland Hayward, January 16, 1940.) This is an exaggeration on the side of virtue, but it is substantially true that drinking did not affect his efficiency for some time in Hollywood.

12. To FFL, October 8, 1937; *Letters*, pp. 19-20.

13. To Mrs. Richard Taylor, September 27, 1937.

14. To Helen Hayes, September 16, 1937; *Letters*, p. 555. To FFL, February, 1938; *Letters*, p. 22.

15. To FFL, October 8, 1937; *Letters*, p. 18.

16. Budd Schulberg, "Old Scott," *Esquire*, January, 1961, p. 97.

17. To FFL, February, 1938, *Letters*, p. 21; to ———, September, 1935, *Letters*, p. 529. This second letter was never sent, but Fitzgerald was so serious about the passage I have quoted that he copied it into his Notebooks; see Notebooks, O, CU, p. 209.

18. To MP, *ca.* May 14, 1932, *Letters*, p. 229; Budd Schulberg, "Old Scott," *Esquire*, January, 1961, p. 100.

19. *Beloved Infidel*, pp. 294-301.

20. To FFL, October 8 and November 4, 1937; *Letters*, pp. 18-21. Mrs. John Pirie to H. D. Piper, May 12, 1946.

21. James Drawbell, *The Sun Within Us*, pp. 316-17.

22. So at least I have been told by people who knew her at this period in London. She herself reports that at St. Moritz one of these people she thought she was deceiving quietly called her "an adventuress."

23. Except where I have indicated otherwise, my account of the relations between Fitzgerald and Miss Graham depends on the vivid account Miss Graham herself has given in *Beloved Infidel*, pp. 172-338.

24. LT, p. 96. Zelda was supposed to know nothing about Sheilah, but some suspicion — perhaps aroused by her knowledge of how close Fitzgerald's books always were to his experience — must have led her to say of Kathleen: "I confess that I didn't like the heroine [of *The Last Tycoon*], she seeming the sort of person who knows too well how to capitalize the unwelcome advances of the ice-man and who smells a little of the rubber-shields in her dress." (ZSF to Mrs. Bayard Turnbull, November 13, 1941.) Fitzgerald's notes for LT show that even the silver belt with stars cut out of it that Stahr remembers from his first meeting with Kathleen was Sheilah's, though she does not mention it in *Beloved Infidel*.

25. Even this refusal of the authorities to let him on the plane gets into LT, in the episode in the Nashville airport.
26. Mrs. Maurice Flynn to FSF, n.d.
27. To Joseph Mankiewicz, January 20, 1938, *Letters*, pp. 563-64.
28. To MP, April 23, 1938, *Letters*, p. 278; to Gerald Murphy, March 11, 1938, *Letters*, p. 427; to FFL, July 7, 1938, *Letters*, pp. 32-33.
29. To MP, September 3, 1937, April 23, 1938, May 20, 1940, *Letters*, pp. 275, 278, 288.
30. To FFL, November 11, 1938, February 19, 1940; the second of these is in *Letters*, p. 64.
31. Leila Barber to FSF, November 28, 1938; to FFL, *ca.* December, 1938, *Letters*, p. 45.
32. To FFL, October 31, 1939, *Letters*, p. 62.
33. I have based this account of the Winter Carnival trip largely on what Mr. Schulberg has told me and on his two articles about Fitzgerald, "Fitzgerald in Hollywood," *The New Republic*, March 31, 1941, and "Old Scott," *Esquire*, January, 1961. See also *Beloved Infidel*, pp. 271-72. In dealing with this episode Mr. Turnbull says that Mr. Schulberg was "celebrity-conscious" and unable to "help feeling a little superior to this derelict 'genius' " (*Scott Fitzgerald*, pp. 296-97). I do not know the evidence on which Mr. Turnbull bases this unfavorable judgment of Mr. Schulberg, but it is perhaps worth reporting that during all the many times I have discussed Fitzgerald with him he has never shown anything but admiration and affection for Fitzgerald.
34. To MP, January 4, 1939, *Letters*, pp. 282-83.
35. To MP, July 19, 1939.
36. "I think I can honestly say that the 1939 attack of T. B. was fictional. He was drinking heavily at the time and preferred to have as few people as possible know about it. Specifically, he tried to spare Scottie or rather to conceal from her the fact that he drank so much, so he referred to his confinement as T. B." (Francis Kroll Ring to AM, June 14, 1948; Mrs. Ring was Fitzgerald's secretary throughout this period). See also *Beloved Infidel*, p. 278.
37. See *Beloved Infidel*, pp. 210, 234-35, 269.
38. To MP, January 3, February 25, 1939. The second of these is in *Letters*, p. 284.
39. To MP, October 20, 1939.
40. To Harold Ober, July 19, 1939.
41. To Kenneth Littauer, n.d., *Letters*, p. 588.
42. "News of Paris," though written in 1939 or 1940, was not published until after Fitzgerald's death, when it appeared in *Furioso*, Winter, 1947.

CHAPTER XVI

1. *Collier's* offer was for $2,500 for each installment of six or seven thousand words. As Fitzgerald planned the novel — though not as he actually wrote what he got written — this offer meant $20,000 or $25,000 for the complete serial (Littauer to FSF, October 10, 1939). Later, however, Perkins estimated that *Collier's* might go to $30,000 (MP to Scribner, October 16, 1939).
2. To FFL, October 31, 1939, *Letters*, p. 61.
3. Francis Kroll Ring to AM, June 14, 1948.
4. Littauer to FSF, November 28, 1939; to MP, November 28, 1939.
5. Unidentified, September 18, 1939.
6. Kathleen's uncertainty about Americans and her looking like "pink and silver frost" (pp. 115, 116) are about all Fitzgerald took from the story for the novel. It was rejected by the *Post* and *Cosmopolitan* and finally published in *Collier's*, April 16, 1949.
7. To FFL, Winter, 1939.
8. To Leland Hayward, January 16, 1940. The story about the producers' cabal is in Schulberg's *What Makes Sammy Run?*
9. To FFL, January 25 and April 11, 1940; *Letters*, pp. 64 and 68.
10. To William Dozier, May 15, 1940.
11. To MP, May 20, 1940; *Letters*, p. 288. To Katherine Tighe Fessenden, May 29, 1940; *Letters*, p. 601.
12. To FFL, June 15, 1940; *Letters*, p. 80.
13. Bennett Cerf, "Trade Winds," the *Saturday Review of Literature*, August 16, 1947.
14. To FFL, June 20, 1940; *Letters*, p. 83.
15. To FFL, September 14, 1940.
16. To ZSF, October 19 and 23, 1940; *Letters*, pp. 127 and 128.
17. To FFL, December 7, 1940; *Letters*, p. 99.
18. This comment is among the notes for LT.
19. The reviewers quoted here are James Gray, the St. Paul *Dispatch*, October 27, 1941; Stephen Vincent Benét, the *Saturday Review of Literature*, December 6, 1941; Margaret Marshall, the *Nation*, February 8 and November 8, 1941; *Time*, November 3, 1941. The most penetrating reviews were Benét's and James Thurber's in the *New Republic*, February 9, 1942.
20. At the time of Thalberg's death Fitzgerald had written a friend: "Thalberg's final collapse is the death of an enemy for me, though I liked the guy enormously. . . . I think . . . that he killed the idea of either Hopkins or Frederick March doing 'Tender Is the Night.'" (To Mr. C. O. Kalman, September 19, 1936.) See "Crazy Sunday."
21. To FFL, October 31, 1939; *Letters*, p. 61. Behind Fitzgerald's portrait of Cecilia is a good deal of Budd Schulberg's past as well

as of Scottie. When he showed Schulberg the opening chapter of LT, he said, "I sort of combined you with my daughter Scottie for Cecilia. . . . I hope you won't mind" (Budd Schulberg, "Old Scott," *Esquire*, January, 1961, p. 101).

22. LT, p. 3.
23. The quotations in this paragraph are from LT, pp. 160, 71, 131, and from the ms. version of a scene — later dropped — which came just after the studio flood.
24. LT, p. 125.
25. TSOP, p. 52.
26. *Gatsby*, pp. 113-14.
27. TITN, p. 102.
28. LT, p. 15.
29. To FFL, August 24 and February 26, 1940; CU, pp. 299 and 290. The first of these letters is in *Letters*, p. 91.
30. From the notes for LT.
31. LT, pp. 19, 121. See also the note printed by Mr. Wilson on pp. 134-35.
32. The quotations in this paragraph are from LT, pp. 13, 49, and 106.
33. LT, pp. 30-33. Boxley is based on Aldous Huxley.
34. The quotations from LT in this paragraph occur on pp. 101 and 69.
35. To MP, December 13, 1940; *Letters*, p. 280.
36. Frank Scully, *Rogue's Gallery*, Hollywood, 1943, pp. 268-69.
37. This story has been reported to me as coming from Alan Campbell, who was then Dorothy Parker's husband.
38. The *Saturday Review of Literature*, December 6, 1941, p. 10.

FITZGERALD'S
PUBLISHED WORK

THE FOLLOWING LIST of titles is not, in the technical
sense, a bibliography. It is a chronological list of the first
publications of Fitzgerald's books and of his periodical writings. To have included every edition and issue of Fitzgerald's
books would have increased the size of the list inordinately
and required technical bibliographical descriptions of a minuteness which seems out of place here. For similar reasons
I have limited the periodical list. It does not include reviews,
interviews, letters to the editor, or jokes written for the
Princeton *Tiger*. It does not include reprintings of stories in
English magazines, or American reprint magazines, short story
collections, or textbooks. It does not include movie scripts,
where the problem of ascription is very difficult; it does not
include plays, movie or radio scripts made from Fitzgerald's
work by other writers.

Unless an item in the periodical list is otherwise identified,
it is a short story. I have abbreviated *The Saturday Evening
Post* to Post. Wherever an interesting point about an entry is
known to me, I have made a note of it in a parenthesis after
the entry. The name of a character in such a parenthesis indicates that the story is one of a series of which this character
is the central figure. Initials indicate the volume in which the
story was reprinted by Fitzgerald (TSOP = *This Side of
Paradise*; FP = *Flapper and Philosophers*; TJA = *Tales of*

the Jazz Age; ASYM = *All the Sad Young Men;* TR = *Taps at Reveille).*

BOOKS

This Side of Paradise, Charles Scribner's Sons, New York, 1920.

Flappers and Philosophers, Charles Scribner's Sons, New York, 1921. Contains: The Offshore Pirate, The Ice Palace, Head and Shoulders, The Cut-Glass Bowl, Bernice Bobs Her Hair, Benediction, Dalyrimple Goes Wrong, The Four Fists.

The Beautiful and Damned, Charles Scribner's Sons, New York, 1922.

Tales of the Jazz Age, Charles Scribner's Sons, New York, 1922. Contains: The Jelly-Bean, The Camel's Back, May Day, Porcelain and Pink, The Diamond as Big as the Ritz, The Curious Case of Benjamin Button, Tarquin of Cheapside, O Russet Witch, The Lees of Happiness, Mr. Icky, Jemina.

The Vegetable or from President to Postman, Charles Scribner's Sons, New York, 1923.

The Great Gatsby, Charles Scribner's Sons, New York, 1925.

All the Sad Young Men, Charles Scribner's Sons, New York, 1926. Contains: The Rich Boy, Winter Dreams, The Baby Party, Absolution, Rags Martin-Jones and the Pr — nce of W — les, The Adjuster, Hot and Cold Blood, "The Sensible Thing," Gretchen's Forty Winks.

Tender Is the Night, Charles Scribner's Sons, New York, 1934.

Taps at Reveille, Charles Scribner's Sons, New York, 1935. Contains: BASIL: 1. The Scandal Detectives, 2. The Freshest Boy, 3. He Thinks He's Wonderful, 4. The Captured Shadow, 5. The Perfect Life; JOSEPHINE: 1. First Blood, 2. A Nice Quiet Place, 3. A Woman with a Past; Crazy Sunday, Two Wrongs, The Night of Chancellorsville, The Last of the Belles, Majesty, Family in the Wind, A Short Trip Home, One Interne, The Fiend, Babylon Revisited.

The Last Tycoon, edited by Edmund Wilson, Charles Scribner's Sons, New York, 1941.

The Crack-Up, edited by Edmund Wilson, New Directions, New York, 1945. Contains: Echoes of the Jazz Age, My Lost City, Ring, "Show Mr. and Mrs. F. to Number ——," Auction — Model 1934, Sleeping and Waking, The Crack-Up [The Crack-Up, Handle with Care, Pasting It Together], Early Success, The Note-books, Letters.

PERIODICALS

1915

Shadow Laurels, Nassau Literary Magazine, April.

The Ordeal, Nassau Literary Magazine, June.

1916

To My Unused Greek Books (verse), Nassau Literary Magazine, June.

Jemina, Nassau Literary Magazine, December (by "John Phlox, Jr.").

The Usual Thing, Nassau Literary Magazine, December (by "Robert W. Shameless").

The Vampiest of Vampires, Nassau Literary Magazine, December.

Our Next Issue, Nassau Literary Magazine, December.

1917

The Debutante, Nassau Literary Magazine, January.

The Spire and the Gargoyle, Nassau Literary Magazine, February.

Rain Before Dawn (verse), Nassau Literary Magazine, February.

Tarquin of Cheepside, Nassau Literary Magazine, April.

Babes in the Woods, Nassau Literary Magazine, May.

Princeton, the Last Day (verse), Nassau Literary Magazine, May (TSOP, p. 168).

Sentiment and the Use of Rouge, Nassau Literary Magazine, June.

On a Play Twice Seen (verse), Nassau Literary Magazine, June (TSOP, p. 147).

The Cameo Frame (verse), Nassau Literary Magazine, October.

The Pierian Spring and the Last Straw, Nassau Literary Magazine, October.

1918

My First Love (verse), Nassau Literary Magazine, February.

Marching Streets (verse), Nassau Literary Magazine, February.

The Pope at Confession (verse), Nassau Literary Magazine, February.

City Dusk (verse), Nassau Literary Magazine, April.

1919

Babes in the Woods, The Smart Set, September (TSOP, pp. 73-78. See Nassau Literary Magazine, May, 1917).

The Debutante, The Smart Set, November (TSOP, pp. 179-93. See Nassau Literary Magazine, January, 1917).

A Dirge (verse), Judge, December.

1920

Porcelain and Pink, Smart Set, January (TJA).

Head and Shoulders, Post, February 21.

Benediction, The Smart Set, February (FP. See The Ordeal, Nassau Literary Magazine, June, 1915).

Dalyrimple Goes Wrong, Smart Set, February (FP).

Myra Meets His Family, Post, March 20 (the revision of a rejected story written in April, 1919, called "Lilah Meets His Family").

Mister Icky, Smart Set, March (TJA. See The Usual Thing, Nassau Literary Magazine, December, 1916).

The Camel's Back, Post, April 24 (TJA).

Bernice Bobs Her Hair, Post, May 1 (FP).

The Ice Palace, Post, May 22 (FP).

The Offshore Pirate, Post, May 29 (FP).

The Cut-Glass Bowl, Scribner's Magazine, June (FP).

The Four Fists, Scribner's Magazine, June (FP).

The Smilers, Smart Set, June (the revision of a rejected story written in June, 1919, called "Smile, Smile, Smile" and "A Smile for Sylvo").

May Day, Smart Set, July (TJA).

Who's Who: F. Scott Fitzgerald (article), Post, September 18.

The Jelly-Bean, Metropolitan Magazine, October (TJA).

The Lees of Happiness, Chicago Tribune, December 12 (TJA).

This Is a Magazine (article), Vanity Fair, December.

1921

Jemina, The Mountain Girl, Vanity Fair, January (TJA. See Nassau Literary Magazine, December, 1916).

Tarquin of Cheapside, Smart Set, February (TJA. See Nassau Literary Magazine, April, 1917).

His Russet Witch, Metropolitan Magazine, February (TJA).

The Beautiful and Damned, Metropolitan Magazine, September, October, November, December; February, March, (1922).

1922

The Popular Girl, Post, February 11 and 18.

Two for a Cent, Metropolitan Magazine, April.

The Curious Case of Benjamin Button, Collier's, May 27 (TJA).

The Diamond as Big as the Ritz, Smart Set, June (TJA).

What I Think and Feel at Twenty-Five (article), American Magazine, September.

Winter Dreams, Metropolitan Magazine, December (ASYM).

1923

Dice, Brass Knuckles and Guitar, Hearst's International, May.

Imagination and a Few Mothers (article), Ladies Home Journal, June.

Hot and Cold Blood, Hearst's International, August (ASYM).

The Most Disgraceful Thing I Ever Did (article), Vanity Fair, November.

1924

Making Monogamy Work (article), Metropolitan Syndicate, January.

Our Irresponsible Rich (article), Metropolitan Syndicate, February.

The Cruise of the Rolling Junk

(article), Motor, February, March, April.

Gretchen's Forty Winks, Post, March 15 (ASYM).

The Moment of Revolt that Comes to Every Married Man (article), McCall's, March.

How to Live on $36,000 a Year (article), Post, April 5.

Diamond Dick, Hearst's International, April.

The Third Casket, Post, May 31.

Absolution, American Mercury, June (ASYM).

"The Sensible Thing," Liberty, July 5 (ASYM).

The Unspeakable Egg, Post, July 12.

John Jackson's Arcady, Post, July 26.

Wait Till You Have Children of Your Own (article), Woman's Home Companion, July.

What Do We Wild Young People Want for Our Children (article), Woman's Home Companion, July.

Rags Martin-Jones and the Pr — nce of W — les, McCall's, July (ASYM).

How to Live on Practically Nothing a Year (article), Post, September 20.

The Flapper's Little Brother (article), McCall's, December.

1925

The Pusher in the Face, Woman's Home Companion, February.

The Baby Party, Hearst's International, February (ASYM).

Love in the Night, Post, March 14.

Our Own Movie Queen, Chicago Tribune, June 7 (largely writ-

ten by Zelda Fitzgerald).

My Old New England Farm House on the Erie (article), College Humor, August.

One of My Oldest Friends, Woman's Home Companion, September.

The Adjuster, Red Book, September (ASYM).

A Penny Spent, Post, October 10.

What Became of Our Flappers and Sheiks (article), McCall's, October (with Zelda Fitzgerald).

Not in the Guidebook, Woman's Home Companion, November.

1926

Presumption, Post, January 9.

The Rich Boy, Red Book, January and February (ASYM).

The Adolescent Marriage, Post, March 6.

How to Waste Material (article), Bookman, May.

The Dance, Red Book, June.

1927

Your Way and Mine, Woman's Home Companion, May.

Jacob's Ladder, Post, August 20.

Love Boat, Post, October 8.

A Short Trip Home, Post, December 17 (TR).

Princeton (article), College Humor, December.

1928

The Bowl, Post, January 21.

Magnetism, Post, March 3.

The Scandal Detectives, Post, April 28 (TR. Basil Duke Lee).

Looking Back Eight Years (article), College Humor, June (with Zelda Fitzgerald).

A Night at the Fair, Post, July 21 (Basil Duke Lee).

The Freshest Boy, Post, July 28 (TR. Basil Duke Lee).

He Thinks He's Wonderful, Post, September 29 (TR. Basil Duke Lee).

Who Can Fall in Love After Thirty (article), College Humor, October.

The Captured Shadow, Post, December 29 (TR. Basil Duke Lee).

Outside the Cabinet-Makers, Century Magazine, December.

1929

The Perfect Life, Post, January 5 (TR. Basil Duke Lee).

Ten Years in the Advertising Business (article), Princeton Alumni Weekly, February 22.

The Last of the Belles, Post, March 2 (TR).

Forging Ahead, Post, March 30 (Basil Duke Lee).

Basil and Cleopatra, Post, April 27 (Basil Duke Lee).

A Short Autobiography (article), New Yorker, May 25.

The Rough Crossing, Post, June 8.

Majesty, Post, July 13 (TR).

At Your Age, Post, August 17.

The Swimmers, Post, October 19.

1930

Two Wrongs, Post, January 18 (TR. Josephine).

Girls Believe in Girls (article), Liberty, February 8.

Salesmanship on the Champs-Elysées (article), New Yorker, February 15.

First Blood, Post, April 5 (TR. Josephine).

The Millionaire's Girl, Post, May 17 (largely written by Zelda Fitzgerald).

A Nice Quiet Place, Post, May 31 (TR. Josephine).

Bridal Party, Post, August 9.

A Woman with a Past, Post, September 6 (TR. Josephine).

One Trip Abroad, Post, October 11.

A Snobbish Story, Post, November 29 (Josephine).

1931

The Hotel Child, Post, January 31.

Babylon Revisited, Post, February 21 (TR).

Indecision, Post, May 16.

A New Leaf, Post, July 4.

Emotional Bankruptcy, Post, August 15 (Josephine).

Between Three and Four, Post, September 5.

A Change of Class, Post, September 26.

Echoes of the Jazz Age (article), Scribner's Magazine, November.

A Freeze-Out, Post, December 19.

1932

Diagnosis, Post, February 20.

Six of One, Red Book, February.

Flight and Pursuit, Post, May 14.

Family in the Wind, Post, June 4 (TR).

The Rubber Check, Post, August 6.

What a Handsome Pair, Post, August 27.

Crazy Sunday, American Mercury, October (TR).

One Interne, Post, November 5 (TR).

1933

One Hundred False Starts (article), Post, March 4.

On Schedule, Post, March 18.

More than Just a House, Post, June 24.

I Got Shoes, Post, September 23.

Ring (article), New Republic, October 11.

The Family Bus, Post, November 4.

1934

Tender Is the Night, Scribner's Magazine, January, February, March, April.

"Show Mr. and Mrs. F. to Number ——" (article), Esquire, May and June (with Zelda Fitzgerald).

No Flowers, Post, July 21.

Auction — Model 1934 (article), Esquire, July (with Zelda Fitzgerald).

New Types, Post, September 22.

In the Darkest Hour, Red Book, October (The Count of Darkness, Part I).

Her Last Case, Post, November 3.

Sleeping and Waking (article), Esquire, December.

1935

The Fiend, Esquire, January (TR).

The Night Before Chancellorsville, Esquire, February (TR).

Lamp in a Window (verse), New Yorker, March 23.

Shaggy's Morning, Esquire, May.

The Passionate Esquimo, Liberty, June 8.

The Intimate Strangers, McCall's, June.

The Count of Darkness, Red Book, June (The Count of Darkness, Part II).

Zone of Accident, Post, July 13.

A Kingdom in the Dark, Red Book, August (The Count of Darkness, Part III).

1936

The Crack-Up (article), Esquire, February.

Pasting It Together (article), Esquire, March.

Too Cute for Words, Post, April 18 (Gwen).

Fate in Her Hands, American Magazine, April.

Handle with Care (article), Esquire, April.

Image on the Heart, McCall's, April.

Three Acts of Music, Esquire, May.

Inside the House, Post, June 13 (Gwen).

The Ants at Princeton, Esquire, June.

Author's House, Esquire, July.

Afternoon of an Author, Esquire, August.

An Author's Mother, Esquire, September.

"I Didn't Get Over," Esquire, October.

"Send Me In, Coach," Esquire, November.

1937

An Alcoholic Case, Esquire, February.

Trouble, Post, March 6.

Ode to Parnassus (verse), New Yorker, June 5.

The Honor of the Goon, Esquire, June.

A Book of My Own (article), New Yorker, August 21.

The Long Way Out, Esquire, September.

The Guest in Room Nineteen, Esquire, October.

Early Success (article), American Cavalcade, October.

In the Holidays, Esquire, December.

1938

Financing Finnegan, Esquire, January.

1939

Design in Plaster, Esquire, November.

Strange Sanctuary, Liberty, December 9.

The Lost Decade, Esquire, December.

1940

Pat Hobby's Christmas Wish, Esquire, January (Pat Hobby).

A Man in the Way, Esquire, February (Pat Hobby).

Boil Some Water — Lots of It, Esquire, March (Pat Hobby).

Teamed with Genius, Esquire, April (Pat Hobby).

Pat Hobby and Orson Wells, Esquire, May (Pat Hobby).

The End of Hate, Collier's, June 22.

Pat Hobby's Secret, Esquire, June (Pat Hobby).

Pat Hobby, Putative Father, Esquire, July (Pat Hobby).

Homes of the Stars, Esquire, August (Pat Hobby).

Pat Hobby Does His Bit, Esquire, September (Pat Hobby).

Pat Hobby's Preview, Esquire, October (Pat Hobby).

No Harm Trying, Esquire, November (Pat Hobby).

A Patriotic Short, Esquire, December (Pat Hobby).

1941

On the Trail of Pat Hobby, Esquire, January (Pat Hobby).

Fun in an Artist's Studio, Esquire, February (Pat Hobby).

On an Ocean Wave, Esquire, February (by "Paul Elgin").

Two Old Timers, Esquire, March (Pat Hobby).

Mightier than the Sword, Esquire, April (Pat Hobby).

Pat Hobby's College Days, Esquire, May (Pat Hobby).

The Woman from Twenty-One, Esquire, June.

Three Hours Between Planes, Esquire, July.

Gods of Darkness, Red Book, November (The Count of Darkness, Part IV).

1947

The Broadcast We Almost Heard Last September, Furioso, Fall.

News of Paris — Fifteen Years After, Furioso, Winter.

1948

Discard, Harper's Bazaar, January.

The World's Fair, Kenyon Review, Autumn (a chapter from an early version of Tender Is the Night).

1949

The Last Kiss, Collier's, April 16 (see The Last Tycoon).

INDEX